SAVE THE CAT!
WRITES A
young adult
NOVEL

SAVE THE CAT!
WRITES A
young adult
NOVEL

The Ultimate Guide to Writing a YA Bestseller

JESSICA BRODY

Based on the bestselling
Save the Cat! by Blake Snyder

TEN SPEED PRESS
California | New York

CONTENTS

Opening Image
Where We Begin . . .

Once upon a time, many many years ago, there was a tiny little corner of the bookstore, with an even tinier little sign that read "Young Adult." (You might have passed it on your way to the bathroom.) It consisted of a handful of shelves and maybe a hundred or so titles, and milling about its tiny little selection were a few teenagers searching for their next read.

Then came books like *Twilight*, and *The Hunger Games*, and *Divergent*, and *The Fault in Our Stars*, and *The Hate U Give*, and so many others. The genre exploded. "Young adult" became a household term. And that tiny little corner of the bookstore began to grow and spread—like Alice after consuming too many of Wonderland's finest "Eat Me" cakes—until it was one of the most dominant sections of the bookstore, filled not just with teenagers anymore, but readers of all ages.

And the best part? Young adult wasn't (and still isn't) technically a *genre*. It's an age categorization. Which meant *anything* was fair game. Paranormal, dystopia, romance, comedy, drama, thriller, horror, mystery—they all fit into those ever-expanding shelves.

In short, young adult fiction became a book industry gold rush. Publishers scrambled to acquire rights to the next runaway bestseller, movie studios filled their slates with films helmed by actors barely out of high school, book festivals catering to young adult fiction popped up around the globe, authors were sent on worldwide book tours.

And readers still couldn't get enough. They were hungry for more.

Today, the mad rush to market might have died down a bit, but "young adult" is still as popular as ever. And it continues to diversify and grow year over year, attracting some of the most talented writers in the industry and tackling some of the most challenging and important topics of our generation, like racism, gender identity, inequality, injustice, abuse, disease, sex, addiction, and more.

While trends in the young adult category might come and go, three things remain clear: young adult fiction is here to stay, the world is still hungry for good young adult stories, and we need more writers to tell them.

Which brings us to this book.

The Biggest Problem Writers Have

Why did you pick up this book?

Have you always dreamed of writing a young adult novel and don't know where to start? Have you *tried* to write a young adult novel in the past and quit halfway through? Or finished one but couldn't publish it or sell it to readers? Or perhaps you picked up this book because it has a cute cat on the cover and you like cats and are interested in saving them. (If this is the case, you might want to put the book back down now. It's not really about saving cats, but we'll get to that in a minute.)

Or perhaps you're like I was more than a decade ago, when I stared down at my first finished novel and my drawer full of rejection letters and it became painfully clear to me that despite all the time and effort and passion that had gone into that novel, I didn't have the slightest clue how to craft a good *story*.

Humans are born with a passion for well-told stories. But writers, unfortunately, are not born *knowing* how to write them (an egregious universal oversight in my opinion). Sure, there are a handful of writers out there who sit down at a computer with a seed of an idea and three weeks later emerge with an elegantly structured novel with taut pacing, compelling character development, and a satisfying ending without even trying. (We don't really like those writers.) But for the 99.9 percent of the rest of us, we have to work at it. *Hard.* We have to study the secrets of story structure. We have to dissect other novels and analyze their intricate inner workings. We have to *learn* how to develop an elegantly structured novel with taut pacing, compelling character development, and a satisfying ending.

And that's exactly what I did, more than a decade ago, when I picked up a screenwriting guide called *Save the Cat!* by Blake Snyder. I learned what a good story was and how to write one. I have since sold more than twenty novels to major publishers such as Simon & Schuster, Penguin Random House, and Macmillan. My books have been translated into more than twenty languages, and several have been optioned for film and television.

Wait a minute, did you just say Save the Cat! *is a screenwriting guide?*

That I did. The original *Save the Cat!* book was written for screenwriters, but here's what I found: story is story, whether it appears on a big screen, a small screen, or an eBook screen, or in an old-fashioned book made out of real paper (which, yes, young adults do still read—voraciously!). And once I discovered that the Save the Cat! method worked well for novels, I wanted to share it. I wanted to do for other novelists what Blake Snyder did for me.

Which is why, in 2018, I published the first novel adaptation of the Save the Cat! method, called *Save the Cat! Writes a Novel*. And now I've updated the method even more specifically for young adult novelists.

Think of this guide as your crash course in storytelling. The ultimate guide to writing a young adult bestseller. By the time you finish reading this book, you will know what makes up a good story and why, and more important, you'll know how to apply that to your own young adult fiction, so that you can start crafting memorable, unputdownable stories that resonate with teen readers.

Because here's the harsh truth: no matter how good of a writer you are, no matter how masterfully you can string together sentences, no matter how witty your dialogue, how evocative your prose, how vivid your descriptions, how unique your literary voice, if you can't craft a good *story*, readers won't stick around until the end. I'd even venture to say they won't stick around past page 50.

I told you it was harsh! But if you didn't hear it from me, you'd hear it from someone else, like a book reviewer online. And trust me, I'll be nicer about it.

Since publishing *Save the Cat! Writes a Novel*, I have been blown away and humbled by the response. I continue to get messages daily from authors who have used this method to write novels, finish novels, revise novels, fix novels, bring novels back from the dead, get novels represented by literary agents, and sell novels to readers, publishers, and even movie producers! These are not authors who were born knowing how to tell a story. These are authors like you and me who just needed a little help.

I'm certain that Save the Cat! can help you as well. We might not be saving any literal cats, but we're saving writers. And that's an important job too!

What Exactly Is Save the Cat?

Save the Cat! is a blueprint. Yes, like the thing you need when you build a house. And that's the perfect metaphor. Houses can look very different from the outside, but they all have certain things in common, right? Walls, windows, doors, a roof. Certain elements must be present for the house to stand upright (instead of sloping dangerously to the left which, trust me, makes it very hard to arrange furniture). Story works the same way. On the outside, our stories are very different, but crack them open and you find they are built upon a very similar foundation. A similar structure. In fact, without this structure, they don't stand at all. They collapse.

Is this structure new? Am I teaching you some groundbreaking, fancy-pants, postmodern, innovative way to tell a story? No, in fact, it's the opposite. This common story structure has been around for a very long time. Since before we were even writing stories *down*. If you study successful stories throughout time (and I have!), you'll find this structure exists in almost all of them.

Blake Snyder recognized this pattern in movies, and I recognized it in novels, leading me to believe that it's some kind of "secret storytelling code" (whoa!). So, no, we're not reinventing the storytelling wheel here; we're simply noticing which storytelling elements already resonate with readers and audiences and using those same elements to craft successful stories of our own.

So it's a formula?

Uh-oh. There's that dreaded *F*-word.

Many writers hear words such as "blueprint" or "pattern" and automatically translate that to "formula." They worry that following a structure method like Save the Cat! will cause their novel to feel formulaic or predictable. And no one wants that, right?

Or do they?

Here's the thing. Humans are wired to respond to certain storytelling elements told in a certain order. We've been responding to them since our earliest days, when our primitive ancestors told stories around campfires. You could almost say it's in our DNA. Whenever a reader picks up a book, they enter an invisible contract with the writer. "I will give you hours, days, and maybe even weeks or months of my precious time. But in exchange, you have to give me what I'm expecting. Sure, I want surprises and twists along the way, but I came here for a story, and I have an innate understanding of what that means."

Therefore, in order for you, the writer, to fulfill your end of the invisible contract, there are certain things you *must* include in your story for it to be defined in the reader's mind as a story. These things are what make up the secret storytelling code. So, in a way, yes, it *is* a formula. But it's a formula your readers *want*. And it's your job to make it your own. Just as so many brilliant and famous young adult writers have done before you. Writers such as Suzanne Collins, S. E. Hinton, Nicola Yoon, Veronica Roth, Lois Lowry, John Green, Angie Thomas, Meg Cabot, Marie Lu, Neil Gaiman, Markus Zusak, Cassandra Clare, Leigh Bardugo, and so many more.

These great names have built dynamic, surprising, unpredictable, unique stories on a *familiar* foundation and have gone down in history for it. I've found the secret storytelling code in almost all their novels. And we'll be using the Save the Cat! method to analyze many of them so you can see it for yourself.

The bad news is, you might never be able to read a novel the same way again (sorry!). The *great* news is, you'll know exactly how to structure a well-told story, again and again and again, with any idea, any genre, any character you can possibly dream up. And *that*, I think, is pretty dang cool.

But What Does It Have to Do with Cats?

Oh, right. I almost forgot about the cat.

One of the things that writers love about Blake Snyder's original screenwriting book is his cleverly titled tips on how to avoid common storytelling pitfalls. "Save the Cat" is one of those tips.

Essentially, it says that in order to get your audience in sync with your main character, there must be something redeemable, sympathetic, or likable about them. No, they don't have to *be* likable, but they must have at least one trait or perform one act that quickly gets the audience on the character's side and convinces them to stick around for two hundred, three hundred, even four hundred–plus pages.

Sure, they could *literally* save a cat, like from a tree, a burning building, or a shelter. Or they could help an old lady cross the street, leave a big tip at a restaurant, have a sick relative who relies on them, struggle with a tragic backstory or mean-spirited guardian. The possibilities are endless.

So, no, they don't have to actually save a cat. There are many ways to get the reader to root for your main character (which we'll talk about in the next chapter). But I would just like to point out that on the very first page of *The Hunger Games* by Suzanne Collins, Katniss tells us about the time she tried to drown a cat, but after her sister relentlessly begged and cried, she decided to (*cough, cough*) *save* him instead.

Is "Save the Cat!' the most important tip you'll find in this book? No. But it has the best name, so we put it on the cover. It is, however, indicative of the kind of storytelling advice you can expect from this guide and this method.

Do We Really Need a Book Just for Young Adult?

I asked myself this very question when I sat down to write this book. Is young adult really that different? Does it warrant its own novel-writing guide? And after studying the structure and character arcs of hundreds of young adult novels (and writing more than fifteen of my own), I decided that these stories are unique enough and have specific enough qualities to necessitate a book dedicated to them.

Young adult (or "YA") is defined—in the industry and in this guide—as fiction targeted to (and appropriate for) readers ages twelve through eighteen. And that usually means the protagonist of the story is the same age. This age category is often confused with "middle grade," which is fiction targeted to and appropriate for readers ages eight through twelve, typically featuring protagonists of the same age. For novels where the protagonist's age straddles the line, like *The Book Thief* by Marcus Zusak and *The Giver* by Lois Lowry (both featuring twelve-year-old main characters), you can defer to the publisher's product page and the section of the bookstore where the book is currently being shelved. By those indicators, both are young adult.

Simply put, these are stories told through the eyes of teenagers (or near-teenagers) that explore what it means to be a teenager (in the real world, a fantasy world, two hundred years ago or two hundred years from now).

While the structure of a young adult novel is similar to the structure of any other novel, the filter through which we tell young adult stories is unique. Anyone who's ever been a teenager will probably agree. It's a time in your life when emotions are raw, experiences are new, friendships are tested, drama is high, the boundaries of identity are being pushed and formed, independence is just within reach, and the world feels both limiting and limitless at the same time.

There's a reason young adult novels are among the best-selling books in the publishing industry. It's a transformative age, and, as we'll soon see, storytelling is *all* about transformation. Which means these tales are hitting a storytelling sweet spot (for both young and not-so-young readers alike).

In other words, YA is its own novel-writing beast, and it does warrant its own guide, if for no other reason than to laser-focus our study of story structure using exclusively young adult examples. In this book, we will crack open tons of popular and successful young adult novels and analyze how and why they work so you can apply these discoveries to your own writing and craft young adult bestsellers worthy of sitting on the shelf beside the best of them.

If you chose to write a young adult novel simply because you thought it might be *easier* than writing a novel for adults, I think you'll be disappointed. It might actually be harder. I'll tell you why.

Young adult fiction, in general, tends to have tighter plotting, faster pacing, and smaller word counts, which means there's very little room for error. Every page matters. Teens are used to and expect well-structured novels; it's as simple as that. With all the other things they've got going in their lives—school, extracurriculars, college applications, homework, friends, crushes, parents, bingeable TV, video games (sheesh!)—it's a miracle they're able to read at all! They have neither the time nor the patience for a novel that doesn't grab them instantly and hold their attention to the very end.

And what do you know? That's *exactly* what the Save the Cat! method is designed to do. Because it originated as a screenwriting method, it leans heavily on the same kind of visual elements, fast pacing, and airtight structure that we would expect from a movie. It's *designed* to keep audiences riveted from start to finish, no matter what else is going on in their lives.

So, in a way, a young adult edition of Save the Cat! feels almost essential.

How to Make This Book Work for You

I'll be honest. You will probably not use this book in the same way as other writers.

The inner workings of stories might be the same, but the inner workings of writers definitely are *not*. We all approach the creative process in different ways. You might be a hardcore "plotter," someone who likes to outline and plot out *everything* before you write even a single word of your first draft. Or you might be a staunch "pantser," someone who prefers to discover the story as you go and "write by the seat of your pants" as they say. Or, maybe you're somewhere in the middle (a "plontser?").

Either way, this book *will* work for you. It's all a matter of how and *when* you use it. If you're a plotter, you might find yourself reaching for this book at the start of your novel-development process, when you're laying out your route, brainstorming your options, and trying to decide where to go and how to get there. If you're a pantser, you might find this book to be more helpful as a revision tool, after you've written a first or second draft and need help sorting through what you have and making it all work. Or you might find yourself reaching for this book *throughout* the novel-writing process, when you're stuck or stalled out or could use some extra inspiration.

Bottom line, the structure has to get added in somewhere. And this book will help you do that.

Let's talk about how.

I have been teaching the Save the Cat! method for a long time, through in-person workshops, online courses in my Writing Mastery Academy, and now books. And over the years I've developed what I believe to be the most logical, intuitive, and effective way to teach writers how to structure their novels.

Which means, I urge you to read this book in order. I know, I know, you are a rebel! You're writing *YA*, after all! But trust me on this. I have structured this guide very purposefully, to give you the best possible chance of success.

If you're just starting out the novel-development process and all you have is a seed of an idea, this book will systematically guide you through the steps to take that seed and grow it into something magnificent. If you're stuck in the middle of a novel and just want to know how to fix it, this book will help you diagnose the problem, which I'm 95 percent certain goes deeper than you think it does.

In other words, it's all connected. Your plot, your structure, and your character transformation. Or what I like to call the Holy Trinity of Story.

You're on a complex and often arduous journey that can be very hard to navigate without a confident guide and a trusty road map.

So here it is:

- **CREATING YOUR STORY-WORTHY HERO:** In chapter 1, we'll talk about the main character or "hero" of your young adult novel, who they are, and how to make sure they are truly worthy of being the star of your story.

- **BUILDING YOUR SAVE THE CAT! BEAT SHEET:** In chapter 2, we'll break down the fifteen beats (or plot points) of the famous Save the Cat! Beat Sheet (your story structure blueprint) in great detail, with loads of examples from popular YA fiction, so you can use those beats to construct your own young adult masterpiece that is at once riveting and transformative!

- **CUSTOMIZING YOUR BEAT SHEET:** In chapter 3, we'll go *beyond* the basic foundation of story structure and look at ways that you might customize your beat sheet to make it work for you, including writing in multiple points of view. This is where I've put my advanced storytelling tips and my answers to the most popular questions of novelists using the Save the Cat! method, to help you customize the method, if necessary, to your story.

- **IDENTIFYING YOUR GENRE:** In chapters 4 through 14, we'll pinpoint the genre of your novel using the ten Save the Cat! story genres. These are not your typical genres (sci-fi, drama, comedy, and so on). Instead, the Save the Cat! story genres are broken down by type of character transformation and/or central theme. This will help you see your plot and character through a specific story lens and further develop your novel using the essential genre ingredients to make it successful. We'll also study the structure of ten popular young adult novels (one for each story genre) using the Save the Cat! Beat Sheet and the genre ingredients, so you can see how the Save the Cat! method applies to some of today's most successful YA fiction.

- **SELLING YOUR NOVEL:** In chapter 15, we'll move past the writing of your novel and into the selling of your novel. Using all the strategies outlined in this book, we'll put everything together to distill your story down to a one-page description (the synopsis) and, furthermore, into a one-*sentence* description (the logline) that you can use to pitch agents, editors, publishers, readers, and even movie producers.

- **GOING BEYOND THE FIRST BOOK:** Finally, in chapter 16, we'll explore how to use Save the Cat! to craft a successful young adult *series* and study the structures of popular series of different lengths.

Are you excited to get started? I certainly am.

I've designed this book to emulate a writing workshop, walking you step by step through the process of developing (or fixing!) your novel from start to finish. And to ensure you're always on the right track, I've included exercises and checklists at the end of key chapters. This will help you hold yourself and your story accountable. Or if you prefer to work with a critique partner or group, feel free to use the checklists to help critique each other.

Either way, the goal of this guide is to help you brainstorm, write, and/or revise the best possible story you can. Whether you've got a full draft of a novel finished, or you're still staring down that terrifying first blank page. Whether you've spent months fleshing out a character or world, or you're just flirting with the twinkle of a new idea.

It's never too late or too soon to start.

So let's go!

Creating Your Story-Worthy Hero
How to Craft Characters That
Teen Readers Will Care About

Before we can talk about *what* happens in your novel, we have to talk about *who* it's about. You'll soon find that these two things are intimately related. The *who* is the anchor of your story's construction, not to mention your reader's guide through the story. So regardless of what stage of the novel-development process you're at now—brainstorming, outlining, writing, revising, pulling your hair out trying to find the perfect word to describe the sky—I urge you to put all of that aside. Clear your desk of all the sticky notes, and your head of all the noise, and just focus on one thing for now:

Your **hero.**

That's what we'll be calling your main character from here on out. Because it just sounds more important, doesn't it? It sounds *cool*. And if you're going to be asking your reader to read two-hundred-plus pages about this person (or animal, mythical creature, cyborg, or whatever), they better sound cool. They better be *worthy* of those pages.

So how do we create heroes who are interesting, memorable, relatable, and more important, who readers want to read about? Simple!

You give them three very crucial things:

1. **A PROBLEM** (also known as a flaw that needs fixing)

2. **A WANT** (also known as a goal that the hero is pursuing)

3. **A NEED** (also known as a life lesson to be learned)

By starting the process with these three things, and focusing your creative energy on them now, you'll be amazed at how easily and fully you hero starts to take shape in your mind. And how seamlessly you'll be able to build or revise the plot around them later.

So let's see what we're dealing with here.

A Problem

When was the last time you met a teenager who had life all figured out? Better yet, when was the last time you met *anyone* who had life all figured out? Exactly.

A **flawed hero** is essential to a flawless plot, especially in young adult fiction, when we're exploring some of the most tumultuous, dramatic, and transformative years of our lives. Perfect heroes are about as realistic and believable as perfect humans . . . who, by the way, don't exist. Therefore they shouldn't exist in your story either.

But what does it mean to have a "flawed hero"? It means a hero who has a problem. Or better yet, *lots* of them. The best hero is one whose life is *riddled* with problems, both on the outside *and* on the inside.

Just look at Celaena Sardothien in *Throne of Glass* by Sarah J. Maas. When the novel begins, she's enslaved in a salt mine prison, which sounds pretty grim to me. She's also secretly grieving the tragic massacre of her family, which has hardened her and made her resistant to forming real connections with people.

Or look at Avery Grambs in *The Inheritance Games* by Jennifer Lynn Barnes. She has problems to spare! She's poor, works hard to make ends meet, has a father who's out of the picture and a mother who died, and now lives with her sister . . . except for the times she has to sleep in her car because her sister's deadbeat boyfriend moves back in. Oh, and by page 3, she's accused of cheating on a test because the principal can't bring himself to believe that someone like Avery could possibly do well. So she's also the victim of class discrimination.

Talk about problems!

The trick is to not let your hero's problems stay contained to just *one* aspect of their life. You want those problems to spread, infect, wreak havoc everywhere.

In *I Am Not Your Perfect Mexican Daughter* by Erika L. Sánchez, Julia Reyes feels like she doesn't fit into her Mexican American family and has trouble living up to the saintlike status of her "perfect" older sister, Olga. This has contributed to anger issues and undiagnosed depression. Julia is constantly acting out, not just at home (where she's frequently grounded by her mother), but at school too (where she's frequently sent to the principal's office). And all of these problems are only exacerbated by Olga's death as Julia struggles to process her grief.

As hard as it can be to riddle your hero's life with problems right from the start of the story, it's also essential. A flawed hero is what gives your story *purpose*. If you write a novel about a character who doesn't (desperately!) need some change in their life, your reader just won't care. It's as simple as that.

We turn to stories to be inspired by characters who fix problems, improve their lives, overcome fears and flaws. Teen readers want to read novels that take deeply imperfect heroes and make them a little *less* imperfect. How do I know? Because that's what almost *every* successful young adult novel does.

Do you think Calaena Sardothien pushes people away forever? Do you think that Avery Grambs spends the rest of her life in poverty, wishing for something better, or that Julia Reyes feels angry and powerless for the whole book?

Of course not! But we must have problems in order to fix them. We must start somewhere that gives us a place to *go*.

If, after only a few pages, your reader is thinking something along the lines of *Whoa, this person's life is a mess. I wonder how it will turn out for them*, then voilà! You've done your job. You've effectively *engaged* your reader. Because a reader who wonders is a reader who keeps reading.

A Want

But if your hero is just sitting around, stewing in their problems, and doing nothing to try to solve them, then *you've* got a problem as well. Heroes need to be proactive right from the start of the story. And there's a very easy way to make them proactive.

By giving them something to **want**.

A goal to pursue.

Your hero *knows* they've got problems (or maybe they don't know, and that's one of their problems!). Now ask yourself, *What are they doing to try to fix those problems? What do they* think *will improve their life?*

That is their goal. That is what they're actively pursuing (at least at the start of the novel). And it can be almost anything. To get accepted to a dream college. To solve a mystery. To catch the evil creature that's been ravishing nearby villages. To get back together with an ex. To get a million followers online.

Now, will this thing *really* fix your hero's life? Probably not, but that's not the point. The want gives your hero something to *do* and gives *you* something to write. But most important, the want gives the reader something to root for.

This girl wants to stop her family from being deported (The Sun Is Also a Star *by Nicola Yoon*). *I wonder if she'll be able to do it!*

This guy wants to keep his online relationship a secret (Simon vs. the Homo Sapiens Agenda *by Becky Abertalli*). *I need to find out if he succeeds!*

This bounty hunter wants to catch a criminal so she can pay off her overdue rent and keep herself from getting evicted! (Warcross *by Marie Lu*). *Now I* have *to keep reading.*

And that's the secret, my friend. Simple yet effective. Time-tested. Readers keep reading when you give them something to read *for*. When you give your hero a goal.

GOALS MUST BE TANGIBLE

The key to crafting a successful character goal, however, is that it must be *tangible*. Concrete. Meaning, the reader must be able to understand not only what the goal is, but more important, when and if the hero gets it or loses it.

If Natasha gets that deportation order canceled, we *know* her goal has been achieved.

If Simon's secret relationship with "Blue" gets out, we *know* his goal has been lost.

If Emika doesn't catch that criminal, she'll likely be out on the street.

The problems start happening when the author makes the goal too nebulous, vague, or intangible.

For example, "My hero wants to be happy" or "My hero wants closure" or "My hero wants independence" are not tangible goals. Because they're not specific enough. They're not trackable. How do we know when and if your hero is happy or has experienced closure or feels independent? We don't.

But we can make intangible goals tangible by giving them concrete qualities.

Like "My hero will feel independent *when* they get their driver's license."

Or "My hero will be happy *when* they track down their missing sibling or claim their birth right as the heir to the throne."

Now the goal is trackable. Now we'll know when it's been gained or lost.

Again, these things probably won't *really* make your hero happy or truly fix their life, but for now, it's enough to get your hero off their butt and into action from the very first page. Because your hero's goal is what gives your story momentum from page one.

It's very difficult to write a novel about a hero who's just wandering around trying to get closure. What exactly are they *doing* to achieve that closure?

So ask yourself: *What does my hero want? What are they pursuing that they* think *will improve their life? Is it trackable?*

And I'm sorry, but the excuse "My character is a teenager who's been grounded" isn't a reason to not make your hero proactive. Teen heroes might still be under the control of their parents (depending on the story), and they might have *slightly* less agency than an adult character, but that doesn't mean your hero shouldn't still be proactive. It just means you have to get more creative.

Look at how strict and controlling Julia's mother is in *I Am Not Your Perfect Mexican Daughter*. Amá is constantly grounding Julia and telling her what to do and how she should live her life. But does that stop Julia from doing *anything*? Not really. She still writes poetry (because she *wants* to move to New York and be a writer). And later, despite knowing her mother would disapprove, she still actively tries to track down proof that Olga wasn't as "perfect" a daughter as everyone thought she was.

Which brings up a good point about goals. They can and often *do* change as the story goes on. We'll talk more about when and why a hero's goals might change in the next chapter, but for now we can give our heroes trackable things to want right from the start, even if those things are replaced later on.

WHAT'S STANDING IN THEIR WAY?

Now, just because your hero *wants* something doesn't automatically mean they'll get it. At least not without a fight. While we're thinking about our hero's goal, we also should be thinking about *why* the hero hasn't achieved this goal yet.

What is standing in their way?

Is it a nemesis or antagonist (an actual person working against your hero)? Like Martin in *Simon vs. the Homo Sapiens Agenda*, who discovers Simon's secret email relationship with Blue and threatens to expose him.

Or is it just general conflict (external or internal forces working against your hero) that's standing in your hero's way? Liesel Meminger in *The Book Thief* by Markus Zusak desperately *wants* to read the book she stole. What's standing in her way? Her own illiteracy. Emika Chen in *Warcross* wants that bounty so she can pay off her overdue rent. What's standing in *her* way? Other bounty hunters who are after the same reward.

For every want or goal we give our hero, there should be an equal or opposite force holding the hero back from achieving it. Why can't Natasha in *The Sun Is Also a Star* just walk into a US immigration office and *stop* the deportation from happening? Well, for starters, US Citizenship and Immigration Services doesn't work that way. It's not that simple. And if it were, there would be no story. Nothing left for the reader to root for.

So, while it's important to give your hero goals, it's equally important to make sure your hero doesn't achieve those goals too easily. And in some cases, they don't achieve them at all.

That's right: much to the dismay of our heroes, goals aren't always achieved in the end. Some are. Some aren't. Emika's rent does eventually get paid off and Liesel gradually learns to read, thanks to the help of her foster father. But Natasha isn't able to stop her family from being deported to Jamaica, and eventually Simon's secret does get out.

But here's the cold, harsh truth about heroes and what they *think* will fix their life: they're almost always wrong.

Heroes, like humans, prefer quick fixes. A Band-Aid slapped over a wound. And that's exactly what goals are. They're temporary solutions. As good as it might feel to get accepted to your dream college, solve a mystery, catch an evil creature, reunite with an ex, or pass that million-follower mark online, it's not the real answer. It never was.

The Book Thief was never truly about Liesel learning to read or even about stealing books! The story goes much deeper than that, exploring a young girl's struggle to feel powerful in the powerless world of Nazi Germany. And the whole purpose of Natasha's journey in *The Sun Is Also a Star* was not about deportation; it was about who she met along the way and what she discovered about herself in the process.

All stories have a deeper meaning, something that goes beyond just what the hero wants—or thinks will fix their life. Because all heroes, regardless of whether they achieve their goal, eventually have to do real, life-changing, soul-searching work. Eventually, they have to fix their life the *right* way. That's why, in addition to a problem and a want, you must give your hero what is arguably the most story-worthy quality of all . . .

A Need

It's time to pull out the leather couch and play shrink, because it's your job to not only diagnose what's *really* wrong with your hero's life but cure it as well.

The problems and flaws that we talked about earlier were just symptoms of something bigger. A deeper issue that the hero is facing.

We call that deeper issue the **"shard of glass."**

The shard of glass is an emotional (and sometimes physical) wound buried deep within your hero's psyche. Maybe it's been there for a few months, maybe years, maybe longer. But skin has now grown over it, leaving behind a psychological scar that causes your hero to behave the way they do and make the mistakes they make (flaws!).

And this shard of glass—this deep-seated wound—is the *real* problem that needs to be fixed by the end of the story.

How did the shard of glass get there? Why is the hero so flawed? What happened to make them the way they are?

Is it a death not properly grieved, or even a massacre of the hero's entire family, like in *Throne of Glass*? Is it the hero's upbringing in a certain family, group, or society, like Will's gang-torn neighborhood in *Long Way Down* by Jason Reynolds, or Cady's wealthy, image-obsessed family in *We Were Liars* by E. Lockhart? Or perhaps it's an overbearing, judgmental, or disapproving parent (always a popular choice in YA!) like Julia's mother in *I Am Not Your Perfect Mexican Daughter*. (Hey! That shard of glass is even referenced in the title!)

Or maybe your hero's shard of glass originated from somewhere else entirely. It's completely up to you. Regardless of where it came from, this real problem is usually part of the hero's backstory, meaning it happened before the story began, and now it's working behind the scenes, messing up your hero's life and generally sabotaging their happiness, like faulty code in their operating system.

Does the hero know that the shard of glass is there? They might, they might not. But chances are they don't fully understand how deep it's buried or just how much damage it's really been causing them.

At least not *yet*.

But you, the author, must know. And better yet, you must know what it will take to remove that shard of glass (or at least confront it), repair that faulty programming, and truly fix your hero's life. In other words, you must know what your hero really *needs*.

What life lesson must they learn to conquer their flaws, heal the wounds caused by their shard of glass, and emerge from this story a changed and improved person? That is the ultimate definition of the hero's **need**, and the third and biggest question you must ask yourself as you write your novel.

The need is the very soul of your story. It's what gives your novel substance. And it's what your novel is really *about*.

Throne of Glass isn't really *about* a deadly competition to become the king's champion (although that's a very cool premise!). It's about a girl who needs to learn to let people in and make real human connections, despite the tragedy of her past.

The Inheritance Games isn't really *about* a race to solve an epic puzzle hidden in a dead billionaire's mansion (although that certainly makes us want to read the book!). It's about a girl who needs to grieve the loss of her mother and discover her own self-worth in a world that expects very little of her.

Even *The Fault in Our Stars* by John Green isn't *about* a teen girl dying of cancer who falls in love for the first time (although we're moved to tears by that hook!). It's about a teen girl who learns, *through* love, how to enjoy her life—even though she's dying.

This is the real stuff that great young adult fiction is made of. And whether they realize it or not, this is what teen readers are looking for when they pick up a book. Sure, they want romance and space battles and epic fights for the throne. But they also want a story that's *about* something. They want *transformation*.

But how do you make that happen?

A STORY VERSUS B STORY

In short, you must craft a plot that's *designed* to change your hero.

There's a very intimate relationship between plot and character, which we'll explore deeply throughout this book. For now, it's important to know that your hero's want or goal is a crucial part of the *external* story, which in Save the Cat! terms is called the **A Story**.

The A Story *is* the plot. It's all the flashy stuff that's happening on the surface. On the *outside*. Like hunting down a hacker in a virtual reality game (*Warcross*), spying for the resistance (*An Ember in the Ashes* by Sabaa Tahir), or working for a chaotic catering company (*The Truth About Forever* by Sarah Dessen).

Essentially, it's the exciting stuff! The cool stuff!

But while all that flashy stuff is going on, something is also happening to your hero on the inside. They're growing, changing, learning things about themself they never knew. They're gradually transforming as a result of the plot. We call this the B Story or *internal* story.

You can't have one without the other, though. You can't have a novel that's all plot and no transformation. What would be the point? What would we have to resonate with? And you can't have a novel that's all transformation and no plot. What would be triggering that transformation? What would your hero be reacting *to*?

The A Story, what the hero wants, is only half the equation. The true substance of your novel is found in the **B Story**: what the hero needs.

While hunting down a hacker in a virtual reality game in *Warcross*, Emika learns an important lesson about distinguishing reality from the illusion that others want you to see. *While* spying for the resistance in *An Ember in the Ashes*, Laia learns an important lesson about bravery and finding the courage not to run away from your fears. And *while* spending the summer working for a chaotic catering company in *The Truth About Forever*, Macy finally learns how to embrace the chaos of her own grief and deal with it head-on, instead of hiding from it.

Maybe the better word isn't "while" but "because."

All internal stories (B Stories) happen *because* of the external story (A Story). All life lessons are learned *because* of the plot.

The life lesson is the deep, soul-searching journey your hero didn't even know they were on, one that will eventually lead them to an answer they didn't even know they were looking for. And it should be something universal. Something relatable to any reader, particularly a teenaged one.

Now if that sounds like an impossible task (*How am I supposed to know what's universal and relatable to a teenager!?*), I've got some good news for you. Better yet, I've got a *list*.

TEN UNIVERSAL LIFE LESSONS

After studying a *lot* of young adult novels, I've discovered that almost all of them have a need that is derived from one of the following ten universal life lessons.

- **FORGIVENESS**: of self or of others
- **LOVE**: including self-love, family love, romantic love
- **ACCEPTANCE**: of self, of circumstances, of reality
- **FAITH**: in oneself, in others, in the world, in the universe, in God
- **FEAR**: overcoming it, conquering it, finding courage
- **TRUST**: in oneself, in others, in destiny, in the unknown
- **SURVIVAL**: including the will to live
- **SELFLESSNESS**: including sacrifice, altruism, heroism, and overcoming greed
- **RESPONSIBILITY**: including duty, standing up for a cause, fighting against injustice, accepting one's destiny
- **REDEMPTION**: including atonement, accepting blame, remorse, and salvation

If you're worried that choosing something from this list is going to make your novel feel cliché or formulaic, I invite you to look at in a different way. These are the ten lessons that unite us as humans. That remind us we're not alone. And when so many teens are struggling through what is often the loneliest period in their life, that's an important reminder.

That is why we write young adult fiction.

To touch lives, to change lives, and sometimes even to *save* lives.

And if you're thinking *I don't* need *a need. I don't want to* lecture *teens with a life lesson. I just want to entertain them with a good thriller or fantasy adventure*, then consider this:

The most successful thrillers or fantasy adventures in the young adult market have a universal life lesson buried somewhere within them. It might not be as obvious or as front-and-center as some other character-driven novels, but it's there. Don't believe me? Check out the beat sheet for *Wilder Girls* by Rory Power (horror/thriller) on page 358 or *Children of Blood and Bone* by Tomi Adeyemi and *Six of Crows* by Leigh Bardugo (fantasy adventures) on pages 214 and 249. They all feature a hero (or multiple heroes) who goes into the story flawed and comes out the other side transformed in some way.

The flashy and exciting A Story might be why the reader picks up the novel in the first place, but it's the internal B Story that will resonate with them long after it's over.

More Heroes, More Problems

Now that you're fully versed in what makes a hero story-worthy, your own hero might already be starting to take shape in your mind. But you might be wondering the same thing that many writers wonder at this stage of the process: *What if I have more than one main character? Does that mean I have more than one hero?*

The short answer is: *yes*.

Let's break it down. As I said before, young adult fiction has some of the most complexly structured stories on the market today. And part of that complexity stems from novels that feature more than one narrator, also called a "point of view" (POV). We'll talk more about writing from multiple perspectives in chapter 3, Customizing Your Beat Sheet, but for now, just know that whenever you have multiple points of view in your story, it typically means that you have multiple heroes in your story. This is a popular choice for many young adult authors and has resulted in some phenomenally successful and award-winning novels, including *Six of Crows*, *The Sun Is Also a Star*, *Children of Blood and Bone*, and *One of Us is Lying* by Karen M. McManus.

But as you can probably imagine, if you have more than one hero, you have more than one *everything*. More than one set of problems (and flaws!), more than one want, more than one need, more than one character transformation, and possibly even more than one set of plot points to trigger those character transformations.

That can be a lot to keep track of. But if you can pull it off, the result will be nothing short of masterful.

Look at the mystery/thriller *One of Us Is Lying*, which features not one, not two, but *four* heroes, each with problems, wants, and needs of their own. Addy is too emotionally dependent on her boyfriend (flaw), something she learned from her mother and sister (shard of glass) and has to learn how to be her own person (need), all the while trying to keep her boyfriend from discovering she kissed someone else (want). Bronwyn puts too much pressure on herself to succeed academically (flaw), partly because of her family's accomplishments and her sister's past struggle with leukemia (shard of glass). This pressure has led her to cheat on a test to secure her spot at Yale (want), but in the end, it's coming clean and cutting herself some slack that will truly set her free (need). Since Nate's addict mother left him (shard of glass), he's careful to keep everyone at a distance (flaw) while trying to make ends meet for himself and his father (want), but it's his relationship with Bronwyn that will eventually teach him how to let down his guard and let people in (need). And Cooper is terrified of what will happen if his friends and family find out he's gay, especially his strict, conservative father (shard of glass), so he hides his true self from everyone (flaw) and focuses on his lifelong goal of becoming a professional baseball player (want), until his secret is revealed and he's forced to embrace who he really is, instead of hiding from it (need).

Oh, and there's a whole murder mystery going on in the A Story too. *Wow, right?*

But it works well in this story because the premise of the novel is all about figuring out which one of them has secrets and which "one of [them] is lying." (It turns out, all of them are, something we know only because we've seen the story through all of their perspectives.)

The choice of whether to include more than one hero in your novel should ultimately be about what will best serve *your* story, not about what other writers in the industry are doing. For every successful, masterfully structured multiple-hero novel, there is an equally successful and masterfully structured novel with only one hero, like *The Hunger Games* by Suzanne Collins, *The Fault in Our Stars*, *We Were Liars*, *The Hate U Give* by Angie Thomas, and *Red Queen* by Victoria Aveyard.

Sometimes focusing on one hero is the best way to tell *that* hero's story. Remember, every time you add another hero to your novel, you have fewer pages to devote to each hero's journey (both external and internal).

Regardless of how many heroes you choose to feature in your novel, I still urge you to pick what I call the "one true hero." It's kind of like choosing your favorite child, which I know you're not supposed to do. But in this case, I promise it's okay (and you don't have to tell your other heroes). The one true hero is like the top-billed star in a movie. Whose name appears at the top of your book's poster? Who is this novel *mostly* about?

Let's find out.

Who Is Your One True Hero? (Choose Wisely!)

Remember, there's an intimate relationship between character and plot. Every hero has one true plot that is destined to transform them, and every plot has one true hero that it is destined to transform. Your job is to play matchmaker and make sure the right character winds up in right plot.

First psychiatrist, now matchmaker!? Yes, you're a very busy bee.

Why is it so important to get this right? Well, because a failed match can easily equate to a failed novel.

Your plot should be the *only* plot that can transform this hero. And this hero should be the *only* hero who can be transformed by this plot (or at least the hero who is *most* transformed by it). And that's how we make our decision about who our "one true hero" is. We ask ourselves: Who has the *most* to learn? Who has the furthest to go, the most growing to do, the biggest obstacles to overcome? In short, who will get the most out of this story?

There's a good reason Aristotle (and not Dante) is the hero and narrator of *Aristotle and Dante Discover the Secrets of the Universe* by Benjamin Alire Sáenz. Dante is much quicker to realize his feelings for Aristotle and accept who he is. Aristotle is much more resistant to change, more stubborn, and therefore much more suited to be the hero of this story. Without this story, who knows what might have become of him?

If you're writing multiple points of view with multiple heroes, choosing your one true hero might be harder. Yes, all of your heroes should have compelling character transformations, but whose is the biggest? This is often (but not always) the POV we read first in the novel.

In *Children of Blood and Bone*, Zélie is the hero we meet first and the one who changes the most. While the other two heroes (Amari and Inan) also experience transformative arcs (Amari finds courage in herself and Inan breaks free from his father's brainwashing), Zélie's arc is the one that's front and center in the story. Her lessons in faith and nonviolence are given the most page time by the author and result in the biggest changes for the world of Orïsha, in which the story is set.

On the other hand, in *The Sun Is Also a Star*, we (briefly) meet Daniel first, but Natasha is arguably the hero who grows the most. Yes, Daniel has an impressive character arc of his own (learning to confront his parents and take control of his own life), but we're introduced to Natasha as someone who doesn't believe in love or destiny (flaw), is angry at her father for being a silly dreamer who has made countless mistakes (shard of glass), and is desperately trying to fix one of those mistakes by stopping her family from being deported (want). But by the end of the novel (which takes place in a single day) Natasha has forgiven her father, has accepted her own destiny, is in awe of the universe's interconnectedness, and is in love. That's one heck of a transformation.

Even if you're writing only one POV, I still urge you to ask yourself whether you've chosen the *right* POV, the *right* hero. You don't want to get halfway through writing your novel only to realize you've picked the wrong hero. You'll end up trying too hard to make it work, forcing the hero into the plot like a square peg into a round hole, and the story will end up feeling contrived.

I've seen it happen with countless authors. They'll complain that the story is just not working, but they can't figure out why.

And then a light bulb goes on. There's this *other* character, a side character, a throwaway character, a villain, a character with a single line of dialogue, who fits the story more organically, and voilà! Problem solved. Novel saved.

So even if you think you know who your one true hero is, I'm going to ask you a very important question: *Are you sure?*

Your answer could make all the difference.

And if you're still having trouble deciding, consider this: Who can serve as the best guide for the reader? Sometimes that means the character with the least amount of prior knowledge about your world, allowing the reader to discover it through the hero's eyes (like Clary Fray in *City of Bones* by Cassandra Clare, who is introduced to the world of Shadowhunters right along with us). Sometimes that means the character with the most unique perspective on the story (like Avery Grambs in *The Inheritance Games*, who is not swayed by the wealth and affluence that has shaped so many members of the Hawthorne family).

Whoever you choose, your reader will be searching for that guide. That one true hero to latch on to. They'll be trying to figure out what kind of world this is, what the rules are, who the key players are, how should they *feel* about everything that's happening. But most of all, your reader will be trying to figure out how this story will affect them. How will it change them? And they'll find that answer in how it changes your hero.

Okay, so you've got a story-worthy hero (or more than one!) with a problem, a goal, and a need; what now?

Now it's time to set them loose in your plot and see how they do. But don't worry, it's not as scary as it sounds.

And, thankfully, we have a very trusty road map.

EXERCISE: IS MY HERO STORY-WORTHY?

- Who is the hero of your story?
- What is their big problem or flaw? (They can have more than one!) Remember, flaws start internally (from that metaphorical shard of glass) and manifest into external problems in your hero's life.
- How is this problem or flaw affecting your hero's life/world?
- What is causing this problem or flaw? What is the shard of glass? (Time to psychoanalyze, Dr. Author!)
- At the start of the novel, what does your hero want? What is their goal? (What do they *think* will fix their life?)
- How has your hero been actively pursuing this goal?
- Why haven't they achieved this goal yet? (This roadblock can be internal, external, or both!)
- What does your hero actually need? What is their life lesson? (What will *really* fix their life?)
- Is your hero the character who changes the *most* in the novel? (If not, is there another character who might be more story-worthy?)

CHECK YOURSELF!

- ❏ Does your chosen hero change more than any other character in the novel?
- ❏ Is your hero's problem or flaw specific?
- ❏ Does the hero's problem or flaw create a desperate need for change?
- ❏ Is your hero's goal tangible and concrete? (Will we, as readers, know when or if they achieve it?)
- ❏ Is there something standing in the way of your hero achieving that goal? (If not, the goal is too easy!)
- ❏ Is your hero's need (or life lesson) universal? Would a random person on the street understand it?

Building Your Save the Cat!
Beat Sheet
A Fifteen-Step Blueprint for a Flawlessly Structured Novel That Works

Crack open any well-written young adult novel and you'll find there are actually *two* stories going on: an external story or **A Story** (also called the "plot"), and an internal story or **B Story** (also called the "character transformation"). The external story, as we've discussed, is where all the *exciting* stuff happens: battles for the crown, road trips, breaking into secret labs, confrontations in the school hallway, solving murders, first kisses, first *other* things. It's the stuff that's happening on the outside. Stuff you can *see*. But it's the internal story where all the *important* stuff happens: flaws are conquered, fears are overcome, wounds are healed, and lessons are learned. It's the stuff that's happening on the inside. Stuff you can *feel*.

Together, these two stories weave and blend and twirl in a beautiful, romantic dance called "structure." That's the first time you've ever heard anyone describe structure as "romantic," isn't it? But it *is* romantic when you think about it! Your hero and your plot are destined to be together. Meant to be. It's written in the stars! Because without the carefully chosen elements of *your* plot, your hero would never transform. And without a hero who needs to transform, there would be no reason for your plot.

So how do we choreograph this dazzling *pas de deux* of structure? Welcome to the Save the Cat! Beat Sheet!

It's your trusty guide, your blueprint, your cheat sheet to structure. And it's about to become your very best friend as well.

Often, when we think about the undertaking of writing a novel, we become paralyzed. *I have to write* how *many pages?* And *they have to make sense?* It's like getting into a car in New York City and deciding you're going to drive to Los Angeles. Chances are, you wouldn't do that without a map. Or better yet, a whole GPS system with turn-by-turn instructions to keep you on route.

That's what the Save the Cat! Beat Sheet is. It's a map. It tells you where the turning points are, where the ups and downs in the road are, where to stop to rest and where to rev the engine. It tells you how to get from the first page to the last page—start to finish—while still taking your passenger (your reader) on the ride of their life.

But it's not just about plot. This beat sheet is also your guide to crafting a character transformation that resonates.

In other words, the Save the Cat! Beat Sheet is designed to turn you into a master storyteller.

And here's the best part: it doesn't matter *when* or *how* you use it—as an outlining tool before you start writing, as a revising tool after you've already written, or as a jump start after you've wandered five hundred miles off course during your first draft and are now sitting stranded on the side of the road, wondering why you thought this detour to explore the best friend's uncle's backstory as a potato farmer was a good idea. The Save the Cat! Beat Sheet is here to help you stay on course or get back on course.

So let's unfurl this map and see where we're going.

The beat sheet is broken down into three "acts" (or parts), which are further divided into fifteen total "beats" (or plot points). Coming up, we'll go deep into each act and beat (with examples!), but first, it's helpful to see the entire beat sheet laid out as an overview.

So here's a quick summary of all fifteen beats and where they belong in your novel.

ACT 1

1. **OPENING IMAGE (0% TO 1%):** A "before" snapshot of your hero and their world.

2. **THEME STATED (5%):** A statement made by a character (typically not the hero) that *hints* at what the hero's arc will be (that is, what the hero must learn/discover before the end of the book). Also referred to as a life lesson.

3. **SETUP (1% TO 10%):** An exploration of the hero's status quo life and all its flaws, where we learn what the hero's life looks like before its epic transformation. Here we also introduce other supporting characters and the hero's primary goal. But most important, we show the hero's reluctance to change (aka learn the theme) while also hinting at the stakes at risk should the hero *not* change.

4. **CATALYST (10%):** An inciting incident (or life-changing event) that happens to the hero, which will catapult them into a new world or new way of thinking. An action beat that should be big enough to prevent the hero from being able to return to their status quo Setup world.

5. **DEBATE (10% TO 20%):** A reaction sequence in which the hero debates what they will do next. It's usually presented in the form of a question (such as "Should I go?"). The purpose of this beat is to show the hero's reluctance to change or how momentous the change will be.

ACT 2

6. **BREAK INTO 2 (20%):** The moment the hero decides to accept the call to action, leave their comfort zone, try something new, or venture into a new world or new way of thinking. It's a decisive *action* beat that separates the status quo world of Act 1 from the new upside-down world of Act 2.

7. **B STORY (22%):** The introduction of a new character or characters who will ultimately serve to help the hero learn the theme. Also referred to as a helper character, this can be a love interest, nemesis, mentor, family member, friend, or other.

8. **FUN AND GAMES (20% TO 50%):** This is where we see how the hero is faring in their new world. They're either loving it or hating it. Succeeding or floundering. Also called the promise of the premise, this section represents the *hook* of the story (why the reader picked up the novel in the first place).

9. **MIDPOINT (50%):** Literally the middle of the novel, where the Fun and Games culminates in either a false victory (the hero has thus far been succeeding) or a false defeat (the hero has thus far been floundering). Something should happen here to raise the stakes and push the hero toward real change.

10. **BAD GUYS CLOSE IN (50% TO 75%):** If the Midpoint was a false victory, this section will be a downward path where things get progressively worse for the hero. If the Midpoint was a false defeat, this section will be an upward path where things seem to get progressively better for the hero. But regardless of path, the hero's deep-rooted flaws (or internal bad guys) are closing in as tension, stakes, and conflicts mount.

11. **ALL IS LOST (75%):** The lowest point of the novel. An action beat where something happens to the hero that, combined with the internal bad guys, pushes the hero to rock bottom.

12. **DARK NIGHT OF THE SOUL (75% TO 80%):** A reaction beat where the hero takes time to process everything that's happened thus far. The hero should be worse off than at the start of the novel. This darkest hour is the moment right before the hero figures out the solution to their big problem and learns the theme or life lesson.

ACT 3

13. **BREAK INTO 3 (80%):** The "aha!" moment. The hero realizes what they must do to not only fix all of the problems created in Act 2, but more important, fix themself. The arc is *nearly* complete.

14. **FINALE (80% TO 99%):** The hero proves they have truly learned the theme and enacts the plan they came up with in the Break Into 3. Bad guys are destroyed, flaws are conquered, lovers are reunited. Not only is the hero's world saved, but it's a *better* place than it was before.

15. **FINAL IMAGE (99% TO 100%):** A mirror to the Opening Image, this is the "after" snapshot of who the hero is after going through this epic and satisfying transformation.

Or, if you're more of a visual person, here's a nifty graphic for you:

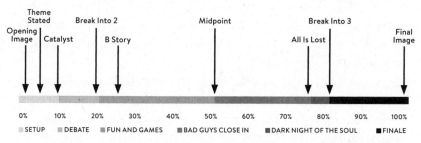

Voilà! This is your road map to transformation. Your guide to crafting a compelling story. Don't leave home without it! But also, don't worry if any of these beats seem confusing or nebulous right now. This entire chapter is dedicated to the beat sheet, which means we're going to be exploring each beat in detail. By the end of this chapter, you'll be so well-versed in structure, you'll be able to write a novel in your sleep. (Okay, not really, but how cool would that be?)

And to further solidify this magical beat sheet thing, I've broken down *ten* novels in depth later on in the book, so you can see how all the beats come together to masterfully construct some of the most successful and beloved young adult books on the market.

What Goes Where

You might have noticed in our beat sheet overview, there were percentages noted next to each beat. These percentages tend to cause a lot of stress and anxiety among writers, so let's deal with that right off the bat (no panicked writers allowed on this journey!).

I've read *a lot* of novels. And after analyzing the structure of hundreds of modern and classic novels, what I found was that the fifteen beats tended to fall *roughly* in the same place for each story, regardless of genre or age group. For instance, I found that some sort of big, life-changing event (aka the "Catalyst") came roughly 10% of the way through the story, and that about 20% of the way through the story, the hero entered a new world or tried something new (Break Into 2), and at about 75% of the way through the story, the hero hit some type of rock bottom or low point (All Is Lost). This is how I became certain that there *was* in fact a secret storytelling code hidden beneath the surface of almost all popular fiction.

I took my findings and averaged them to create the percentages you see in the pages in this book. Which means there are novels where the beats come earlier than the percentage markers I've provided, and novels where the beats come later. Remember, these percentages are *guidelines*, based on novels that are already successful. They are not set in stone. The beat sheet police are not going to knock down your door and confiscate your laptop if your Break Into 2 beat comes a few pages late. Or early.

But guidelines should *guide* you. Your beats should *roughly* match these percentages if you want your story to follow the template that readers are accustomed to reading. They can also keep you on track and help you diagnose potential pacing and structure problems. If you find that your Catalyst doesn't come until 30% of the way through your novel, your story is probably dragging and you risk losing your reader's attention. If you find that your All Is Lost is coming at 60% (instead of closer to 75%), that's a sign you haven't effectively built up to that moment and the impact of such a crucial, life-changing beat might fall short.

To help keep you on track as we dive into the beat sheet in more detail, I've included a reminder of these guidelines at the start of each beat, along with a recap of what the beat is for. I call it the "beat cheat sheet" (because I like rhyming things). So let this cheat sheet be a comfort to you, not a source of stress.

Calculating Your Beats

How do you know exactly where *your* beats fall? Well, that can be tricky if you're in the outlining phase or are still writing the first draft. My recommendation is to start with an *estimated* total word count or page count for your story and work from there.

For instance, if you estimate your story will be 80,000 words (a fairly average length of a young adult novel), then your Catalyst would ideally come around the 8,000 word mark (10% of 80,000), your Break Into 2 would come around the 16,000 word mark, the Midpoint around the 40,000 word mark, and so on. (If you don't want to do the math, I have a beat sheet calculator at JessicaBrody.com/stc-calculator.)

If you need help estimating the total length of your novel, check out these handy tables, which feature some publishing industry standard lengths (from "Wrestling with Word Counts" by Sarah Diamond, www .scbwi.org/wrestling-with-word-counts) for young adult novels as well as the estimated lengths of a few popular YA novels in different genres.

YOUNG ADULT NOVELS	WORD COUNT	PAGE COUNT
Publishing Industry Standard (contemporary fiction)	60,000 to 85,000	240 to 360
Publishing Industry Standard (speculative fiction)	70,000 to 100,000	280 to 400
The Giver by Lois Lowry	43,617	174
The Fault in Our Stars by John Green	65,752	313
The Sun Is Also a Star by Nicola Yoon	70,180	384

To All the Boys I've Loved Before by Jenny Han	78,662	355
The Hunger Games by Suzanne Collins	99,750	399
Warcross by Marie Lu	108,750	416
Children of Blood and Bone by Tomi Adeyemi	154,280	544

The key, however, is to be flexible. Stories change. They're pesky like that. Remember, you can always adjust as you go. I've never written a novel that turned out exactly the same length as I estimated. And for that matter, I've never written a novel that matched the beat sheet I started with. But I find it helpful to start with a guideline and an estimate, so I have something to write *toward*. Like road markers on this long, cross-country journey we call storytelling.

So, are you ready to put an end to all of your plotting problems?

Let's beat it out.

Act 1

You might have heard of the three-act structure before, but in Save the Cat! terms, we like to define the acts as "worlds." Three worlds that your hero will journey through en route to becoming the person they need to become. The purpose of Act 1, which we call the **thesis** world or "status quo" world, is to give your hero a place to begin. Something to grow *from*. And to give your readers a solid understanding of who your hero is and what their life is like before the epic transformation that awaits them. Because without an understanding of where your hero has been, it's difficult for your readers to appreciate how far they will go.

So we *show* them.

1. OPENING IMAGE

OPENING IMAGE > THEME STATED > SETUP > CATALYST > DEBATE

WHAT DOES IT DO? Provides a quick "before" snapshot of your hero and their world.

WHERE DOES IT GO? 1% (This is the first scene or chapter of your novel.)

If you were to capture your hero's flawed existence in one snapshot, what would it look like? That's exactly what the Opening Image is. It's the "before" picture in the quintessential before-and-after comparison. Which means, yes, there will be an "after" picture at the end.

The Opening Image is your reader's first glimpse at your hero and their world. And you know what they say about first impressions? You never get a second chance to make them. So we want to make sure this Opening Image grabs the reader and helps them understand exactly what kind of journey they're about to go on and *who* they're going on it with.

Which is why the Opening Image is also where we set the tone, style, mood, and voice of the novel. Is your story a comedy? Then your Opening Image should be pretty dang funny. Is your story a dark fantasy? Then your Opening Image should be dark and fantastical. Is your story a suspense thriller? Then thrill us! Put us on the edge of our seats right off the bat.

But there's a reason this beat is called the Opening *Image* and not, say, the Opening Monologue or Opening Info Dump. The word "image" reminds us, as writers, to be visual. Put the reader right into the scene. Don't just tell us about your flawed hero. *Show* us your flawed hero in action! This is the fastest way to hook a reader, by dropping them right into an active scene. This forces the reader to become an active part of the scene themself.

In the opening scene of *Divergent* by Veronica Roth, we're dropped right into Beatrice's status quo world as her mother cuts her hair. It's the only time she's allowed to look at herself in a mirror. With this one snapshot, we get a taste of this world (it's not like our own) and Beatrice's place in it as a member of the selfless Abnegation faction. We learn that she will soon have to choose which faction to join permanently, and the choice is haunting her, because she secretly wants to leave Abnegation, which would mean abandoning her family.

In the Opening Image of *Aristotle and Dante Discover the Secrets of the Universe* by Benjamin Alire Sáenz, we meet Aristotle on the morning of his fifteenth birthday as he lies in bed feeling lonely and miserable, listening to a radio DJ play "La Bamba" and thinking about how sad it is that Richie Valens died young. Our first impression of Aristotle? He *definitely* needs some change in his life!

These are successful Opening Images because they give us a glimpse of what we are getting into and the kind of journey we are about to embark on. And because they give us a glimpse of the hero's flawed life.

All of this happens in one scene because this beat is what we call a **single-scene beat**. It takes place over the course of one scene or chapter. It's an important distinction to make because there will be other beats along the way that are **multi-scene beats**, meaning they span multiple scenes or chapters of your novel. But for the Opening Image, we get only one snapshot. One chance to make a first impression. So, what's yours going to be?

My advice: focus on the hero's flaws and problems.

In *The Hate U Give* by Angie Thomas, one of Starr's biggest problems at the start of the novel is that she feels out of place in her two worlds (her mostly Black neighborhood and her mostly white private school). So where does author Angie Thomas put her in the Opening Image? In one of those two worlds—a party in Garden Heights—feeling . . . you guessed it! Out of place!

And in the sci-fi tech thriller *Warcross*, one of Emika's biggest problems is the three months of rent that's overdue on her apartment. So how does author Marie Lu *show* us this problem? By opening with a scene of Emika trying to pay off her rent by bounty hunting a criminal who's been illegally betting on the popular virtual reality game Warcross. Not only does this introduce us to Emika, her big problem, and her initial goal, but it also gives us a glimpse of the sci-fi world Lu has built in the novel.

Remember back in chapter 1 when you brainstormed your hero's flawed life and all their problems? Well, in the Opening Image you choose one of those problems (or several) to highlight and show your hero dealing with it. If your hero struggles with confidence, show us! Choose the perfect snapshot that captures that struggle. If your hero has attachment issues, how can that come through in a single scene? Perhaps your hero is shown throwing away something that most people would consider sentimental, like a photograph or a yearbook. Or perhaps they're shown quitting a sport that they're actually really good at.

All of these types of images are essentially *clues* for your reader. Little nuggets of information that lure the reader into the story and get them thinking. *Why are they throwing away that sentimental photograph? I bet there's a story behind that!*

The more *visual* clues you can drop for your reader, the more active and engaged they will be in your story right from the start. The Opening Image is the first place to start dropping those clues and giving your reader a hint of who this hero is as the story begins.

That way, when the reader reaches the end of the novel, or the Final Image (an opposite or **mirror beat** to the Opening Image), they can truly appreciate how far the hero has come and how much work you've done as the writer to bring them there.

2. THEME STATED

WHAT DOES IT DO? Briefly hints at the transformative journey that your hero will take and the flaw(s) they will eventually conquer.

WHERE DOES IT GO? 5% (Or ideally somewhere in Act 1.)

With the Opening Image, we gave the reader a good look at who the hero is at the start of the story. Now we're going to give the reader a hint at who the hero is going to *become* by the end. What will this epic journey of transformation entail? Where are we ultimately going?

That is the function of the Theme Stated beat.

It's a **single-scene beat** that happens early in the story (usually *within* the Setup beat), when the hero's need or life lesson is *subtly* hinted at or touched on, usually by a secondary character.

Ooh. Sounds clever, right? It is. If it's done well. So, let's break down how to do that.

Remember that every story is about transformation (or should be!). Every story takes a flawed hero and makes them *less* flawed. The Theme Stated references that transformation with a little nod to what the hero **needs** to learn by the end of the story in order to overcome their flaw.

Like "Sometimes when people talk, they don't always tell the truth," stated by Aristotle's mom in *Aristotle and Dante Discover the Secrets of the Universe* (10). Or "when / you're walking in the nighttime, / make sure the nighttime / ain't walking into you," stated by Will's mom in *Long Way Down*, a novel in verse by Jason Reynolds (40). Or "learn to look at the *whole* of something, not just the parts," stated by Emika's dad in *Warcross* (33).

And how do you like that? By the end, all of these heroes learn exactly these lessons.

Aristotle learns not only how to speak his own truth, but also to decipher truths that are not spoken. Will learns through his brother's death how to rise above the Rules of his neighborhood and not let the darkness get him too. And Emika learns that people aren't just good or bad; those are merely parts of a whole. Reality is more complex.

If you missed the impact of these quotes when you read these specific novels, that's actually a good thing. The theme should not be stated in an obvious, over-the-top way. You don't want to shine a giant spotlight on this beat, screaming, "Look over here! This is the big life lesson of my book!" This beat works best when it's done slyly. Covertly. Even *deviously*. Yes, I'm encouraging you to be devious. Mostly, I'm encouraging you to be *creative*. If you can subtly state your hero's ultimate life lesson in such a way that your reader doesn't even realize they've read it, that's a winning Theme Stated.

We're planting a seed in the reader's mind. So by the end of the novel, when the hero learns that exact lesson you hinted at earlier, on some subconscious level the reader thinks, *Well, that was brilliant.*

Let's just call it like it is. It's reader manipulation. The very best kind.

Don't be confused by the term *theme*, though. In Save the Cat! terms, the Theme Stated refers to your hero's need or life lesson.

The Truth About Forever by Sarah Dessen, for example, has many themes in the traditional, Honors English–class sense of the word: death, identity, family, perfection, and so on. But for the sake of its masterfully crafted beat sheet, the Theme Stated comes on page 34, when Macy's boss, Delia, says, "Ah, a girl with all the answers," subtly referencing Macy's flaw of wanting to control everything. But does Macy listen and start letting go of control right then and there? No! Otherwise, the book would be over on page 34. For Macy, control and the illusion of perfection is how she's managed to get through her father's death in one piece. Eventually, though, after a chaotic summer of working at a catering company, falling in love, and meeting new people, she will learn that she *doesn't* have all the answers and she *can't* control everything, and that's okay. But she has to experience a whole external story (A Story) to get there.

That's what I love most about the Theme Stated beat. The hero is essentially being given a hint to the real answer, the real solution, the thing that will ultimately fix their life (right up front)! And what do they do with it? They ignore it! Not because they're stupid or stubborn (okay, maybe they're a little stubborn), but mostly because they're not *ready* to hear it yet. They've got a bunch more living and learning to do (a whole novel's worth!) before they can fully embrace what they need and change for good.

Heroes tend to be resistant to transformation. At this point in the story, they don't *want* to change. So it's often useful to have the theme stated by a secondary character, or someone the hero can believably ignore—like a teacher, a random schoolmate, a fellow passenger on an airplane, an overbearing parent, or even a nemesis. It's not a hard-and-fast rule, but it's much easier for a reader to believe that the hero would ignore a secondary character than someone they're close to. In young adult fiction, not surprisingly, themes are often stated by adults, which makes sense because this is a time in a teenager's life when they're trying to figure things out on their own and listening to an adult figure might undermine their blossoming independence.

But your theme doesn't have to be stated to them outright. It can also appear in a book your hero is reading, in a newscast on TV, in an advertisement on your hero's social media feed. What's important is that it's done quickly and discreetly and that your hero rejects it.

Why does the hero typically reject or ignore the theme? It's realistic. It's *human*. We humans rarely change just because some random person on the street tells us to. We rarely change because *anyone* tells us to. It takes a lot to get a person to change their ways. Which is why, throughout the rest of this novel, we're going to throw a lot at your hero—dystopian governments, treasure hunts, cafeteria drama, intergalactic battles, life-threatening illnesses, vampires!—but it's all in service of helping your hero *realistically* learn and grow.

That's storytelling, my friends.

Creating exciting external events (plot) that organically trigger internal change (transformation).

Now, if you're thinking *Wow, Jessica, it sounds so simple!*—it is! But if you're thinking *Wow, Jessica, it sounds impossible!* don't worry. I'm going to guide you every step of the way. And here's a little secret to set your mind at ease.

You *already* have your theme.

Remember when I told you to think about who your hero is, why they're flawed, and what they need to learn in order to pull out that shard of glass and fix those flaws? Well, guess what? That need—that life lesson—*is* your theme. Now you simply have to figure out who's going to state it and how.

3. SETUP

WHAT DOES IT DO? Sets up your hero's life and their status quo world before everything changes.

WHERE DOES IT GO? 1% to 10% (This beat usually takes up the first tenth of the novel.)

The Setup is where we continue to build our hero's status quo world and all of its problems. In this beat, we expand upon the initial "snapshot" of the Opening Image and reveal the *whole* picture, giving our reader a solid understanding of who this hero is before their epic transformation, so that they can fully appreciate all the change that's yet to come.

There's a lot to do to accomplish that, but thankfully you get multiple scenes or chapters to do it, because this is a **multi-scene beat**, unlike the Opening Image and Theme Stated, which were each a single scene. And trust me, you're going to need those multiple scenes to get the work done, so let's roll up our sleeves and find out what's happening here.

Hero and Goal

First up, we need to establish the hero of the story (or heroes, in the case of multiple points of view). Your hero is at the helm of this ship, and this whole storytelling universe revolves around them. (Don't let it go to their head.) So it's important for our readers to understand *who* this character is. What is their personality? What are their tics? What are their likes and dislikes? Who populates their life? Any characters who are important to your hero's world should be established in this beat. We call these characters the A Story characters because they represent the **A Story** (also known as the "external story"), as opposed to the B Story character we'll meet in a later beat.

But arguably one of the most important things to establish in the Setup is your hero's goal. Remember in the last chapter, we talked about what your hero **wants**. Well, one of the fastest and most effective ways to introduce a hero to a reader is to show that hero pursuing that want. What we want says a lot about us, and having a *tangible* goal right from the start of the story not only gives the story momentum but also gives your reader something to latch on to.

We're immediately drawn into *The Sun Is Also a Star* by Nicola Yoon because we want to find out if Natasha can stop her family's deportation. And we're immediately drawn into *Warcross* because we want to find out if Emika can earn enough money to pay off her overdue rent.

But the hero's goal here in the Setup doesn't have to be life-changing, with massive stakes. It can be something as simple as yearning after a crush, like Cady in *We Were Liars* by E. Lockhart, or wanting to learn how to swim, like Ari in *Aristotle and Dante Discover the Secrets of the Universe*. Just make sure it's important to your hero right now.

Remember, the hero doesn't have to pursue this goal throughout the *entire* story. Goals often change, as we'll see in upcoming beats. But when we first meet this character, what are they after? What do they *think* will fix their life?

The Things that Need Fixing

It's also important in the Setup beat to show just how much your hero's life needs to be fixed. How imperfect is this world? *Why* is this story so essential? We show this by riddling our hero's world with problems. Problems create urgency, and urgency gives readers a reason to keeping reading. In Save the Cat! terms, we call these problems the **things that need fixing**. It's a laundry list of things that aren't working or just generally not great about the hero's life or world.

The hero is poor, has to pick pockets to survive, hates the elite ruling class of "Silvers," feels hopeless that things will ever change, and is probably going to be sent off to war where her brothers are already fighting (Mare in *Red Queen* by Victoria Aveyard). The hero is frustrated by her mother's strict rules and conservative beliefs, she's constantly being compared to her "perfect" older sister who is now dead, her algebra teacher picks on her (Julia in *I Am Not Your Perfect Mexican Daughter* by Erika L. Sánchez).

These things are not just thrown into the Setup willy-nilly. They serve a very important purpose. They become checkpoints along the journey. We can use these things to demarcate change. As we move through the story, we can keep returning to this list and asking, *What about now? Is Mare still poor and feeling hopeless about the world? Does she still hate all Silvers? Does Julia still think her sister is perfect?*

Although not all of these things have to be fixed, we as writers can use the "things that need fixing" to check our plotting. If enough items on this list are not resolved, we're not doing enough to transform our hero and their world.

And let's not forget about the *big* thing that needs fixing, the source of your hero's flaws: the **shard of glass**. How is that psychological wound manifesting in your hero's life? What challenges or conflict is it creating? We also use the Setup to visually cue the reader that there's an internal story to be told here too. Something that goes deeper than what's happening on the outside.

In *The Book Thief* by Markus Zusak, it's Liesel's shard of glass (the loss of her brother and mother) that causes her to feel powerless. But the author doesn't just come out and *say*, "Liesel felt powerless," because that's not as interesting. Zusak reveals the wound manifesting by showing Liesel stealing her first book, having nightmares and wetting the bed, and starting fights at school. And yet, despite all this stealing and fighting, Liesel is not *unlikable*. All of these manifestations of her shard of glass make her sympathetic, despite some of her so-called *less* desirable traits.

And that, right there, is the spirit of "Saving the Cat!" It doesn't have to be an actual cat that's rescued (though it certainly can be). Rather, it's the moment (or series of moments), typically found in the Setup beat, where the writer goes out of their way to get the reader on the hero's side. Either by giving the hero a sympathetic quality, a relatable problem (or nemesis), or a glimpse into *why* they behave the way they do, or by having them do something specifically redeeming.

Like Avery buying a homeless man breakfast in *The Inheritance Games* by Jennifer Lynn Barnes, or Mare saving up money to buy her sister earrings, despite barely having enough to buy food or keep the lights on in *Red Queen*.

Having a "Save the Cat!" moment or moments in the Setup beat is not a requirement, but if you have a hero who might be hard to sympathize with or if you want to make doubly sure your reader will get behind your hero, taking the extra time to establish your hero as someone the reader will definitely root for might be worth the effort.

If you're thinking, *This is lot to do in one beat*, you're right. It is. But it can be done. And here's a nifty trick to help you accomplish it.

Home, Work, and Play

A great way to check all the boxes of the Setup beat and show off the breadth of your hero's world is to give us scenes (or partial scenes) that take place in various aspects of the hero's life. We call these aspects "home," "work," and "play." Home is the hero's homelife, where and how they live, what their family dynamic is like. Work is what the hero is forced to do every day. If you're writing a contemporary young adult novel, that is probably high school, or maybe an after-school job. And play is what your hero does for fun. How they unwind, who they hang out with, and what their social life is like. Showing us glimpses of these three facets of the hero's life gives us a nice full picture of the status quo world and allows you to show how your hero's flawed existence is affecting everything.

Think about Avery in *The Inheritance Games*. Her problems don't stay contained to one aspect of her life. She lives with her sister's deadbeat boyfriend and often has to sleep in her car (home). To make ends meet, she has a part-time job in a diner (work) and hosts illegal poker games in the school parking lot (play). All of this is revealed in the first thirteen pages of the novel! When it's done well like this, we not only get a really good sense of who this hero is in their status quo world, but also get a sense that something *needs* to change or this hero is doomed.

Take it a step further and add what's called a **stasis = death** moment. This is a moment in the Setup that shows change isn't just needed, it's *imperative*. Otherwise, things are going to get *really* bad, maybe even fatal.

In *Warcross*, Emika arrives home in the Setup to find an eviction notice pinned to her door. She now has three days to pay her overdue rent, or she'll be homeless. In *The Hate U Give*, when the party Starr is attending is broken up by gunshots, her friend Khalil says, "Can't have a party without somebody getting shot" (page 16). This is a world that *needs* to change and a hero who *needs* to help bring about that change.

We use the Setup to not only build the status quo world but also drop hints that it's not working and we can't stay in it for long. Something has to happen. Something big.

And it will . . .

4. CATALYST

WHAT DOES IT DO? Disrupts the status quo world with a life-changing event.

WHERE DOES IT GO? 10% (Or earlier.)

The Catalyst is the first major turning point of the story. It's a **single-scene beat** that will crash through the status quo world and send the story spiraling in a new direction.

Prim's name is called at the reaping (*The Hunger Games* by Suzanne Collins), Julia discovers evidence that her dead sister was not the perfect daughter everyone thought she was (*I Am Not Your Perfect Mexican Daughter*), Khalil is shot by police (*The Hate U Give*), Macy's boyfriend tells her he wants to take a "break" (*The Truth About Forever*), Edward saves Bella's life, revealing he has superhuman speed and strength (*Twilight* by Stephenie Meyer), Cady wakes up after a mysterious accident she can't remember (*We Were Liars*).

The Catalyst is one of the easiest beats to identify in a novel because it often comes without warning and almost always turns the story on its head (or at least it should!). The Catalyst's primary purpose is to stop the status quo world in its tracks, or at the very least derail it. Because it's hard to continue like nothing has happened after your sister is called to participate in a fight to the death, or a mysterious boy blurs before your very eyes, or your boyfriend calls it quits. I mean, you could *try*, but you'd just be deluding yourself.

And that's the key marker of an effective Catalyst and a good way to test if you have one: can your hero easily go back to the way things were before and pretend this never happened? If the answer is no, you've got yourself a strong, healthy Catalyst there. If the answer is yes (or even *maaaaybe?*), then you might want to up your Catalyst game. Because if the hero *can* easily go back to the way things were before the Catalyst, you risk your reader wondering, *Why don't they?*

The Catalyst is the pivotal moment when life changes. It's a call to action. A wake-up call (sometimes literally—Catalysts often come as an unexpected phone call in the middle of the night). Everything else in the story, including every decision your hero makes from here on out, will stem from this one beat. So, no pressure, right? But we can achieve all of this if we just make the Catalyst big enough that the hero has no choice but to move forward.

Admittedly, that task is easier to accomplish when the Catalyst comes in the form of bad news, like a breakup, an arrest, or a devastating diagnosis. After all, people often don't change unless something bad happens to them. Adversity leads to powerful transformation. And events that seem bad at the time can often lead to a better, brighter future. But Catalysts don't have to be unequivocally *bad* to be effective.

Sometimes the Catalyst comes in the form of an opportunity that's presented to the hero. Like the invitation to compete to be the king's champion in *Throne of Glass* by Sarah J. Maas or the mysterious job offer that Emika receives from billionaire tech mogul Hideo Tanaka in *Warcross*. Sometimes the Catalyst is the reveal of a hidden ability, skill, or status that the hero didn't know about, which could mean good news or bad news. Like when Beatrice discovers that she's a Divergent, a rare person who doesn't conform to the factions of society (*Divergent*). And sometimes the Catalyst is just downright awesome (or seemingly so), like the unexpected inheritance that's mysteriously bequeathed to Avery in *The Inheritance Games*.

In a novel where a love story is the primary storyline, the Catalyst is often the first meeting of the love interest (even if they don't seem like the love interest at the time). Because it's this *person* who will send the story in a new direction. Think *The Sun Is Also a Star*, *Aristotle and Dante Discover the Secrets of the Universe*, or *When Dimple Met Rishi* by Sandhya Menon (that Catalyst is even in the title!).

And some novels even have *two* Catalysts (also called a **double bump**). In *Red Queen*, Mare's world is sent spiraling when her best friend, Kilorn, is conscripted to fight in the war, and then things get even more chaotic when she discovers that she has the ability to control lightning, something her status as a "Red" should not allow. (For more on double bumps, see chapter 3, Customizing Your Beat Sheet).

But what all of these Catalyst have in common—good or bad, single or multiple—is that all are *external* things that happen *to* the hero.

Catalysts are a key part of the **A Story**, so they are almost always an action or event that happens to the hero, rather than some kind of internal realization inside the hero's head. If, when crafting your beat sheet, you reach the Catalyst and start writing "My hero realizes . . ." or "My hero thinks . . ." stop right there. Heroes will have plenty of time to realize and think about things in the next beat. For now, we want this stuff to be happening *to* the hero, outside of their head.

Remember our romantic dance of structure? The careful weaving of external story and internal story? This is where we start to see it really pick up. Storytelling is essentially just a series of choreographed steps: *external* events, which trigger *internal* realizations, which inspire *proactive* decisions. One, two, three, one, two, three. On and on we waltz. With each external event and internal realization it triggers, we get closer to the *ultimate* internal realization and the ultimate transformation.

But I'm getting ahead of myself.

For now, let's just focus on making your Catalyst as big and life changing and status quo destroying as possible.

5. DEBATE

WHAT DOES IT DO? Shows how resistant your hero is to change and/or prepares your hero for the Break Into 2.

WHERE DOES IT GO? 10% to 20% (This beat takes us from Catalyst to the end of Act 1.)

You just threw your hero a giant curveball. Now they need time to react to it. This is a **multi-scene beat** in which your hero has a chance to gather their thoughts, weigh their options, and *debate* what to do next.

That's why the Debate is usually centered around a question, often a variation of "What do I do?" or "Should I stay or go?" or just "What does this mean?"

What will Julia do with the items she found in her dead sister's bedroom? (*I Am Not Your Perfect Mexican Daughter*) What faction will Beatrice choose? (*Divergent*) How will Mare save her best friend from conscription? (*Red Queen*)

We give our heroes this opportunity to think, reflect, and gather more information because it's only natural. It's only human, therefore it's *realistic*. When life throws us curveballs, we don't always know exactly what to do next. Or even if we do, it's not always an easy decision to make, or we don't always have all the information to make it. There are things to consider, stuff to prepare, questions to answer.

In *Long Way Down*, after Will's brother, Shawn, is shot in the Catalyst, Will debates what to do next, which includes going to the drawer where Shawn kept his gun, trying to figure out who shot Shawn, and informing us about the Rules of his neighborhood, which dictate that he take revenge. After Starr is the only witness to Khalil's shooting in *The Hate U Give*, there's a literal Debate (among members of her family) about whether she should speak up and step forward as a witness.

People rarely change overnight or make big, life-changing decisions without at least taking a moment to reflect on the situation. Therefore, skipping this important beat runs the risk of your story feeling contrived.

But the Debate isn't always centered around the question of what the hero will *do* next. Sometimes it's centered around gathering information that might help the hero later decide on a course of action. Like when Bella researches myths and legends to figure out what exactly Edward Cullen is in *Twilight*, and Avery researches Tobias Hawthorne trying to figure out why a perfect stranger would name her in his will in *The Inheritance Games*.

After Hideo Tanaka contacts Emika with the job offer in *Warcross*, she wonders, *Is this for real? Or a prank?* Then, when she's flown to Tokyo to meet with Tanaka himself and it becomes clear that it *is* real, the Debate changes to, "What exactly does the job entail?"

In novels where the love story is at the forefront, the Debate might center around the question of the couple's fate. "Will Natasha and Daniel ever see each other again?" (*The Sun Is Also a Star*) "How will Ari's summer change with Dante in it?" (*Aristotle and Dante Discover the Secrets of the Universe*)

And sometimes the Debate beat is more of a preparation for what happens next, in which the hero mentally, physically, or emotionally prepares for the next beat. In *Throne of Glass*, Celaena spends very little time debating whether she will join the competition. That decision was easy. Now she has to actually get to the city where the competition takes place, a journey lasting a few weeks. Along the way, she learns some things about her fellow travelers, including her escort, Prince Dorian, and we, the readers, learn some things about the world and its lore.

Remember, you get multiple scenes to have this Debate play out, and the sky is the limit in how you do it. In *We Were Liars*, as Cady struggles to piece together what happened the night of her accident, she spends some of this beat writing her own allegorical fairy tales as a creative way for her to process (Debate!) what happened to her the past summer.

Another great strategy for fleshing out your Debate is to bring your hero back to home, work, and play, to show how this decision or question is weighing on them in various aspects of their life. Perhaps other characters can chime in here too and help the Debate process along. This is also an effective way to show how the status quo world is already changing. By taking your hero back to familiar places, you're proving to them (and the reader) that they really can't go back to the way things used to be, as much as they might want to. That part of their life is over. They can only move forward.

And forward they will go. Into the great unknown. Into a whole new world.

Act 2

There are several make-or-break moments in a story where the reader will likely stop reading if they're not executed correctly. The first is the Catalyst. If nothing exciting or unexpected happens to the hero, eventually the reader will give up, because the story is going nowhere. The second moment is when the story enters Act 2.

Why do many readers jump ship at this point?

Because the author didn't make Act 2 different enough from Act 1. So once again, it felt like the story was going nowhere.

Act 2 is designed to be the opposite of Act 1. The inverse. If Act 1 was the **thesis** world, then Act 2 should be the **antithesis** world. It should feel completely new, unfamiliar, and *different*. That's why we also call it the "upside-down" world to remind us of how much it should contrast from the status quo world we just left.

If you do that—if you build an Act 2 world that makes a reader go *Now, this is new*—then you've got this in the bag. And you've also probably got a reader who's going to stick around to find out what happens in this new and unfamiliar place.

6. BREAK INTO 2

WHAT DOES IT DO? Brings the hero into the upside-down world of Act 2, where they will fix things the *wrong* way.

WHERE DOES IT GO? 20% (Before you get one-quarter of the way through your novel, there should be a clear Act break.)

Adventure! Excitement! Romance! Mysteries! Quests! It all starts here, in this second major turning point of your novel, as we *break* from the status quo world and step into the upside-down world.

The Break Into 2 is a **single-scene beat** that marks the exit from an old way of life and an entrance into a new way of life. It's only one scene because this is simply the moment of decision or the moment of action when the hero takes the first step across the Act 1/Act 2 threshold.

Think about it this way: if the Debate was a question, then the Break Into 2 is typically the answer to that question.

Will Starr in *The Hate U Give* speak up about what she saw? Yes! She agrees to talk to the police and is suddenly thrust into the middle of a growing race controversy that's quickly spreading across the country. What a change for a girl who spent her Act 1 world trying to *hide*.

What faction will Beatrice in *Divergent* choose? At the Break Into 2, the day of the Choosing Ceremony arrives, and Beatrice declares she will leave her family and join the brave and daring Dauntless, a faction that couldn't be more different from the passive, selfless Abnegation in which she grew up. She even changes her name shortly after, shedding Beatrice and becoming the new, dauntless "Tris."

This is the moment where the hero bids goodbye to their status quo world and enters a new one.

Keep in mind, however, that heroes don't physically have to *go* anywhere to enter a new world—which is fortunate, because it can be difficult when you're dealing with teenage heroes who are bound by their parents' rules and limited in their ability to travel. Journeys into the unknown don't require physical or geographical distance. An upside-down world can be found in one's own town or even one's own home, simply by trying something new, venturing into a new way of thinking, or taking on a new job or "mission."

In *The Truth About Forever*, after Macy's boyfriend calls for a break in their relationship, her solution is not to go anywhere new. But she does decide to accept a job at a catering company that is the embodiment of chaos and disorganization, which takes her far, far away from the structured, organized life she led before.

And In *Long Way Down*, Will's answer to his Debate is to grab Shawn's gun, ride the elevator to the ground floor of his building, and shoot the man who he thinks shot his brother. It's a building he's lived in all of his life, and yet this elevator ride feels very different with a gun tucked into his waistband and a new "mission" guiding him.

These beats are effective for two reasons: (1) there is a clear and defined *break* from Act 1 to Act 2, and (2) there is a proactive decision or move being made on the part of the hero.

A Proactive Decision

The key word here is "proactive." This beat is never as impactful (or exciting!) when the hero isn't in the driver's seat of the decision. Even if it's as simple as agreeing to have coffee with a new boy—the moment that marks the start of Natasha and Daniel's relationship in *The Sun Is Also a Star*—or Aristotle introducing his new friend, Dante, to his parents in *Aristotle and Dante Discover the Secrets of the Universe*.

We don't want our heroes to be pushed, tricked, coerced, dragged, or forced into Act 2. We want them to take that step of their own free will. Why? Well, it proves that this is a hero worth reading about! This is a hero who is willing to go somewhere new or try something new. This is a hero willing to change, even just a little bit.

Heroes can drag their feet and be resistant to change all they want in Act 1 (you could say that's what Act 1 is for!), but that's over now. It's time for heroes to grow up, get their butt in gear, and do something proactive. I realize that can be difficult to achieve when you're dealing with a hero who's only fourteen or fifteen and still limited by what they can realistically accomplish on their own, but teenagers are crafty.

A proactive hero is *especially* important in young adult novels because it's a time in a person's life when independence is just within reach. When boundaries are constantly being tested. When the yearning for freedom and choice is a constant fixture in life. So use that to give your hero agency. And there's no better place to do it than here at the Break Into 2.

Fixing Things the Wrong Way

But let's take a closer look at these proactive decisions. There's something they all have in common. They all feature a hero who is being motivated by something they *want*, not something they *need*. Remember the difference? External wants are what the hero *thinks* will fix their life. Internal needs are what will *really* fix their life.

In *I Am Not Your Perfect Mexican Daughter*, when Julia decides to investigate the truth about her sister's secret life at the Break Into 2, is she doing it because she started to empathize with her mother and learn how to connect with her? Of course not. That comes *way* later. She's doing it because she *wants* to know if her sister really was the perfect Mexican daughter everyone thought she was. She's doing it because she thinks this truth will ease her burden of being such a disappointment to the family.

And in *Divergent*, when Beatrice chooses Dauntless as her faction, is it because she's realized the power she holds as a Divergent and has embraced the complexity of her identity? No. She just *wants* to prove that she's brave and fits in somewhere. In fact, she's trying to *hide* who she really is and repress any of her Abnegation tendencies, because she thinks of them as a weakness, not a strength.

That's why I like to call Act 2 **"fixing things the wrong way."**

In *Red Queen*, after Mare's ability to control lightning is revealed, she accepts a bargain with the king to pretend to be a long-lost orphan of a Silver family, to keep the Reds from revolting. In exchange, she demands that her family be protected, her brothers returned from war, and her friend be exempt from conscription. She agrees to this not because she recognizes her power to bring about real change in the world (*need*), but because she *wants* to protect those she loves.

But we certainly can't fault Mare, or any heroes, for fixing things the wrong way. They're trying. They're making an effort. They did, after all, bravely leave their Act 1 world behind, and that's not nothing. But they haven't had enough experience (or plot!) to know how to fix things the right way. They haven't had enough *external* events to trigger the right *internal* realizations.

But they're on their way!

When it comes down to it, the decision that's being made here, at the Break Into 2, is a Band-Aid. It's a temporary solution to slap over the wound so they can try to ignore it for a little bit longer. It's not going to fix anything for *real*. Because the shard of glass is still buried in there, the real problem still needs to be dealt with. The theme still needs to be learned.

And it will be. Just not yet . . .

But fixing things the wrong way is where all the fun happens. It gives us adventures through space, epic fantasy battles, mysterious treasure hunts, drama in the cafeteria, and *lots* of kissing! It's what gives us the external story—the A Story—because it's all being motivated by external things (wants).

The Act 2 Goal

So, what decision is *your* hero making here? What external goal are they pursuing as they strive to fix things (the wrong way)? From here on out, I'll be referring to this as the **Act 2 goal**. Keep in mind, it doesn't have to be the same goal they were pursuing in Act 1. The Break Into 2 is a common place for goals to change. After all, the Catalyst just threw a giant wrench into things; it's reasonable to think that could derail your hero's goals too.

In *Warcross*, after Emika accepts Hideo's job offer, her goal is no longer to pay off her rent (that's already been taken care of by her new employer); now her goal is the job itself: to track down a criminal named Zero who has hacked into Warcross. And in *We Were Liars*, Cady's goal as she arrives back on Beechwood Island after a full year away is no longer about her crush on Gat; it's about returning to the location of the accident to try to remember what happened.

The Act 2 goal can also be a spin-off or modification of the Act 1 goal. In *Throne of Glass*, Celaena still wants her freedom, but now she has a different path to get it (the king's champion tournament).

Regardless of what type of goal you choose, I can't stress enough how important it is to define this goal for yourself at the Break Into 2. This Act 2 goal is going to be the thread that holds your story together for at least the next 30% of the novel, possibly longer. It's going to be not only storytelling fuel to propel you forward, but also a rudder that keeps you pointed in the right direction and informs so many decisions you will make from here on out. Many writers flounder in the writing of Act 2 because they don't have a clear and defined goal at the start of it, so they end up floating around aimlessly, trying to find a direction. Decide what your hero's Act 2 goal is, make it tangible, and make it trackable.

You will thank me later, I promise.

7. B STORY

WHAT DOES IT DO? Introduces the character who will somehow represent the B Story/internal story/theme and help your hero learn it.

WHERE DOES IT GO? 22% (Usually happens right after the Break Into 2 but can come earlier. Just make sure it happens in the first 25% of the novel.)

A whole new world needs a whole new cast of characters to populate it. You can introduce as many new characters as you need to in Act 2, but this **single-scene beat** is about introducing one very special new character, called the **B Story character**, also known as the "helper" character.

Before we get into exactly who this character is and their role in the story, let's review our definition of the B Story. In Save the Cat! terms, the B Story is defined as the internal story, the character transformation, the *growth* that the hero experiences as a *result* of the A Story (the external story).

But how do you show something that's happening on the *inside* of a character? How do you tell a story of internal transformation in an effective, engaging, and visual way?

Enter the B Story character!

In a nutshell, the B Story character is a character who will directly or indirectly help your hero learn their theme. Essentially, it's a character who will *represent* the B Story. Which means their very existence is a visual reminder of the internal journey your hero is on.

Now that doesn't mean the B Story character appears on the page spouting thematic soliloquies or lectures about life lessons to be learned. That would be a little on the nose. Not to mention didactic, which we all know teens *loooove*. (#sarcasm.)

Like the Theme Stated, we wield this tool subtly, with careful, creative brushstrokes. And there are lots of fun ways to do that.

For instance, your B Story character can represent the theme by being a total embodiment of it. Like Wes in *The Truth About Forever*, who says he doesn't like perfect, he likes flaws (something Macy has to learn), or Four in *Divergent,* who, as we discover by the end, is *also* Divergent and *also* originally from the Abnegation faction. But instead of rejecting his divergence, which Beatrice tries to do, he embodies it, embracing the virtues of all factions (he even has each faction's symbol tattooed on his back). Four believes "selflessness and bravery aren't that different" (336), and he teaches Beatrice how to embrace the Divergent factions within herself.

Your B Story character can also represent the theme by highlighting your hero's flaws, thus shining a spotlight on what needs to change. Like Gat in *We Were Liars,* who is Cady's love interest and the only person on the island who isn't part of the Sinclair family. As an outsider, he has a different perspective on how the family behaves, the entitlement and privilege they possess, and the way they sweep truth under the rug—something that will prove to be very important to not only help Cady remember what happened that night of the mysterious accident, but how she can overcome it as well.

Or maybe your B Story character represents the theme by being the opposite of it, thus sharing some of your hero's qualities and holding up a mirror to your hero's flaws. Like Cal, the crown prince and one of Mare's love interests in *Red Queen*. While Mare needs to learn a valuable lesson in harnessing her own power, Cal lets his be controlled by his father. Mare and Cal also both find themselves trusting the wrong people—namely Cal's brother—and being betrayed by them.

It's important to note that while love interests are a popular choice for B Story characters in young adult fiction, you have options. The B Story character can be a friend, a mentor, or even a nemesis or enemy. Or they can be a nemesis in disguise! Like Hideo Tanaka, the famous billionaire founder of Warcross, and Emika's love interest, who turns out to be the true villain of the story (*Warcross*). Who your B Story character is and how you use them is up to you; just make sure that they are fulfilling their primary function: to help guide the hero toward their theme in some shape or form, even if that's not done directly, purposefully, or even with the best intentions.

Another requirement of the B Story character is that they should be a product of the Act 2 world.

This means the character wouldn't have come into the hero's life (or wouldn't have become important in the hero's life) if it weren't for the hero's Break Into 2. Think about it. If the B Story character represents the theme and the theme could have been learned without ever leaving the status quo world, then what's the point of the story? Once again, we're subconsciously hinting to the reader that change is imperative. That hanging out in Act 1 isn't an option. And that this upside-down world—as scary, magnificent, fantastical, romantic, frustrating, magical, or terrifying as it is—is the only way to real growth and true transformation. And we can accomplish this by building the B Story character (the thematic helper character) out of the fabric of the Act 2 world.

In *Divergent*, Beatrice meets Four only because she chose Dauntless at the Break Into 2. In *Warcross*, Emika meets and falls in love with Hideo only because she accepted his job offer. And even though Macy met Wes *before* she accepted the part-time job offer at Wish catering, it's because of the Break Into 2 beat that they're able to get closer and become important to one another. So, even if your B Story character existed in Act 1, make sure that their purpose or role changes in some way as a result of Act 2.

Multiple B Story Characters

Can you have more than one B Story character?

Yes!

We call these **twin B Story characters** (like Ilsa Hermann and Max Vandenburg in *The Book Thief*). You can even have **triplet B Story characters** (like in *Red Queen* where Cal's B Story duties are shared with Maven, the other love interest, and Julian, one of Mare's teachers at the palace).

But a word of warning: don't start throwing in extra B Story characters just because you can and it's fun. To deserve this extra-special role, remember they must, in some way, be a product of the Act 2 world and they must in some way represent the theme and help the hero learn it. But what's additionally important is that they each help the hero learn the theme in a *different* way. Otherwise, why do you need both?

In *The Book Thief*, when Liesel steals a book from a Nazi book burning at the Break Into 2, the only person who notices is Ilsa Hermann, the mayor's wife. Liesel's relationship with Ilsa changes many times throughout the novel, but eventually Liesel discovers that Ilsa is someone who succumbed to her own feelings of powerlessness when her son died years ago. Now she sits in her library full of books that she refuses to read. She's literally surrounded by the power of words but does nothing to harness it. She is someone who has *failed* to learn the same theme that Liesel needs to learn and thus helps Liesel learn it. At the end of the story, it's Ilsa who gives Liesel a blank book to write her *own* words in and says, "Don't punish yourself . . . Don't be like me, Liesel" (524).

Max Vandenburg, on the other hand, also teaches Liesel about finding your own personal power, but in a different way. As a Jewish man hiding in Liesel's basement, he is someone whose power has been stripped away, yet he finds his own way to stand up to Hitler by having imaginary boxing matches with him. Liesel and Max bond over their mutual feelings of powerlessness (represented by their nightmares) and their mutual love of words.

So, does all this helping and theme-learning happen in this one beat? No, that would be impossible, as it's a single-scene beat. This is simply where your B Story character is first introduced or first enters the story in a real way. Remember, you still have to juggle the A Story (the external story) and any A Story characters who are still in the picture.

Your B Story character will continue to appear throughout the second and possibly even third act. And because they represent the theme, every time they do appear, you are reminding the reader (ever so *subconsciously*, of course) that this story isn't just about the external stuff. There's a deeper meaning here too.

It's subtle. It's manipulative. It's *writing*.

8. FUN AND GAMES

WHAT DOES IT DO? Delivers on the promise of the premise of the novel and shows us how your hero is faring in the new Act 2 world (either having fun or floundering).

WHERE DOES IT GO? 20%–50% (This beat spans the entire first half of Act 2.)

Pick up any novel from your bookshelf. Go ahead. I'll wait.

Got it? Good. Now, turn to the back cover or the inside jacket flap and read the description of the book. What you might not realize as you read it, and what you may have never realized in your many years of reading book descriptions, is that you're most likely reading about the Fun and Games beat.

How can I be so sure? Because the Fun and Games is where we find what's called the **promise of the premise**. The "hook." In other words, the reason a reader picked up the book in the first place.

Readers pick up *Red Queen* because they're promised the story of a lowly Red who's thrust into the dangerous world of the Silver elites. Readers pick up *The Sun Is Also a Star* because they're promised a whirlwind romance between a girl who refuses to believe in destiny and a boy who's put all of his faith in it. And they pick up *Warcross* because they're promised an epic thrill ride through a virtual reality video game led by a teen bounty hunter.

In other words, readers pick up a book because they are promised an Act 1 hero in an Act 2 world. That's the premise of any good novel!

But it's not enough to simply *have* a premise. You also have to deliver on it. And that's what the Fun and Games beat is all about. It's a **multi-scene beat** where we show your Act 1 hero in an Act 2 world. This is where we actually get to *experience* that dangerous world of Silver elites, that whirlwind romance and all of its chemistry, that Warcross championship and the hunt for the hacker within it.

In fact, that's how the beat got its name. Not necessarily because the hero is having fun (although they certainly can be), but because it's fun to read about. Anytime you put an Act 1 hero in an Act 2 world, it's automatically *fun*. And because the hero is still chasing after something they *want*, not something they need, this beat is all about fixing things the wrong way, which usually makes for some pretty entertaining fiction.

So in this beat, your job is to deliver on the promise of *your* premise.

Now, that might *sound* easy, but this is where most writers struggle in the storytelling process, and sadly, it's where most writers give up. But not anymore! Because I'm going to tell you *exactly* how to fill these pages (30% of your novel!) and how to make sure they're awesome, compelling, intriguing, dynamic, and of course, unputdownable!

Upward Paths and Downward Paths

First up, you need to answer a very important question:

How is your hero faring in this Act 2 world?

Are they loving it or hating it? Are they excelling or struggling? Does Act 2 generally improve upon their life or make it worse? Are they having fun or floundering?

The answer to this question will affect the rest of the second act (roughly 60% of the novel). So yeah, *kinda* important.

If you've decided that your hero's life is generally going to improve in this beat, you're writing what's called an **upward path** Fun and Games (in which the general direction is toward success).

On the other hand, if you've decided that your hero's life is generally going to get worse in this beat, you're writing a **downward path** Fun and Games (in which the general direction is toward failure).

Since Break Into 2 in *Warcross*, Emika is ten million dollars richer, an overnight celebrity, and the first wild card pick in the "wardraft." As she trains with her team, she also seems to be making progress in her Act 2 goal of tracking down Zero, the hacker she was hired to catch, *and* developing a closer relationship with Hideo Tanaka, her B Story character. Definitely an upward path.

Same goes for Cady in *We Were Liars*, who, after returning to Beechwood Island for the first time since her accident, is happy to be reunited with her friends (the "Liars") and rekindle her relationship with Gat. She even starts to get some of her memories back from "summer fifteen," the year of the accident, as she makes her upward path toward the Midpoint.

Conversely, the Fun and Games of *Divergent* is a downward path as Tris struggles with the Dauntless initiate training, suffering bruises from the fights and severe bullying from the other initiates. In fact, we can track her progress with the initiation rankings. Throughout this beat, Tris continues to rank near the bottom.

Similarly, in *The Hate U Give*, despite Starr speaking to the police about Khalil's innocence, the officer who shot him is not arrested, triggering riots in Starr's neighborhood. And in her personal life, her parents are fighting more, and Starr is still struggling to keep her two worlds apart, which becomes harder to do as Khalil's story gains publicity and attention. It's a clear downward path toward the Midpoint.

The Bouncing Ball

Note that the upward path and downward path are *general* directions. Not absolutes. After all, 30% of nothing but up, up, up, or down, down, down makes for a pretty dull reading experience, not to mention predictable.

Despite her upward path, Emika in *Warcross* still deals with her fair share of conflict, including struggling in her training with the team, a dangerous journey into the Dark World, and the discovery that Zero is a bigger threat than she first believed. And despite her downward path, Tris in *Divergent* still has some promising moments, like winning her first fight, getting picked first for capture the flag, and winning the respect of her fellow initiates when she bravely takes on a daring zip line from the top of a thousand-foot building.

You have to mix it up with what I call the **bouncing ball** narrative. Your hero is up, your hero is down. Things are going well. Things are not going well. The hero makes a breakthrough, only to hit a brick wall on the other side. Up, down, up, down. That's how you keep a reader on the edge of their seat and the pages turning.

Tracking Your Act 2 Goal

To help you decide whether your hero is on an upward path or a downward path, it might be helpful to think about your Act 2 goal. Remember back in the Break Into 2 when I urged you to come up with one? Well, the Fun and Games is where that goal plays out.

So how is your hero faring in terms of their goal? Are they making strides toward it, or is the goal moving further away? Does it seem like they might eventually achieve it? Or is it seeming more and more hopeless?

In *Red Queen*, even though Mare struggles with life in the palace as a Silver, her goal to try to harness and use her newfound ability tracks upward. She even discovers she has the ability to *create* electricity, not just manipulate it, something no one else can do, proving she is "Not Red. Not Silver. Something else. Something *more*" (140). And later, when she joins the Scarlet Guard who plan to attack the Silvers at the Parting Ball, this new goal also tracks upward.

On the other hand, in *I Am Not Your Perfect Mexican Daughter*, Julia's goal of finding the truth about her seemingly perfect sister does *not* go well as she runs into continual dead ends, making this a downward path.

This is how you will primarily fill the pages of this beat. With the pursuit of your Act 2 goal. It's going to be the thread that holds your story together and guides you and the reader toward the Midpoint, and it's going to be the storytelling fuel that keeps your creativity tank topped off and never dry. When you start thinking about Act 2 in terms of the hero's goal, you will always have something to write about and you will always have a *direction* to write in.

You create scenes for your Fun and Games by asking yourself: *What is my hero doing to achieve their goal? What obstacles are they hitting that force them to swerve and try something else? What conflicts are they encountering that might hinder their progress? What kind of characters are they meeting who might help—or not? What smaller goals are being spun off from the larger goal?*

In *Throne of Glass*, Celaena's goal is to win the tournament and become the king's champion, a very trackable goal because it's divided into a series of tests that Celaena must train for and pass. These comprise the primary scenes of this beat. But the goal becomes a lot more difficult when other competitors start turning up dead, and she starts falling in love with the captain of the guard *and* the crown prince.

In *Long Way Down*, Will's goal is to get to the ground floor of his apartment and shoot the boy he's convinced killed his brother. But with every floor he stops on, a ghost boards the elevator with Will, each one a victim of gun violence and the Rules that Will is so determined to follow. And each one in some way challenges Will's decision to seek revenge, serving as emotional conflict with the goal.

Weaving in Subplots

But the Act 2 goal is not *all* that's going on in this beat! Don't forget about the B Story character you introduced. What is happening with them? Are they helping or hindering your hero's goal? Or are they simply serving as a break from the goal?

This beat is also where you might introduce or further other sub-plots, like friendships, romances, drama with the parents, problems at school or work, or anything else that's important to your hero's story. In *I Am Not Your Perfect Mexican Daughter*, Julia isn't *just* attempting to track down the truth about her sister's secret life. She's also hanging out with friends, kissing a boy she doesn't really like, sneaking out of the house to attend a party, cleaning houses with her mother, fighting with her parents about the upcoming quinceañera that they're planning against her will, and getting grounded—a lot.

When you look at it that way, 30% of the novel doesn't seem like enough!

But it is.

After all, we can't stay in the Fun and Games forever. Just like the Catalyst that booted us out of the Setup, something is coming to boot us out of the Fun and Games as well.

Something that will send the story in a new direction yet again.

9. MIDPOINT

WHAT DOES IT DO? Marks the middle of the novel with either a false defeat or a false victory while at the same time raising the stakes of the story and shifting the direction of the narrative.

WHERE DOES IT GO? 50%

Welcome to the biggest turning point of the novel. It's a bear of a beat, but I promise you're going to love it.

The Midpoint is essentially a crossroads of many things in your story. Think of it like the Grand Central Station of plot threads. There's a lot going on and a lot to keep track of, but it's arguably one of the most important beats, and when done well, it can elevate your storytelling to new heights.

The Midpoint is aptly named, not only because it marks the middle of the book. It also marks the middle of Act 2 and the middle of the hero's character transformation. Both very important middles.

Whenever I reach the middle of a novel that I'm reading, I can immediately tell if the author has failed to harness the power and magic that is the Midpoint. The novel will lack focus and feel scattered. The plot will meander, and threads won't come together in meaningful ways.

Some authors jokingly refer to the middle of the book as the "muddle" because it can be a messy thing to write. But not anymore! Not with your handy road map at the ready.

So let's crack open this beast and see what we're dealing with.

The Midpoint is a **single-scene beat** that sends the story in a new direction. But there's a lot to do in this single scene to make the Midpoint as dynamic and impactful as it can be.

Essentially, all great Midpoints should:

1. Show the hero experiencing either a false victory or a false defeat

2. Raise the stakes of the story

3. Shift the story from the wants to the needs

Let's break this down.

A False Victory or False Defeat

We can pretty much check this box because you've already been working toward this.

I have? You have.

Remember your Act 2 goal, the one you were tracking in the Fun and Games with either an upward path or a downward path? Well, both those paths lead right to here. They are designed to drive your narrative straight toward the Midpoint.

If your hero was on an upward path in the Fun and Games, your Midpoint will be a **false victory**. Meaning your upward path has culminated in some kind of success.

At the Midpoint of *Warcross*, there's a literal victory as Emika's team wins their first official game of the tournament. Although Emika's primary Act 2 goal is to track down Zero, she also *wants* her team to win, so this feels like a pinnacle of the upward path she's been on.

Similarly at the Midpoint of *We Were Liars*, Cady notes, "Life feels beautiful that day. The four of us Liars, we have always been. We will always be . . . Here, in some way, we are young forever" (135). Despite her headaches and the still-unsolved mystery surrounding her accident, Cady is back with her friends and happy. It feels like the high point of the summer.

On the other hand, if your hero was on a downward path in the Fun and Games, then your Midpoint will be a **false defeat**. Meaning, your downward path has culminated in some kind of failure.

When a giant tank rolls into the neighborhood of Garden Heights at the Midpoint of *The Hate U Give*, it feels like the bottom of the downward path that Starr has been on. Her testimony to the police did nothing. The anonymous blog she started did nothing. Her neighborhood is a war zone. And there still has been no justice done for Khalil. Meanwhile, one of her Garden Heights friends, Kenya, is putting pressure on Starr to speak out (publicly) about the shooting.

And in *Divergent*, when Tris goes into her first fear simulation (getting attacked by crows), it feels like a defeat for her. She struggles with the simulation, sobbing afterward and telling Four she wants to go home. This is the moment she feels the *least* brave, the furthest from her Act 2 goal of proving that she belongs in Dauntless. She's basically giving up.

To put it *very* simply, in false victory Midpoints, the hero gets something they want, and in false defeat Midpoints, the hero loses something they want.

But that word, "want," is exactly why they're both *false*.

Remember, this story was never about what the hero *wants*. It's about what they *need*.

Divergent was never about fitting *into* Dauntless; it's about embracing the fact that she doesn't fit into any faction. She's a Divergent, and it's a strength, not a weakness. And *Warcross* was never about winning the game or even about catching the "bad guy." It's about Emika learning to see the whole picture and the deeper, more complicated truths that picture reveals about what it truly means to be "bad" or "good."

So either your hero went after something they wanted, and it didn't work out (false defeat), or it did work out (false victory), but the victory isn't what they thought it would be. They still feel incomplete. Empty. It didn't fix their life the way they thought it would.

Why? Because they still haven't learned the theme! They're still the same flawed hero they were in Act 1.

Even though Starr in *The Hate U Give* took an important step in her transformation by agreeing to talk to the police about the shooting, by the Midpoint it's clear she's *still* hiding. And even though Cady in *We Were Liars* thinks she's happily reunited with the Liars, she has *still* failed to remember that her friends died in a fire two years ago. This has all been happening in her imagination as she struggles to process her grief. It's a *literal* false victory.

The false victory and false defeat both serve the same purpose: to shine a big ol' spotlight on the fact that the story isn't over, so this external thing the hero was after must not be the deeper purpose of the story. There must be something *more* here.

And, of course, there is.

To send our heroes toward their deeper purpose (the need), it's not enough to simply have a false victory or false defeat. Something else must happen here at the Midpoint. Something big enough to *push* your hero into the second half of Act 2 and closer to their final destination: real change.

Which brings us to the second thing all great Midpoints should do.

Raising the Stakes

Up until now, your hero has been piloted by what they want. It's driven them this far. But as we've established with either a false victory or false defeat, it's not enough. They need to start focusing on the real stuff. And we, the writers, need to help them do that by throwing something in their path that *forces* them to change course and start heading in the right direction (toward their ultimate transformation).

The raising of the stakes is essentially you saying to your hero, "It's no longer Fun and Games, buddy. Things are getting serious. You better get your act together and stop messing around."

In *Warcross*, Emika's first victory is almost immediately interrupted by an attempt on Hideo Tanaka's life. In *Throne of Glass*, another competitor turns up dead. And in *Red Queen*, moments after the Scarlet Guard's plan to attack the Parting Ball succeeds (false victory), a surprise bomb goes off, signaling Mare that she's been betrayed.

This is why I personally like to call the Midpoint the "s**t just got real" beat.

Because it raises the stakes of the story in an exciting, thrilling, and usually unexpected way. And in raising the stakes (physically, emotionally, or both!) you make it harder for your hero to go backward, consequently pushing them *forward*.

But introducing a deadly threat isn't the only way to do that, and that strategy might not work for the genre you're writing. Fortunately, there are lots of ways to raise stakes. I find that most stake-raising moments fall into one of these five popular categories:

1. Love Story Ramp Ups

A first kiss, a first "more than kiss," a first declaration of love. These are all things that take the relationship to the next level, making it harder for your hero to run away, hide, or return to who they were before. They're *exposed*, and that's scary.

In *The Sun Is Also a Star*, Natasha and Daniel share a passionate kiss in a norebang (Korean karaoke room). It marks a false victory in Natasha and Daniel's relationship, but also raises the stakes by making things a lot more complicated. Especially for Natasha. What if she *can't* stop her family from being deported? Will she have to say goodbye to a boy she's starting to fall in love with?

Ramping up the love story pushes your hero even further out of their comfort zone and puts more pressure on them to change. Of course, they can still mess up the relationship (and they probably will), but they can't just walk away now. At least not without consequences.

2. Ticking Clocks

Nothing puts more pressure on a hero than time. Once you announce that there's a limited time period, it gives your plot a boost of adrenaline and, of course, raises the stakes.

Ticking clocks can come in all shapes and sizes: an upcoming test, event, game, or performance that will determine the hero's future; a leak in the fuselage of the spaceship with only hours of oxygen remaining; a diagnosis that gives a patient months or even weeks to live; the discovery that the killer, if not caught, will strike again in five days.

Did you get anxious just reading those? That's the point! A ticking clock forces your hero to focus on what's really important and make some tough calls.

In *The Hate U Give*, it's revealed at the Midpoint that the district attorney is preparing to take Khalil's case in front of a grand jury and that Officer One-Fifteen's father is going to do a television interview on his son's behalf. These are ticking clocks for Starr, pushing her to make her biggest, boldest decision yet: to do a live interview herself and tell the world what she saw.

3. Big Parties, Celebrations, Competitions, or Public Events

Why are there so often big events or parties right at the Midpoint—like the Parting Ball at the Midpoint of *Red Queen* or the first competition at the Midpoint of *Warcross*?

Because a **Midpoint party** is a great way to raise the stakes! It forces the hero to step out of their comfort zone and be "on display." They're exposed now, and *that* is scary. Perhaps your hero has been technically *existing* in their upside-down Act 2 world but not quite embracing it. Perhaps they're still longing for the comforts of Act 1. Perhaps they've just been phoning in this whole Act 2 business. Well, once they've been revealed for all to see (at a big party, celebration, or event), it's much harder to pretend.

In *I Am Not Your Perfect Mexican Daughter*, the false defeat Midpoint happens at Julia's quinceañera, a party she doesn't want and where she feels completely out of place. Not to mention, Julia *knows* this party isn't for her, but for her dead sister, Olga. This only intensifies her feelings of inadequacy and causes her to lash out at one of her aunts. This party not only spotlights how out of place Julia feels among her family but also highlights just how resistant she's become to empathizing with her mother's grief (her theme). And it shows how Julia's wants are overshadowing her needs. Instead of facing her grief head-on, she uses the party to further her Act 2 goal of finding out the truth about Olga.

4. Spilled Secrets

Spilled or revealed secrets are also a great way to raise emotional and personal stakes. This might happen purposefully or accidentally. So many secret crushes, secret backstories, and secret truths are revealed at the Midpoint.

In *The Truth About Forever*, this is the beat when Macy and Wes initiate a game of "Truth." Wes tells Macy about the crime he committed that got him sent to reform school, and Macy, for the first time ever, speaks about the day her dad died and confesses the guilt she feels. It's a big step for both of them, especially for Macy, because it's hard to go back into hiding after you've revealed something so personal about yourself.

Secrets are typically a sign that the hero hasn't yet changed the right way. Because secrets are usually kept out of fear. Fear of exposure, ridicule, not being accepted, or any other personal consequences. And for that reason, they are great ways to show and track flaws. Because secrets tend to be connected to flaws. And revealing them forces the hero to start facing up to those flaws in a real way.

When writing for teens, secret spilling can be a very effective storytelling tool. This is an age when readers are starting to experiment with new things and new identities and are often afraid of the consequences should any of that come to light. Secrets are effective at not only building intrigue from the start of a story, but also paying off that intrigue with stakes-raising moments when those secrets are revealed. Like I always say: "When all else fails, add a secret!"

5. Major Plot Twists

Who can resist a good plot twist? I certainly can't! That's why you'll find one in almost all of my Midpoints.

A major, game-changing plot twist is a great way to raise the stakes, because what you're saying to the hero and the reader is, "You *thought* you knew what this story was going to be, but think again!" It's a curveball. It forces the hero to rethink, refocus, replan, re-everything!

Tragedy strikes, a new clue to a mystery is uncovered, a dead character is not really dead! You'll find some of the biggest plot twists in literature right here at the Midpoint. These **Midpoint twists** tend to be *big*. They must be, because their purpose is to yank the hero out of the Fun and Games, away from what they thought they wanted, and send them down a new path, into a brand-new beat.

In *The Inheritance Games*, just as Avery discovers a key clue in the puzzle she's been trying to solve throughout the Fun and Games (false victory), gun shots ring out in the forest and Avery is almost hit. Looks like someone *really* wants to keep her from solving this puzzle. Talk about a twist! This literal Fun and Games of *The Inheritance Games* has just turned deadly.

So those are five common types of Midpoints. Of course, you're not limited to these five. Be creative! Flex those storytelling muscles. Raise the stakes in a way that makes sense to *your* story. You're also not limited to just *one*.

Look at the Midpoint of *Scythe* by Neal Shusterman. Our two heroes, Citra and Rowan, arrive at the Vernal Conclave (public event) to compete in their first apprenticeship test, and when they both purposefully fail (in order to help the other), one of the Scythes of the New Order (led by the antagonist) decrees that, at the end of their training, the winning apprentice should be forced to kill the loser (time clock *and* a Midpoint twist). Oh, and right before this, Citra and Rowan kissed (love story ramp-up!).

Whew! All of that in one Midpoint!

You'll notice what all of these stakes-raising moments have in common: they send the story in a new direction. After the exciting Midpoint of *Scythe*, Citra and Rowan's mentor kills himself and the two are separated and sent to train under different mentors. After Natasha and Daniel kiss in the norebang in *The Sun Is Also a Star*, she forces herself to *refocus* on her goal of stopping the deportation, reminding herself that she can't fall in love with someone if she's going to be kicked out of the country in less than twenty-four hours.

All of these Midpoints pushed the hero out of one beat and into the next. Just like the Catalyst! The Midpoint is another external event that triggers an internal realization that will inspire a proactive decision on the part of your hero. And the waltz waltzes on!

As you brainstorm your own stakes-raising moment, always remember your end goal. *Why* are you raising the stakes? The answer should be to push the hero forward and closer to real change. To make it even harder for them to go back to the way things were. And by doing this, you're essentially *shifting* the story from the wants to the needs.

Which is the third and final thing that all great Midpoints should do.

Shifting from Wants to Needs

After Tris's seemingly catastrophic fear simulation in *Divergent*, Four reveals that she actually did better than any of the other initiates, unveiling a hidden skill she didn't know she had but that she will continue to use to her advantage in the pages to come. This skill, as we'll soon learn, is a result of her divergence, so in a way, by using it, she's getting closer to embracing this part of her instead of pushing it away—which is exactly what she *needs* to do.

It's a subtle **shift from wants to needs.**

At the Midpoint of *Long Way Down*, the elevator stops on the fifth floor and Will's dead Uncle Mark enters. He challenges Will, asking why he's here and pressuring him to stop playing around and answer the question. Uncle Mark plays out Will's revenge plan like a movie, forcing Will to really absorb what he's about to do and recognize the consequences of his actions. In essence, Mark is *shifting* Will from his wants to his needs.

Of course, that doesn't mean that on the very next page Will, Tris, or any hero suddenly goes, *Aha! I've recognized all my flaws and now know how to fix things the right way!* Otherwise, the book would be over shortly after the Midpoint. But these heroes are *gradually* making their way *toward* that realization. Or perhaps even learning a small piece of their larger theme at this moment.

For that reason, a new goal is often introduced here at the Midpoint, or shortly thereafter in the next beat. This can also be a spin-off goal or a side goal. Or even just a modification or new perspective on the existing Act 2 goal.

After Avery is shot at in *The Inheritance Games*, she hasn't abandoned her goal of solving Tobias Hawthorne's puzzle, but she also has a new goal of figuring out who was trying to kill her. After Hideo's life is threatened at the Midpoint of *Warcross*, Emika's goal of finding Zero remains the same, but the stakes of that goal have changed. She's no longer just looking for a hacker; now she's looking for a potential murderer.

Without something new being introduced here (or in the next beat), or the plot shifting in some way, the Midpoint won't feel as effective. If the hero could continue on their same path after this, following the same goal in the exact same way, you know that your Midpoint isn't big enough.

This new or modified goal is proof that the plot did, in fact, pivot here. That we *are* being sent in a new direction. And that we are shifting, ever so subtly, from the wants to the needs.

We can really drive this shift home and represent it visually by having the A Story characters and the B Story characters intersect here in some way. Maybe they're all at the Midpoint party (like in *Scythe*). Maybe the B Story character is the character who helps bring about the shift (like Four does for Tris in *Divergent*). Maybe the stakes-raising moment directly affects the B Story character (like it does for Hideo in *Warcross*).

By having the **A and B Stories cross** or interact in some way (through its representative characters), we are subtly hinting to the reader that things are changing. The wants are starting to take a back seat to the needs and the hero is getting closer to finally fixing things the right way.

More reader manipulation? Absolutely! Isn't that the best part?

The Crossroads of All Crossroads

So there you have it. The solution to the muddle. The magical Midpoint where we show a false victory or false defeat, raise the stakes, and shift the story from wants to needs.

By now you might be thinking, *Wait a minute; all this happens in* one *scene?*

And while technically yes, this is a single-scene beat and it *can* happen in one scene, it can also be accomplished in several smaller scenes grouped close together. But the idea is that all of this happens around the 50% mark. And the closer together you can group these elements, the more effective they will be, the straighter your structure will feel, and the less clunky, meandering, and "muddly" your middle will seem.

If you want an inspiring example of a Midpoint where everything happens in *one* scene, be sure to read the full beat sheet for *The Hunger Games* (page 295).

In the end, though, don't beat yourself up if this beat takes multiple tries to get right. My Midpoints are the most rewritten beats of my novels. As I've said, it's a bear of a beat. But once you crack it, you'll breathe a huge sigh of relief as you feel the structure of your whole story fall satisfyingly into place.

10. BAD GUYS CLOSE IN

WHAT DOES IT DO? Provides a place for your hero to rebound after a false defeat Midpoint or fall down after a false victory Midpoint, all while the conflict, stakes, and tension are mounting and internal bad guys (flaws) are closing in.

WHERE DOES IT GO? 50% to 75%

If it's feeling like Act 2 is disproportionately longer than Act 1, you're right. Act 2 is 50% of the novel. Which is why I like to think of Act 2 as having two subacts, Act 2A (everything before the Midpoint) and Act 2B (everything after the Midpoint).

This might help you as we move into this next beat, as it should feel like we've entered new territory here. Bad Guy territory.

Now, if you're already thinking, *I don't have bad guys in my story! I'm writing a quiet, contemporary novel!* I've got news for you. *Every* story has bad guys. They just might not be defined in the way you're used to defining them.

The Bad Guys Close In beat is a **multi-scene beat** that spans 25% of the novel (coming in second place for longest beat!) It was originally named after the classic sequence in an action film when the bad guys regroup (after having been temporarily defeated by the hero at the Midpoint) and come back with a vengeance.

The title of this beat confused me for years. Then I realized something essential. The stereotypical "bad guy" is just conflict personified. What if, instead, we thought of this beat as "conflict closes in?" Aha! Light bulb! Essentially, this is the part of the book where the conflict builds, the stakes continue to rise, the tension ratchets up, and things get more intense for your hero.

In *Red Queen*, after the Parting Ball at the Midpoint, everything intensifies for Mare. She's forced to leave the city she calls home and travel to the unfamiliar capital, her allies are being picked off one by one, and when drops of her blood are discovered in the palace, the threat of her being exposed as a Red (not the Silver she claims to be) only increases.

And in *The Sun Is Also a Star*, after their passionate kiss at the Midpoint, Natasha and Daniel step outside the safe cocoon of the norebang, and the conflict of real life crashes down around them. Natasha confesses to Daniel that she's in danger of being deported *today*, which leads to a fight and their eventual separation.

Like a continual tightening of a screw, we want our plots to build with tension and intensity in this beat and our heroes to feel like the walls are closing in around them. Because we have to keep constant pressure on them and push them toward that moment of real change.

Failure to increase the conflict in this beat can cause the second half of your novel to lose momentum—and potentially lose readers as well. But keep in mind, there are different types of conflict.

There's external conflict. That's the obvious kind. The stuff that's happening on the outside of the hero, the stuff you can see. Like battles with natural elements, institutionalized prejudice, enemy kingdoms, supernatural abilities, or technology gone rogue. And of course, battles against *literal* bad guys, like bullies, nemeses, mean teachers, parents who just don't get it, evil rulers, evil robots, evil hordes of zombies or killer wasps (basically there's no limit to who or what can be evil). All of these options are technically *bad guys*, or **external bad guys** to be more specific.

But there's also that internal conflict. The stuff that's happening *inside* your hero. The stuff you can *feel*. Like battles with your own identity, beliefs, motivations, or sense of self. And of course, there's always battles with the hero's flaw or emotional wound left behind by their shard of glass. That's the primary internal conflict of this entire story. And every page that your hero doesn't learn their life lesson (that is, conquer that flaw), this battle gets more and more intense.

All of these options are technically bad guys too. They're **internal bad guys**.

So, yes, I guarantee your novel has bad guys. Or at least it should. Because it has conflict. Both external and internal.

But here's where things get *really* interesting.

Your Bad Guys Close In beat is going to look different depending on whether you had a false victory Midpoint or a false defeat Midpoint.

Remember, the Midpoint is a turning point, sending the story in a new direction. Let's take a look at what that means. If you have a false victory Midpoint, then your Fun and Games was an upward path, which means this beat should feel like a **downward path** (a new direction). On the other hand, if you have a false defeat Midpoint, then your Fun and Games was a downward path, which means this beat should feel like an **upward path**.

That's what a turning point does. It *turns* the trajectory of the story. It pivots the plot.

So let's see what each option looks like.

Downward Paths

A downward path Bad Guys Close In is pretty easy to conceptualize. After a victory at the Midpoint, things feel like they're getting progressively worse for the hero. And life is generally on a downward trend. (With a few bouncing balls thrown in to keep things interesting, of course.)

This is where we see Emika in *Warcross* coming up against more danger and more threats as her obsession with tracking down Zero grows. She's even recruited by Zero, who threatens her when she rejects him (external bad guys). Meanwhile, her relationship with Hideo is heating up but ends up becoming another source of conflict when a picture of them kissing is broadcast to the world, resulting in a public backlash against both of them.

In *We Were Liars*, the high point of Cady's summer at the Midpoint is immediately followed by darker days, in which her friends no longer want to leave Cuddledown house (where they've all been staying) and

Mirren grows increasingly sicker. Cady's imaginary world (in which her friends are still alive) is crumbling as the truth seeps in. But things aren't just bad in the present. As Cady remembers more about that tragic summer, she also remembers how bad things had gotten within her family as well. Like the constant fights over money and inheritance that eventually inspired Cady and her friends to set fire to the house.

Upward Paths

An upward path Bad Guys Close In is just the opposite. After a defeat at the Midpoint, things feel like they're getting progressively *better* for your hero. Things are working out. Strides are being made toward their goal(s). And life is generally on an upward trend (minus the bouncing balls, of course!).

This is where we watch Tris climb to the top of the rankings in *Divergent*, using her ability to manipulate the simulations to her advantage. But even as things progress in terms of her goal of proving she belongs in Dauntless, there's still plenty of conflict closing in. Her number-one ranking attracts dangerous enemies, and she starts to uncover a plot to overthrow the government.

And in *The Hate U Give*, Starr's upward path sees her speaking up more, using the power of her voice, instead of hiding. Her TV interview becomes one of the most-watched interviews in the network's history; she testifies in front of a grand jury, and she even stands up to her racist friend, Hailey, for the first time. Yet, despite this, the tension is still ratcheting up at every turn, like when Starr is threatened by the King Lords gang, warning her *not* to speak up.

Internal Bad Guys

However, regardless of what path your hero is on, whether things are getting progressively better here or worse, those *internal* bad guys—those unchecked flaws—are always closing in. And they're closing in fast.

In *I Am Not Your Perfect Mexican Daughter*, life seems to improve for Julia after the Midpoint. She starts to apply for college (putting her closer to the independence she so desperately craves), she starts dating a boy who shares her love of poetry, and she even finds the proof she's been looking for that her sister was not the perfect daughter everyone thought her to be (Act 2 goal). But through all of this, she hasn't yet addressed her grief or her anger, which are still seeping through the cracks of her happiness and even sabotaging her new relationship.

Remember, a hero's flaws are like faulty code in their operating system. They can go unnoticed for a while, but gradually more and more errors appear, making it harder to operate normally. If flaws aren't dealt with—if life lessons aren't learned and shards of glass aren't removed or confronted—those errors will continue to pop up, until eventually the whole system shuts down.

And what do you know? That's exactly what's going to happen.

Because that's what this beat is ultimately designed to do. Regardless of upward path or downward path, those internal bad guys are still in there, working behind the scenes in your hero's psyche, making it nearly impossible for your hero to find any true contentment.

This beat is designed to gradually but steadily push your hero closer and closer to their darkest moment. Their lowest of the low.

Total system-wide failure.

11. ALL IS LOST

WHAT DOES IT DO? Illustrates your hero's rock bottom (lowest moment) of the story.

WHERE DOES IT GO? 75%

Ever heard the old adage that no one really changes until they've hit rock bottom? Well, welcome to rock bottom. Your hero has hit it. They've tried everything else—entered new worlds, attempted new ways of doing things, met new people, pursued the thing they thought would fix everything—yet they've still failed.

The All Is Lost is a **single-scene beat** in which something happens *to* your hero to knock them down and bring them to their lowest point yet. Notice the emphasis on the word "to." Like the Catalyst, this is an external beat. And, like the Catalyst, there's usually a sense of *surprise*. Something the hero (and the reader) wasn't expecting. Because of this, the All Is Lost is another beat that's typically easy to spot in novels.

Breakups, deaths, groundings, betrayals, firings, failed battles, and friendship-ending fights are some popular choices.

What do all of these have in common?

Loss.

The hero must *lose* something here. There must be a sense of failure. Whether it be related to the goal the hero is pursuing or something else. Like Natasha's failure to stop her family from being deported in *The Sun Is Also a Star*, or the grand jury's decision *not* to indict the officer who shot Khalil in *The Hate U Give*.

Or perhaps the hero *does* achieve a goal, but in doing so, they're plunged into their darkest hour or most perilous situation yet. Like Tris in *Divergent*, who is accepted into the Dauntless faction as the number one–ranked initiate (Act 2 goal) only moments before leaders of the Erudite faction use embedded transmitters to turn all the Dauntless into sleepwalking soldiers and she and Four are captured. Or Cady in *We Were Liars*, who finally remembers what happened the night of the accident (Act 2 goal), only to realize it was a fire that she alone survived.

The only way your hero can believably change the *right* way is if the wrong way doesn't work. And since Act 2 was all about changing the wrong way, this beat must come with a sense of failure. Otherwise, why would your hero try anything else?

One of the reasons many manuscripts fall apart at the end is because the writer didn't bring their hero low enough. They didn't build in *enough* failure, enough loss, enough of a rock bottom. They weren't hard enough on their hero. So when they tried to write a resolution with a satisfying character transformation, it just fell flat. It didn't feel believable. Why would the hero change if nothing all that bad happened to them? Why would they try anything else if what they were doing before was working pretty well?

The All Is Lost is another major turning point of the story. In the same way we use the Catalyst to push our heroes out of their Act 1 world, we must use the All Is Lost to push our hero out of the Act 2 world and into yet another world. The world of Act 3, where they will finally, *finally* learn the theme and fix things the *right* way.

But if that All Is Lost isn't big enough—if all is not really *lost*—then it just won't work.

So don't be afraid to mess things up for your hero here. Bring 'em down! Bring 'em low!

A Sense of Blame

There are a few ways you can make sure that your All Is Lost is as impactful as it can be. First, build in a sense of blame for the hero. The All Is Lost should be (at least indirectly or partially) the hero's fault. Even though the event is happening *to* them, the responsibility should be partially theirs. After all, they tried to change the wrong way, they failed to recognize or deal with their internal bad guys (those pesky flaws that are still hanging around), and they didn't learn their life lesson. So why shouldn't it be their fault? They ignored the bigger issue!

Because Mare in *Red Queen* still hadn't learned her life lesson about harnessing her own power, she lets that power be stolen by someone she trusts, someone who has been using her this whole time. Maven, one of Mare's love interests, ends up betraying not just her, but the whole kingdom, and Mare is powerless to stop it. This all might have been avoided if Mare hadn't trusted the wrong person.

The more sense of blame you can attach to your hero for the predicament they find themselves in, the more serious and grim the predicament will feel. And it has to feel serious and grim. It has to feel bigger than any other beat, including the Catalyst, because it's the beat that's going to eventually lead to real change.

The Catalyst was a fluke. A random event. A rare piece of bad (or good!) luck. This beat, this event, is *personal*.

And that will automatically make it more impactful.

The Whiff of Death

The second thing we can do to drive home the sense of loss here and believably set up the epic transformation that's coming is to insert what's called a **whiff of death**.

Nothing feels lower, darker, or more hopeless than death. Which is why it's no coincidence that many characters die or come close to death here at the All Is Lost. This beat is where Rue dies in *The Hunger*

Games, where Dante is beaten to within an inch of his life for kissing another boy in *Dante and Aristotle Discover the Secrets of the Universe*, where Julia attempts to commit suicide in *I Am Not Your Perfect Mexican Daughter*, where the elevator opens one final time and Will's dead brother Shawn (the one who started it all) steps inside in *Long Way Down*.

A popular character to die or leave in this beat is the mentor, someone who has been a role model, guide, or source of strength for your hero throughout the journey. What will the hero do without them? How will they cope? How will they go on? Survive? Defeat the villain? Save the city? Win the war? This is why killing the mentor is effective. It forces the hero to (eventually) realize that they have what it takes to go it alone. That the mentor already gave them the strength, courage, and wisdom they need.

In *The Book Thief*, the All Is Lost comes when Papa is sent away to war as punishment for helping a Jewish prisoner marching through town. He's been Liesel's confidante, supporter, and mentor since the story began, and now he's just . . . gone. And after Max left in the Bad Guys Close In, it feels even *worse*.

Even if you don't include a literal death here, there are plenty of creative ways to evoke the feeling of death. A whiff of death could be the death of a friendship, the death of an idea, the death of a relationship. These are all metaphorical deaths. In *Warcross*, Zero bombs the Phoenix Riders' dorm at the All Is Lost, which is a literal whiff of death, and steals all of Emika's virtual memories of her father—a more metaphorical whiff of death, as it feels like she's losing her father all over again.

We can also *hint* at death by pointing out the dead flowers in the garden, visiting a grave site, or evoking the memory of a death. Like in *The Truth About Forever* when Macy visits the hospital for the first time since her dad died and it conjures up all the grief she hasn't yet dealt with.

But we don't add death just to add death. We don't kill off characters callously because it works and we want our stories to resonate.

The death is symbolic here. Whether it's literal or not, it's an important metaphor to impart to our readers.

Something has to end so that another thing can begin. Something has to die so that it can be reborn anew.

The All Is Lost is essentially where the old world/character/way of thinking finally *dies* so that eventually a new world/character/way of thinking can be born.

It's yet another external event that will trigger an internal realization, which will inspire the biggest, most important decision of the hero's life.

In our romantic waltz of structure, this is the event that will lead to the epic Finale.

But before any of that can happen, your hero has some very important soul-searching to do.

Because before they can change, they have to reflect.

Before they can act, they have to *react*.

They have to cry and stomp their feet and shout at strangers and generally fall into pits of despair.

Up next: the ever-important wallowing beat.

12. DARK NIGHT OF THE SOUL

WHAT DOES IT DO? Shows how your hero reacts to the All Is Lost and how they eventually break through to a resolution.

WHERE DOES IT GO? 75%–80% (This beat takes us to the end of Act 2.)

For every action, there is a reaction. For every Catalyst, there is a Debate. And for every All Is Lost, there is a . . . *Dark Night of the Soul*.

This beat is hands-down the most fun one to say. Go ahead, say it aloud, in a deep, booming, movie-trailer voice. You'll feel better about the world afterward.

Like the Debate, the Dark Night of the Soul is a **multi-scene beat** during which the hero is given some time to react and reflect on what just happened.

They're given time to mourn or *grieve* their loss.

In *The Book Thief*, Liesel and Rosa both mourn the absence of Papa, who's been sent off to war. In *We Were Liars*, as all the memories of the fire flood in, Cady mourns the loss of her friends, feeling like she's losing them all over again, then locks herself in her room, refusing to come out. In *Red Queen*, after Mare is betrayed and arrested at the All Is Lost, she cries alone in her cell, feeling stupid and used and helpless. In *The Sun Is Also a Star*, after Natasha gets the news that her family will be deported, she and Daniel walk solemnly back to her house, as she thinks about how much she'll miss New York . . . and him.

I call this the "wallowing beat," because that's often what characters do here. They wallow in their defeat. They mope around, sulk, cry, and maybe even write sad poetry or listen to angry music.

But people grieve loss in different ways; that's why wallowing is not your only option here. Some characters get *angry*. Like Ari in *Aristotle and Dante Discover the Secrets of the Universe* who, after learning about the attack on Dante, brutally beats up one of his attackers. Or Starr in *The Hate U Give* who, after the grand jury failed to indict Officer One-Fifteen, leaves for Garden Heights to join the riots.

Only *you* know how *your* hero will react to everything that's happened. But remember that heroes often feel the furthest away from their life lesson here. Whatever progress they've made toward learning their theme feels lost after their rock bottom. And they feel even worse off now than at any other point in the novel.

Compare the Aristotle we see here to the Aristotle we met in the Opening Image—lying in bed, listening to the radio, feeling lonely and miserable. Over the course of Act 2, he's ventured out of that status quo world; he's met and has been *changed* by Dante; and now, as Dante lies in a hospital bed, within an inch of his life, it feels even *worse* than where he started.

Return to the Familiar

In the Dark Night of the Soul, heroes often have the feeling *What was the use of even trying if this is where it got me?* Which is why in this beat heroes will commonly try to move *backward*. They get back together with an ex, they go back to an old house, they reunite with old friends. In some way, they try to reconnect with their Act 1 self.

I call it the **Return to the Familiar**. Why does it happen *so* often in the Dark Night of the Soul? Because it's a *fantastic* way to show the hero (and the reader) just how far the hero has already come and how much this journey has already changed them. They've been to the upside-down world of Act 2, for heaven's sake! They've met B Story characters and survived plot-altering Midpoints! Whether they realize it or not, they're not the same person as they were when they left Act 1.

And this proves it.

In *The Truth About Forever*, after she's grounded at the All Is Lost, Macy tries to go back to the person she was at the start of the summer, studying for the SATs and being the reliable and controllable daughter her mom wants her to be. She and her mother fall into their same old rhythm of not talking about things (especially difficult things, like their mutual grief). Macy even considers getting back together with Jason, the very boy who asked for a break at the Catalyst. But she misses her new friends, and as she remarks on page 306, "It was like it was another person, some other girl."

Heroes are desperate at this point. It's only natural for them to try to seek safety in something known and familiar. Especially in the face of defeat or tragedy. Humans do it all the time. So heroes do it too.

A variation on the return to the familiar is to have your hero get something they've been wanting (possibly from the start), only to find they don't want it anymore. Like in *Warcross*, when Hideo gives Emika the ten-million-dollar bounty she's been chasing since the Break Into 2—the whole reason she's even *here*—but after everything that's happened, it doesn't feel important anymore.

When you put your hero back into their status quo world, or bring some aspect of that world back, you're essentially shining a giant spotlight on the fact that they don't fit in anymore. They're a stranger in a place that once felt so safe and familiar. Even if they wanted to, they can't go back to the person they were before. Attempting to return to the status quo world is just another Band-Aid. It won't fix the real problem underneath. And your hero sees that pretty quickly.

The Dark Night Epiphany

Regardless of how your specific hero reacts, every Dark Night of the Soul beat is essentially the same thing. It's the darkness before the dawn. The defeat before the breakthrough. The last moment before the *real* change occurs.

That's why this beat often comes with what I call the **Dark Night Epiphany**. It's a revelation moment that happens somewhere within the Dark Night of the Soul (usually toward the end). The hero suddenly sees something in a new light. Like a final clue to a mystery, a truth they've been overlooking this whole time, a thread that ties everything together. It's the final puzzle piece falling into place. The final turn of the microscope lens that brings the whole picture into focus.

Emika realizes that Zero is using rigged artifacts in the final championship game to upload a virus to every Warcross user (*Warcross*). Aristotle learns the truth about his violent brother, whom his parents never talk about (*Aristotle and Dante Discover the Secrets of the Universe*). Julia learns the tragic story of her Amá's border crossing, which gives her a whole new perspective on her mother, the sacrifices she made, and the reason she is the way she is (*I Am Not Your Perfect Mexican Daughter*). And Tris's mother reveals she is *also* a Divergent and explains why they are such a threat to the factions, leading Tris to embrace her divergence as a strength, not a weakness.

This Dark Night Epiphany is symbolic of everything that's happening in this beat. Because although it might not look like it from the outside, your hero is not just grieving in this beat. They're not just wallowing or stomping around. There's some very important work going on *inside* your hero. Whether they realize it right away or not, this moment of failure and defeat is forcing them to take a closer look at themself, analyze their life choices and everything they've tried and failed to achieve thus far. Essentially, your hero is being forced to break open their operating system and take a look at that faulty code that's been messing up their life and causing problems.

They're being forced to see their flaws for what they are. Manifestations of a much deeper wound. Scars that have grown over the shard of glass.

We talked about how external events trigger internal reflections. Well, this is the biggest internal reflection that's going to happen in the whole novel. Because it's the reflection that's going to lead to the ultimate resolution. The All Is Lost was a single event, action, or moment, and then it was over. Now that the hero has time to reflect on it, they can start to see it for what it really was. A wake-up call.

No more avoiding the real issue; no more fixing things the wrong way.

It's time to rip off that Act 2 Band-Aid, face the wound underneath, and *finally* heal it.

Act 3

If Act 1 was the thesis world, and Act 2 was the antithesis world, then Act 3 is the **synthesis** world. This is where everything comes together. Where plot threads fuse, intertwine, and resolve. Where A Story characters and B Story characters join forces. And where the hero becomes the new and improved version of themselves, combining who they were in Act 1 with their trials and tribulations in Act 2. Or in other words:

Who the hero was in Act 1 + What they've learned in Act 2
= Who they will become in Act 3

Isn't it glorious?

The Midpoint might have been the important *crossroads* of all things, but Act 3 is the satisfying *blending* of all things. This is where broken relationships are mended, transgressions are forgiven, wounds are healed, bridges are rebuilt, and the waltz of structure reaches its grand Finale. Act 3 is where the wisdom and life lessons of the B Story combine with the all the excitement and sizzle of the A Story to create something magnificent. When executed well, these can be some of the most exciting, rewarding, satisfying pages of your novel. So let's see how it's done.

13. BREAK INTO 3

WHAT DOES IT DO? Brings the hero into the synthesis world of Act 3, where they will finally fix things the *right* way.

WHERE DOES IT GO? 80%

After hitting rock bottom at the All Is Lost, going through a Dark Night of the Soul and realizing their Dark Night Epiphany, the hero is inspired to make a decision.

The Break Into 3 is the Eureka! beat. The huzzah! beat. The "By George, I think they've got it" beat. It's when the hero, thanks to everything they've encountered in Act 2, realizes what they have to do to not only fix whatever messes they've made in Act 2 but, more important, fix themself.

All the lows and highs and struggles and conflict and thematic lessons from the B Story character have led to this, our final turning point.

The Break Into 3 is literally a break*through*. In this **single-scene beat,** the hero either figures out what they have to do and/or takes the first step toward doing it.

Tris realizes she knows how to shut down the simulation that's controlling the Dauntless and, drawing on her strengths as an Abnegation *and* a Dauntless, creates a plan to do it (*Divergent*). Natasha realizes her problem isn't the deportation, but the resentment she feels for her father's mistakes, and she finally confronts him (*The Sun Is Also a Star*). Emika finally tells her teammates the truth about why she's here and creates a plan to infiltrate the final championship game to stop Zero from deplozying the virus (*Warcross*). Cady returns to Cuddledown house, where the Liars have been "staying," finally ready to say goodbye (*We Were Liars*).

At the Break Into 2, your hero tried to fix things the wrong way, only to discover that the things that really mattered weren't actually fixed. Their problems followed them. Because their *real* problems were never *out there*; they were always *in here*. Inside of them.

And now that they realize that, they'll have to **fix things the right way.**

Which is exactly what they'll do.

But how? Good question!

The Act 3 Goal

Remember at the Break Into 2 when I told you to think of an Act 2 goal to help keep you on track? Well, Act 3 comes with its own goal. Even if you don't reveal what that goal is to the reader right away (which is actually a very handy trick for keeping readers engaged), the **Act 3 goal** will be essential in structuring, tracking, and writing a compelling third act.

Once again, this can be the same goal your hero has been chasing down the whole time (maybe now they're just pursuing it in a different way thanks to everything they've learned in Act 2). Like in *The Inheritance Games*, where Avery is still trying to solve the puzzle hidden within the Hawthorne mansion, but it's only now that she's gathered all the clues from Act 2 (and stumbled upon the final clue in the Dark Night Epiphany) that she knows where to go next. Or it could be a brand-new goal. Like in *I Am Not Your Perfect Mexican Daughter*, where the goal is no longer to prove her sister wasn't perfect, but to heal her relationship with her mother.

This goal could be directly related to the hero's theme and proving that they've learned it, like in *The Hate U Give* when Starr joins the protests, grabs the bullhorn, and uses her "weapon"—her voice—to tell the world what she saw, no longer hiding. Or perhaps the goal is related to a big game, event, battle, test, or performance that the story has been leading up to in which the hero has to prove that they have what it takes to win, save the day, or persevere. Like in *The Truth About Forever* when Macy brings together her Act 1 world (mom) and Act 2 world (catering company) to save her mother's big gala event from disaster, but not before finally building up the courage to open the present her father gave her before he died, proving she's ready to face up to her grief (theme).

However you do it, the whole point of Act 3 is to not only fix any external problems that need to be fixed, but also to prove that the hero has learned their life lesson and can come out of this journey transformed.

Of course, that doesn't all happen in *this* beat. After all, you have roughly 20% of the book to accomplish this feat of brilliance. This is just the single scene (or perhaps even single page or paragraph!) where your hero first decides to act and/or takes the first step of that action. And just like at the Break Into 2, this moment should feel decisive and clear. Even if the reader doesn't quite know yet what you have in store for them or what the big plan is, they should *feel* that change is coming once again. Except this time, it's the *right* kind of change.

14. FINALE

WHAT DOES IT DO? Shows the hero executing their Break Into 3 plan, resolving the problems created in Act 2, and proving that they've learned the theme and have been transformed.

WHERE DOES IT GO? 80% to 99%

If the Break Into 3 was the inspiration of the plan, the Finale is its *execution*. It's one thing for your hero to say, "I know what I need to do to fix all these problems and, more important, fix myself!" it's quite another for them to, you know, actually *do* it.

So you could think of the Finale as the "Putting their money where their mouth is" beat.

And it's not going to be easy. It's not going to be quick. At least it shouldn't be if we want to leave our readers with a sense of satisfaction at the end.

That's why the Finale is a **multi-scene beat** that takes us through the trials, tribulations, and obstacles (both external and internal!) that your hero must face in order to prove that they have what it takes to save the day and save themself.

With the Break Into 3 being a single scene, and the Final Image (the last beat) being a single scene, the Finale is the bulk of Act 3. It's 20% of your novel! And I'll be honest with you, writing it can often feel like swimming the English Channel. After you've finally gotten out of the seemingly never-ending stretch of Act 2, it's normal to feel tired. It's normal to feel daunted, like you've got nothing left in the creative tank.

And sadly, far too often, writers take the easy way out. They write a quick little Finale that wraps up everything swiftly and easily, and they call it done. Which will only lead to disappointment for your reader. You've come this far! Don't wimp out on me now!

Thankfully, I've got something to help you (you knew I would, didn't you?).

Allow me to introduce you to your favorite new storytelling tool. The thing that's going to save your third act and make it just as dynamic, exciting, rewarding, and emotionally impactful as the rest of your novel.

It's called the **Five-Point Finale**.

The Five-Point Finale breaks down your Finale beat into five sub-beats or "points." If the Finale is a swim across the English Channel, then these five points are the buoys that plot your course. They give you ever-important markers to keep your Finale on track toward a satisfying ending. And they give *you*, the writer, rest stops along the way, to catch your breath and regather your strength.

The Five-Point Finale works under the assumption that all Finales are essentially about the same thing: storming a castle!

Don't worry; the castle is a metaphor (you don't have to go back to page 1 of your novel and insert a castle).

The castle can be anything. A game, event, or public spectacle like the championship game in *Warcross*, the execution in the arena in *Red Queen*, or the big gala in *The Truth About Forever*. The castle can be a protest, like in *The Hate U Give*; a building, headquarters, or stronghold, like in *Divergent*; or a house or dwelling where something emotionally difficult must be accomplished, like Cuddledown house, where Cady must say goodbye to her friends in *We Were Liars*, or Natasha's apartment, where she must confront her father in *The Sun Is Also a Star*. The castle can also be less of a physical place and more of a concept or idea, like a wrong the hero must right or a truth they must face, like in *I Am Not Your Perfect Mexican Daughter* and *Aristotle and Dante Discover the Secrets of the Universe*.

It can also be a literal castle.

So, what is *your* castle? Well, it's your Act 3 goal! And the Five-Point Finale is a blueprint that will help you track that goal, to ensure you're delivering an exciting and satisfying ending to your novel that doesn't feel rushed or too easy.

Basically, the castle represents your hero's plan to do whatever it is they've decided they need to do at the Break Into 3. And the Five-Point Finale helps you masterfully execute that plan to ensure you're crafting the most compelling third act possible.

So let's see what it's all about.

Point 1: Gathering the Team

Before any castles can be stormed, or any plans can be implemented, there's usually some preparation required. This can be a literal gathering of the team, where the hero calls upon allies, troops, or even just a few friends to help out. This is a great place to bring A Story characters and B Story characters together (if they're still speaking to your hero—or still alive—after the All Is Lost!) or in some way blend your Act 1 and Act 2 worlds.

This is the moment in *Divergent* when Tris recruits her dad and brother (Act 1 world), to help her storm the Dauntless headquarters (Act 2 world) to shut down the simulation that's turning all the Dauntless members into sleepwalking killing machines. This clever synthesis is also a nod to Tris's theme of embracing all parts of her Divergence: Abnegation (represented by her dad), Erudite (represented by her brother), and Dauntless (represented by herself).

What kind of bridges were burned in Act 2 that your hero now has to mend in order to gather their team? This is a great opportunity to show growth. That's why this beat is also a reconciliation beat. Before your hero can storm their "castle," they need help, and in order to get help, they might have to make amends.

In *The Truth About Forever*, after Macy rallies her "team" of friends from the catering company to help save the gala, she has one last person to "gather." Her mother. Macy shows growth in this sub-beat when, instead of trying to find the right words to say to her mom (which she's failed to do all summer), she simply embraces her, for once, letting her know exactly how she's feeling, "without thinking first" (352).

But heroes don't always have to storm a castle with a team. Some heroes storm a castle on their own. Which is why this beat can also be any other type of preparation. Like a Gathering of the Tools, Amassing of the Weapons, or even just a Mapping of the Route.

In *Warcross*, because the team has already been gathered, Emika spends this sub-beat in the Dark World, acquiring the illegal artifacts that they'll need to enact their big plan to "storm" the final Warcross game and stop Zero from activating the virus.

Essentially, whatever needs to be done in order to enact this big plan is done here.

Point 2: Executing the Plan

Now that the hero is properly prepped, it's go time! Let's storm that castle!

In this sub-beat, the hero works together with their team to execute their plan and achieve their Act 3 goal. And of course, it's not easy. (When is it *ever* in good storytelling?) It's hard! There are roadblocks, challenges, obstacles. *Conflict!* But fortunately, thanks to point 1, your hero and their team are *prepared*. They're overcoming those obstacles and hurdling over those roadblocks.

Despite the pouring rain, Macy and her friends move the gala inside and kick off a great party (*The Truth About Forever*). Emika glitches herself into the game and, with the help of her team, starts deactivating the rigged artifacts (*Warcross*). Tris and her team jump onto a train bound for the Dauntless headquarters and dodge guards and other dangers in search of the control room (*Divergent*). One by one, Cady says an emotional goodbye to the Liars (*We Were Liars*).

If your hero has a team, make sure they're pulling their weight in this sub-beat. What special skills, technology, knowledge, or wisdom do they bring to the endeavor? Why are they even on this quest? This is a great place for side characters to have their moment in the sun and where you'll often see their fun quirks pay off. Unique skills are *finally* rewarded. Devices that were once thought to be worthless are suddenly the thing that gets the hero and the team out of a jam.

It's also where a lot of side characters make a self-sacrifice. Maybe it's a literal sacrifice, and they die in the name of the goal, like Tris's dad in *Divergent*, who leads the guards away and is killed so Tris can reach the control room. Or maybe it's just a metaphorical sacrifice, and they take the blame or the detention slip or the wrath of the parents so that the hero can continue on. In *We Were Liars*, as Cady says goodbye to each of the Liars, they all accept their share of the blame for the fire, and this "sacrifice" helps unburden Cady of some of her guilt and grief.

However it happens, the **team member sacrifice** has a deeper meaning and an important storytelling function: it forces the hero to face the final challenges all on their own, proving that they really do have what it takes. The less help the hero has in the final pages, the harder it is for them, and the more rewarding it is to read.

But regardless of who does what in this sub-beat and who's still around by the end of it, the important thing to note here is that this is the hero's *first* attempt to fix things the right way. And yes, the emphasis on *first* is important. Heroes should never succeed on their first attempt. Because where's the fun in that? It's too easy!

But heroes should definitely *think* they can succeed on the first attempt. That's what this sub-beat is all about: your hero believing (perhaps foolishly) that they're ready for this. After all, they gathered their team, they got their tools, they mapped their route. What could go possibly wrong?

Point 3: High Tower Surprise

The hero has stormed the castle, snuck past the guards, climbed the steps to the highest tower only to find . . . what they seek is not even there! And the bad guys have led them straight into a trap!

This is the moment where Tris opens the door to the control room to find . . . Four at the controls, trapped in a simulation like all the other Dauntless (*Divergent*). This is the moment when Emika successfully destroys the second Artifact to win the game and stops Zero's plan, only to find that the real villain is not Zero, but Hideo, the man she's been falling in love with (*Warcross*).

Compared to any conflict you've thrown at your hero so far, this is the *big* one. The one the hero is least expecting. The one that brings the whole plan to a screeching halt. It could be an external conflict, like Macy's ex-boyfriend showing up just as the gala is going well (*The Truth About Forever*), or it could be internal conflict, like Cady's struggle to say goodbye to her friends—especially her B Story character, Gat (*We Were Liars*).

Regardless of what your Act 3 goal is, it's clear it's not going to work. At least not in the way the hero originally thought.

The purpose of the High Tower Surprise is to ensure that your Finale has conflict and nothing feels too easy. It's also meant to show how overconfident and naïve your hero really was. It was never going to work the way they planned! What were they thinking?

So, yes, this moment should feel like a failure. A surprise curveball that knocks them off their game and their goal. If this is feeling familiar, it should. The High Tower Surprise is yet another Catalyst! Another external event in the waltz of structure. And by now we all know what *those* are followed by . . .

Point 4: Dig Deep Down

You got it! Reflection! Dang, you're getting good at this structure thing!

Like the Debate that followed the Catalyst, and the Dark Night of the Soul that followed the All Is Lost, the Dig Deep Down is the moment in the Finale when the hero and their team (if there are any of them left!) are stuck. With no backup plan. No way out. No hope. They'll never achieve what they set out to achieve now.

And then . . . something magical happens.

When Tris comes face-to-face with a mentally hijacked Four who is set on killing her, she is alone and completely out of options. She knows she can't bring herself to kill him, so what can she do? "*My father says—used to say—that there is power in self-sacrifice,*" she thinks on page 476, right before she hands the gun to Four, drawing on the Abnegation virtue of selflessness. But instead of shooting, Four wakes up. How? Four doesn't know. "I just heard your voice," he says. So Tris's father was right. There *is* power in self-sacrifice. Something Tris could learn only after embracing that part of herself, embracing her divergence.

You can call it magic. Or you can just call it good character development, but this is where the hero digs deep down and finds something within themselves. Strength they never knew they had. A piece of wisdom they never knew what to do with. A key (whether it be physical or metaphorical) that unlocks something they never knew was locked.

When Emika learns that Hideo has used the final game to activate a program that can control people's minds, she *partially* understands his motivations for doing it (to stop people from committing heinous crimes and to "force" the world to be a better place). She recognizes the *good* in it. But also the bad. Having learned her theme, she now sees the *full* picture, not just the individual parts, and decides she can't support him in his quest to take away free will.

The High Tower Surprise was a test. A test of willpower, courage, inner strength, maybe even faith. Has the hero really learned the theme? Have they really overcome those internal bad guys and conquered those flaws once and for all? Or has this all been a bunch of big, fancy talk?

Well, here's where they prove it.

If the Break Into 3 was a recognition that there *is* a shard of glass, then this moment is when the hero digs deep down and *removes* the shard of glass for good, proving that they really have healed.

Here is where Macy in *The Truth About Forever* finally realizes that she doesn't want to live a controlled, predictable life. When her ex-boyfriend shows up and suggests they make a list of all the things they want out of a relationship, she tells him it won't work. Because "sometimes things just happen. That aren't expected. Or on the list" (366).

Here is where Cady in *We Were Liars* goes back to Cuddledown house and starts to clean it from top to bottom, symbolically clearing away her grief and the remnants of her summer with the Liars (which existed only in her imagination). When she's done, she draws a picture of her friends and mounts it on the fridge. Their deaths are remembered and out in the open, no longer buried in her mind, and they will not be forgotten.

Whatever you choose to do here, it should be something the Act 1, status quo hero *never* would have done (or never even *could* have done). They didn't have the skills, the wisdom, the experience. They didn't have the wild ride through the upside-down world of Act 2 and all its challenges, thematic characters, and rock-bottom failures. They didn't have the inspiration of a Break Into 3 and then the personal test of a High Tower Surprise. But now they do. And now they can prove to the reader and themself that it was all worth it. That they truly were story-worthy after all.

This sub-beat can also be called the **Touched by the Divine** moment. And I don't necessarily mean divine in the spiritual or religious sense here (although depending on your story, it certainly *can* be). I mean divine in the very *human* sense of the word. What does it mean to be human?

Forgiveness.

Love.

Acceptance.

Faith, fear, trust, survival, selfishness, responsibility, redemption.

The meaning you've chosen to highlight is the very theme you've been working so hard to thread through your entire story. And what do you know? It's those same universal themes we talked about way back in chapter 1.

But what really causes a human being to forgive? To love? Accept? Is it external plot points crafted into a beat sheet? Well, that helps. And it certainly makes it more *believable*. But there's gotta be something else involved, right? Something that goes beyond just plot points. Something that brushes up against those deeper life questions.

Something *divine*.

So yes, there is a bit of ineffableness about this beat. And when done well, it can be one of the most resonating moments of a novel.

When Tris selflessly hands over that gun in *Divergent*, we feel something. When Emika stands up to Hideo and vows that she won't support his plan, even if it *was* crafted out of a desire to do good, something resonates in us.

Neither of these books are pitched to readers as having deep messages about the human experience. Yet it's still in there. Because whether readers realize it or not, deep down, it's what they want.

Nay, it's what they *need*.

It's not until your hero digs deep down that they can come up with a solution of what to do next. A new plan. The external event of the High Tower Surprise triggered this internal reflection, which will again inspire a proactive decision. We're about to see our romantic one-two-three waltz of structure take its final step.

Will this new plan work?

Only time will tell. But one thing's for certain: it's going to require a leap of *faith*.

Point 5: The Execution of the New Plan

Your hero leaps into action one last time. There's no net to catch them. But they don't need one anymore. They have something better. They have their *theme*. They've learned their life lesson, they've conquered their flaws, they've come out of this a transformed person. Whatever happens now is just icing on the cake.

And that makes the triumph of this beat so much sweeter.

This is where your hero puts their new plan into action, and it works!

Tris and Four shut down the simulation, steal the hard drive, and escape the Dauntless compound (*Divergent*). Macy runs from her ex-boyfriend (who represents her former, overly controlled self) and straight to Wes (who represents her new, embracing-the-chaos-of-life self) and kisses him (*The Truth About Forever*). Cady writes one final fairy tale in which she recognizes the ugliness of tragedy and acknowledges that she hasn't lost *everyone* she loves—she still has family who are alive and real and can become a more important part of her story (*We Were Liars*). And Emika vows to stop Hideo (a new plan that will carry over to the second book in the duology) and then returns to her team's dorm, where one final twist is revealed: Zero is Hideo's brother (*Warcross*).

Often called the **climax** of the story, this is the resolution, the moment of victory where the goal is won. Or maybe the goal is lost, but it doesn't matter, because the hero has already won. Even if you've chosen to end the Finale with a failure (that is, not a happy ending), there's a lesson to be learned in that too. For your hero *and* your reader. Because something changed here. We didn't just run around in circles and come out the other end the same as we started. We went somewhere. And we're forever transformed by that journey.

So there you have it: the Five-Point Finale! The climatic and cinematic finish to your stunning masterpiece of structure. The beat that will skillfully tie together the exciting and thrilling adventure of your external story with the poignant and moving transformation of your internal story, leaving your reader truly riveted.

Prepare to take a bow.

In short, it works because it ensures that your ending feels *earned*.

No one wants to read about a hero who Breaks Into 3 with a plan and then on the next page achieves that plan with no conflict whatsoever. It's boring. It's predicable. It cheats the reader out of the exciting, satisfying ending they deserve. And frankly, after all the work you've done so far, it cheats you out of the ending you deserve too.

That's the beauty of the Five-Point Finale. It helps you chart a course through the long and arduous waters of this beat that is guaranteed to have your reader clinging to the edge of their seat in suspense, panic, despair, a swell of emotion, and finally a shuddering breath of relief.

Teens are some of the most voracious readers on the planet. Which means they know a good book when they find it. And they *love* to gush to everyone when they do, making them the best members of your marketing team *ever*. So give them something to gush about. Give them a Finale worth telling their friends about.

Can there be more than five points in your Finale? Yes! Depending on how long your Finale is and how many Act 3 goals you have, you might find yourself with multiple High Tower Surprises, multiple plans, and multiple conflicts standing in the way. These longer, more intricate Finales tend to appear in sci-fi, fantasy, or action/adventure stories, where there are more bad guys to defeat, but there's no rule that a contemporary story can't have more than five points too.

Is the Five-Point Finale absolutely necessary? No. I've read Finales that don't include all five points that feel just as impactful. Sometimes a hero doesn't need a team or supplies and can just launch right into point 2 (Executing the Plan). Sometimes the High Tower Surprise doesn't lead to an entirely *new* plan but simply forces the hero to Dig Deep Down and find the strength to continue with the existing plan.

(For more variations on the Five-Point Finales, check out the ten full beat sheet breakdowns coming up in chapters 5 through 14.)

Just like the rest of the beat sheet, these five points are here to *guide* you, to give you a blueprint of how to craft a successful story that will resonate with readers all the way to the end.

Don't think of the five points as creative chains that bind you; rather, think of them as suggestions to *inspire* you.

In the end, you write the novel you want to write. You tell the story you want to tell.

But if you're getting feedback from early readers or agents or editors like "great story but the ending felt rushed" or "resolved too easily," you know where to turn.

15. FINAL IMAGE

WHAT DOES IT DO? Provides an "after" snapshot of your hero and your hero's life to show how much they've changed.

WHERE DOES IT GO? 99% to 100% (This is the final scene or chapter of your novel.)

We've reached the very last beat and the very last *scene* of your novel! It's the Final Image. And just as the name suggests, it's a **single-scene beat** that *shows* us who your hero is *after* this huge transformative journey is complete.

What does your hero's life look like now? How far have they come? What have they learned? How much have they changed and grown and healed? They just went through upside-down worlds and rock bottoms and dark nights of the soul. They've faced down external bad guys and the even more scary, *internal* bad guys, removed shards of glass, and fixed things the right way. What do they have to show for it? What parting image do you, the writer, want to leave your readers with?

These are the questions to ask yourself when crafting your Final Image.

If the Opening Image was the "before" snapshot, then this is the "after" snapshot, and the further apart you can make these—the more drastic the change—the better the book.

Think about how far Tris has come in the final scene of *Divergent*. She has "no home, no path, and no certainty" (487). And her world has been torn apart, with the factions of Abnegation and Dauntless both broken. Yet through it all, by embracing her divergence, she has already become braver than she ever imagined she could be.

Or think about how different Aristotle's life is in the final scene of *Aristotle and Dante Discover the Secrets of the Universe*, compared to the Opening Image. As Ari lies in his pickup truck with Dante, gazing at the summer stars, we know he is no longer alone and miserable. He has discovered the secret truths of his own heart and let those truths transform him.

This final scene is your chance to prove to your reader that this journey was worth the effort. That we went somewhere! This hero was worthy of this story and your attention, and here's the proof. Look how much they've *changed*.

Look how far Starr Carter has come from the girl who didn't fit in anywhere, didn't want to make waves, to the girl who's now an activist, promising in her last lines to never be quiet again (*The Hate U Give*).

Mirror Beats

We call the Opening Image and Final Image **mirror beats** because they tend to mirror each other in some way. Some authors choose to create more literal mirrors, with the Opening Image and Final Image set in the exact same place or setting; or on the exact same important day, perhaps a year later; or some other type of mirror, so you can really *see* how the hero has changed. Like how Julia is looking at Olga in a coffin in the Opening Image of *I Am Not Your Perfect Mexican Daughter*, and then in the Final Image is looking at the ultrasound picture of the baby no one knew Olga was carrying when she died. In the former, Julia is disapproving of what she sees, consumed by angst; in the latter, she is clinging to this lost piece of her sister, reflecting on all she's discovered about herself in the process of finding it.

These can also be called "bookend" images because they provide nice, matching beginning and end caps to this journey. Some authors choose to simply invoke a similar feeling as the Opening Image or call back to something from the first scene to serve as the mirror.

In the Opening Image of *Warcross*, Emika is a lone bounty hunter, working for herself, trying to pay off her rent. In the Final Image, however, she's teaming up with another bounty hunter for a greater purpose: to stop Hideo. The mirror shows us two bounty hunting jobs, but a very different hero.

Your Final Image doesn't *have* to mirror the Opening Image, but it should be visual. Just like in the opening scene, the more visual you can make this beat, the more effective it will be. If you simply *tell* the reader that this hero has changed, you cheat the reader out of a fun, satisfying reading experience. If you *show* them, on the other hand, and give them the opportunity to piece things together themself, the final pages of your story will feel like a triumph. Something earned. Something worth talking about.

That's how you engage a reader. By inspiring them to say, "Would you look at that? Everything is so *different*."

You can have all the fancy explosions and battles and romantic interludes you want, but what good is an explosion if there's nothing personal at stake to be lost? What good is a battle if it's not fought for a deeper purpose? And what good are romantic interludes if they don't push our emotional boundaries and pull at our heartstrings? All of that is signed, sealed, and delivered to your reader *through* your hero. So if nothing changed, what was it all for?

If you set up a flawed hero in Act 1, take them on a wild ride through the upside-down world of Act 2, bring them so low they have no choice but change the right way in Act 3, and then cap off that journey with a Final Image that *proves* that the hero was transformed and that this was all worth it, I guarantee you, your reader will have no choice but to feel transformed as well.

The Transformation Machine

Ta-da! There you have it, my friend. The Save the Cat! Beat Sheet. Your fifteen-step cheat sheet to writing a novel that will resonate, engage, enchant, delight, move, and inspire readers. No matter what genre you're writing in.

The beat sheet can also be called **the transformation machine**, and by now you can probably see why. It's designed to transform heroes. "Step right up, ladies and gentlemen, and witness the magic of the transformation machine! A flawed hero goes in one end and poof! comes out the other end *transformed*! Look how much better their life has become! Look at those choices they're making now! Aren't they a beaut'?"

Or as I like to think of it: the Save the Cat! Beat Sheet takes an imperfect hero and makes them a little *less* imperfect.

Are we fixing every flaw? No. Are we perfecting humans? Impossible! Humans will never be perfect. So heroes can't be either. It's unrealistic to go into the beat sheet thinking you're going to fix every problem, every flaw, every bad thing in your hero's life. Since when does *that* ever happen? But you're going to fix at least one. And it's going to be a big one. It's going to be the most important one in the hero's life at this moment.

And the beat sheet is your guide to fixing it in an exciting, dynamic way that leaves readers breathless.

So, how do you feel?

Inspired? Motivated? Maybe a little overwhelmed?

If that's the case, don't worry. It's perfectly natural. There was a *lot* jammed into this chapter, and it might take a moment (or several) to sink in. But fear not. This is not the end of our master class on structure. As you continue through the rest of the book, things will start to come together, if they haven't already.

And I'm *sure* you have questions.

Like "What happens if I'm writing an antagonist story?" And "What do I do with multiple points of view?" And "Where do I put prologues and flashbacks and backstory?"

The beat sheet is the foundation of structure. Of course, there will be ways to build on it, tweak it, and customize it. Which is why coming up next is a chapter called "Customizing Your Beat Sheet," which breaks down all the most common ways to bend the "rules" of structure.

But it's important to learn the foundations first, so you know exactly *what* you're customizing and, more important, *why*. Learn the rules. Study what makes stories work, gain a firm understanding of structure before you set off to write the "exception."

Then, in chapters 5 through 14, we'll be taking everything you've learned so far and applying it to ten popular young adult novels so you can see the entire beat sheet (customizations and all!) in action. That's right: ten full-length novel beat sheets to explore and study exactly how the beats play out in different genres and story types, with different heroes who have different flaws, different bad guys, different worlds, different everything!

I hope that by reading these beat sheets you'll see that this stuff is pretty universal. These beats appear in almost all successful young adult novels because they form a pattern of story. That's why I call them the "secret storytelling code." And the more you see and recognize this pattern, the easier it will be for you to craft it into your own work. So I urge you to read all the beat sheets, even if the genre doesn't match your own. Because it's helpful to see how these beats not only appear in stories you love but appear in their own unique way, with the author's own creative interpretation of classic story structure.

It's also helpful to read each beat sheet so you can see the range of where the beats fall. As I've mentioned, the percentages for each beat are guidelines, based on averages. As you read the beat sheet breakdowns, you'll discover that not all heroes Break Into 2 at the 20% mark. Not all themes are stated at 5%. Not all B Story characters are introduced at 22%. And some Catalysts come later or earlier than the 10% mark.

But regardless of these slight variations, the beats are all in there. And hopefully by now you can see why they kind of *have* to be.

These beats are inspired by life itself.

You might even go as far to say that it's not just a storytelling code, it's a *human* code.

That's probably why it works.

Where Do I Start? Tips on Using the Beat Sheet

If you *are* feeling a little overwhelmed by everything you've read in this chapter, here are some final pieces of advice on tackling the beat sheet before we move on.

First, you don't have to tackle the beats in order.

In fact, I rarely do. It can be sort of daunting to sit down and see that giant expanse of beats stretched out before you. Not to mention, in order to know where to begin, sometimes you need to first know where you're going.

That's why, after figuring out who my hero is (and their problem, want, and need), I usually start the plotting process with the five foundation beats of the story.

THE FOUNDATION BEATS

These are the five foundation beats that pivot the story and send it in a new direction:

- Catalyst (10%)
- Break Into 2 (20%)
- Midpoint (50%)
- All Is Lost (75%)
- Break Into 3 (80%)

These are also the single-scene beats that the multi-scene beats are strung between (that is, the Debate connects the Catalyst and the Break Into 2; the Fun and Games connects the Break Into 2 and the Midpoint; and so on). So it can be easier to brainstorm these beats first because they feel like tent poles you can nail into the ground and erect the other beats around. Once you establish these beats, the other beats fall into place naturally. Once I know what the goal is going to be when my hero Breaks Into 2 and I know my Midpoint is going to be a false victory, I can start crafting my upward path Fun and Games with that information in mind. And once I know how the hero will fix things the *right* way at the Break Into 3, it become easier to start thinking about where they have to start to get there and then construct my Opening Image and Setup.

I also recommend the foundation beats if you're someone who wants to create a *loose* outline of your story before you begin writing. These beats can help you craft what I call a "starter beat sheet." It's not a full-on outline; it's just a starting point. And if you're finding that your first drafts meander too much, these five foundation beats can help direct your story and keep you on track, or at least headed in the right direction!

Which brings me to my next piece of advice:

The beat sheet is not *just* for outlining.

REVISING A NOVEL WITH THE BEAT SHEET

As I mentioned way back at the start of the book, this method is very flexible, and you might find yourself using it at different stages in your novel-writing journey.

If you're a "pantser," for instance (someone who likes to write by the seat of their pants—also called a "discovery writer"), and the idea of outlining *anything* makes you break out into a cold sweat, then you can use the beat sheet as a revision guide. In other words, put this book away until you've got a first draft to work with. Then come back to this chapter and see what beats you have, what beats you're missing, what beats need to come earlier or later, and what beats need to be fleshed out or reengineered completely for maximum impact.

If you're using this book as a revision guide, you might even create *two* beat sheets. A **before** beat sheet (what your story looks like now) and an **after** beat sheet (what you intend your story to look like after the next draft). Then you can use the after beat sheet as a step-by-step revision plan.

BUT WAIT! THERE'S MORE . . .
WAYS TO USE THE BEAT SHEET

But the beat sheet isn't just an outlining or revising tool. It's also a tool for helping you get unstuck. Perhaps you've started a first draft and had lots of momentum at the beginning (which is natural). You were excited, you had ideas, you had *inspiration*, and then suddenly you had *nothin'*. It's like it all just dried up, and now you're stuck somewhere in the novel and have no idea what to do or where to go next. Come back to this chapter. Read the beats again. I wouldn't be surprised if it illuminates exactly where you went off course and, more important, how to get back on.

One other way that I love to use the beat sheet is to test-drive new ideas. Have you ever had a novel idea that you thought was simply *brilliant*, but then you start writing it only to discover a hundred pages later that it's not so brilliant and there's no way you can sustain this idea for the rest of the story? That's where the beat sheet might have saved you some time and stress. Sometimes, when I get a new idea, I sit down and see how many beats I can *roughly* sketch out (and I'm talking *rough* here—a few bullet points apiece, if that). If I can come up with at least eight or nine of the fifteen beats, I know I can make the story work. On the other hand, if I'm struggling to even figure out a few, I know I have to either retool the idea or make a follow-up call to my muse and ask for something else.

By test-driving new ideas with the beat sheet, you can assure yourself that you're not pouring your heart and soul and precious time into an idea that goes nowhere. You can be confident before you start that the idea "has legs," as they say in the movie biz. Meaning it can go the distance and carry you across the finish line. Even if the beats you brainstorm end up changing throughout the writing process (and many of them probably will), you know you at least have the inspiration and ideas you need to make it to the end.

LAYING IT ALL OUT: USING THE SAVE THE CAT! BOARD

Finally, if you need even *more* structure or you're more of a visual learner, allow me to introduce you to the Save the Cat! board.

It's a visual way to see all your beats at once and even start laying down individual scenes within those beats.

You can use a physical cork board (the bigger the better!) or a digital one (check out the Save the Cat! Story Software at SavetheCat.com for a digital board that's designed to work with this method).

The board is divided into four rows, which represent Act 1, Act 2A (up to the Midpoint), Act 2B (after the Midpoint), and Act 3.

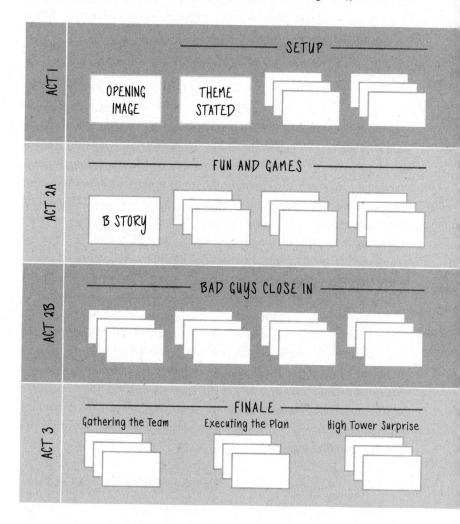

(If you're using a physical board, masking tape is a great way to divide your board.)

The board is then populated with "scene cards" (index cards that each represent a single scene or piece of information in your novel). It helps to lay out your single-scene beats first and then start filling in the multi-scene beats between them.

And voilà! Here's what you get:

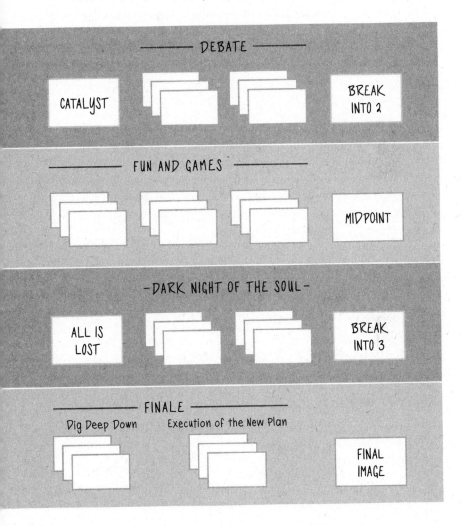

Now, isn't that helpful? (And so dang pretty!)

I don't know about you, but looking at that just makes my little structure heart sing.

It really does help to *see* how those single-scene beats and multi-scene beats work together. Although I should note that the number of cards depicted here is just for illustration purposes. It's not a limit or requirement. Depending on your story, you might have more or less.

If you want a guideline, aim for about thirty cards for every 25,000 words or 100 pages of your story. So, for a 75,000-word novel, you might end up with approximately ninety cards in your story.

But if you're still brainstorming, then throw that guideline out the window. Go bananas. Create as many cards as you want! You can always delete, change, or move cards later.

And that's the beauty of the board. The cards are *moveable*. The story is *moldable*. You can zoom out and see the full picture, which can be *so* helpful when you're stuck on page 132 obsessing over the color of your hero's front door and its symbolic significance for *everything*. The board helps you get your head out of the trees and focused back on the forest. There'll be plenty of time for trees and symbolically colored front doors later. Right now, let's just worry about the structure.

EXERCISE: THE TRANSFORMATION TEST

Is your hero's transformation as big as it can be? Have you hit all the beats hard enough?

Use this handy Self-Workshop Checklist to make sure your beats pass the transformation test!

Opening Image

- ❏ Is your Opening Image *one* scene or one group of interconnected scenes?
- ❏ Is your Opening Image *visual*? (Are you showing, not telling?)
- ❏ Is one or more of your hero's flaws evident in this scene?
- ❏ Have you established the tone, style, and voice of your story?

Theme Stated

- ❑ Does your theme relate to your hero's need or life lesson?
- ❑ Is your theme stated by someone (or something!) *other* than the hero?
- ❑ Have you stated your theme in a subtle, creative way?
- ❑ Can your hero easily and believably dismiss this theme?

Setup

- ❑ Have you shown at least one thing that needs fixing in your hero's life?
- ❑ Have you introduced other supporting characters (A Story characters)?
- ❑ Have you effectively illustrated the hero's status quo world?
- ❑ Did you clearly establish your hero's want or external goal somewhere in this beat?
- ❑ Have you shown your hero in more than one area of their life (such as home, work, and play)?
- ❑ Are your hero's flaws evident in this beat?
- ❑ Have you created a sense of urgency that imminent change is vital (stasis = death)?

Catalyst

- ❑ Does the Catalyst happen *to* the hero?
- ❑ Is it an *action* beat? (No revelations allowed here!)
- ❑ Is it impossible for the hero to go back to their normal life after this?
- ❑ Is the Catalyst big enough to break the status quo?

Debate

- ❑ Can you sum up your Debate with a question? Or if it's a preparation Debate, have you clearly defined what your hero is preparing for and why?
- ❑ Have you created a sense of hesitation in your hero?

Break Into 2

- ❏ Is your hero *leaving* an old world behind and entering a new one?
- ❏ If your hero isn't physically going somewhere, are they trying something new?
- ❏ Is your Act 2 world an upside-down version of your Act 1 world?
- ❏ Is the break between Act 1 and Act 2 clear and distinct?
- ❏ Does your hero make a *proactive* move or decision to enter Act 2?
- ❏ Is your hero making a decision based on what they *want*?
- ❏ Can you identify why this is the wrong way to change?
- ❏ Have you established a clear Act 2 goal?

B Story

- ❏ Have you introduced a new love interest, mentor, friend, or nemesis character?
- ❏ Can you identify how your B Story character (or characters) represents the theme?
- ❏ Is your new character in some way a product of the upside-down Act 2 world?
- ❏ If you have multiple B Story characters, do they represent (or teach the hero) the theme in different ways?

Fun and Games

- ❏ Do you clearly show your hero either succeeding (upward path) or floundering (downward path) in the new world?
- ❏ Have you created ups and downs (bouncing ball) along that path?
- ❏ Have you shown your hero pursuing their Act 2 goal?
- ❏ Have you delivered on the promise of your premise?
- ❏ Have you visibly illustrated how your Act 2 world is the upside-down version of your Act 1 world?
- ❏ Are you weaving in other subplots (like the B Story)?

Midpoint

- ❏ Can you clearly identify either a false victory or a false defeat?
- ❏ Have you raised the stakes of the story enough to push the hero into the next beat?
- ❏ Do your A (external) and B (internal) stories cross in some way?
- ❏ Can you identify a shift from the wants to the needs (even if it's subtle)?

Bad Guys Close In

- ❏ Is the path of this beat a direct opposite of your Fun and Games? (That is, if your hero was on an upward path in the Fun and Games, are they on a downward path here? And vice versa?)
- ❏ Have you upped the conflict, stakes, and tension in this beat?
- ❏ Have you established a new or modified goal that the hero is pursuing (or a new approach to their existing goal)?
- ❏ Have you shown or identified how the internal bad guys (flaws) are working against your hero?

All Is Lost

- ❏ Does something happen *to* the hero in this beat?
- ❏ Is your hero in some way responsible for what happens here?
- ❏ Is your All Is Lost *big* enough to push your hero into Act 3? (That is, have they really hit rock bottom?)
- ❏ Have you built in a sense of loss and/or a whiff of death?
- ❏ Does this beat feel like another Catalyst for change?

Dark Night of the Soul

- ❏ Is your hero reflecting on something in this beat?
- ❏ Is this beat leading your hero toward an epiphany?
- ❏ Does your hero's life seem worse off than it did at the beginning of the book?

Break Into 3

- ❏ Does your hero learn a valuable *universal* lesson (theme) here?
- ❏ Does your hero make a proactive decision to fix something?
- ❏ Is the decision based on (or inspired by) what your hero needs?
- ❏ Have you established an Act 3 goal for the hero to pursue?
- ❏ Can you identify why this is the *right* way to change?
- ❏ Is your Act 3 world a synthesis of Act 1 and Act 2?

Finale

- ❏ Does your hero struggle to enact their plan? (That is, does your Finale have conflict?)
- ❏ Is there a Dig Deep Down moment when your hero proves they've really learned their theme?
- ❏ Do the A Story and B Story somehow intertwine in this beat?

Final Image

- ❏ Is your Final Image *one* scene or collection of interconnected scenes?
- ❏ Is your Final Image *visual*? (Are you showing, not telling?)
- ❏ Is it evident how your hero has *transformed*?
- ❏ Does your "after" snapshot somehow mirror your "before" snapshot (Opening Image)?

Customizing Your Beat Sheet
You've Learned the Rules . . .
Now Let's ~~Break~~ Bend 'em!

"But what about . . . ?"

These are the three words that begin about 85% of the questions I get from writers learning to use the Save the Cat! method to tell better stories.

But what about . . . multiple points of view, prologues, flashbacks, backstory, villain stories, Catalysts that come on the first page?

Yes, yes, there are a lot of "what abouts."

What these questions are really asking, though, is, "How do I customize the beat sheet and make it work for *my* story?" Which is a valid question that I will definitely attempt to answer as extensively as I can (within the page-count limits my publisher gave me).

By the time you read this chapter, you should be familiar with all the "rules." You know the ins and outs of the beat sheet—the basic story structure—and now you can start thinking about what you're going to *do* with it. How you're going to *bend* those rules and make them your own. Yes, the rules *can* be bent. Despite the rigidity of the word "structure," don't forget that storytelling is still an art form and we still need to bring our creativity, personality, voice, perspective, experience, and *interpretation* to the table. Otherwise, we could probably just program a computer to write novels, and then we'd all be out of a job. (Although I hear they're working on that now, which is quite terrifying.)

All the full beat sheet examples I've included later in the book highlight an author who has taken the basic story structure and made it their own. And you can do the same.

Let's look at some *common* ways the Save the Cat! method can be adapted, tweaked, expanded, and customized to fit your story.

An important thing to note before we begin: this chapter and the strategies included are completely optional and by no means required. The Save the Cat! Beat Sheet, broken down in the previous chapter, is *all* you need to craft a compelling story, as evidenced from the multitude of successful examples we analyzed. Most likely not *all* of these customizations will apply to you and your story, and there's a strong chance *none* of them will. In which case you are more than welcome to skip them. So think of this chapter as more of an à la carte menu to choose from, when and *if* you need to customize the basic beat sheet.

What About Multiple Points of View? Tracking More Than One Hero Through the Beat Sheet

Having multiple points of view is an especially popular choice in young adult fiction. So let's talk about how to work with the beat sheet when you're juggling more than one narrator (also called "point of view character").

The first step is figuring out which of your narrators are actually heroes and not side characters. It's quite possible to give a side character a perspective in the story. (It's quite possible to do anything! This is fiction! This is YA fiction!)

In *The Sun Is Also A Star*, Nicola Yoon dedicates several short chapters to the perspective of minor characters we never hear from again. But it's purposeful, because the story is about the interconnectivity of everything, so we need to see how one person affects the next, who affects the next, and so on. Similarly, in *Wilder Girls* by Rory

Power (full beat sheet on page 358), the author uses a side character's sporadic POV to widen our understanding of the world, the theme, and the threat of the dangerous virus that's been ravaging the island of Raxter.

In the Save the Cat! methodology, a character is counted as a hero when they are given attention in the story equal (or roughly equal) to that given the primary hero. That means equal page time, equal plot focus, and, most important, equal transformation. Any character who fits these criteria is probably a hero and should be treated as such (like with a raise in pay and their own dressing room). Anyone else, you can probably relegate to the position of "side character" (shared dressing rooms, lower pay, no dental).

But that doesn't mean side characters can't have wants and needs of their own! They often do. They're just probably not going to be a central focus of the story.

Once you figure out who's been given "hero status" and who hasn't, it's time to sort out your beat sheet situation.

When writing a young adult novel with multiple points of view, there are three primary options: a **single-track** beat sheet, a **multi-track** beat sheet, and a **blended-track** beat sheet.

Let's break 'em down.

SINGLE-TRACK BEAT SHEETS

A single-track beat sheet (also called a "team beat sheet") is when your heroes act together and experience the majority of the story together, as a team. This would be novels like *One of Us Is Lying* by Karen M. McManus (full beat sheet on page 334) and *Six of Crows* by Leigh Bardugo (full beat sheet on page 249).

The heroes are part of a group, and the story is mostly about what happens to the group and less about the individual journeys. You can tell whether you're dealing with a single-track beat sheet by looking at the major turning points of the story, namely the Catalyst, Break Into 2, Midpoint, All Is Lost, and Break Into 3. Do the same beats affect *all* the heroes at once?

In *One of Us Is Lying*, the Catalyst (Simon is dead!) affects all four of the heroes, as they were all in the room with him when he had his deathly allergic reaction. The Break Into 2 is when they are all named as suspects and thrust into the murder investigation. Essentially, they *share* beats. They're on the same story "track." Which means you need only one beat sheet for the story, because the beats are shared.

But you *do* have to decide how the beats affect each of your heroes and push them toward their (*different*) transformations. For example, in *One of Us Is Lying*, after Simon is pronounced dead, the Debate question is the same (what happened to Simon?), but all of the characters react differently because they're different people with different flaws and unique character arcs, and we see those reactions through their respective points of view.

In other words, for single-track beat sheets, the beats themselves are typically the same for all heroes but trigger different transformations.

MULTI-TRACK BEAT SHEETS

On the other hand, you're dealing with a multi-track beat sheet when your heroes all experience *different* beats, effectively putting their stories on different "tracks."

These tracks might overlap for some of the beats (for example, heroes might share a Catalyst or a Midpoint), or perhaps the tracks overlap for a few chapters during longer beats (like the Fun and Games or Bad Guys Close In). Of course, the characters can still *interact* with each other throughout the novel, but for the most part, they are experiencing different yet *connected* stories. And that's a key word for multi-track beat sheets. *Connection*. What is it? Is it a thematic connection? (Multiple characters learning the same life lesson or exploring multiple perspectives on a theme.) A world connection? (Multiple characters experiencing different parts of a world.) Maybe an aftermath connection? (Multiple characters experiencing the aftermath of a major event but in completely different ways.) Or something else?

In *The Sisterhood of the Traveling Pants* by Ann Brashares, we have four heroes experiencing four different summers, connected by a special pair of pants. In *An Ember in the Ashes* by Sabaa Tahir, we see both Laia and Elias navigating their own beats and goals, connected by the location of Blackcliff Military Academy, where Laia is sent in as a rebel spy and Elias is participating in the Trials that will decide the next emperor.

My coauthor, Joanne Rendell, and I also employed multi-track beat sheets in the first book of our System Divine trilogy, *Sky Without Stars* (a sci-fi retelling of Victor Hugo's *Les Misérables*). In the novel, three heroes are living very different lives on our French-inspired planet and experiencing very different beats. But they are connected by the threat of a looming revolution, which brings them together for chapters at a time while their beat sheets remain relatively separate.

With multi-track beat sheets, because you are dealing with multiple sets of beats, you'll need multiple beat sheets. But keep in mind that the beats don't have to occur simultaneously. Many novels that fall into this category have staggered beats, meaning one hero might be Breaking Into 2 while another is still in their Setup, one might be experiencing their All Is Lost while another is already in their Finale. It all depends on how and when you introduce each hero in the story and how much page time you give them.

BLENDED-TRACK BEAT SHEETS

And finally, you have the option of *blending* the two methods, when some parts of your story are on a single track while others are on a multi-track. This is by far the most complex method and it's not for the faint of heart! (Faint of plotter?) It can be a *lot* to keep track of.

There are no limits to how creative you can get with blended-track beat sheets. You could craft a story where the first act of the novel is on a multi-track (your heroes are separated and experience different beats), the second act is on a single track (the heroes come together and share beats), and the third act is back on a multi-track (the heroes break apart to tackle their own Finales). Or you can have the stories fusing and dividing multiple times throughout the novel.

Think of your heroes' stories like railroad tracks that are constantly crossing, merging, and separating again. Which means your beat sheets will do the same!

Before you get dizzy and pass out from the mind-bogglingness of it all, let me assure you that it's a very common type of storytelling in young adult. It's been done, and done well, so you have lots of examples to study.

Take a look at *All the Bright Places* by Jennifer Niven, *Eleanor & Park* by Rainbow Rowell, *Five Feet Apart* by Rachael Lippincott, or *When Dimple Met Rishi* by Sandhya Menon to study examples of blended beat sheets with two points of view. In all of these stories, the two heroes are falling in love, which means their beat sheets are naturally coming together, but they are also living their own lives with family, friends, school, or summer activities, which means their beat sheets are also diverging.

Connection is key here too. You must figure out what exactly is bringing these beat sheets (and heroes) together and what's driving them apart.

In novels like *Far from the Tree* by Robin Benway and *Clap When You Land* by Elizabeth Acevedo, heroes discover long-lost family members they never knew about, which becomes the driving force in how the beat sheets merge and diverge. In *Children of Blood and Bone* by Tomi Adeyemi (full beat sheet on page 214), the heroes are brought together by a common goal and thrust apart by conflicts that stand in the way of that goal.

And to add even another level of complexity (hey, you asked the question!), blending can also mean that while one or two heroes are on a multi-track beat sheet, *other* heroes are on a single-track (team) beat sheet. My coauthor and I wrestled that beast to the ground in the second and third books of our System Divine trilogy. In *Between Burning Worlds* (book 2), while two of our heroes (Marcellus and Alouette) are on a mission to another planet to stop a deadly weapon (team beat sheet), the other hero (Chatine) is back on the home planet of Laterre with a beat sheet of her own. Then the three beat sheets intersect for a shared Finale. In *Suns Will Rise* (book 3), we decided to torture ourselves even more by adding two more heroes (and points of view) and loads more merging and diverging. Marcellus and Chatine start out together on a team beat sheet, while Alouette and our new narrators, Cerise and Etienne, have beat sheets of their own. Then, at her Break Into 2, Chatine joins Etienne for a mission, and they become a team with a team beat sheet all the way through their joint Dark Night of the Soul, while Alouette, Marcellus, and Cerise are still on their own tracks, experiencing their own beats. However, after Alouette and Marcellus *share* a Midpoint, Cerise joins them toward the end of her Bad Guys Close In, and those three team up for a joint All Is Lost and Dark Night of the Soul. Until finally, *all* five heroes come together for a team Finale!

Don't try this at home, kids. I'm a professional!

Actually, on second thought: *Do* try it at home! Experiment, play around, find what works for you and your story. And don't be afraid to tear that story up *multiple* times and stitch it back together *multiple* times.

My advice when attempting a blended-track beat sheet: write a *separate* beat sheet for each hero, then see how and where those beats overlap and merge or where they *could* overlap and merge.

Multiple POV writing can be a wild ride, with beats flying around like marbles in a game of Hungry Hungry Hippos, but don't forget the primary purpose. You're telling this story to transform your heroes! Which means, in all of this (controlled) chaos, there still needs to be a compelling character arc. That is our first and foremost goal. If you lose sight of that, it won't matter what track you're on, because the story *will* crash.

Remember, there's no rule that says you *have* to write multiple points of view or have multiple heroes.

Bottom line: don't do it just because "all my friends are doing it." We all know how well that turns out. Tell *your* story, and tell it well. And if you don't tell it well the first time, tell it again, and again, and again until you get it right.

What About Early (or Late!) Catalysts? Modifying the Catalyst Beat

Do the beats always have to come in the same order every time? Do they ever get turned around, swapped, or moved?

The short answer is yes, but it depends on the beat.

Some beats kind of *have* to come in the right order, because they are results of previous beats. You can't have a Debate until you have a Catalyst to debate about. You can't have a Fun and Games until you Break Into 2, where the Fun and Games takes place. You can't have a Bad Guys Close In without a Midpoint to shift the direction of the plot. And you can't have a Finale until you're in Act 3.

But one beat that does get moved around often in novels, particularly in young adult novels, is the Catalyst. Either because the author wants it to come *way* sooner (like as soon as the first page) and use it to hook readers. Or because the author has so much Setup work to do, the Catalyst has to be pushed back to make room. I've done both, and there are benefits and risks to both. So let's take a look.

EARLY CATALYSTS

For Catalysts that come very quickly—way before the 10% mark—there's not a lot of time to build and flesh out the status quo world before it's torn apart. Yet early Catalysts are not necessarily a bad thing. They are great devices for hooking a reader early. Not to mention, if you're seeking the traditional publishing route and trying to sign with an agent, some agents will read only the first ten to thirty pages of a novel before deciding whether they want to read more, which means you better get *something* exciting into those first thirty pages!

For whatever reason, there are plenty of successful young adult novels with a very early Catalyst, as early as the first scene or chapter. *I Hunt Killers* by Barry Lyga opens on the crime scene of a murder in a small, quiet town; in *The Book Thief* by Markus Zusak, Liesel's brother dies within the first ten pages; in *City of Bones* by Cassandra Clare, Clary meets demons and demon hunters in the first chapter; and in my own novel *52 Reasons to Hate My Father*, the book starts right after my teen heiress hero has crashed her five-hundred-thousand-dollar Mercedes convertible into a convenience store on Sunset Boulevard.

So how do you balance the first act when the Catalyst comes so quickly? The very same way that these authors (and I) did: **blend and bump.**

The blending comes by merging the Setup and the Debate. You can use the hero's reaction to the Catalyst to help establish the status quo world, by showing how the Catalyst is affecting it. It's basically having your Debate do double duty. In *I Hunt Killers*, Jazz's reaction to the Catalyst (the murder) is what gives him the opportunity to bring the reader up to speed about his famous serial killer father, Billy Dent, who's now in prison, and how his father shaped his status quo world and the town of Lobo's Nod, which has been peaceful since Billy's arrest. It also provides us with insight into Jazz's relationship with the town sheriff, who's become a kind of father figure to him.

In *The Book Thief*, the early Catalyst shows us how a new status quo world was built around this event. Liesel's life with her foster care parents, the Hubermanns, is shaped by this grief. And in *City of Bones* and *52 Reasons to Hate My Father*, the hero tries to ignore what happened at the Catalyst and move on with their status quo life, which allows for some Setup work to be done in the Debate. Like establishing Clary's life with her single mom, her mom's best friend Luke, and Clary's friendship with Simon (*City of Bones*). Or establishing Lexington's fraught relationship with her billionaire father, the superficial nature of her friendships, and the comfort and solace she finds with her dog (*52 Reasons to Hate My Father*). However, in both of these novels, the heroes find that the Catalyst is not so easily ignored. And eventually it will catch up to them with what's called a **double bump.**

The double bump is a popular device used in novels with an early Catalyst, or novels featuring heroes who just need a little extra *coaxing* out of Act 1. It serves as a second Catalyst that *pushes* the hero into the Act 2 world. In *City of Bones*, Clary finds it impossible to ignore the existence of demons when her mom is kidnapped by one (second Catalyst), compelling her to step into the world of Shadowhunters (Break Into 2) and learn more about their ways.

In *The Book Thief*, the double bump is used to upset the new status quo world that was built in the aftermath of the first Catalyst. For Liesel, the start of World War II changes everything for her new family and town and is the impetus that inspires her to start stealing (Break Into 2). Similarly, in *I Hunt Killers*, when Jazz offers to help the police with their investigation into the murder (wants) and the sheriff refuses (double bump), it's enough to motivate Jazz to start his own investigation (Break Into 2).

To see the **blend and bump** strategy in all its glory, check out the beat sheet for *Stargirl* by Jerry Spinelli on page 274.

LATE CATALYSTS

Late Catalysts come with a big warning label. It's much harder to get a reader to stick around when nothing really "big" happens for forty, fifty, sixty, or even more pages. Trust me, no wants to read sixty pages of Setup, regardless of how beautiful or funny or voice-y the writing is. In a day and age when we *all* have a shorter attention span (including teens), it's important to get to the Catalyst as fast as you can, while still checking the boxes of an effective Setup.

However, there are some scenarios where a late Catalyst might be unavoidable. One being basic math. After all, a 500-page novel that follows the beats to the letter puts the Catalyst on page 50, which is a lot of pages of Setup.

If you find yourself in one of these scenarios (and you've already done all you can to trim your opening chapters and get to the Catalyst faster), there are a few strategies you can try to keep your readers engaged and turning pages until the Catalyst arrives and the story is kicked into high gear. Let's take a look at them.

The Cryptic Allusion

A great way to pull a reader into the story, especially if you're dealing with a late Catalyst, is to *allude* to the Catalyst to come, without actually spelling out what it is. This can happen in a prologue (see more on prologues later in this chapter), a flash forward, or by simply telling the story in past tense, from the POV of a narrator who's looking back in time with the unique perspective of having already seen all the events of the story.

You might drop small hints that a Catalyst is forthcoming, like, "Before the phone call came, I was a different person" or "I'll never forget the night the man in the trench coat knocked on my door and handed me the key." Then back up in time to tell the events that led up to this moment.

The pull of this tactic is the reader's desire to find out what this big event is that you've alluded to, leaving you time to not only set up your status quo world, but drop even more hints as you do!

In *We Were Liars* by E. Lockhart, the hero, Cady, alludes to the Catalyst on page 4 when she tells us about all the things she *used* to be (blond, strong, pretty) and then reveals, "It is true, I suffer migraines since my accident." We know something big is coming (this mysterious accident), and it's going to change Cady in many ways. And we keep reading to find out what it is.

I also employed this tactic in a small half-page prologue of my novel *The Geography of Lost Things*, which begins "By the time the messenger arrived at our front door, Jackson had already been dead two weeks." What did the messenger bring? Who is Jackson? Well, the Catalyst will soon reveal all, but before I get there, I jump back in time and catch the reader up on all the events that happened *before* the messenger arrives—in my Setup.

The Looming Catalyst

Another effective way to keep your reader engaged until the Catalyst comes is to drop hints that only the reader notices but the hero doesn't. Or if they do, they ignore them. This creates the effect of a Catalyst looming in the future that the reader can *sense* coming.

In *The Sun Is Also a Star*, because the novel is narrated by both Daniel and Natasha, we get a sense that they're going to meet. As these two strangers go about their day, we foresee their paths converging before they actually meet at the Catalyst on page 50.

I also employed this tactic in my young adult novel *In Some Other Life*, whose Catalyst doesn't come until page 48, when the hero, Kennedy, walks in on her boyfriend cheating with her best friend. It's a huge shock to her, but I'm sure that savvy readers are able to pick up on the clues I dropped that this affair has actually been going on for a while. The idea is that readers will start to theorize about the looming Catalyst and keep reading to see if they were right.

Readers love to play detective. They delight in picking up on subtle clues that the writer leaves them. It's a little game that readers and writers play, each trying to outsmart the other. The writer leaves the clue, wondering if the reader will catch it. The reader picks up a clue, wondering if the writer expected them to find it. Talk about reader engagement!

Mini Catalysts

If you're dealing with *long* pages of Setup, try populating those pages with a few smaller mini catalysts leading up to the big Catalyst (with the capital C). These mini catalysts (also called bumps) act as little explosions in the hero's life, each serving to push the hero closer to Act 2.

In *To All the Boys I've Loved Before* by Jenny Han (full beat sheet on page 151), before Lara Jean's secret love letters are sent out in the Catalyst on page 64, she experiences smaller mini catalysts that disrupt her status quo world. Like her sister Margot breaking up with her long-time boyfriend Josh (who has become part of the family) and then Margot leaving for college in Scotland (which was expected but still sends shock waves through Lara Jean's life).

In my novel *Unremembered*, the Catalyst that finally pushes the hero into Act 2 doesn't come until around page 50, when my hero (who survived a plane crash with no memories) is tracked down by a boy who tells her that her life is in danger and that she was never actually on the plane. It's this encounter that encourages her to Break Into 2 and go investigate the plane crash herself, but it serves more as a "last straw" in a long line of mysterious events (mini catalysts) that are all pushing her toward the same decision. First, the plane crash itself (which opens the book), then a boy who seems to appear in her hospital room in the middle of the night, then the discovery of a strange, barcode-like tattoo on her wrist. These are all little explosions in the hero's life, well timed to go off at just the right moment and have just the right impact to move her forward little by little, until she's ready to fully accept that things are not what they seem and to seek the truth.

So, yeah, the Catalyst is a slippery little beat that can and often *will* move around to fit the specific story you're telling. The key is to adjust the other beats around it to make sure you're still doing your job to set up Act 1 effectively so that when the hero does Break Into 2, the reader can tell, right away, what an upside-down world it truly is.

What About Prologues? Reimagining the Opening Image

Since the Save the Cat! method was originally created for screenwriters, there are some glaring gaps when it comes to adapting it for novelists. And the one I'm asked about a lot is in relation to prologues. How do they fit? Where do they fit? *Do* they fit?

They do.

The trick is figuring out *whether* you need them, and if you do, how to make them work for you and your beat sheet.

A prologue is defined as a "separate introductory section of a literary work," which I interpret to mean a piece of narrative that is set apart from the main story in some way and for a good reason. The key here is a *good* reason.

To me, a prologue is most effective when it feels *different* from the main storyline. Either because of tone, POV, perspective, timeline, or some other attribute. But to justify the use of a prologue, you need to ask yourself, *What purpose does it serve for the reader's experience?*

Maybe you're flashing forward to a point in the future, to give the reader a hint of what's to come or flashing back into the past, to give the reader a unique perspective on your character's backstory or world. Maybe you want to show the POV of another character besides your hero, because their perspective will prove important somehow. Maybe you want to tease the reader with something that *will* happen later in the plot, like a Catalyst, Midpoint, All Is Lost, or even Break Into 3. A prologue that reveals the hero's tone or emotional state when they're further along in the story (and therefore further along in their transformation) might serve as an interesting contrast to the hero's tone at the start of the story.

All of these feel like *good* reasons to have a prologue. If the prologue doesn't feel separate from and important to the story, then you might not need it. I can't tell you how many prologues I've written into the first draft and then deleted in revisions because I had first *thought* it was important to the story, but really it was just me figuring things out. (My novel *A Week of Mondays* had a record-breaking *five* deleted prologues. But I *had* to write them. If only to figure out I didn't *need* them.)

So what beat in the Save the Cat! Beat Sheet is the prologue? Is it the Opening Image? Or something else? Well, it really depends on the *function* of your prologue. Is it serving to introduce your hero in a way that gives the reader their first glimpse of who the hero is, what their flaws might be, what their goals might be, or other crucial information? Then, yes, I would consider that your Opening Image.

However, if your hero isn't even mentioned in the prologue, or they play a very small part in your prologue, I would say that's not your Opening Image, but rather a teaser or sidebar to your story. I consider the Opening Image beat to be your reader's first *illuminating* glimpse at the hero of your story (or one of them, if you have multiple heroes). So if we don't meet your hero in a significant way until chapter 1, then *that* would probably serve as your Opening Image and should check all the boxes of an effective one. And the prologue becomes more like a Pre-Opening Image.

Or maybe you want to look at it as *two* Opening Images, one to establish the tone of the story or something important about your world (the prologue) and one to establish the hero (chapter 1). And that's fine too. As long as you *are* establishing your hero in a visual, engaging way, there's no reason why you can't first use a prologue to do whatever you're needing it to do.

How you *define* it is pretty irrelevant, as long as you get the job done.

In *Twilight*, author Stephenie Meyer uses a prologue as a flash forward. We get a very short (one-page) glimpse at the Finale beat, when Bella has left the safety of her protectors (Jasper and Alice) to save her mother from the vampire James. Of course, we don't know that at the time. All we get is a sense of looming danger, which draws us into the story and gives us a hint of the stakes. Then, in the next scene (chapter 1), we're introduced to Bella with an Opening Image.

In *Shadow and Bone*, author Leigh Bardugo uses her prologue (a third-person flashback) to give us information on Alina's childhood in the orphanage of Keramsov, her friendship with Mal, and most important, the Grisha examiners who came to test Alina for magical powers and, as we learn later, somehow *missed* Alina's ability to summon light (a rare and mythical power in this world). So we're getting all sorts of good stuff here: worldbuilding; backstory; a dark, fantastical tone; even a mystery, which in my book qualifies it as an Opening Image.

In *The Sun Is Also a Star*, author Nicola Yoon uses her prologue to introduce us to the theme of the novel: destiny. An unidentified narrator shares a Carl Sagan quote about baking an apple pie from scratch and explains that to truly make it "from scratch" you would need to invent everything in the universe—atoms, black holes, suns, moons, farming, even the printing press—all the way back to the Big Bang. Because it's all connected. This is an indirect reference to the Theme Stated and the life lesson that one of the heroes, Natasha, will learn. Then, over the next *two* chapters, we get our two Opening Images for the two heroes.

Because the prologue is purposefully set apart from the rest of the story, it can serve many different functions and also hint at many different beats. Just be sure you really do have a good structural or thematic reason for the prologue and can justify including it. After all, it's your reader's first impression of your story. If it's not necessary, you lose out on the opportunity to hook your reader with something else that *is* necessary.

What About Flashbacks and Backstory? Weaving in Creative Character Development

Where do flashbacks and backstory belong in the Save the Cat! Beat Sheet? Is there a specific beat or beats where these elements go? The short answer is there is no hard-and-fast rule. There's no one beat that is the ultimate "flashback" beat. But there *are* places in the beat sheet where these literary devices work *better*.

First, some definitions. A *flashback* is typically a scene in your novel that takes place *before* whatever is currently happening in the story. Which means it almost always takes the reader *out* of the current timeline. It's usually distinguished from the current scene by italics or a new heading with a date or time stamp, or by using key transition words that cue the reader you're traveling into the past. Like, "He remembered a time when . . ." or "Her mind drifted back to . . ." or "They flashed back to . . ." Flashbacks are usually used to develop your characters (showing the reader who they are and why), reveal or highlight the theme of the novel, create context for the story, or build and establish stakes (by showing the reader why a specific plot point in the present is so impactful, because it is connected to a past event).

Backstory, in contrast, is an overarching term that encompasses *anything* that happened in the character's past (before the novel began). The **shard of glass** that we talked about back in chapter 1 is part of your hero's backstory (and can be shown to the reader using a flashback).

So a flashback is a *part* of a character's overall backstory.

But whether you use flashbacks to convey backstory or not, giving your reader information about your character's past and why they behave the way they do is important. When used sparingly and strategically, it can provide context and clarity and even create empathy for unlikable characters (another way to save the cat!).

But where do you do this?

Most likely, you're going to deliver backstory (through flashbacks or other means) in the multi-scene beats. So we're talking the Setup, Debate, Fun and Games, Bad Guys Close In, Dark Night of the Soul, and Finale. The single-scene beats (especially those **foundation beats** that pivot the plot) are best kept in the present. For example, a Catalyst that sets the story into motion is *probably* going to happen in the present, not the past, unless there's a very compelling reason. Like, perhaps, your hero is an amnesiac whose memories are slowly returning and one specific memory serves as the incident that incites everything.

Likewise, the Midpoint, which raises the stakes of the story and pivots the direction of the plot, is *probably* going to happen in the present as well. Same goes for the All Is Lost and those beats where the hero is making a decision and taking action (Break Into 2 and Break Into 3). These beats work best in the present, as they're dictating where the story goes next.

In the Setup, on the other hand, you are literally setting up your hero and their world, so perhaps a little sprinkling of backstory here—maybe a flashback or two—will help accomplish that. And notice I said "sprinkling." Backstory is most compelling to read about when it's sprinkled in here and there, not dumped in all at once (especially at the start of the story). Give the reader *just* enough for them to understand what's happening in the present, but always leave them wanting *more* backstory, not less.

In the Setup of *To All the Boys I've Loved Before* (full beat sheet on page 151), the hero, Lara Jean, flashes back on the day her mom died, leaving her older sister, Margot, to take care of the family. It's a short scene but serves its purpose well: to give us context about this family's dynamic, the tragedy they all share, and the stakes of Margot's monumental decision to leave home and go to college in Scotland.

Similarly, the Debate beat is *designed* for contemplation and internal reflection, making it a fitting place to perhaps dive into the past for a moment, to show how that past might influence the big decision coming up in the Break Into 2.

In the Debate of *If I Stay* by Gayle Forman (full beat sheet on page 316), we see the first of many flashbacks in the Debate, after Mia's family suffers a terrible car accident. As Mia tries to figure out if her out-of-body experience is real or not, she flashes back to a happier time in her life. Forman uses flashbacks here and throughout the novel to give us context for the big thematic choice that lies at the heart of Mia's story: *Should I stay or go?*

In general, the multi-scene beats are good places to weave in backstory because you have *time*. You have *pages*. Remember how long that Fun and Games was? It might be nice to give the reader some short breaks from the A Story (external story) here by diving into the hero's past and revealing some important backstory, especially if it relates to the B Story (internal story).

In *Six of Crows* by Leigh Bardugo (full beat sheet on page 249), as soon as the team is on the ship and sailing toward Fjerda to infiltrate the Ice Court (Act 2 goal), the author spends some time exploring the heroes' backstories, providing us with well-placed flashbacks that help us better understand the complex pasts that have shaped them into who they are today, which not coincidentally is one of the themes of the novel (how tragedies of our past shape our present). Bardugo effectively continues these flashbacks in the Bad Guys Close In, Dark Night of the Soul, and even sparingly in the Finale.

The operative word with backstory and flashbacks is always *necessity*. Nothing slows a plot more than unnecessary backstory. Backstory should be used to explain a character's behavior, raise the stakes of the plot, help reveal the theme, inform the events of the present, or connect to the present storyline in another meaningful way. The rule is if the story doesn't make sense without it, then it's necessary. If you can lift it out and the story still works, then you probably don't need it.

What About Villain and Antagonist Stories? Crafting Negative Arcs and Reverse Beat Sheets

Do heroes always have to change for the *better*? No! And here's where we start to get into some fun with villains and antagonists as the "heroes" of our stories. Villain origin stories have become popular in young adult fiction; some of the best-known examples are *The Ballad of Songbirds and Snakes* (a *Hunger Games* prequel) by Suzanne Collins, *And I Darken* by Kiersten White, *The Young Elites* by Marie Lu, and *Fairest* (a novella set in the Lunar Chronicles world) by Marissa Meyer.

These stories still feature main characters who transform. They just don't transform into a *less* flawed version of themself. They typically transform into a *more* flawed version of themself. The flaw, rather than being conquered and overcome, is perverted, amplified, and allowed to consume. Villain stories explore what happens when a deeply rooted flaw (or shard of glass) serves to turn the hero to the "dark side."

So, do you need a whole different beat sheet to accomplish this feat?

Nope. You can use the same one, but the purpose of the beats might change.

Let's look again at those foundation beats that pivot the plot: Catalyst, Break Into 2, Midpoint, All Is Lost, and Break Into 3.

Ask yourself: How do these beats guide my hero toward the *opposite* of the theme? How do I push my hero toward not emotional growth, but emotional deterioration? How can I introduce a flawed hero in Act 1 and use Acts 2 and 3 to show them succumbing to their flaws instead of overcoming them?

In *The Ballad of Songbirds and Snakes*, we meet flawed hero Coriolanus Snow (who will eventually become President Snow in the Hunger Games trilogy). He is ambitious, proud, jealous, and obsessed with safeguarding the reputation of his family name, a trait he received from his morally bankrupt father (**shard of glass**). When the districts rose up against the Capitol several years ago, the Snow munitions empire fell. Coriolanus's parents both died, and so did the family's fortune. This has turned Coriolanus very angry toward the districts. Now he can barely afford to feed and clothe himself (**problems**) and desperately **wants** to win a cash prize from mentoring the winning Hunger Games tribute so he can go to university. But his hopes are dashed when he gets assigned Lucy Gray, a tribute from the worst district—12 (Catalyst). There's no way *she* can win. Or can she?

As Coriolanus Breaks Into 2, taking on the challenge of mentoring this tribute, he ends up falling for her and ultimately leads her to winning the Games (false victory Midpoint). But when it's revealed he cheated (fixing things the wrong way), he's punished by being sent to District 12 as a lowly Peacekeeper, dashing his dreams of ever going to university. That's where his downward path really puts pressure on him and his flaws. How far will Coriolanus go to preserve his reputation and his pride? To what depths will he sink to see the Snow family name restored?

Now, if this were a typical beat sheet with a positive arc, he would overcome his legacy of greed and corruption and put human life and decency *above* his pride and ambition. But it isn't. So instead, when

Coriolanus is put to the test and discovers that his friend and fellow Peacekeeper is plotting with rebels, he turns him in, watching him hang for his treason at the All Is Lost. He gets another shot at redemption in the Finale, when he escapes District 12 with Lucy Gray after she's wrongfully convicted of murder, but the moment she reveals that she knows what he did to his friend (High Tower Surprise), he turns on her too, choosing once again to succumb to his flaws and prioritizing his ambition and pride. Instead of digging deep down to prove he's learned the theme, he digs deep down and proves he hasn't. Lucy Gray runs, and he shoots into the trees, not sure if he hit her, but also not really caring. He has become the villain.

His negative arc lands him exactly where he wants to be: on top. The Final Image shows us Snow at university, studying under Dr. Gaul (his depraved mentor), with a "bright" future in the Capitol. He is financially *better* than he was at the start, but morally worse, having done atrocious things to get there.

For a full example, check out the beat sheet (on page 214) for *Children of Blood and Bone* by Tomi Adeyemi, in which one of the three heroes experiences a negative arc.

The beat sheet is designed to transform heroes, but that doesn't necessarily have to be for the good. It's all about customizing those beats to make them work for you, subverting the standard story structure to serve *your* purpose and deliver *your* message. Because whether your hero changes for worse or for better, there's still *something* for the reader to glean here. There's still a universal theme that deals with what it means to be human.

Which makes the most important question for you to answer not whether the arc is positive or negative; it's what are you trying to *say*?

Those are the most common ways to customize the beat sheet, which I've collected over the years from my own writing and reading, and from working with thousands of authors through online webinars, in-person workshops, and my Writing Mastery Academy. But this is by no means a comprehensive list. Because there will always be another "what about?" There will be ways to bend the "rules" of story structure. Or at least *modify* them to make them work for you.

Hey, this whole Save the Cat! novel thing *exists* because I read a screenwriting guide and thought, *I can make that work for novels.*

Which is why I urge you to *play.* Have fun. Be creative. I've given you the foundations and the tools—now go build something amazing. And when all else fails, get studying. Find novels like your own and learn from how other authors have taken the basic structure and made it work for their specific story.

And what do you know? That's what the next chapters of this book are all about.

Identifying Your Genre
The Ten Save the Cat! Story Genres

Pop quiz! What do the following three young adult novels have in common?

The Giver by Lois Lowry
An Ember in the Ashes by Sabaa Tahir
Long Way Down by Jason Reynolds

If you said, "They all have the fifteen beats!" then congratulations, a gold star for you!

But what if I told you that in addition to all of these novels having the same fifteen beats, they are all the same *genre*?

Nonsense! you might think. *One is a science fiction classic, one is a fantasy adventure, and one is a contemporary novel in verse!*

That's right. And yet, they are same *type* of story.

Allow me to explain.

In chapter 2, we studied the mechanics of story in general. We broke down story into an easy-to-follow template (the Save the Cat! Beat Sheet) so we could study how successful stories work and use that blueprint to craft our own. Now it's time to drill a little deeper into story and look at the mechanics of how different *types* of stories work so that we can, once again, break them down into easy-to-follow templates and use those templates to craft the most compelling, successful version of that story that we can.

Here's a secret. Readers don't want to read anything *new*.

Yes, they want to read something creative, something inventive, something with a twist!

They want a story that *looks* new, but still *feels* familiar. In other words, they just want the same thing, only different.

Don't believe me? I'll prove it. Over the next ten chapters, I'll break down ten different genres that nearly *all* novels fit into . . . from the beginning of time. These are not your mother's genres, like sci-fi, fantasy, comedy, drama, and romance. Those are categorizations of style and tone. The genres we'll be studying in this book are categorizations of *story.*

So, appropriately, they're called the Save the Cat! story genres.

And they help us determine what *kind* of story we're trying to tell, what *type* of transformation our hero is undergoing, and what central theme or question we're setting out to explore.

I like to think of the story genres as *filters.* (Yes, like the kind you put on your Instagram pictures to make us even *more* jealous of your recent beach vacation.) Story is story. The fifteen beats are the fifteen beats, no matter what type of story you want to tell. But the story genres put a slightly different *filter* on that basic story template, highlighting different things and changing the contrast of different beats.

As you study the ten story genres, you'll start to see that, in almost all the novels included in each genre, certain elements or conventions appear over and over again. Like patterns. Like a code! (There's that word again!) Just as the fifteen beats were a codification of story in general, the Save the Cat! story genres are a codification of ten universal story types. Which means they distill thousands of years' worth of literature into ten easy-to-follow templates.

Shut the front door!

Right?!

Now it's just a matter of figuring out where *your* story fits, so you can study the key elements of your genre, make sure you're including all of them, and determine how you can put a new twist on those elements to really make your story stand out. In other words, so you can give us the same thing—only different.

We all want to write "original" stories, but the truth is there's no such thing. We're all recycling the same ten stories over and over, just putting our own unique spins on them. All the young adult novels you read and love, all the novels that are flying off the shelves at the bookstores, all the novels that are snatching up six-figure book and movie deals are not original at all.

Now, you can choose to look at this as depressing and hopeless; you can even stomp your feet and say, "No! I'll show you! I'll write something that no one has ever written before!" Or you can choose to look at this as a *huge* relief. I've just taken the burden of the impossible off your shoulders. You can't write an original story, so don't even try.

Wow, don't you feel *so* much better?

What you *can* write, however, is a *fresh* story. That's really what readers want. A fresh take on an age-old story type.

And over the next ten chapters, I'm going to show you exactly how to deliver one.

Overview of the Ten Story Genres

I hope that by now you're getting excited to learn more about these magical ten genres that are going to make your life so much easier. So here's a quick overview. After that, there's an entire chapter devoted to each one, including a full-length beat sheet of a novel from that genre.

1. **RITES OF PASSAGE:** A hero must endure and come to terms with the pain and torment brought about by life's common challenges (death, separation, loss, addiction, coming of age, tragedy, and so on).

2. **BUDDY LOVE:** A hero is transformed by the existence of someone else; this includes (but is not limited to) love stories, friendship stories, and pet stories.

3. **INSTITUTIONALIZED:** A hero enters or is already entrenched inside a certain group, institution, establishment, or family and must make a choice to join, escape, or destroy it.

4. **SUPERHERO:** An extraordinary hero finds themself in an ordinary world and must come to terms with being special or destined for greatness.

5. **GOLDEN FLEECE:** A hero (or team) goes on a road trip or quest of some type (even if there's no actual road), in search of one thing

(usually a prize or destination) and winds up discovering something else: their own self.

6. **FOOL TRIUMPHANT:** An underestimated underdog hero is pitted against some kind of "establishment" and proves a hidden worth to society.

7. **DUDE WITH A PROBLEM:** An innocent, ordinary hero suddenly finds themself in the midst of extraordinary circumstances (and danger) and must rise to the challenge.

8. **OUT OF THE BOTTLE:** An ordinary hero is temporarily "touched by magic," usually involving a wish fulfilled or a curse bestowed, and the hero learns an important lesson about appreciating and making the most of "reality."

9. **WHYDUNIT:** A crime is committed and a mystery must be solved by a detective (of some kind), during which something shocking is revealed about the dark side of human nature.

10. **MONSTER IN THE HOUSE:** A hero (or group of heroes) must overcome some kind of monster (supernatural or not), in some kind of enclosed setting (or limited circumstances), and someone is usually responsible for bringing the monster into being.

Ta-da! There they are. Ten universal story genres to fit any novel, even yours.

While some of these genres are more popular in young adult than others (the most popular probably being the first five), you can find *all* of these genres in the young adult section of the bookstore today. And because fads in YA come and go so quickly, I urge you to never write to a trend. Just because right now you might notice that Fool Triumphant stories are few and far between, that doesn't mean tomorrow they won't be the hot new thing.

Tell the story you want to tell. Write the tale that inspires you. And use the following genre templates to make sure you get it right. Think of these templates as your cookbook. Find the recipe you want to make, study the basic genre ingredients, and then figure out what seasonings and flavors to add to make it *yours*.

Let's go back to those three novels I listed at the start of the chapter.

The Giver is about a boy who discovers that the idyllic community he's living in is not so idyllic and plans to escape so he can bring about change. *An Ember in the Ashes* is about two teens living under the oppressive Empire: a rebel spy who seeks to expose its secrets and a soldier who seeks to escape it. And *Long Way Down* is about a teen growing up in a gang-torn neighborhood who mentally battles against the Rules that dictate he shoot his brother's killer.

Have you figured out what story genre they fit into yet? Have you noticed how they all feature a hero who is entrenched inside a certain group, institution, establishment, or family and must make a choice to join, escape, or destroy it? They're all Institutionalized stories!

How about these three young adult novels?

Six of Crows by Leigh Bardugo, about a band of teen thieves who take on an impossible heist; *An Abundance of Katherines* by John Green, about two teens who go on a road trip to escape heartbreak; and *Warcross* by Marie Lu, about a teen hacker who tracks a criminal through a virtual reality game competition.

Notice the elements they all have in common.

They all feature a hero (or team) who goes on a road trip or quest of some type, in search of one thing, and winds up discovering something else—their own self! They're all Golden Fleeces!

Is it just me, or is that ridiculously fun? (It might just be me.)

But wait a minute, you might be thinking. *Does that mean that Lois Lowry, John Green, and Jason Reynolds all sat down with their genre guides and started checking boxes of ingredients?* Who knows? Only they know the answer to that. I'm here to tell you that it doesn't matter.

The boxes are still checked.

The same goes for the fifteen beats of the beat sheet. Whether an author is *consciously* following the template is irrelevant. Because they still did it.

Some chefs can cook without a recipe and it still tastes perfect. Some of us (*most* of us, in fact) need those templates. We need a cheat sheet! And if that includes you, then welcome to the cheaters club, my friend. I've been a proud, card-carrying member for more than fifteen years and twenty novels now. And I promise you there's nothing wrong with needing a little guidance.

If you know you're setting out to write a Rites of Passage story, for instance, then I highly recommend you *read* Rites of Passage stories. Any writing teacher will tell you that if you want to be a better writer, you have to be a better reader. But now, with the Save the Cat! genres, you can find stories similar to yours, which share common ingredients, and study those stories specifically. This is especially useful when you get stuck. I can't tell you how many times the Save the Cat! genre guides have helped me bust out of a plotting blockage.

But the Save the Cat! genres don't only help you *write* your book; they might help you sell it as well. Regardless of your writing goals—traditional publishing, self-publishing, or even sending your finished novel to a few friends—you're going to have to *pitch* it to someone. I guarantee you, somewhere along the way, someone is going to ask, "What's it about?" And you're going to have to tell them— *succinctly*—in a compelling way that makes them want to read it. Trust me, that's no easy feat. (Which is why I've included a whole chapter later in this book on how to pitch and sell your novel.)

But here's the thing. When someone asks what your book is about, they don't really want to hear the entire story beat for beat (I can tell you *that* from experience). What they really want to know is: How is it the *same* as something I've already read, and how is it *different*?

What they're really asking for is the story genre! (Without even realizing it!)

Of course, that doesn't mean you're going to start off saying, "Well, it's an Out of the Bottle . . ." because that's probably not going to make much sense to anyone who hasn't read this book (yes, you're now part of the secret club with its own secret language! If you're lucky, I'll even teach you the handshake).

Instead, you're going to use what the publishing industry calls "comparable titles" or just "comps" for short. And you'll find those comps in your story genre.

So instead of saying, "Well, it's an Out of the Bottle story . . ." you can say something like, "Well, it's like *Before I Fall* by Lauren Oliver, but it's a comedy, and instead of reliving the day of her death over and over, the hero continuously relives the day her boyfriend broke up with her."

But don't bother writing that novel. I already did. It's called *A Week of Mondays*, and that's how exactly how I pitched it.

The story genres. Learn 'em. Use 'em. Love 'em.

Final Note: Bleeding Genres

Before I release you into the great expanse of the Save the Cat! genre guides and beat sheets, I want to offer a quick word of warning.

It's *very* easy to get hung up on identifying the genre of something. Whether that be your own novel or one of the novels I've included as examples. You might even be panicking because your novel fits into *many* genres. I'm here to tell you that you're not alone. Most novels can fit into several genres.

Long Way Down by Jason Reynolds is the perfect example. The majority of this novel-in-verse takes place during an elevator ride in which Will, the hero, is riding the seven floors down to the lobby of his building with the plan to shoot the man who just shot his brother. During this elevator ride, we learn "the Rules" of Will's neighborhood, which include "Always seek revenge." Each floor the elevator stops on, a ghost boards with Will, someone else who was killed by gun violence and who has a story to tell.

You'll remember I classified this tale as Institutionalized, as that's where it most resonated with *me*. You may have read it and had a completely different interpretation because you're a different person. For instance, I could also see this as an Out of the Bottle because the ghosts feel very much like a temporary magical curse that's bestowed on Will to teach him an important lesson (similar to *A Christmas Carol* by Charles Dickens, which I classify as an Out of the Bottle). But there's also some Golden Fleece vibes going on here. The elevator ride could be interpreted as a "road," and the ghosts make up the team that Will picks up on his way to a destination (the ground floor), during which he learns something about himself. It could even be a Rites of

Passage, as the story deals with a hero coming to terms with the death of his brother.

But in the end, it was the emphasis on the Rules of Will's neighborhood (or institution) that struck the biggest chord with me and inspired me to place it in the Institutionalized camp. Whether that's how you read it, I don't know. Whether that's what Jason Reynolds intended, I *really* don't know!

But isn't that one of the joys of storytelling? You write something, you put it out there, and it takes on a life of its own. It impacts people in different ways because it's fed through the myriad of different filters and experiences that readers bring to the relationship. And since novels are complex by nature, chances are they're going to bleed into multiple genres.

The point is: it doesn't matter! Don't panic. It's not about getting it *right*. It's about making it easier on *you*, the writer. The genres are meant to guide you, not to send you spinning into dizzying circles trying to puzzle it out, when you could be spending that precious time *writing*.

When my coauthor, Joanne Rendell, and I were writing *Between Burning Worlds* (the second book in a young adult sci-fi trilogy pitched as "*Les Misérables* in space") we started out thinking it was an Institutionalized story. The first book in the series was an Institutionalized, so that made sense to us.

Then the problems started.

We rewrote that book over and over and over and just couldn't seem to get the story to "click" into place. No matter how many times we refigured the beat sheet, the story just felt *unfocused*. Until one day, when I was complaining about it to a writer friend, I just happened to mention the *quest* that two of the heroes go on to stop a deadly weapon, and that's when it hit me.

Quest. Team. Destination.

"It's a *Golden Fleece*! We've been trying to cram the book into the wrong genre!"

No wonder it wasn't working. No wonder it lacked focus. Once we unlocked the genre, we were able to focus the beats around the

Golden Fleece elements, which caused the rest of the story to *finally* fall into place.

That's what the genres are meant to do, my friends. That's why we study them. Not so we can debate with each other, dig in our heels, and swear that *we're* right. And certainly not so we can make our own lives miserable. The genres help us unlock our story and figure out what we're trying to say. And *then* make it easier to say it.

Moral of the story: different novels in a series can have different genres, *and* the genre can change (multiple times) during the writing process. For that matter, if you have multiple points of view, you might even have multiple genres going on at once, one for each POV (although in these situations, I'd urge you to focus on the genre of your "one true hero" to keep your reader from feeling like they're being tugged in too many directions).

As you read the next ten chapters and study the genre guides, remember to go easy on yourself. Cut yourself some slack. Cut *me* some slack. My genre categorizations are not the end-all-be-all verdict that shall go down in the annals of storytelling wisdom (if there is such a thing, which I doubt). They're simply here to help you recognize the patterns, see the similarities, find the code. And if you disagree, great! That means you're looking at the stories in a new way, which will ultimately help you write your own.

So if you're caught between two or even three story genres for your own work, ask yourself what *feels* best to you. Which ones resonates with *you*? What kind of story do you *want* to tell?

In the end, that's all that really matters.

Rites of Passage
Sometimes Life Is the Biggest Conflict of All

If there's one story genre that we can be sure will never go out of style in young adult fiction, it's the Rites of Passage. These are stories that deal with the trials and tribulations of simply being *alive*.

Death, puberty, separation, breakups, addiction, illness, identity crises, tragedy, and coming of age. This genre centers on life's "passages" and the roadblocks that stop us in our path and force us to reexamine who we are. And there's arguably no other time in a human life when these passages feel more fresh, raw, immediate, and pressing than adolescence.

As evidenced from some timeless classics, bestsellers, and award-winners, like *The Book Thief* by Marcus Zusak, *The Poet X* by Elizabeth Acevedo, *The Catcher in the Rye* by J. D. Salinger, *I Am Not Your Perfect Mexican Daughter* by Erika L. Sánchez, and *Simon vs. the Homo Sapiens Agenda* by Becky Albertalli, among so many others.

The teenage years are some of our most volatile. New experiences and emotions are coming at us daily, we're discovering and forging new identities, and new worldviews are overshadowing the worldviews of our parents and adult mentors.

In other words, what an amazing time in which to set a story!

Ask any teenager to tell you about their life, and I'm willing to bet you'll hear a Rites of Passage story. And that's why this genre is so universal, across centuries, cultures, races, genders, and ages. We've *all* been there. We've all suffered through life's curveballs. We've all been forced to adapt or change to overcome life's biggest challenges.

And that's the premise at the heart of every Rites of Passage novel: growing up.

It can often be the hardest test of all.

Rites of Passage tales tend to be stories about grief, because they're often stories about loss and overcoming it. But loss can come in many forms: loss of a life (death), loss of a friendship or relationship (separation), loss of childhood or innocence (coming of age). But just because these are stories of loss doesn't mean they are necessarily all *sad* or told with heavy, drama-laden narratives. How your hero handles the loss and narrates their Rite of Passage depends on the hero and the voice you've gifted them with. So, yes, this genre can include comedies too.

Regardless of the tone, the necessary ingredients of this story genre remain the same. They all contain (1) **a life problem**, (2) **a wrong way to attack the problem,** and (3) a solution to the problem that involves **an acceptance of a hard truth** the hero has been avoiding.

Let's break down each of these ingredients one by one so as you craft your own Rites of Passage, you can be sure you're checking the right boxes and getting the most impact out of your tale of life's woes.

A LIFE PROBLEM

In these types of stories, the life problem is *usually* something unavoidable. Just another part of being human. Death is a popular choice in this genre, as it's such a mysterious yet inevitable part of life. In *I Am Not Your Perfect Mexican Daughter*, Julia deals with the death of her older sister and the pressure to fill her role as the perfect daughter. In *I'll Give You the Sun* by Jandy Nelson, the twin heroes (Noah and Jude) both deal with the car accident that took their mother's life, and in *We Were*

Liars, E. Lockhart gives us a twist on the genre, as Cady doesn't even realize she's grieving the loss of her friends until close to the end of the novel. But the whole premise is still centered around that grief.

Similarly, separation is something we *all* have to cope with at some point. Whether it's a devastating breakup, a best friend moving away, or some other difficult parting, who among us hasn't had to say goodbye to someone we weren't ready to say goodbye to? In *Crank*, Kristina is dealing with not only her parents' divorce but also her father's eight-year absence since then. In *To All the Boys I've Loved Before*, Lara Jeans deals with her older sister's going off to college in Scotland and all the responsibilities that fall on her shoulders in the wake of it.

The struggle with identity is another life problem that features prominently in Rites of Passage tales, especially of the young adult variety—whether that be sexual identity, gender identity, social identity, cultural identity, religious identity, or something else. In a time of life when bodies and hormones are changing, worlds are broadening, social groups are dissolving and reforming, it's only natural that we'll find conflict here. In *Simon vs. the Homo Sapiens Agenda*, Simon knows he's gay, but he's not out to his friends and family. Throughout the novel, he struggles to keep his budding online relationship with a boy named Blue a secret. And in *If I Was Your Girl* by Meredith Russo, we meet Amanda, a trans teen who is looking for a fresh start at a new school after being brutally attacked and bullied for coming out in her old school.

Other common life problems include illness, addiction, or the classic coming of age. In *The Poet X*, Xiomara deals with the problem of growing up, growing curves, and getting noticed by boys, all under the tight control of a strict religious mother.

In some cases, the life problem might refer to a horrific tragedy in the hero's past—like *Speak* by Laurie Halse Anderson, about a fourteen-year-old girl who was raped the summer before freshman year, or *Girl in Pieces* by Kathleen Glasgow, about a seventeen-year-old girl who tries to piece her life back together after being a victim of teenage sex trafficking. These types of life problems are certainly not unavoidable parts of life, but the act of grieving them is.

The life problem doesn't have to be limited to one thing. In *The Truth About Forever* by Sarah Dessen, the grief Macy experiences over her father's heart attack (death) is compounded by her boyfriend's announcement that he wants a "break" (separation). In *The Book Thief*, Liesel struggles with the death of her younger brother, followed shortly after by a separation from her mother when she's dropped off at a foster home.

Some life problems appear in the form of the story's Catalyst, but it's also common for the life problem to be part of the hero's backstory.

Regardless of what life problem you choose for your hero and where you introduce it, it's there. And it's not going to just go away. It must be dealt with. *How* your hero deals with it, however, is another matter and brings us to our second genre ingredient.

A WRONG WAY TO ATTACK THE PROBLEM

How the hero deals with the life problem usually involves some kind of avoidance of the pain. Like stealing (*The Book Thief*), secret keeping (*Simon vs. The Homo Sapiens Agenda*), drug or substance abuse (*Crank*), dating the wrong person (*The Poet X*), or even denial that the problem exists (*We Were Liars*). Your options are endless. And they aren't necessarily limited to the "real world." Although this genre is mostly found in realistic fiction, there are some exceptions. In *More Happy Than Not* by Adam Silvera, a realistic fiction novel with a speculative twist, the hero, Aaron, is able to attack his life problems the "wrong way" by getting a sci-fi-esque procedure that allows him to forget painful memories.

The word "wrong" isn't a moral judgment of the hero's choices. It stems from the reality that this approach probably won't actually *solve* the problem; it will only bury it, and possibly make it worse. Simon, in *Simon vs. the Homo Sapiens Agenda*, feels he has no other choice but to keep his sexual orientation a secret (because he wants to protect Blue's privacy). But it's this wrong way to attack the problem that ends up complicating everything within Simon's group of friends and making his life messier.

But even though the wrong way to attack the problem probably won't fix the problem, it's the very thing that makes this genre so compelling to read. And often it's what drives the plot forward, because it usually centers around the hero's Act 2 decision and goal.

In *I Am Not Your Perfect Mexican Daughter*, instead of confronting her grief and trying to find common ground with her mother, Julia sets off at the Break Into 2 to prove that her sister, Olga, *wasn't* the perfect daughter everyone believed her to be. The truth won't bring Olga back, and it certainly won't bring her family closer together, but it's the primary driving force of the plot.

While it's true that *all* heroes first try to fix things the wrong way in Act 2, in Rites of Passage stories this wrong way is front and center in both the external and internal stories because the pain of the life problem is so raw and immediate. In these novels, the avoidance of the pain *is* the premise. So much so that it's often referenced in the title. *The Book Thief*, *Crank*, and *I Am Not Your Perfect Mexican Daughter* all speak directly to this genre ingredient. In *We Were Liars*, Cady's "wrong way to attack the problem" is to become a liar to herself, even if she doesn't realize it.

In fact, this genre ingredient is the reason we're drawn to these books in the first place. Readers aren't interested in a book about someone who handles life's problems with grace, humility, and emotional competence. How dull would that to be? We read Rites of Passage stories for the struggle, for the *wrong way*, in hopes that eventually it will lead to the *right* way. Which coincidentally (or not!) is our third genre ingredient.

AN ACCEPTANCE OF THE HARD TRUTH

In the end, this is what all Rites of Passage stories are *about*. Acceptance. And it's usually the acceptance of the very truth or pain that the hero has spent so much time and effort avoiding. Liesel in *The Book Thief* realizes that her true power comes not from the books (and other things) that she steals, but from the words inside of her that she eventually puts into a book of her own. Xiomara discovers a similar power of words through her poetry in *The Poet X*. Julia in *I Am Not Your*

Perfect Mexican Daughter realizes that learning Olga's secrets won't set her free from her mother's harsh rules and impossible expectations; only a deeper understanding of her own grief and her mother's grief will do that. And Simon in *Simon vs. the Homo Sapiens Agenda* ultimately finds the courage to face his fears head-on, and together he and Blue decide to go public with their relationship.

In the end, these stories of life's growing pains leave readers with a similar message: We can't expect life to change, so we'd better change instead. We can't count on tragedy not to strike or grief not to come for us; we can only count on ourselves to get us through the pain when it does. It's a lesson as universal as life itself. Which is probably why publishers of young adult books keep publishing these stories, and readers keep reading them. We've all been held back and knocked down by life's roadblocks and unexpected twists, but the heroes of these tales inspire us to keep going, keep trying, keep growing.

To recap: if you're thinking about writing a Rites of Passage novel, make sure your story includes these three essential ingredients:

- **A LIFE PROBLEM**: a universal challenge such as death, puberty, separation, breakups, addiction, illness, identity crises, and coming of age that often results from nothing more than just being alive.
- **A WRONG WAY TO ATTACK THE PROBLEM**: Your hero can't attack the problem head-on (at least not at first). They usually try to avoid the pain, and that gives the story its premise and momentum.
- **AN ACCEPTANCE OF THE HARD TRUTH**: This is the real solution: facing the pain head-on. Acceptance usually comes with the understanding that it's the hero who must change, not life itself.

POPULAR YOUNG ADULT RITES OF PASSAGE NOVELS

The Catcher in the Rye by J. D. Salinger
Forever by Judy Blume
The Perks of Being a Wallflower by Stephen Chbosky
Speak by Laurie Halse Anderson

The Truth About Forever by Sarah Dessen
Crank by Ellen Hopkins
Elsewhere by Gabrielle Zevin
The Book Thief by Markus Zusak
The Summer I Turned Pretty by Jenny Han
Second Chance Summer by Morgan Matson
Every Day by David Levithan
To All the Boys I've Loved Before by Jenny Han*
We Were Liars by E. Lockhart
I'll Give You the Sun by Jandy Nelson
Simon vs. the Homo Sapiens Agenda by Becky Albertalli
More Happy Than Not by Adam Silvera
If I Was Your Girl by Meredith Russo
Girl in Pieces by Kathleen Glasgow
I Am Not Your Perfect Mexican Daughter by Erika L. Sánchez
The Poet X by Elizabeth Acevedo

* Beat sheet follows.

TO ALL THE BOYS I'VE LOVED BEFORE

BY: Jenny Han
STC GENRE: Rites of Passage
BOOK GENRE: Young adult contemporary
TOTAL PAGES: 355 (Simon & Schuster Books for Young Readers paperback edition, 2016)

It's hard to think "young adult" without thinking "Jenny Han." Her contemporary YA novels are sweet, comforting, heartfelt, and devoured by readers of all ages around the world. *To All the Boys I've Loved Before* has spent more than forty weeks on the *New York Times* best-sellers list and was published in over thirty countries. In 2018, Netflix released the movie adaptation, and its smashing success quickly led to adaptations of the following two books in the trilogy, *P.S. I Still Love You* and *Always and Forever, Lara Jean*. As we study the novel's airtight structure and inspiring character arc, it's easy to see how Han has captured the hearts of so many readers with this heartwarming tale about the trials and tribulations of growing up.

Opening Image (0)

In a prologue, Lara Jean describes her tradition of writing letters to boys she loves as a way of getting over them. The letters are sealed and addressed, then stored in a hat box in her closet, but never sent. Here we meet a girl who lives safely in her imagination, writing letters to boys who will never read them.

Theme Stated (3)

"Your sister suffers from delusions of grandeur," says Josh, the long-time boyfriend of Lara Jean's older sister, Margot. It's meant as a joke, in response to Lara Jean's romanticizing about visiting her sister in Paris during spring break. But the nugget of truth takes root in the reader's mind. Lara Jean *does* suffer from delusions of grandeur, as we'll soon see in the Setup. She's a romantic who prefers to live in her own imagination because it's safer than living in the real world. But eventually she'll have to face up to that real world and accept the fact that change is just another part of growing up.

Setup (1–64)

We enter Lara Jean's status quo world just days before her sister, Margot, is scheduled to leave home to study abroad in Scotland. Since the death of their mom years ago, Margot has been the mother figure to younger siblings Lara Jean and Kitty, often picking up the slack for their OB-GYN father who works odd hours. Lara Jean **wants** to be a good older sister to Kitty and fill Margot's shoes after Margot leaves, but the change is already hard on her. In fact, being overly dependent on Margot is one of the **things that needs fixing** in Lara Jean's life, along with her fear of driving and her anxiety about being in charge after Margot leaves. As Lara Jean wonders, "How can we be the Song girls without Margot?" (15), we get a sense of the **stasis = death** of her situation. Margot's looming departure is the big life problem at the heart of this Rites of Passage story that will force Lara Jean to grow up and face reality.

Margot's departure is also one of the novel's **mini catalysts** or "bumps," each putting increasing pressure on Lara Jean to change before the big Catalyst arrives to push her out of her status quo world. (For more on mini catalysts, see page 126.)

Another bump is Margot's breakup with Josh. He's someone who's always around and feels like part of the family, so the breakup is hard on Lara Jean, made even more complicated by the reveal that she once had a secret crush on Josh—and even wrote him one of her aforementioned unsent love letters. Later, Lara Jean gets into a car accident, which only exacerbates her fear of driving and makes stepping into Margot's role as eldest sister feel more challenging.

Also in the Setup, we see our hero at home, work, and play.

At **home**, we get to know Lara Jean and her family, who are very close. At **work**, Lara Jean is preparing to go back to school for her junior year, which should be interesting after the news that the school's "it" couple—Peter Kavinksy and Genevieve Mitchell—have recently broken up. And at **play**, we meet Lara Jean's long-time friend Chris, who smokes, hooks up with boys she doesn't know, and has been suspended twice—in contrast to Lara Jean's hobbies of baking cookies and scrapbooking. Lara Jean's innocence and inexperience are spotlighted through her stark difference from Chris.

The night before school starts, Josh comes over for dinner, and Lara Jean teases Kitty about having a crush on Josh. Kitty gets angry and storms out. Later, Lara Jean and Josh talk about their first crushes, and Lara Jean admits that hers was Peter Kavinsky (who was also her first kiss in middle school), while Josh admits that his was Lara Jean! This shocks her and stirs old feelings for him that she thought were gone. Though Lara Jean secretly liked Josh first, she still feels guilty and disloyal to Margot for having these feelings. So she sits down to write Josh another never-to-be sent love letter to help her get past them. Here, we see her **flaw** manifesting. Lara Jean refuses to face reality and live in the real world. Her letters are imaginary, one-sided conversations that feel much safer than real-life ones.

But those imaginary conversations are about to become *very* real, and soon she'll have no choice but to face them . . .

Catalyst (64–72)

A few days after junior year begins, Peter Kavinsky confronts Lara Jean about a letter she wrote to him. He shows her an envelope with her handwriting on it, claiming it came in the mail yesterday. The letter is humiliating, describing how she fell in love with him, how hard it was for her to see him with Genevieve, and then listing his worst qualities and accusing him of stealing her first kiss.

Debate (73–106)

How did the letter get mailed? And "what if the others were sent too?" (75). These become the Debate questions, as a mortified and completely panicked Lara Jean races home to find her hat box missing from her closet. Her first instinct is to call Margot for help, but she vows to solve this herself: a first big step in her transformative journey.

After some investigation, she still has no answers.

She tries to avoid Josh, just in case his letter was mailed too, but she doesn't succeed. He corners her at her locker, holding the letter and demanding to talk to her about it. Lara Jean tries to brush it off as no big deal, but Josh is blindsided and confused. When he seems about to confess feelings for *her*, she panics and tells him she's dating someone. Lara Jean picks the first person she spots in the hallway—Peter—and kisses him.

That's when her Debate question becomes: How will she get out of this predicament and keep her feelings for Josh a secret?

Break Into 2 (107–111)

The next day, Peter proposes an arrangement. If they continue to pretend to be a couple, it serves them both: Lara Jean will save face with Josh, and Peter will finally convince his ex-girlfriend, Genevieve, that they're over (**Act 2 goal**).

Lara Jean hesitates, worried about Genevieve's reaction (she's known to spread vicious rumors about people). Peter assures her Gen is all talk, and when he tells Lara Jean that Josh definitely believed the story that they were a couple, Lara Jean agrees. "Okay, let's do it" (111).

B Story (87–88)

Although Peter Kavinsky is introduced in Act 1, he doesn't play a significant role in Lara Jean's present story until she kisses him in the hallway and tells Josh that they're dating. But now that he's in her world, he starts to broaden it in many ways, bringing her out of her shell, pushing her out of her comfort zone, and causing her to see her naivete and innocence for what it is. As Lara Jean's pretend boyfriend, Peter is a perfect embodiment of the theme of imagination versus reality. And as her feelings for him deepen throughout the story, the lines between the two are blurred, putting even more pressure on Lara Jean to grow up and face the real world.

Fun and Games (112–182)

On page 112, Peter and Lara Jean walk into school, hand in hand, for the first time, and we are officially in the upside-down world of Act 2! Lara Jean experiences high school like she's never experienced it before: as the girlfriend of one of the most sought-after boys in school.

How fitting that a girl who prefers to live in a world of make-believe would have a make-believe boyfriend. But that's Act 2 for ya! And Lara Jean is definitely **fixing things the wrong way**. Instead of facing up to the truth about her feelings for Josh, she hides them under the guise of a fake relationship.

That relationship gets off to a rocky start, and Lara Jean even considers calling it off, but once she and Peter set some ground rules—even drawing up a contract—things fall into an **upward path** groove as Jenny Han delivers on the promise of the premise (a fake relationship). We get to enjoy Lara Jean and Peter's fun and teasing banter and the adorable budding relationship of Kitty and Peter, all while Lara Jean still struggles with her responsibilities as the eldest sister, which serve as an effective **bouncing ball**.

Author Han also makes great use of clothes to illustrate Lara Jean's gradual transformation and inner conflict. In trying to find the right clothes to wear as "Peter's girlfriend," Lara Jean suddenly realizes how childish her clothes are. She inhabits the same world (same high school, same house, same closet), yet things are already feeling new and unfamiliar. Later, after school, we see her putting on a comfortable old nightgown (a symbol of her innocence), subconsciously trying to hold on to her status quo life, even as things change around her.

As the Fun and Games continue, Peter brings Lara Jean out of her shell more, taking her to football games and the diner she used to frequent as a third wheel with Margot and Josh, and introducing her to his friends, who seem to really like her. And when Peter helps Lara Jean make cookies for Kitty's PTA bake sale, real chemistry begins to spark between them.

But as Lara Jean's relationship with Peter grows stronger, her relationship with Josh becomes more strained. She wishes they could be friends, but his history with Margot and Lara Jean's feelings for him make it too complicated.

As the story nears the Midpoint, the **emotional stakes are raised** when Lara Jean discovers that Margot had sex with Josh when they were together, something Margot and Lara Jean promised each other they wouldn't do until they were married, or they were "really, really in love and at least twenty-one" (160). Margot's breaking of their sisterly pact is eye-opening for Lara Jean. Suddenly, things that once felt certain in her life are cast into doubt, including how well she knew her sister.

Midpoint (182–194)

Peter brings Lara Jean to a **Midpoint** party on Friday night, to put more pressure on Genevieve to accept that their relationship is over. And it works.

In a **false victory** moment, Genevieve storms out of the room after witnessing Lara Jean sitting on Peter's lap. Lara Jean marks it as a "Success!" (187), and Peter tells her, "You did a good job . . . She's so jealous, it's killing her" (188).

But the **stakes are raised** when Peter and Genevieve get into a fight, leading Lara Jean to think that Peter still has feelings for Genevieve. And later that night, when Peter asks Lara Jean why she's never had a boyfriend, in a **shift from wants to needs**, she admits, "It's scary when it's real. When it's not just thinking about a person, but, like having a real live person in front of you . . ." (192).

Lara Jean comes home to an email from Margot, reminding her of all her responsibilities at home (**A and B Stories cross**). But Lara Jean breezily replies that she's got everything under control.

Bad Guys Close In (195–273)

If the focus of the Fun and Games was the fake relationship, then the focus of the Bad Guys Close In is the real relationship. We've crossed a threshold at the Midpoint; now, over the course of this beat, we will watch the lines between make-believe and reality blur and Lara Jean struggle to tell the difference between the two (**internal bad guys**).

How can she continue to hide from reality (flaw) if she doesn't know what's real and what's fake?

As Peter and Lara Jean spend more time together, their conversations take a more personal turn as well. Peter opens up about missing his dad since his parents' divorce, which Lara Jean can relate to with Margot's absence.

But with this growing closeness comes *real* emotions, namely jealousy. We see the **downward path** in action when Peter calls off a study date with Lara Jean to be with Genevieve, causing Lara Jean to wonder if Peter's plan was less about moving on from Genevieve and more about holding her place. Then, to retaliate, Lara Jean uses Josh to make Peter jealous (a twist on the Fun and Games) by accepting a ride to school with him. Later, when Genevieve spots Lara Jean and Josh eating together at the diner, word gets back to Peter, and he asks Lara Jean to *not* hang out with Josh in public anymore.

Meanwhile, Lara Jean's **internal bad guys** are hard at work. First, she tells Peter not to come over anymore because she's worried that her sister, Kitty, will become too attached to him (subtext, anyone?). Then, after Peter kisses her, Lara Jean realizes not only did she like it, but she also likes *him*. But when he apologizes the next day, claiming he kissed her only because Josh was watching, Lara Jean narrates, "How was I supposed to know what's real and what's not? It feels like I'm the only one who doesn't know the difference" (257).

But let's not forget about the **external bad guy**—Genevieve—who still sees Lara Jean as a threat for "stealing" Peter. As Lara Jean prepares to go on a class ski trip with Peter, her friend Chris warns her not to ski alone because Genevieve is going to be there (foreshadowing, anyone?).

However, things at home are improving. Lara Jean's car comes back from the shop and she faces her fear of driving by taking Kitty grocery shopping and proving she's finally getting a handle on the responsibilities of being the eldest sister and stepping up to take Margot's place.

Maybe in more ways than one, as we're about to see . . .

All Is Lost (274–277)

After helping put up the Christmas tree, Josh confronts Lara Jean about her relationship with Peter, claiming she doesn't act like herself around him. An argument ensues, during which they finally broach the topic they've been avoiding since the Debate: Lara Jean's letter and their feelings for each other.

Josh insists that if Lara Jean had told him that she liked him earlier, things would have been different. He admits that he's been jealous of Peter and then, shockingly, kisses Lara Jean. But perhaps even *more* shockingly, she kisses him back.

She runs to her room, lamenting the fact that she just kissed her sister's ex-boyfriend *and* cheated on her fake boyfriend.

Dark Night of the Soul (278–313)

As Lara Jean deals with the shame of her actions, to make matters even worse, she learns that Peter was with Genevieve the previous night.

Later, when Josh tells Lara Jean that he thinks it was fate that her letters were sent out and that they're meant to be together, she has her first of two **Dark Night Epiphanies**. She realizes she doesn't love Josh anymore. But it's evident that she hasn't yet learned the theme when Josh says he wants to tell Margot about the kiss, but Lara Jean would rather pretend it never happened.

Desperate for things to return to normal (**return to the familiar**), Lara Jean tries to break off the fake relationship with Peter, but he convinces her to keep it up until after the ski trip. However, when Margot comes home for Christmas, it becomes clear that it's impossible for things to go back to normal because so much has changed without Lara Jean's even realizing. The return of her sister shines a spotlight on how much Lara Jean has already grown up and how much the two sisters have lost touch since Margot left.

On the class ski trip, Peter cuddles up to her on the bus, putting on a show for Genevieve, but this time Lara Jean can't handle it. She squirms away from him, which only makes him mad. Later, a fight between them leads to Peter's confession that he likes Lara Jean for real and wants to be her boyfriend. Lara Jean says no, convinced he still likes Genevieve.

Peter accuses her of only liking guys she doesn't have a shot with because she's scared. "You'd rather make up a fantasy version of somebody in your head than be with a real person" (312). And even though she denies it, it hits home. (As it should. It *is* the theme, after all!)

It isn't until Peter leaves that Lara Jean wonders—in her second **Dark Night Epiphany**—if Peter could be right.

Break Into 3 (313)

"I don't want to be afraid anymore. I want to be brave," Lara Jean realizes on page 313. She runs off to find Peter.

Finale (314–355)

POINT 1: GATHERING THE TEAM. Before Lara Jean can be with Peter for real (**Act 3 goal**), she first has to find him and make amends for turning him down. She locates him in the hot tub and confesses that she *does* like him. Then she kisses him. It's amazing, and Lara Jean loves how powerful she feels. When they return to their separate rooms for the night, Lara Jean feels like she's flying.

POINT 2: EXECUTING THE PLAN. Lara Jean and Peter are officially a couple now, and they sit together on the bus on the way home, ignoring the whistles and stares they get from people. But then Lara Jean learns (from Genevieve) that Peter is telling everyone that he and Lara Jean had sex in the hot tub last night. She calls Lara Jean a slut and tells her that Peter dated her only to make Genevieve jealous.

Lara Jean is devastated and furious at Peter. Back on the bus, Peter tells her he didn't start the rumor and asks why she cares about it if it's not true. This is when Lara Jean's life lesson is put to the test. Is she really ready for a *real* relationship and all the real-life conflict that comes with it?

Back home, Lara Jean refuses to return Peter's texts; she shuts off her phone to celebrate Christmas with her family.

POINT 3: HIGH TOWER SURPRISE. Peter shows up unexpectedly and tries to talk to Lara Jean about what happened. She's angry because she thinks he didn't defend her enough to his friends. She accuses him of letting people think they had sex. Peter is angry in return that she doesn't give him enough credit. The argument is interrupted by Josh, who calls Peter a scumbag (after having heard the rumor). The two boys insult each other, and Peter yells at Josh for kissing Lara Jean.

That's when Lara Jean sees Margot standing in the doorway. She heard the whole thing.

Margot accuses Lara Jean of betraying her and runs to her room. Peter tries to comfort Lara Jean, but she kicks him out and hides in the bathroom. When she tries to talk to her sister, Margot won't open the door.

POINT 4: DIG DEEP DOWN. Getting shut out by Margot feels like the worst punishment of all for Lara Jean. She worries that she and her sister will never find their way back to each other.

Lara Jean flashes back on how she and Margot once became so close. After their mother died, they were forced to grow up quickly and take care of Kitty. Through this flashback, Lara Jean examines her **shard of glass,** the reason she's so afraid of the real world. Because the last time she faced it, everything fell apart.

And now everything is falling apart again. She realizes her relationship with her sister was built on grief and responsibility and now it's crumbled. Which means it will have to be rebuilt on something new. Something Lara Jean is finally ready to face.

POINT 5: THE EXECUTION OF THE NEW PLAN. After discovering that Margot told their dad about the ski trip rumors, Lara Jean barges into Margot's room to confront her. Margot accuses Lara Jean of changing too much and failing to take responsibility for the family. She also yells at Lara Jean for betraying her with Josh.

Lara Jean tries to explain, finally revealing the feelings for Josh that she's kept hidden for so long. All of these years she's been forced to pretend, putting her family and her loyalty to her sister before herself. And now she's finally coming clean.

Lara Jean admits to how much she looks up to Margot and how much power Margot has over her. And in a tender moment, Margot deals with some of her own flaws and insecurities when she confesses how hard it's been to be a role model to Lara Jean and Kitty. After she left for Scotland, Margot was hurt that they didn't seem to need her as much as she thought they did.

They collapse into each other's arms.

Later, on New Year's Eve, Lara Jean also comes clean to Kitty, admitting that her relationship with Peter was fake. Kitty has a moment of emotional growth as well, admitting that she was the one who sent out Lara Jean's letters, because she was mad at Lara Jean for teasing her. It seems all three sisters have been hiding truths from each other. But now that they're out, they can have a healthier, more *real* relationship. Lara Jean forgives Kitty, showing she has fully stepped into the role of responsible older sister.

As Lara Jean reads all the notes Peter wrote to her during their fake relationship, she realizes just how real their relationship had become, and that together, these notes make a love letter. She remarks that she can now see the difference between loving someone from afar (status quo Lara Jean) and loving someone up close (new and improved Lara Jean). "When you see them up close, you see the real them, but they also get to see the real you" (354).

She goes outside to light sparklers with Kitty. They see Josh, and he and Lara Jean exchange a smile. Lara Jean has a feeling that everything will be fine between them, and Josh will always be in their lives in some way.

Final Image (355)

In a **mirror beat** to the Opening Image, Lara Jean sits in her room and writes a love letter to Peter.

A real one.

WHY IS THIS A RITES OF PASSAGE?

To All the Boys I've Loved Before contains all three elements of a successful Rites of Passage story:

- **A LIFE PROBLEM:** When her older sister, Margot, moves to Scotland for school, it leaves Lara Jean without the mother figure she's always relied and depended on. This separation, combined with the death of their mother years ago, forms the life problem Lara Jean has to overcome.
- **A WRONG WAY TO ATTACK THE PROBLEM:** Lara Jean has always preferred her imagination over real life (which is too scary to face). So when Lara Jean's love letters are accidentally sent out (including one to Margot's ex-boyfriend, Josh), she starts a fake relationship with Peter to avoid facing up to reality and confronting her feelings for Josh head-on. This avoidance of the pain illuminates the growing and maturing she still has to do in the wake of Margot's absence.
- **AN ACCEPTANCE OF THE HARD TRUTH:** Only when Lara Jean becomes brave enough to face the reality of life head-on (instead of hiding in the safety of her imagination) is she able to have a real relationship with Peter and rebuild her shattered relationship with her sister.

Cat's Eye View

For quick reference, here's a brief overview of this novel's beat sheet.

OPENING IMAGE: Lara Jean describes her tradition of writing unsent letters to boys she loves as a way of getting over them.

THEME STATED: "Your sister suffers from delusions of grandeur" (3). Lara Jean is a romantic who'd rather live in her imagination than in the real world.

SETUP: Since the death of their mother years ago, Lara Jean has relied on her older sister, Margot, to be the mother figure in her life. Now that Margot is leaving for college in Scotland, Lara Jean will have to fill her role for their younger sister, Kitty, something she doesn't feel ready to do. Lara Jean has been secretly harboring feelings for Margot's now-ex-boyfriend, Josh.

CATALYST: Peter Kavinsky confronts Lara Jean about a letter she sent him, describing how she fell in love with him. It would seem her "unsent" letter to him has been sent.

DEBATE: How did it get sent? And were any others sent too? Lara Jean races home to find the letters missing. When Josh confronts her about his letter, Lara Jean panics and tells him she's dating Peter now.

BREAK INTO 2: Peter suggests that they pretend to be a couple so Lara Jean can save face with Josh and he can convince his ex, Genevieve, that they're over (Act 2 goal). Lara Jean agrees.

B STORY: As her fake boyfriend and eventual real love interest, Peter broadens Lara Jean's world, pushes her out of her comfort zone, and helps her realize that it's better to live in the real world than hide in your imagination, however scary it might seem.

FUN AND GAMES: Lara Jean and Peter embark on their fake relationship while Lara Jean also struggles with her responsibilities as the eldest sister at home. As her fake relationship with Peter grows stronger, her real relationship with Josh grows more strained.

MIDPOINT: At a Midpoint party, Genevieve storms out after witnessing Peter and Lara Jean together (false victory), but it leads to a fight between Peter and Genevieve, making Lara Jean believe he still has feelings for Genevieve (emotional stakes are raised). Later, Lara Jean admits that having a "real" relationship scares her (shift from wants to needs).

BAD GUYS CLOSE IN: Lara Jean and Peter's fake relationship slowly turns into a real relationship, which leads to real feelings (including jealousy). Lara Jean starts to push Peter away, afraid of her growing closeness to him. Meanwhile, Lara Jean shows improvements in shouldering her responsibilities at home as the older sister.

ALL IS LOST: Josh confesses his feelings for Lara Jean and kisses her. She kisses him back and then runs to her room, feeling horrible for kissing her sister's ex-boyfriend and cheating on her fake boyfriend.

DARK NIGHT OF THE SOUL: Lara Jean deals with the shame of her actions and tries to break off her fake relationship with Peter, who convinces her to keep it going until the upcoming ski trip. Margot comes home, and Lara Jean realizes how much has changed since Margot left (return to the familiar). On the ski trip, Peter asks Lara Jean to be his girlfriend for real, but she says no, still too scared of a real relationship.

BREAK INTO 3: Realizing she doesn't want to be afraid anymore, Lara Jean sets off to find Peter and be with him for real (Act 3 goal).

FINALE: After reuniting in the hot tub, Lara Jean finds out about a hurtful rumor spread about her and gets angry at Peter for not defending her. When Peter comes over to talk to Lara Jean, he ends up fighting with Josh and yells at him for kissing Lara Jean. Margot overhears it all and runs from the room. After Lara Jean digs deep down to confront her fear of the real world (and the death of her mother), she's able to reconcile with her sister and start anew.

FINAL IMAGE: In a mirror of the Opening Image, Lara Jean sits down to write a (real) love letter to Peter.

Buddy Love
All You Need Is Love . . . or Friendship

Love is in the air! Whether that be romantic love, platonic love, or even the love of a pet or inanimate object, this genre is all about the love. More specifically, Buddy Love!

It's no surprise that this is another hugely popular genre in the young adult space. After all, the teenage years are often when first loves are experienced, new friendships are forged, and one's life is changed by another.

And that's what these stories are all about. Heroes who are changed by someone else.

The biggest identifying marker of a Buddy Love story is that the harbinger of change is usually the introduction of another person. Which is why you'll often find the Catalyst beat of these stories to be the introduction of the "buddy," which sets the plot in motion and sends the story in a new direction.

In *Five Feet Apart* by Rachael Lippincott, Stella's controlled and routine status quo world is turned upside down when she meets Will, a fellow cystic fibrosis patient being treated at the same hospital. And in *When Dimple Met Rishi* by Sandhya Menon, Dimple knows exactly what she wants in life and how to achieve it. But when she meets Rishi (and discovers her parents have arranged for her to potentially marry him one day), her life is never the same.

Although in YA, buddies are most commonly romantic love interests, that's not your only option here. Buddies can come in all shapes, sizes, and species! They can be a new friend who will change the course of the hero's life (as in *Will Grayson, Will Grayson* by David Levithan and John Green, and *They Both Die at the End* by Adam Silvera), a long-lost sibling or relative, or even a pet, wild animal, robot, or inanimate object! Or they can be a friend who turns *into* something more (as in *Aristotle and Dante Discover the Secrets of the Universe* by Benjamin Alire Sáenz).

Regardless of who the buddy is, all Buddy Love stories are, in some way, about completion. One person made whole by another. Or two people being made whole by each other.

But don't be fooled by the words "love story." Just because your story *has* a love story or even a love interest doesn't automatically kick it into the Buddy Love camp. Lots of stories have love interests. The question is whether the love story is the primary story or the secondary story. Is it the *main* plot or one of the subplots? In other words, is the love story your **A Story** or your **B Story**? (For a quick refresher on A Stories versus B Stories, refer to page 21.)

In Buddy Love novels, the A Story *is* the love story. We pick up books like *Five Feet Apart*, *When Dimple Met Rishi*, and *The Sun Is Also a Star* by Nicola Yoon because we want to read about two teens falling in love. That's the **promise of the premise!** That doesn't mean that those love stories can't also speak to the theme or help the hero learn the theme too (after all, A Stories are meant to be external triggers of internal transformation); it just means that Buddy Love stories *usually* feature a B Story character who is *not* the love interest but fulfills that role of "representing the theme." Like the immigration lawyer Jeremy Fitzgerald in *The Sun Is Also a Star*, who alters the destiny of both heroes, Natasha and Daniel, forcing them to face up to (and fix) their flaws. Whereas in other genres (of the non–Buddy Love variety) the love story or friendship story is usually found in the B Story, because it's a subplot rather than the main plot or premise.

If the love story *is* the main plot of your novel, you'll want to make sure you include the three essential ingredients of a successful Buddy Love: (1) an **incomplete hero** (or heroes), (2) a **counterpart** that in some way brings about the completion of the hero, and (3) a **complication** that serves as the primary source of conflict in the relationship.

Let's see what we're dealing with.

AN INCOMPLETE HERO

All novels in this genre feature an incomplete hero who finds completion *because* of another. And while, at their core, Buddy Love is about *two* people, it's important to decide which one of them needs to change the most. Which one is going to receive the title Hero (with a capital *H*)? Chances are, in the case of a single POV novel, it will be the narrator, like in *Twilight* (where the hero is Bella), or *Anna and the French Kiss* (where the hero is Anna). In *Aristotle and Dante Discover the Secrets to the Universe*, while the novel is about both Aristotle and Dante, it's written only from Aristotle's POV. Sure, Dante does have some growing to do, but Ari has further to go and more to discover about himself through this relationship; therefore he gets to wear the "Hero" crown.

You could also choose to tell your story from *both* sides of the Buddy Love equation, giving each Buddy a POV and a full transformation to warrant that POV. These are called **two-handers**, and they're very popular in young adult fiction. Some well-known examples include *The Sun Is Also a Star*, *Eleanor & Park*, *When Dimple Met Rishi*, *Emergency Contact*, *All the Bright Places*, *Five Feet Apart*, and *They Both Die at the End*.

But remember what I said way back in chapter 1: more heroes, more problems. Which means, yes, you will have to have two sets of problems, two shards of glass, two wants, two needs, two transformations, and possibly even two beat sheets to track those transformations. In other words, both heroes have to qualify as an "incomplete hero" in need of change. (For more on multiple POV beat sheets, see page 116.)

There are even some occasions, when you may find *three* heroes in a Buddy Love story—also called a **three-hander**— as is the case in Abdi Nazemian's award-winning novel *Like a Love Story*, which features a love triangle between Reza, an Iranian boy who is struggling to come to terms with (and hide) the fact that he is gay; Art, the boy he falls in love with; and Art's best friend, Judy, who is falling in love with Reza. Author Nazemian gives us all three perspectives and three stellar transformations to match.

A COUNTERPART

Once you decide who your incomplete hero is (or heroes are), it's time to figure out who is going to be their impetus for change, aka the "counterpart." This is the one person (or being) in the world who will eventually make our hero's life complete—or who will bring about the change our hero so desperately needs.

The counterpart typically serves as the driving force for the story's premise, so they better be pretty dang special. Or more specifically, they better be pretty dang special to your *hero*. After all, it's the introduction of this buddy that's going to rip our hero right out of their **stasis = death** slump and into the second act! That's a lot of pressure to put on one person's (or animal's) shoulders.

But it must be done.

Which is why the counterpart of a good Buddy Love is often a little quirky, a little different. Maybe with a unique background, a unique way of doing things, or a unique perspective on something. Whoever they are, they can't be status quo. They're in the story to *break* the status quo! They kind of *have* to be unique.

In *Aristotle and Dante Discover the Secrets of the Universe*, Dante is a breath of fresh air for Aristotle. Everything about him feels new: the way he looks at the world, the books he reads, his courage, and his compassion. And in *Twilight*, Edward is a freaking vampire! That's enough to break most people's status quo.

Or, in the case of the two-hander, the heroes will most likely be each other's counterpart. But again, think about *why* they are counterparts to each other. Why they complement each other, or why they clash so magnificently. What character traits or quirks can only *they* bring out in each other? If the buddies have nothing to learn from each other, what's the point?

In *The Sun Is Also a Star*, Natasha refuses to believe in love or destiny, preferring instead to try to control as much of her life as she can. Daniel, on the other hand, is so controlled by his parents, all he wants to do is throw up his hands and let destiny take the wheel. What perfect counterparts they are! But at first, when these two collide (quite literally in the street), there's not just chemistry; there's disagreement, there's clashes in worldview, there's *conflict*.

Which brings us to our third and final genre ingredient.

A COMPLICATION

What is standing in the way of the buddies getting together or staying together? Is it a person (like Etienne's girlfriend in *Anna and the French Kiss*)? A physical or mental illness (like in *Five Feet Apart*, *The Fault in Our Stars*, and *All the Bright Places*)? A secret that one of the buddies is keeping (like Reza's sexual orientation in *Like a Love Story*)? Or perhaps the complication is societal, cultural, or situational (like the arranged marriage in *When Dimple Met Rishi*, or the fact that both buddies are going to die at the end in *They Both Die at the End*). The complication can also be an emotional or psychological blockage or trauma (like Natasha's refusal to believe in love or destiny in *The Sun Is Also a Star*, or Eleanor's abuse in *Eleanor & Park*). Or even supernatural (like Edward's propensity to drink blood in *Twilight*). Or the complication can simply be a misunderstanding.

But *something* has to be driving a wedge between your buddies, otherwise the story will feel too easy (and too short). And if you try to keep the buddies apart without a clear complication, you run the risk of the story feeling contrived and the ending feeling unearned.

The complication can be present from the start, perhaps keeping the buddies from realizing their true feelings for each other, or it can emerge later, as a way to up the stakes and keep things from getting *too* cozy and comfortable. In *All the Bright Places*, it's not until much later in the story that Violet discovers that Finch is bipolar, which explains some of his recent behavior. But because we, the readers, are given access to Finch's POV, we get a sense of the complication much earlier and can feel it looming in the air. The complication should feel, to your reader, like a storm that's brewing in the distance, threatening to come between these two buddies.

Ironically, though, it's often the complication that brings the buddies together in the first place! Or even *keeps* them together. In *Five Feet Apart*, Will and Stella meet and fall in love only because they're both hospitalized for cystic fibrosis. Yet that's the very thing that's literally keeping them five feet apart. And without Edward's supernatural abilities as a vampire, he never would have saved Bella's life and consequently thrust them together in the aftermath.

Giving your complication multiple layers and multiple functions makes your story sing and your storytelling chops shine. It makes readers grip the edges of the book in both agony and ecstasy, frustration and delight. And it's that same complication that usually drives the Buddy Love stories to their All Is Lost beats. Since the All Is Lost is defined as the hero's rock bottom or lowest point, you'll typically find buddies breaking up, fighting, or in some way separating here. That wedge you've driven between them has grown so wide that, combined with those unchecked flaws, the relationship just can't survive.

And some *don't* survive. Some buddies will mend the rips in the relationship and get back together, and others won't. It's important to note that Buddy Loves don't always have to end with happily ever after. Adam Silvera's bestselling Buddy Love is literally called *They Both Die at the End* . . . and they do. But not before leaving a lasting impact on each other. In *Five Feet Apart*, Stella and Will don't end up together. But Will has saved Stella's life (in more ways than one) and Stella has given Will a reason to keep fighting. And that is enough.

The point of the Buddy Love is not to ensure that the two buddies ride off into the sunset together; it's to ensure that whatever sunset they're riding off into (whether that be the same sunset or different ones), they're riding off as changed people.

In the end, all Buddy Love stories contain a similar message: my life has changed for having known another. And that message resonates.

Because the search for love, for friendship, for companionship is something we can all relate to.

To recap: if you're thinking of writing a Buddy Love novel, make sure your story includes these three essential ingredients:

- **AN INCOMPLETE HERO** who is missing something physical, ethical, emotional, or spiritual. They need one another to be whole or realize their own completeness.
- **A COUNTERPART** who makes that completion come about or has qualities the hero needs.
- **A COMPLICATION**, be it a misunderstanding, personal or ethical viewpoint, physical or emotional hindrance, epic historical event, the prudish disapproval of society, or something else. This is the primary source of conflict in the novel, working to keep the buddies apart but also to pull them together.

POPULAR YOUNG ADULT BUDDY LOVE NOVELS

Twilight by Stephenie Meyer
Will Grayson, Will Grayson by David Levithan and John Green
Anna and the French Kiss by Stephanie Perkins
The Fault in Our Stars by John Green*
The Statistical Probability of Love at First Sight by Jennifer E. Smith
Aristotle and Dante Discover the Secrets of the Universe
   by Benjamin Alire Sáenz
Eleanor & Park by Rainbow Rowell
All the Bright Places by Jennifer Niven
Everything, Everything by Nicola Yoon
The Sun Is Also a Star by Nicola Yoon
When Dimple Met Rishi by Sandhya Menon
They Both Die at the End by Adam Silvera
Emergency Contact by Mary H. K. Choi
Five Feet Apart by Rachael Lippincott
Like a Love Story by Abdi Nazemian
Clap When You Land by Elizabeth Acevedo

* Beat sheet follows on opposite page.

THE FAULT IN OUR STARS

BY: John Green
STC GENRE: Buddy Love
BOOK GENRE: Young adult contemporary romance
TOTAL PAGES: 313 (Penguin paperback edition, 2014)

This novel undoubtedly needs no introduction, but I'll give you one anyway. John Green is known for his quirky, memorable teen characters; witty, irreverent dialogue; and fictional stories that feel so real we can't help but be swept away by them. When a young friend of his died of cancer in 2010, Green was inspired to finish a novel he'd started years before while working in a children's hospital. That novel went on to sell over twenty million copies worldwide. It earned countless starred reviews and was named *TIME* magazine's best fiction book of 2012. In 2014, it also became a blockbuster movie starring Shailene Woodley and Ansel Elgort, bringing in over three hundred million dollars at the box office.

In other words, to exclude it from this book would be criminal. But why all the hype? Well, let's crack it open and find out.

Opening Image (1–6)

Hazel Grace Lancaster is being forced to attend a cancer support group for teens because her mother is convinced she is depressed. Her mother is right. She *is* depressed. She's given up on living or making any real connections with people because she doesn't see the point. Instead, she spends much time alone, watching television and reading her favorite book, *An Imperial Affliction* by Peter Van Houten (a novel invented by author Green, about a girl named Anna who dies of cancer, which literally ends in the middle of a sentence).

As evidenced from her acerbic and sarcastic narration during the support group, our hero, Hazel, is bitter and cynical.

Theme Stated (7)

"Hazel, you deserve a life," says her mother, who wants Hazel to be a normal teenager, make friends, and enjoy her life. Hazel, however, is convinced that there's no point in having a life, let alone enjoying it, because she'll soon be dead.

"I'm a grenade and at some point I'm going to blow up and I would like to minimize the casualties," Hazel tells her mom on page 99. This worldview affects her life from the very start of the novel. But what she **needs** to learn by the end is that she *does* deserve a life. And that life can be lived, even in the face of death.

Setup (6–8)

A short Setup shows Hazel reluctantly attending more support groups, just to make her parents happy. We learn about the multitude of unanswered letters she's written to Peter Van Houten, in an attempt to find out what happened after the end of *An Imperial Affliction* (**wants**). But like so many wants, hers is misguided. She *thinks* that if she can find out what happened to the characters after the protagonist dies, she can ease her own anxiety about what will happen to her parents after she dies.

What this short Setup effectively establishes is that Hazel is a teenager who has given up on life and is just waiting to die. What, after all, does she have to live for?

Well, it's about to walk through the door.

Catalyst (8–14)

There's a new boy at the next support group meeting. And he's hot. After some flirty back-and-forth staring, Hazel learns that his name is Augustus Waters, and although he lost his leg to "a touch of osteosarcoma" (11), he claims he's here only to support his friend Isaac.

This is the event—the meeting of the love interest—that will send Hazel's life spiraling in a new direction. Augustus is charismatic and exudes confidence and optimism (a stark contrast to Hazel's grim outlook). When Augustus mentions his fear of oblivion (dying without leaving a mark), Hazel, uncharacteristically, speaks up at the meeting to tell him to get over it. Everyone dies and is eventually forgotten.

As Buddy Love counterparts should be, they are perfect complements. Two sides of the same flaw: a fear of what they'll leave behind after death, manifested in different ways. Augustus seeks out acts of heroism, in an attempt to leave behind a legacy, while Hazel withdraws from the world in an attempt to leave behind as little damage as possible.

These two souls need each other to bring about their own "completion." While Augustus will help Hazel enjoy the limited time she has left, she will, in turn, help him realize that he doesn't have to save the world to leave behind a legacy. You can do that simply by touching the people in your life.

Debate (14–51)

What will become of this encounter? That's the Debate question, and over the next thirty-seven pages, Hazel and Augustus engage in deliciously witty banter and subtle flirtation. We learn, through their conversations, more about Hazel's cancer and treatment history, including an experimental drug that has kept the cancer at bay (for now). The two also agree to read each other's favorite books. Augustus will read *An Imperial Affliction* and Hazel will read *The Price of Dawn*.

Meanwhile, Hazel spends time at **home** (with her parents), **work** (classes at a community college), and **play** (hanging out with her friend Kaitlyn, around whom Hazel feels uncomfortable because of the fate she's certain awaits her).

Break Into 2 (51–52)

Wondering what Augustus thought of *An Imperial Affliction*, Hazel texts and then calls him, officially kicking off the relationship and the Act 2 world. If Hazel's status quo world was a dreary life before Augustus, then her upside-down world is her life *with* Augustus. And what a new and exciting adventure it will be!

As Hazel remarks on page 52, "Flirting was new to me, but I liked it."

Fun and Games (52–158)

To quote Augustus Waters, "I'm on a roller coaster that only goes up" (11), and that's how this Fun and Games feels. It's an up, up,

upward path as Hazel and Augustus become closer and bring out the best in each other.

They share long phone conversations, philosophical discussions, and the kind of witty banter that author John Green is known for. Perhaps one of the most memorable moments being when Augustus says, "Maybe *okay* will be our *always*," to which Hazel replies, "Okay" (73).

Augustus finishes *An Imperial Affliction* and the two bond over their shared frustration at the abrupt ending. Augustus joins Hazel's quest to find out what happened to the protagonist's family at the end of the story (**Act 2 goal**). But because these answers are not what will truly transform Hazel and help her conquer her flaw, this quest is very much **fixing things the wrong way**.

When Augustus reveals that he's reached out to the author, Van Houten, and that Van Houten has responded, Hazel sends an email of her own, once again asking about the ending. In reply, Van Houten invites her to Amsterdam, where he promises to reveal the information in person. Augustus uses his "dying wish" from the Genie Foundation to secure them *both* a trip to Amsterdam. And the upward path continues.

Meanwhile, however, the **bouncing ball** is still providing plenty of conflict. Augustus's friend Isaac is dumped by his girlfriend just before his scheduled surgery, which will leave him blind. Augustus tells Hazel about his ex-girlfriend who died of cancer, reminding her of her own impending death and that the closer she gets to Augustus, the more it will hurt him when she's gone. No matter how much *fun* she's been having with Augustus, that fear of what she'll leave behind when she dies still haunts her (**flaw**). Then Hazel is sent to the ICU after being attacked by horrible head pain. Despite her pushing him away, Augustus devotedly waits for her in the waiting room. The doctors find no new tumors in her PET scan, but her lungs are filling with fluid. They advise her *not* to travel to Amsterdam.

While in the hospital, Hazel reveals her **shard of glass** to the reader with a flashback to the day everyone thought she was going to die and she overheard her mom say, "I won't be a mom anymore" (117). Those words gutted Hazel, creating her fear of the emotional destruction she'll leave behind when she dies.

But the upward path continues when Hazel's parents reveal that she can still go to Amsterdam as planned. Her doctor made a convincing case that Hazel needs to live her life (theme). It seems her Act 2 goal is headed for success.

Hazel boards a plane with her mother and Augustus. As Hazel and Augustus look out the window at the sunset, we're reminded of their different worldviews. Hazel sees a sun*set*, while Augustus sees it as a sunrise somewhere else. After Augustus confesses that he loves Hazel, he restates her theme. "I'm not in the business of denying myself the simple pleasure of saying true things" (153), reminding her that our days can be enjoyed, even when they're numbered.

But despite feeling something for him too, she's unable to say "I love you" in return.

B Story (67–71)

Speaking of Hazel's theme, it's brilliantly represented by the fictional author, Peter Van Houten, who plays the role of Hazel's B Story character. Although he was technically in Hazel's life from the start of the novel, it's not until Augustus gets in touch with him in Act 2 (page 67) that he enters Hazel's life in a more real, immediate way.

Early on, Hazel says, "Peter Van Houten was the only person I'd ever come across who seemed to (a) understand what it's like to be dying, and (b) not have died" (13). She sees him as a man with the answers, the one person who can ease her fears, when in actuality he's suffering even worse than she is. He is the embodiment of her fears. As someone who has lost a daughter to cancer, Peter represents the dark side of Hazel's life lesson. This is what you become when you let death take over. When you fail to embrace life, as fleeting as it may be.

But by the end of the novel, this is exactly what Hazel will learn, and Peter will be a facilitator of that lesson in more ways than one.

Midpoint (160–176)

On the first night in Amsterdam, Hazel and Augustus go on a romantic date at a fancy restaurant. All dressed up, walking along the canals of a moonlit city, drinking champagne that tastes like the stars, this has

false victory written all over it. Especially because the next day they are scheduled to meet with Peter Van Houten, and Hazel will finally learn what happened to the characters after the end of *An Imperial Affliction*. Peter Van Houten even picks up the check at the restaurant (**A and B Stories cross**).

But Hazel still thinks of herself as a grenade that will eventually blow up and hurt Augustus. The closer they get, the more her flaws remind her of how dangerous it is for her to fall in love. Still, as they sit on a bench overlooking the canal, in a subtle **shift from wants to needs**, Augustus says, "It would be a privilege to have my heart broken by you" (176).

Bad Guys Close In (177–261)

When Hazel and Augustus show up at Peter Van Houten's house, the narrative takes a sudden and very noticeable turn into a **downward path**. Peter is nothing like the wise author Hazel has idealized for so long. He's a disheveled, bitter, mean-spirited alcoholic who refuses to give her the answers she came all this way for. When Hazel pushes him to tell her what happened to the characters in his book, he spitefully replies, "They're fictions . . . Nothing happens to them" (191), and then he insults her.

Later, at a visit to the Anne Frank house, Hazel pushes herself to climb the stairs to the attic, thinking she owes it to Anne because she is dead and Hazel is not (a hint that she is starting to see life as more of a gift than a burden). To further illustrate that we are gradually shifting from wants to needs, at the top, Hazel kisses Augustus, finally giving in to the attraction that she's been fighting since the Catalyst.

The **love story ramps up** even more when the two go back to the hotel and lose their virginity to each other. Hazel has completely let down her guard now, letting Augustus into her life, even though she's still terrified of hurting him when she dies.

But as it turns out, that's not the pain she has to worry about.

Augustus breaks the news that his cancer has returned (**ticking clock**), which raises the stakes of the story and pushes us further along the downward path. He's hospitalized shortly after returning from

Amsterdam, and this time it's Hazel waiting in the waiting room. Their roles are reversed. She is no longer the grenade. He is. But this doesn't push her away. She starts calling him Gus, like his parents do.

As Gus's condition deteriorates, they continue to remind each other of their own personal life lessons. In response to Gus lamenting that his obituary won't be in all the newspapers (referencing his fear of oblivion), Hazel says, "I just want to be enough for you, but I never can be" (241). And Augustus reminds her, "It's a good life, Hazel Grace" (236).

Gus hits a low point (his personal All Is Lost), when he calls Hazel from a gas station at two in the morning covered in vomit after something went wrong with his G-tube. As they wait for the ambulance, in an ironic reference to the name of this beat, Hazel tells him, "There are no bad guys . . . Even cancer isn't a bad guy really. Cancer just wants to be alive" (246). The inevitability of both of their situations is real. And literal bad guys or not, it's closing in fast, putting pressure on both of them to change and combat their own fears about death.

In his personal Dark Night of the Soul, Gus comes home from the hospital in bad shape and falls into despair. He decides he wants to attend his own funeral and asks Hazel and Isaac to deliver eulogies. In her eulogy, Hazel quotes Peter Van Houten: "Some infinities are bigger than other infinities. A writer we used to like taught us that." But she spins the concept and makes it her own, showing not only the effect Van Houten has had on her, but also the effect Gus has had on her. "You gave me forever within the numbered days, and I'm grateful" (260). Hazel is close to learning her theme, but that lesson is about to be tested in a major way.

All Is Lost (261–262)

Augustus's heart stops. In a literal **whiff of death**, Hazel is reminded that this devastation will come to her parents next. Her fear of the emotional wreckage she'll leave behind is stronger than ever, making this moment feel like a loss in more ways than one.

Dark Night of the Soul (262–282)

Hazel's grief is unbearable. In an attempt to **return to the familiar**, she calls Gus's voicemail and listens to the silence after the beep. Since her diagnosis, Hazel has lived with the fear of what life will be like for her loved ones after she's gone. Now, she's experiencing it firsthand, and it's awful.

At the funeral, Hazel gives a different eulogy, reciting one of the quotes of encouragement hanging around Gus's house: "Without pain, we couldn't know joy" (272), but she silently remarks that it's "bull-shit." Whatever progress she's made toward learning this very theme has been washed away by Gus's death and her anger at the universe.

Even though she didn't want to go to the funeral (in fear of seeing a foreshadow of her parents' pain in Gus's family), her mom made her. Peter Van Houten, who flew out for the funeral, tries to make amends for his actions in Amsterdam by offering Hazel an explanation of what happened after the end of his book. But Hazel no longer **wants** this. She's no longer looking for something else or someone else to save her from her fears, which means she's close to completing her transformation.

This reappearance of the B Story character serves as a reminder of what will happen if Hazel doesn't learn her theme. If she lets her sadness and anger turn her bitter, like Peter. Later, after some wallowing in her room, she muses that there are two kinds of adults: those like Van Houten, who are miserable and always looking for someone else to pass their pain on to, and those like her parents, who turn into zombies, doing whatever is necessary to keep walking around. In a **Dark Night Epiphany**, Hazel realizes that she doesn't want to be either.

Break Into 3 (282–283)

A few days later, Hazel learns from Isaac that Augustus was writing a sequel to *An Imperial Affliction* for Hazel, but Isaac has no idea where it is. Hazel realizes there is still something left of Gus in the world and decides she needs to find it (**Act 3 goal**).

Finale (283–309)

POINT 1: GATHERING THE TEAM. Hazel gets in the car, ready to drive to Gus's house, only to find Peter Van Houten sitting in her back seat. He apologizes for being so awful to her in Amsterdam and confesses his own grief over the death of his six-year-old daughter. His bitterness stems from his anger at the universe for taking her—the same bitterness that has been living in Hazel's heart. But not for long. Hazel, in her first sign of having learned her theme, tells him to "Go home. Sober up. Write another novel. Do the thing you're good at" (287).

This moment serves as almost a reverse gathering of the team. Hazel kicks Van Houten out of her car, rejecting her B Story character, and taking on the challenge alone.

POINT 2: EXECUTING THE PLAN. Hazel searches Gus's room and computer for the sequel he was writing, but she can't find it. She asks his parents, who are still deep in mourning, if he had a notebook, but they don't know of one. Before leaving his house, she climbs into his bed and inhales the last lingering traces of his scent, saying goodbye.

POINT 3: HIGH TOWER SURPRISE. Three days later, Gus's dad calls to say they found a Moleskine notebook, but there was no writing in it. However, a few pages were torn out. She looks for the missing pages in the church where the support group is held, but finds nothing.

POINT 4: DIG DEEP DOWN. During support group, Hazel admits that she wants to die. When the leader, Patrick, challenges her, asking why she doesn't die, she first thinks of her "old stock answer" (her status quo world answer): that she wants to stay alive for her parents. But then she realizes, while that is still somewhat true, it's not the whole truth. "I owed a debt to the universe that only my attention could repay, and also I owed a debt to everybody who didn't get to be a person anymore" (295). She's learned this life lesson through her B Story character and through knowing Gus. Loving him *and* losing him.

POINT 5: THE EXECUTION OF THE NEW PLAN. At home, Hazel confesses to her parents that she heard what her mother said in the hospital that night when everyone thought she would die, about no longer being a mother. Here, she is removing her **shard of glass**, the source of her biggest fear about dying.

Her mother reveals that she's been secretly studying to be a social worker so she can help other families affected by cancer. Hazel is overjoyed, knowing her mother will have a life after she dies. She makes her parents swear they will stay together after she's gone, confronting her fears once and for all. Her mother reminds Hazel that she "of all people know it is possible to live with pain" (300). Because she's doing it now.

The next day, Hazel realizes Gus sent the missing pages from his notebook to Van Houten. She writes to his assistant, who promises to go to Peter's house to look for them.

Final Image (308–313)

After visiting Gus's grave with her parents, Hazel returns home to find an email from Van Houten's assistant, who has found the pages and attached a scan of them. The pages contain a letter that Augustus wrote to Van Houten, asking if Van Houten would write a eulogy for Hazel. But Van Houten had nothing to add, so it is Gus who has written Hazel's eulogy, just as she did for him.

In his letter, we see Hazel's influence on Gus and the way he overcame his own fears and learned his own theme. He has realized that in people's quests to leave legacies, they often leave behind destruction and scars instead. His legacy is being loved by Hazel, and that is enough for him. He ends his letter with "you don't get to choose if you get hurt in this world . . . but you do have some say in who hurts you. I like my choices. I hope she likes hers" (313).

And she does.

WHY IS THIS A BUDDY LOVE?

The Fault in Our Stars contains all three elements of a successful Buddy Love story.

- **AN INCOMPLETE HERO:** Hazel has given up on life and is essentially waiting to die, but she's still terrified of the pain she'll leave behind when she does. She is missing the opportunity to live life to the fullest in the numbered days she has left.

- **A COUNTERPART:** Augustus is not scared of what he'll leave behind, but what he *won't*. Obsessed with making a mark and leaving a legacy, he tries to live life heroically and to the fullest, making him the ideal counterpart for Hazel, his worldview the perfect counterbalance to hers.
- **A COMPLICATION:** Cancer is the clear complication in this relationship. In the first half of the novel, Hazel's cancer is keeping the buddies apart (Hazel doesn't see the point in falling in love when she's surely going to die soon). But surprisingly, it's the return of Augustus's cancer that becomes the primary source of conflict in the second half of the novel. Yet the cancer is the very thing that brought them together in the first place, through the support group.

Cat's Eye View

For quick reference, here's a brief overview of this novel's beat sheet.

OPENING IMAGE: Hazel, a bitter and cynical teen, attends a cancer support group because her mother is convinced she's depressed.

THEME STATED: "Hazel, you deserve a life," her mother tells her on page 7. But Hazel is convinced there's no point in having a life (let alone enjoying it) when she'll soon be dead.

SETUP: Hazel attends more support groups and attempts to find out what happened after the abrupt ending of her favorite book, *An Imperial Affliction* (wants). Hazel is worried about the pain and destruction she'll leave behind after she dies.

CATALYST: A new boy attends the next support group meeting . . . and he's hot! Her meeting of Augustus Waters is the event that will smash through Hazel's status quo world and launch this love story into high gear.

DEBATE: What will become of the meeting? Hazel and Augustus flirt and exchange favorite books.

BREAK INTO 2: Wanting to know what Augustus thought of *An Imperial Affliction*, Hazel texts and calls Augustus, officially kicking off the relationship.

B STORY: Peter Van Houten, the author of *An Imperial Affliction*, helps Hazel learn her life lesson by representing the *opposite* of the theme. He is someone who stopped living in the face of death, as it turned him bitter and angry.

FUN AND GAMES: Hazel and Augustus get closer and bring out the best in each other. Augustus joins Hazel's quest to find out what happened after the end of *An Imperial Affliction* (Act 2 goal) and contacts the author, who invites them both to Amsterdam to meet with him. Hazel's cancer gets worse, but her doctors still let her go. Augustus uses his wish from the Genie Foundation to get them there.

MIDPOINT: In a false victory, the two share a romantic, candlelit dinner in Amsterdam the night before they're scheduled to visit Van Houten and finally find out what happened after the end of the book.

BAD GUYS CLOSE IN: Peter Van Houten turns out to be a mean-spirited drunk who insults Hazel and refuses to give her what she came for. Hazel and Augustus have sex for the first time right before he tells Hazel that his cancer is back. His condition continues to deteriorate, and Hazel stays by his side.

ALL IS LOST: Augustus dies, which devastates Hazel and reminds her of what her parents will have to suffer when she dies (whiff of death).

DARK NIGHT OF THE SOUL: Hazel's grief is unbearable. She becomes very angry. She attends Augustus's funeral, where Van Houten attempts to apologize for his actions in Amsterdam. She realizes she doesn't want to become like him (Dark Night Epiphany).

BREAK INTO 3: When Hazel learns that Augustus was writing a sequel to *An Imperial Affliction* for her, she becomes desperate to find it (Act 3 goal).

FINALE: Hazel drives to Augustus's house, but the book is not there. Later, his parents find a notebook with pages torn out of it. At support group, Hazel proves she's learned the theme when she admits to herself that she wants to be alive. When it's discovered that Augustus sent the torn-out notebook pages to Van Houten, his assistant scans them and sends a copy to Hazel.

FINAL IMAGE: The notebook pages contain a letter Augustus wrote to Van Houten about Hazel, in which he says his legacy is being loved by Hazel and that's enough for him. He writes that he hopes Hazel likes the choices she's made too, and she admits that she does.

Institutionalized
Beware the Group!

To join or not to join? That is the question. At least in this genre!

And who can better relate to this quandary than our teenage readers, who might be asking themselves this very question daily, as they scan the cafeteria looking for a group to sit with, decide which clubs to join, which teams to try out for, and question whether to partake of something just because "everyone else is doing it!"

We understand the basic human need to belong, but sometimes the groups we strive to belong to don't have our best interests at heart. And answering "to join or not to join?" is not always as straightforward as it might seem.

Welcome to the Institutionalized genre! Tales that spotlight a specific group of people and the hero's (or heroes') ultimate choice to join the group, leave the group, or take the group down.

But this genre isn't just about contemporary high school cliques and clubs (although it certainly can be). Many a fantasy and sci-fi novel fits in here too. Because the institutions or groups at the center of these tales can come in many forms. You've got your large, encompassing government institutions, like in *The Giver* by Lois Lowry, *Matched* by Ally Condie, *Renegades* by Marissa Meyer, or *Uglies* by Scott Westerfeld. But there are also smaller institutions, groups limited by size or location. The world of the Socs and Greasers in *The Outsiders* by S. E. Hinton explores a small subsection of Tulsa, Oklahoma, and the class conflict that exists there. Similarly, in *Long Way Down*, author Jason Reynolds pulls back the curtain on the violent, gang-torn neighborhood where his hero Will lives. *Moxie* by Jennifer Mathieu explores a single high school where sexism and sexual harassment run rampant and unchecked, even among the administration. And *Far from the Tree*, the National Book Award winner by Robin Benway, explores a three-person institution of siblings who were all adopted as babies. Finally, there are institutions centered around a unifying issue, event, or thematic element. In *Dear Martin*, author Nic Stone explores the racism that exists not only in the hallways and classrooms of Justyce's predominantly white private school, but also in the world at large.

And of course, you're not limited to just one institution. In the fantasy novel *An Ember in the Ashes* by Sabaa Tahir, heroes Laia and Elias are torn between multiple groups—the Empire, the Resistance, the Blackcliff Military Academy, and the Augurs—all with their own rules, agendas, and expectations.

Basically, if you're writing a novel that pits a hero (or heroes) against some type of group, chances are you're writing an Institutionalized story. And in these tales, the hero and the group are equally important and deserve equal focus. Even if your novel is told through only one POV (as with *Long Way Down*, *Dear Martin*, and *The Outsiders*), the group is still front and center, particularly as the hero dives deeper into what it means to be a member of that group and ultimately whether they'll choose to stay, leave, or burn it down.

If this sounds like the very kind of story you're telling, then let's take a look at the three genre ingredients you'll need to ensure that your Institutionalized tale fits in at the cool kids' table while also standing out from the crowd.

To successfully tell this type of tale, you'll need (1) a **group**, (2) a **choice**, and (3) a **sacrifice**.

A GROUP

What kind of institution are we dealing with here? What are the rules? Who are the members? What are the pros and cons of being part of the in crowd? These are the types of questions explored in Institutionalized tales. After all, this group (big or small) will often feel like the whole world to your hero, so we, the readers, need to know what the group is all about and why it's worthy of an entire story centered around it.

This is where you can really let your creativity shine. Whether that be in the uniqueness of the group itself or the unique perspective you bring to it, the way this institution ticks will be one of the ways you draw your reader in.

Look at the Scythedom in Neal Shusterman's sci-fi novel *Scythe*. In a futuristic world where humanity has conquered death, reapers called Scythes are needed to keep the population under control. This group (which the two heroes Citra and Rowan find themselves invited into as apprentices) has its own rules, laws, politics, conflicts, traditions, and rituals. And Shusterman doesn't stop there. Within the Scythedom itself there are factions and rivalries that divide the Scythes into more groups. Institutions among institutions!

Or look at the gang-torn neighborhood in Jason Reynolds's novel in verse, *Long Way Down*, which is dictated by the Rules (with a capital R!): No snitching. No crying. Always seek revenge. It's these rules that have motivated Will to ride the elevator to the ground floor of his building with the intent of shooting the man who shot his brother.

The challenge in designing your group is making it intriguing to the reader while at the same time exposing its cracks and flaws. Even as you peel back the layers of your institution and reveal its darkest corners and shadiest origins, the reader can still understand why it exists in the first place, even if they don't agree with that existence. After all, so many people have already joined this institution. They can't all be irrational! Or can they?

That's the thing about groups. They can lure us in, even in the face of their dark side, even when they prove to be a little (or very) self-destructive. It's that herd mentality that's built into our DNA. But as we've all witnessed at some point in our life, herd mentality can defy logic and reason. Being loyal to a group often contradicts common sense—sometimes even survival—but we still do it.

Which means that when we join the many, despite our better judgment, we often lose a piece of ourselves.

So as you guide us through the world of your chosen group and show us all of its inner workings, we should be asking ourselves: *What would I do if I were in the hero's shoes? Would I join or not? Would I stay or go? Would I conform or fight for change?*

Because that's what your hero will eventually ask.

Which brings us to our second genre ingredient.

A CHOICE

Whether your hero was born into the group, brought into it (sometimes against their will!) or invited to join, sooner or later all Institutionalized heroes are faced with the same decision.

Flock together or fly solo?

While we readers might never know what it feels like to *choose* to be a Scythe's apprentice, or to follow the Rules and seek fatal revenge, we can certainly understand the dilemma of following the pack or forging our own path. The choice is relatable, because human beings have been part of groups since our earliest days. Our ancestors hunted in packs, shared campfires and caves, found safety in numbers. This is why Institutionalized stories—regardless of where or when they take place—are so primal and relatable to teen readers. Teens are weighing the pros and cons of being part of a group every single day.

That said, the choice isn't always *easy* to make. (For your hero or your reader!)

To explore this ingredient further, let's take a look at three common character types that often appear in this genre.

The hero (or heroes) of these stories typically falls into one of two categories: the **naif**, someone brand-new to the institution, or the **brando**, someone already entrenched in the institution (named after the infamously rebellious actor Marlon Brando). And yes, you can have both!

A naif can be a helpful storytelling device for introducing the reader to the institution you're highlighting, because they, too, need to learn the ropes and are often guided and mentored by other characters already well-versed in how it all works. Think of both Citra and Rowan in *Scythe*, whose status as apprentices automatically places them in this camp. They are shepherded around the Scythedom (both literally and figuratively) by their mentor, Scythe Faraday. This construction allows us, the reader, to be organically shepherded around this new world right along with the heroes. In *An Ember in the Ashes*, Laia was born into the Empire (one of several institutions in the novel), but knows very little about the Resistance (who recruits her as a spy) and Blackcliff Military Academy (where she's sent to gather intelligence). As Laia learns more about the rules, the players, and the politics, so do we.

Naifs are often used as the readers' eyes into the world and can be a helpful alternative to the dreaded "info dumping" (when you have to rely on *telling* your reader too much in order to catch them up).

On the other hand, brandos are typically already entrenched in the world and familiar with all the ins and outs. But even as the novel begins, there's something different about them. They don't exactly fit in, or they're already starting to have their doubts. This is Elias's role in *An Ember in the Ashes*. As a senior student at Blackcliff Military Academy and the son of the Commandant, he knows the institution well and is already planning an escape when the novel begins. This character type also describes Will in *Long Way Down*, who doesn't *want* to commit murder, but what can he do? Those are the Rules, and they must be obeyed. It isn't until he rides the elevator with a team of ghosts (all the victims of gun violence) that the institution starts to show its cracks and presents him with the choice he must make before he reaches the ground floor.

Ultimately, however, both the naif and the brando serve a similar role: to explore the institution and all of its flaws, by going up against a third character type: the **company man**. This is a character who *embodies* the system or institution. They buy into it with all their heart and soul (and as a result, it often does corrupt their heart and soul). Look at the Commandant in *An Ember in the Ashes*, who is so entrenched in the Empire and its politics she sacrifices her own son to rise up in its ranks. Or look at Scythe Goddard in *Scythe*, who *enjoys* gleaning (killing) and lobbies to allow Scythes to glean as much as they want (without the limits of a quota).

These characters come off as just a little bit . . . well, *off*. Whether that be deranged, diabolical, or even robotic. That's the result of an unwavering loyalty to the institution, especially an institution that you, the author, are slowly poking holes in. Yet this character is still clinging to the group, despite the dark truths they may or may not know. But the company man is also an effective storytelling device because this character helps *show* those dark sides of the group and speak to the bigger message here: sometimes when we devote ourselves *too* wholeheartedly to the many, we lose our sense of self.

The company man serves as a warning to the hero—*this is what can happen when you join*—but also represents one side of the choice your hero must make (to join or not to join). It's a choice that will often get more difficult as the story goes on, leading to an epic, heart-pounding Finale, featuring our third genre ingredient.

A SACRIFICE

So what's it gonna be? In or out? Them or me?

When it's finally time to choose, the solution is never easy and often comes with a sacrifice of some sort, whether that be a sacrifice of the individual (the hero chooses to *join* the system), a sacrifice of the many (the hero chooses to *escape* the system, which might include a literal or figurative suicide), or a sacrifice of the institution itself (the hero chooses to "burn down" the system).

While the ending is ultimately up to you and the message you want to deliver to the world about the dangers of groups that seek to control us, I will say that *most* young adult novels opt for door number 2 (escape) or door number 3 (burn it down), even if the ultimate sacrifice doesn't happen until the end of a series.

In *Scythe*, Rowan literally sets fire to the building housing Scythe Goddard (the company man) and his followers. And in *An Ember in the Ashes*, Laia and Elias escape Blackcliff Military Academy together at the end, but the author hints that there's much more to come in its sequels, as the two take on the bigger institution of the Empire as a whole. Even *Long Way Down*, with its ambiguous ending, leads us to believe that Will *won't* choose to seek revenge (join); rather, he'll choose to deal with his grief differently, effectively escaping the institution by defying the Rules of his neighborhood. At least, for us as readers, that's the hope.

And that, right there, is the magic word that influences the endings of so many young adult Institutionalized stories. *Hope.*

While it can be historically and culturally significant (not to mention all-too-often *realistic*) to write Institutionalized tales with a less-than-happy ending, where the individual does not survive the lure and power of the establishment, we must, once again, remember our audience. The evidence is scrawled across the bestseller lists. Teen readers like to believe that hope is not lost. That with courage, determination, and the triumph of the human spirit, we can rise up against the institutions that seek to control us, and that, even at a young age, we can change the world.

And if these are the hands we're placing our future in, I really can't think of a better message.

To recap: if you're thinking of writing an Institutionalized novel, make sure your story includes these three essential ingredients:

- **A GROUP**: a government, family, organization, school, neighborhood, faction, community, or uniting issue that is unique and interesting
- **A CHOICE**: an ongoing conflict between the naif and/or brando and the company man, usually revolving around the question "to join or not to join" (for a naif) or "to stay or not to stay" (for a brando)
- **A SACRIFICE**: leading to one of three possible endings: join, burn it down, or escape (including suicide)

POPULAR YOUNG ADULT INSTITUTIONALIZED NOVELS

The Outsiders by S. E. Hinton
The Giver by Lois Lowry*
Uglies by Scott Westerfeld

Catching Fire by Suzanne Collins
Matched by Ally Condie
The Program by Suzanne Young
An Ember in the Ashes by Sabaa Tahir
Scythe by Neal Shusterman
Moxie by Jennifer Mathieu
Far from the Tree by Robin Benway
Long Way Down by Jason Reynolds
Dear Martin by Nic Stone
Renegades by Marissa Meyer
The Belles by Dhonielle Clayton
The Life and Medieval Times of Kit Sweetly by Jamie Pacton
Ace of Spades by Faridah Àbíké-Íyímídé

* Beat sheet follows.

THE GIVER

BY: Lois Lowry
STC GENRE: Institutionalized
BOOK GENRE: Science fiction
TOTAL PAGES: 225 (Houghton Mifflin Harcourt paperback edition,
2014)

Before there was *The Hunger Games* and *Divergent*, before "dystopia"
became a household term, there was *The Giver*, arguably one of the
most famous dystopic novels for young readers. Winner of the Newbery
Medal of Honor and frequently on required reading lists across the
United States, some consider *The Giver* to be a classic. Originally published in 1993, the novel has received countless awards and starred
reviews and has sold more than twelve million copies worldwide.
Despite the hero being twelve years old, the publisher of the novel has
classified this book as young adult, and many critics and educators
agree that, due to its graphic content and mature subject matter, it's
more appropriate for older audiences. Which might be one reason the

producers of the film adaptation, starring Meryl Streep and Jeff Bridges, decided to age-up the hero to sixteen.

But regardless of the hero's age, when we peel back the cover and take a peek at the structure of this Institutionalized favorite, it's easy to see why this story continues to resonate year after year, decade after decade, with generation after generation.

Opening Image (1–6)

Jonas, our hero, rides his bike home from school, trying to decide the perfect word for how he feels about the upcoming Ceremony of Twelve. He experiences a memory of a time he felt "frightened"—when an unidentified aircraft had flown over the community and everyone was sent indoors. In a single scene, the author paints a picture of a safe, protected, and disciplined community where precise language is used as a form of control. By controlling the language, the community can better control the people. As the **brando** of the institution, Jonas hasn't started to question anything about his surroundings . . . yet.

Jonas decides that he feels "apprehensive."

Setup (6–50)

Jonas's community operates on the idea of "Sameness," something we learn through the novel's longer-than-usual Setup. Most choice has been eliminated, along with emotion, pain, happiness, sexual "stir-rings," and other human experiences. Job assignments and matches between spouses are also decided by the community.

Through Jonas's home, work, and play, we learn more about his world and the rules of the institution. At **home**, we see Jonas participating in the "telling of feelings" with Mother, Father, and younger sister Lily. The nightly ritual feels ironically robotic. Jonas's father, a "Nurturer" (and the company man of this tale) brings home a baby from the Nurturing Center who is not thriving, in order to give him some extra attention. Gabriel quickly becomes a temporary part of the family unit, but it is against the rules to keep him. At **work**, Jonas goes to school and volunteers at the House of the Old. Here we learn that sick babies, the elderly, and rule breakers are "released" to go live

Elsewhere, although no one (including Jonas) knows exactly where that is. Soon, at the annual Ceremony of Twelve, Jonas will receive his permanent job assignment. And at **play**, Jonas hangs out with his friends Asher and Fiona. When he has a sexual dream about Fiona, his mother identifies it as "the stirrings" and gives him a pill to curb the feelings.

Jonas seems perfectly content to live in this institution. He tries hard to follow the rules and be the ideal citizen. But small cracks are starting to show, poking holes through his status quo world. In a **stasis = death** moment, Jonas flashes back to a time he saw something strange happen to an apple he was tossing back and forth with Asher. Later, we'll learn that because of Sameness, no one sees color in this world, but somehow Jonas saw the apple turn red.

Theme Stated (40)

"All lives *are* meaningful," says a woman named Larissa as Jonas is helping her bathe in the House of the Old. It's a party line that she's reciting, and ironically, in Jonas's community, it's a lie. But Jonas is still too entrenched in the system to realize that.

Yet it's exactly what he *will* come to realize by the end of this novel. That all lives are meaningful, but the community's decision to move to Sameness and take away choice and individuality has stripped lives of that meaning.

This statement is also a subtle nod to the "Institutionalized" choice that Jonas will soon face. Will he decide that community is fine the way it is? That eliminating choice and individuality is worth it for the sake of control and peace? Or will he decide that all lives *are* meaningful and that meaning shouldn't be sacrificed for the good of the group?

Catalyst (51–81)

The day of the Ceremony of Twelve finally arrives, and Jonas is feeling eager and apprehensive about his job assignment, but strangely, Jonas's name is not called. Everyone in the auditorium grows antsy with curiosity, wondering if the Chief Elder made a mistake.

There is no mistake. It's announced that Jonas has been selected to become the next Receiver of Memories, a very rare job that is assigned only when the current Receiver is ready to retire. The elder explains that Jonas has all the qualities of a Receiver: integrity, courage, and the "Capacity to See Beyond"—which no one understands, including Jonas.

Jonas is proud and grateful as the crowd chants his name, but he's also filled with fear and uneasiness. He doesn't know what this means, but he seems to understand that his life will never be the same again.

Debate (82–90)

The long Setup leaves fewer pages for the Debate, so Lowry keeps this beat short and sweet and uses it to explore Jonas's curiosity and apprehension about his mysterious assignment.

"What [will] become of him?" is the question the Debate centers around (81). Or in other words, what does this assignment entail?

He learns about the last girl to be assigned the job of Receiver. It was ten years ago, and it did not end well. According to Jonas's parents, she was not well-suited for the job, and she disappeared. This reveal builds some intrigue and stakes around the new life that awaits Jonas.

But things are already changing. The walls of Jonas's status quo world are already crumbling as he gets his first peek behind the curtain of the institution he's been raised to believe in wholeheartedly.

In reading the job file he's been given, he discovers new rules that pertain uniquely to this assignment: he's not allowed to discuss his training or talk about his dreams, nor is he allowed to request release. But other rules of the community no longer apply to him. For instance, he's now allowed to ask any question of anyone. And, most shockingly of all, he's allowed to lie.

Break Into 2 (91–100)

Jonas's first day of his new job assignment arrives. The moment he walks through the doors of the Annex (the domain of the Receiver), he enters the upside-down world of Act 2. Here he will gain access to knowledge he didn't even know existed and answers to questions he never even thought to ask.

As the new Receiver, Jonas will be given memories. Not just of people's lives in the community, but *all* memories, of all people beyond and even *before* the community. This weighty undertaking comes with great wisdom and great joy, but also devastating sorrow.

B Story (94–100)

As Jonas enters the Annex, he meets the Giver, who represents everything Jonas will learn along his internal journey: namely, the importance of choice. Throughout Act 2, we'll learn about the history of Sameness in the community and how it has all but eliminated choice. People became complacent, docile, and obedient, but they lost their ability to feel true emotion, see color, and experience real happiness.

With the help of the Giver, Jonas will awaken to horrible truths about the institution he's come to believe in, which will present him with his ultimate **choice** and sacrifice: to join the institution, leave it, or burn it down. As the B Story character, the Giver will help guide Jonas toward this decision and the personal transformation that comes with it.

Fun and Games (100–135)

The receiving of memories begins. The Giver starts with innocent, pleasurable memories like snow and sledding down a hill. Although there are hints at more painful memories to come, for the most part this beat is an **upward path**, full of exploration and wonder. Jonas learns about color and starts to see it everywhere. But he also gets glimpses of the loneliness this job entails. The Receiver holds all the wisdom but can share it with no one.

Jonas's theme about choice is restated by the Giver on page 120, when he talks about the community's decision to move to Sameness many years ago. "We gained control of many things. But we had to let go of others." Here we see that Jonas has already begun to grow when he vows that this decision was a mistake. But he still waffles about his faith in the institution, which is evident weeks later when he wonders what would happen if the community let people make *bigger* choices and they chose wrong. "We really have to protect people from wrong choices," he decides on page 124, proving that he still hasn't learned the theme and still has more growing to do before he can make his fateful choice about the fate of the institution.

Despite the Fun and Games of experiencing all of these new memories, emotions, and colors, there are hints of darker things to come. When the Giver gives Jonas a memory of an elephant being poached for its tusks, Jonas starts to understand the pain that comes with this job.

Midpoint (135–139)

Despite this, Jonas is enjoying his new role as the Receiver and the wisdom it brings (**false victory**). But the **stakes are raised** when the Giver gives Jonas his first memory of true physical pain: a sledding accident resulting in a broken leg. Jonas is in agony as he receives the memory, and when he goes home later that night, he realizes that no one in his family has ever experienced such pain before. It makes him feel desperately lonely.

Bad Guys Close In (139–181)

Jonas receives more and more painful memories, including that of a completely foreign concept: war. During this **downward path**, the Giver explains that the Receiver must endure these painful memories so that the rest of the community doesn't have to, and to provide wisdom and advice in important matters. Jonas starts to feel desire for things to change, but also hopelessness that they never will. And when the Giver gives him the powerful memory of love (another foreign concept), Jonas enjoys it immensely but is also saddened by the realization that real love can't exist within Sameness. When he asks his parents later if they love him, they don't understand what the question means and reprimand him for using imprecise language.

Back at home, Gabriel, the baby Father brought home, is not showing signs of improvement, and Jonas is worried he'll be released to Elsewhere (a practice which he's starting to doubt is as pleasant and harmless as he's been told). When Jonas discovers he can transmit some of his new memories to Gabriel (to soothe him to sleep), he starts to realize what power he really does have. This moment marks an important step in Jonas's transformation: breaking the rules and making an active choice to put an individual ahead of the community. In another moment of defiance, Jonas stops taking his pills for the Stirrings, allowing him to feel all of his new emotions and colors more fully and vividly.

Jonas's new wisdom affects him more personally as the beat goes on, representing a closing in of his **internal bad guys**. But Jonas is not the first to experience them. The Giver tells Jonas about the previous Receiver, a girl named Rosemary who couldn't handle all of the grief and pain that came with the job. She requested to be released, and the memories she'd received were returned to the community. This is the first time Jonas realizes that there *is* a way to give back memories (and with them, choice) to the community. What will he do with this information? Time will tell. But the Giver does warn Jonas that with the amount of memories Jonas now has, the result of giving them back to the community would be catastrophic.

All Is Lost (182–189)

In response to Jonas's curiosity about the ceremony of releasing, the Giver plays Jonas a recording of a release that his father performed earlier that day on a twin that was born in the Nurturing Center. In a **whiff of death**, Jonas watches as his father injects the baby with a lethal toxin and the baby dies. His father's role as the **company man** is most evident here as he emotionlessly disposes of the tiny body down a chute.

The horrors of what the community will do to maintain Sameness are devastating for Jonas. But this low point is also an important moment in his transformation, raising the personal stakes and pushing him closer to making his ultimate choice about what to do with the knowledge he's gained.

Dark Night of the Soul (190–193)

Jonas is hysterical, sobbing uncontrollably. He realizes his father has become so brainwashed by the community he doesn't even comprehend what he's done. Without memories, he doesn't have the emotional capacity to fully understand death.

In a reverse **return to the familiar**, Jonas refuses to go home, knowing how painful it would be to try to return to his old life. He pleads with the Giver that they must do something. The Giver admits that training Jonas for the past year has given him hope that maybe things *can* change. And something Jonas said has given him an idea . . .

Break Into 3 (194–197)

The Giver and Jonas talk late into the night making a plan (Act 3 goal). We won't know exactly what it is until it all unfolds in the Finale, but we know that it involves Jonas's escape from the community. We also get a hint of the stakes: if the plan fails, Jonas will die.

But Jonas is ready to take the risk. The All Is Lost has pushed him to the realization that "If he stayed, his life was no longer worth living" (194). Jonas has learned his theme about what makes life truly meaningful. And it isn't Sameness. He has made his choice.

Finale (197–224)

POINT 1: GATHERING THE TEAM. The next day at school, Jonas goes over the plan in his head, gearing himself up and providing the reader with the following details about what it entails:

- Leading up to the next Annual Ceremony, the Giver will transfer to Jonas as many memories as possible of strength and courage to help Jonas on his journey.
- Meanwhile, Jonas will stock up on food and supplies.
- On the morning of the Annual Ceremony, Jonas will leave his bicycle by the river to make it look like he's drowned.
- While everyone is distracted with the ceremony, the Giver will drive Jonas out of the community in the trunk of his car.
- Once Jonas is gone, all his memories will be returned to the community and they will have to bear the weight of it.
- The Giver will stay behind to help them cope.

In essence, Jonas will escape the community in order to "burn down" the institution of Sameness. With this choice, his will not be the only life affected; the whole community will feel the consequences of his actions.

POINT 2: EXECUTING THE PLAN. But they never get to execute their plan, because not two days later, Jonas learns from his father that the Nurturing Center is planning to release Gabriel. Jonas cannot let Gabriel die. The empathy and compassion he's acquired over the past year forces him to create his *own* plan—without the Giver's help. Instead of receiving *memories* of strength and courage (as planned), Jonas will have to rely on the real thing.

After stealing his father's bicycle, Jonas takes off into the night with Gabriel. In a mirror to the Opening Image, search planes fly overhead, but the fear Jonas feels now is raw and complete. Instead of obediently running back inside as he did in the Opening Image, Jonas keeps going, proving he's broken free from the brainwashed community member he once was. As he ventures farther away from Sameness, the landscape begins to change. For the first time, he experiences real hunger and real pain. But that pain is juxtaposed with the joy of seeing real birds, wildflowers, and waterfalls.

As his memories fade, he hopes it means they're being returned to the community.

POINT 3: HIGH TOWER SURPRISE. It begins to snow, making the journey more difficult. The hunger is worse than ever, and Gabriel becomes less responsive. It seems certain they will die out here, and for a moment, Jonas considers it as an option.

POINT 4: DIG DEEP DOWN. But Jonas knows they've come too far to give up now. Even though many of his memories are now gone, he digs deep down to find a last remaining memory of sunshine. He gets an urge to keep it and save himself, but that urge is overcome by the love he knows he is capable of feeling for another human being. He transmits the memory to Gabriel, and it ends up warming them both (a possible metaphor for how love is not selfish and ends up shining back on the giver as well as the receiver).

POINT 5: THE EXECUTION OF THE NEW PLAN. Jonas trudges on. Abandoning his bike, he carries Gabriel up a steep hill, fighting to find scraps of warm memories to keep them alive. When he runs out of other people's memories, he turns to his own. Memories of his friends, family, and the Giver. He is flooded with joy and warmth, remembering that he is not alone. He reaches the top of the hill.

Final Image (224–225)

Jonas recognizes the scenery from the very first memory the Giver gave him. He finds a sled, and he and Gabriel slide down the hill toward the houses below. They are filled with colorful lights, music, and what he is sure will be love.

This is Elsewhere.

But what *is* Elsewhere? A quaint village outside of the community? Or an afterlife? Do Jonas and Gabriel die? Or do they survive? Author Lowry leaves the ending ambiguous.

But Jonas has fulfilled his Act 3 goal: releasing the memories (and therefore the gift of choice) back to the community. We may never know for sure what has become of Jonas. But that's what a life of choice and emotion is. It's unpredictable. It's ambiguous. It's uncertain. And that is beautiful.

WHY IS THIS AN INSTITUTIONALIZED STORY?

The Giver contains all three elements of a successful Institutionalized story.

- A GROUP: The community is a dystopian institution parading itself as a utopia. Although it is a place without war and pain, it's also a place without other human emotions like love. Sameness has taken away all choice and individuality.
- A CHOICE: The more Jonas (the brando) receives memories from the Giver and learns about real human emotion, the more he realizes that the community is not the idyllic place he once believed. But what can he do about it? When his father (the company man) coldly euthanizes a newborn baby, his choice becomes clear.
- A SACRIFICE LEADING TO ONE OF THREE POSSIBLE ENDINGS: Join, burn it down, or escape. Jonas sacrifices himself and the memories he's received by running away in order to restore the memories to the community. In his sacrifice, he hopes that Sameness will be "burned down," individuality and choice will be returned, and life will have true meaning.

Cat's Eye View

For quick reference, here's a brief overview of this novel's beat sheet:

OPENING IMAGE: Jonas feels apprehensive about the upcoming Ceremony of Twelve and remembers a time when an aircraft flew over the community and he felt frightened.

SETUP: We're introduced to Jonas's community, which operates on the principle of Sameness. Nearly all choices have been stripped away from the inhabitants; there are very strict rules governing every aspect of life; and sick babies, the elderly, and rule breakers are "released" to live Elsewhere. Jonas (the brando) buys into the institution but also is starting to see things that others do not. At home, his father (the company man) brings home a baby, Gabriel, from the Nurturing Center.

THEME STATED: "All lives *are* meaningful," says Larissa on page 40. In this community it's a lie, but it's exactly what Jonas needs to learn in order to make the difficult choice to bring free will and individuality back to the community.

CATALYST: The Ceremony of Twelve arrives and Jonas is given an unexpected job assignment. He is to become the new Receiver of Memories, a mysterious role that people know very little about.

DEBATE: What does this assignment entail? And how will Jonas's life change? As he reads his job file, he discovers that new rules apply to him and certain old rules no longer apply to him.

BREAK INTO 2: Jonas enters the Annex (the domain of the Receiver) and into a whole new world, where he'll soon be given all the memories that have been stripped away from the community, including those from *before* the community even existed.

B STORY: Upon entering the Annex, Jonas meets the Giver, who will not only give Jonas the memories but also help him learn his life lesson about the importance of choice and individuality.

FUN AND GAMES: The receiving of memories begins, mostly positive ones. Jonas marvels in all of the exciting new things he's experiencing. But a few negative memories also hint at darker things to come.

MIDPOINT: Jonas is enjoying his new role as Receiver (false victory), but the stakes are raised when he receives his first memory of physical pain. When he realizes his family has never experienced such a sensation, he feels lonely.

BAD GUYS CLOSE IN: Jonas receives more and more painful memories (downward path), including that of war. But he also experiences the memory of love for the first time, which both delights and saddens him (bouncing ball). Jonas learns the previous Receiver couldn't handle the job and asked to be released, at which time her memories were returned to the community.

ALL IS LOST: Jonas learns the truth about "releasing" when the Giver shows him a recording of his father euthanizing a newborn baby (whiff of death).

DARK NIGHT OF THE SOUL: Jonas sobs hysterically, realizing how his father has been brainwashed by the community. He asks the Giver what they can do, and together they sit down to make a plan.

BREAK INTO 3: Although the plan is not yet revealed to the reader, the risks of danger are great. But Jonas feels ready to take them, because he knows "If he stayed, his life was no longer worth living" (194). He has learned his theme about what makes life meaningful and has made his choice.

FINALE: The plan was for Jonas to escape the community in the trunk of the Giver's car (which would release all of his new memories back to the community), but the plan goes awry when Jonas learns that Gabriel is to be "released." Instead, Jonas escapes with Gabriel on a bicycle. The journey is long and arduous, but he feels his memories fading, returning to the community, and hopes he has done his part to bring about change.

FINAL IMAGE: Jonas reaches Elsewhere. Is it a quaint village or an afterlife? We may never know. But with true choice and emotion comes beautiful ambiguity.

Superhero
Tales of the "Chosen One"

Imagine the scenario: You're fifteen years old. You're picked on in the hallways, singled out for being "weird," or you're simply overlooked, too unremarkable to even be *noticed*. And then, out of the blue, someone appears and tells you you're special. You're different. You've been *chosen* for a higher purpose. And all those other ignorant fools just don't get it.

If this is sounding like a familiar fantasy, you're not alone.

Which is probably why this genre is *so* dang popular among teen (and adult!) readers. I've basically just described the plot of nearly *all* superhero tales, one of the most iconic, thrilling, and aspirational of all the Save the Cat! genres. These tales play on our human desires to be special, to overcome great obstacles, to do good and fight evil, and maybe even to save the world!

Now, of course, not all of us are built for world saving (I'll be the first to admit I would much rather die in a zombie apocalypse than be called upon to fight the zombies), but we can still be inspired to be better versions of ourselves by reading about those who are. Which is why this genre calls for a very specific type of hero. A hero who is *destined* for greatness—whether they like it or not.

And despite the title of the genre, we're not just talking about classic comic book heroes in capes and tights (although that's how the genre got its name). The (super) heroes of this genre come in many varieties. From those with magical or fantastical abilities, like Mare in *Red Queen* by Victoria Aveyard or Juliette in *Shatter Me* by Tahereh Mafi; to those with abilities created by science, like Max in *Maximum Ride: The Angel Experiment* by James Patterson; to those with super "powers" more grounded in reality, like Tris in *Divergent* by Veronica Roth, and Jazz in *I Hunt Killers* by Barry Lyga. Then there are superheroes who are super just by virtue of the fact that they are destined for bigger, better things, like Cinder in *Cinder* by Marissa Meyer, who is destined to be the Lunar queen, or Katniss in *Mockingjay* (Hunger Games #3) by Suzanne Collins, who is destined to be the leader of a revolution.

In the end, all these stories share a common trait: they are the tales of a "chosen one" who is ultimately different from the rest of us. In fact, of all the Save the Cat! story genres, the heroes of this genre are typically the *least* like the rest of us, which means in order to make them relatable, we have to show how being great isn't always so . . . well, so great. And that's the truth! Being bestowed with magical powers, special abilities, an unrivaled mind, steadfast ambition, or even an unwavering faith in a certain mission or destiny often comes with a price: the curse of being misunderstood by those around you.

And *that's* something we can *all* relate to, whether we're destined to be zombie fighters or zombie dinner. At some point in our lives, we've all been faced with the gut-wrenching challenge of being different, feeling different, or being misunderstood.

But the thing that sets superheroes apart is not *only* their "superness," but also their courage and determination to rise up and pursue their destiny with all that they have, despite the impossible odds and treacherous obstacles thrown in their way. Because honestly, how many of us, if faced with those odds, would actually have what it takes (and be willing to give up what it takes) to triumph? Probably very few of us. Which is what makes the superhero stand apart and be worthy of this story.

Superhero novels are often tales of sacrifice. These heroes know in their heart of hearts what path they must take (or they will eventually). They know how hard it will be. And they will do whatever it takes to succeed. And *that* is what really makes them super.

If it's *your* destiny to succeed as a superhero writer, all the *power* to you! Just be sure you're including the three genre ingredients: (1) A hero with a special **power**, (2) a **nemesis** who stands opposed to the hero, and (3) a **curse** that the hero must suffer as a price for their greatness.

Let's break 'em down.

A POWER

The power is what makes the superhero special and sets them apart from the rest of us (or the rest of their world). And as we've discussed, it doesn't necessarily have to be magical! Although it certainly can be, and that's always a popular choice in young adult fiction, particularly fantasy novels. In *Shatter Me*, Juliette has the ability to kill with just her touch. In *Red Queen*, Mare (a poor girl with red blood) discovers she has the ability to manipulate lightning and electricity, a power that should be possible only for those with silver blood. This automatically makes her special among the Reds. But when it's discovered she can also *create* electricity (something no one else can do), she becomes special among the Silvers as well.

A superhero's power can also be man-made, originating from science, like Max's ability to fly—given the avian DNA that's been grafted into her human DNA—in *Maximum Ride: The Angel Experiment*.

But a superhero doesn't have to have *literal* powers to be super. Sometimes the power is a unique skill that they've honed, or a gifted mind. In *I Hunt Killers*, Jazz is the son of the notorious serial killer Billy Dent, who is now locked away in prison. But Billy has already left his mark on Jazz by raising him to follow in his footsteps. This has given Jazz a unique ability to understand serial killers, which he's vowed to put to use *catching* them, not becoming one as his father intended.

Or sometimes the power is simply a mission to do good or a destiny to be great. Katniss Everdeen in *Mockingjay* starts the novel reluctant and hesitant to do anything to help the rebels' cause. But her status as the Mockingjay is powerful and makes her destined to be the face of the revolution—if she's courageous enough to accept that destiny.

Your hero could also have a combination of powers. Eragon in *Eragon* is destined to be a great dragon rider and save his world, a destiny that *comes* with the bestowal of magical abilities.

Keep in mind that your hero might not even know that they're special at the start of the story. Their power might be something buried, lost, forgotten, or untapped. As is the case with Tris in *Divergent*, Mare in *Red Queen*, and Alina in *Shadow and Bone* by Leigh Bardugo (all of whom discover their "specialness" at the Catalyst beat). Which is why there's a common moment in many superhero stories (typically in Act 2) when the hero undergoes a name change or transformation of some type. This is the moment when the hero assumes their new superhero identity or disguises themself to fit in. Like when Mare is given the fake Silver name Lady Mareena Titanos in *Red Queen*, or Beatrice renames herself as Tris in *Divergent*.

Regardless of your hero's power or when they learn about it, it's what makes the hero more than human, more than the rest of us. And it's not something that can stay hidden for long. Eventually it will attract attention (if it hasn't already).

One person (or creature!) in particular is bound to take notice.

A NEMESIS

The nemesis is the character who directly opposes the hero. They often have abilities that match the hero's (or even surpass the hero's), but those abilities are typically self-made, or the result of extreme effort, which usually involves plotting, manipulating, or scheming. While the superhero seems to have come about their specialness naturally or even effortlessly, the nemesis has to *work* for what they have. Think about Queen Elara in *Red Queen* or the Darkling in *Shadow and Bone*, both of whom have had to scheme and plot their way to positions of power. Elara is rumored to have killed the former queen to put herself on the throne. And when Mare's powers—which were revealed by *accident*—threaten her plans, she again has to plot her way to the top.

That's the burden of the nemesis. They have to try so dang hard. Because essentially what the nemesis lacks is the one quality that makes for every great superhero: good old-fashioned *faith*.

The superhero doesn't have to try so hard because they already *know* they're special. Or if they don't know at first, they will eventually. In fact, it may even be a big part of their B Story: finding that faith in themselves. Conversely, the nemesis has to rely on their machinations, their evil deeds, and their minions (there are almost *always* minions!). They might *seem* special, but really it's a façade. And they'll do whatever it takes to keep the illusion alive, because whether they accept it or not, deep down the nemesis knows they aren't the real hero. They're the wannabe. And wannabes *always* have to try harder.

In *I Hunt Killers*, the nemesis is a serial killer called the Impressionist. And doesn't that name say it all? He's copycatting the infamous murders of serial killer Billy Dent (who was named the Artist). He's literally a copy of Billy and, by extension, Billy's son, Jazz (the hero).

In *Mockingjay*, President Snow has to use all kinds of tricks and schemes to try to defeat Katniss, including brainwashing Peeta to turn against her. Because deep down, he knows Katniss is dangerous. She possesses a natural power (the ability to rally people) that he's had to murder and cheat and intimidate to obtain.

The superhero is a thorn in the nemesis's side, so one of the nemesis's goals is almost always to kill, convert, or neutralize the superhero so that they can continue pursuing their nefarious plans (and boy, do they have plans!).

The hero/nemesis relationship is so fascinating and complex because there's often a connection between the two. Maybe it's a common goal (with two very different approaches). Mare and Queen Elara in *Red Queen* both *want* to stop the unrest between the Reds and the Silvers, but while Mare's approach involves empowering the Reds, Elara's approach is about subjugating them further. Or maybe it's a common wound from their past that has turned them into very different people in the present, like Cinder and Queen Levana in *Cinder* who both suffered serious burn wounds from fires as children. The more you can align your hero and your nemesis with a common bond, the more nuanced and compelling the battle between the two. There's a reason that the Darkling in *Shadow and Bone* can summon *darkness* and Alina can summon *light*. It makes them true adversaries. And when there's a connection between your superhero and your nemesis, the sparks *really* fly in the final battle.

Yes, there *must* be a final battle. An epic showdown that pits superhero against nemesis. This is usually found in the Finale beat of a standalone novel. However, if the book is the first in a series (as many YA Superhero novels are), there will probably still be a battle at the end of the first installment, albeit a slightly less conclusive one. At the end of *Red Queen*, Mare escapes the arena where Queen Elara and her son, Maven, force her to fight to the death. That threat is dealt with—for now. At the end of *Shadow and Bone*, Alina leaves the Darkling alone in the Shadow Fold with the flesh-eating volcra, but because there's two more books in the series, we *kinda* suspect that's not the end of him. At the end of *Eragon*, Eragon kills Durza, but he still has to deal with Durza's boss (King Galbatorix), whom we haven't even met yet. One nemesis steps aside to make room for a bigger, *badder* nemesis.

Regardless of when your *final* battle takes place, it's important to note that superheroes don't always survive it. Sometimes they must make the ultimate sacrifice so that their nemesis can be defeated. But that doesn't mean they weren't victorious. After all, the point of any story is transformation. So as long as they went somewhere internally, their external fate becomes almost irrelevant. (But be warned. Teen readers are often very disappointed and very *vocal* about that disappointment, when their favorite superheroes don't make it to the end of a novel or series.)

But why do teen readers get so attached to these characters? That's where our third (and possibly most important) genre ingredient comes into play.

A CURSE

Being "super" is not always all it's cracked up to be. And with every power comes a price. Also called the curse.

The curse is what balances out the superhero's power and makes them feel, well, *human*. The curse makes us *like* the hero of your superhero tale. Or better yet, fall in love with them!

Having the genius mind of a serial killer, for instance, doesn't exactly make you the top candidate for prom king, as Jazz in *I Hunt Killers* will likely tell you. The people of his small town of Lobo's Nod distrust Jazz, knowing who his father is. Not to mention, author Lyga saddles Jazz with a very challenging guardian—a nasty, senile grandmother who's constantly confusing Jazz for his father. We may not know what it's like to be the son of a serial killer, but we can relate to being an outcast and navigating difficult relatives!

The curse is usually some variation of being misunderstood. By nature, the superhero doesn't fit in, and that often attracts negative attention. We build this curse into our superhero stories to take these characters down a peg, give them a weakness (especially at the beginning) because it ensures the reader won't roll their eyes and mark the book as DNF (did not finish) before they reach the Catalyst because "what do I have in common with a *superhero*?"

Imagine if Mare's ability to generate and manipulate lightning had been discovered before the book began. The main story might have opened up with Mare already powerful, confident, and living a luxurious life with the Silvers, which would have made her a lot harder to root for (not to mention giving her nowhere to go!). Instead, she starts out as a lowly Red, desperate to keep her family fed and keep her best friend from being sent to war. She may not seem "super" at first, but by the time those powers are revealed, we're already rooting for her.

The curse is just another form of reader manipulation. (Our own writerly superpower!) But be careful not to swing too far the other way. If you make your hero's life *too* cursed, or *too* pathetic, the reader might just give up. So, as with all good superpowers, use this one wisely.

A popular way to balance out the curse is by employing a common superhero character type called the **mascot**—someone (or something) who is unwaveringly loyal to the hero, like a sidekick, companion, friend, animal, or even robot buddy! Think about the dragon Saphira in *Eragon*, the android Iko in *Cinder*, or Mare's sister Gisa in *Red Queen*. The mascot's two primary purposes are (1) to balance out some of the negative attention that comes from the curse and get us on the hero's side (after all, *this* character likes them, so there must be something to root for), and (2) show us how different the hero really is, usually by contrast to the mascot themself (who is *not* super and does *not* have the same powers as the superhero). They're also often used as comic relief characters, like in *I Hunt Killers*. Jazz's best friend, Howie, is an awkward, lovable hemophiliac who can always be counted on to help Jazz with whatever risky schemes he gets up to and who sees Jazz as his own person (not the son of a serial killer).

If you can pull off the Superhero genre well, you will become nothing short of super to your hordes of adoring fans and readers. It's a hugely popular and successful genre of novels in the young adult space, and teen readers are always hungry for more.

Because although teens may turn to these tales to escape their normal life and dream of a better one, and although they may have fantasies of sprouting wings, flying with dragons, wielding lightning, hunting killers, and everything in between, the real message comes through loud and clear: Even superheroes have real-world problems. And if they can overcome them, so can I!

To recap: if you're thinking of writing a Superhero novel, make sure your story includes these three essential ingredients:

- A POWER bestowed on your hero, even if it's just a destiny for greatness or a mission to be or do good
- A NEMESIS who directly opposes your hero and who possesses equal (or even greater!) force, but who is the self-made version of the hero and lacks the faith to truly be "the one"
- A CURSE for the hero to overcome (or succumb to) as the price for who they are, which makes your hero relatable to us mere mortals

POPULAR YOUNG ADULT SUPERHERO NOVELS

Eragon by Christopher Paolini
Maximum Ride: The Angel Experiment by James Patterson
City of Bones by Cassandra Clare
Mockingjay by Suzanne Collins
Divergent by Veronica Roth
Miss Peregrine's Home for Peculiar Children by Ransom Riggs
Shatter Me by Tahereh Mafi
Cinder by Marissa Meyer
I Hunt Killers by Barry Lyga
Shadow and Bone by Leigh Bardugo
Origin by Jessica Khoury
Legend by Marie Lu
Red Queen by Victoria Aveyard
Children of Blood and Bone by Tomi Adeyemi*

* Beat sheet follows.

CHILDREN OF BLOOD AND BONE

BY: Tomi Adeyemi
STC GENRE: Superhero
BOOK GENRE: Young adult fantasy
TOTAL PAGES: 525 (Henry Holt hardcover edition, 2018)

Tomi Adeyemi took the publishing world by storm when she arrived on the young adult scene with her debut novel, *Children of Blood and Bone*, a fantasy novel inspired by West African mythology and Yoruba culture that examines racism, oppression, and violence. After receiving one of the "biggest YA debut novel publishing deals ever" (according to the deal announcement in *Deadline*) the book went on to debut at number one on the *New York Times* bestseller list and remain on the list for over two years. Its sequel, *Children of Virtue and Vengeance*, also debuted at number one. The myriad of praise and starred reviews applaud the novel for its inspired worldbuilding, complex characters, powerful themes, and of course, stellar plotting. The book's three heroes and three points of view weave and overlap beautifully, making this an inspiring example of a blended-track beat sheet complete with three intertwining Five-Point Finales! (For more on multiple POV beat sheets, see page 116.)

Opening Image/Zélie (1–20)

After a short prologue in which Zélie flashes back to the day her mother was hung from a tree by the king's soldiers for using "the magic of death" (1), we meet Zélie today, as a young woman in the oppressive kingdom of Orïsha. It's the graduation match for Zélie's secret training in the art of the staff (a weapon of self-defense), and in this single scene we learn about her **wants** (to graduate and earn her staff), one of her biggest **flaws** (a quick temper that often gets her and her family in trouble), and many of the **things that need fixing** in Zélie's world, namely the oppressive rule of King Saran, who levies a tax on divîners (majis whose powers have not yet been activated) in order to keep them weak. Zélie is a divîner.

After Zélie incites a near-violent encounter with the king's guards who arrive to collect more taxes, Mama Agba (Zélie's trainer and mentor) tells Zélie about the history of Orïsha, providing the reader with some important worldbuilding. We learn about the different maji clans, their abilities, and how magic was lost eleven years earlier when maji were hunted and killed in an event called the Raid (referenced in the prologue). Now magic is believed to be dead, but hatred and violence against divîners (marked by their white hair) still remains in the kingdom.

Mama Agba ends the story with a reminder of why they train in the art of the staff. "It avoids rather than hurts, it hurts rather than maims, it maims rather than kills—the staff does not destroy" (16). It's a lesson in nonviolence that Zélie will spend the rest of the novel learning.

Theme Stated/Zélie (18)

"When your opponent has no honor, you must fight in different ways, smarter ways," Mama Agba tells Zélie. It's a response to Zélie losing her temper with the guards and a specific message about the theme of nonviolence, directed at Zélie.

Zélie, who has "inherited [her mother's] rage" (18), feels powerless in the face of the oppressive monarchy and is quick to turn to violence as a response. Eventually, though, she will learn to harness a different kind of power, one that is about to awaken within her. As in many superhero stories, Zélie will not only have to come to terms with her specialness (her maji power and destiny to restore magic to Orïsha) but also learn how to have faith in that power and wield it wisely.

Setup/Zélie (21–74)

Zélie's brother, Tzain, arrives with news that something has happened to Baba, their father. They rush through the floating city of Ilorin to find him thrashing in the water. After Tzain dives in to save him, Baba explains that he went fishing to raise money for the divîner tax but lost the boat. Without money to pay the tax, Zélie will be sent to the stocks (the kingdom's workforce), the equivalent of a death sentence (**stasis = death**). Zélie gets the idea to go to Lagos (the capital) to sell a recently caught sailfish (new **goal**). She and Tzain saddle up Nailah, their lion-aire ryder (and Zélie's superhero mascot), and take off for the market.

Opening Image and Setup/Amari (32–39)

Amari, the king's daughter and princess of Orïsha, suffers through tea with her mother, who finds ways to criticize her in nearly every sentence. A single scene serves as both the Opening Image and the Setup, giving us a glimpse at Amari's world and all the **things that need fixing**. She feels like a prisoner in her life. She's rarely allowed to leave the palace. She grew up under the strict rule of her father, King Saran, who used to make Amari spar with her brother Inan (the pride of the family, recently promoted to captain). Her only friend is a divîner servant named Binta, who Amari soon discovers has been ominously summoned to the throne room to meet with the king.

Catalyst, Debate, and Break Into 2/Amari (39–46)

With three heroes, beats are often condensed into a handful of scenes, as is the case with Amari's Catalyst, Debate, and Break Into 2, which all happen within half a chapter. While looking for Binta in the throne room, Amari overhears Commander Kaea reporting to the king about lost artifacts (a scroll and a sunstone) washing up on shore and activating latent abilities in divîners, turning them into maji. They have the scroll, but the sunstone was stolen and is now missing.

Amari watches on, mesmerized, as Binta is forced to touch the scroll, activating her magic. But Amari is also conflicted by her ingrained belief that magic is evil. The king plunges a sword into Binta's chest, sending Amari into a spiral of grief. She follows the guard who delivers the scroll to Commander Kaea's room, and after a short Debate in which she thinks of Binta, she decides to steal the scroll (Break Into 2).

Theme Stated/Amari (40)

Amari's personal theme is about courage. While overhearing the conversation in the throne room, she remembers what her father used to say to her when he forced her to spar with her brother. *"The maji will come for you. When they do, you must be prepared"* (40).

King Saran has been grooming both his children to be warriors, believing that pitting them against each other will make them stronger and give them a better chance to fight against the maji (who are the enemy in his eyes). But Amari's always felt weak and useless, especially in the face of her father. Throughout the novel, she'll come to realize that she *is* prepared and *does* have what it takes to be a strong fighter. She has just been pitted against the wrong enemy her whole life.

Setup (cont'd)/Zélie (21–74)

Once at the marketplace in Lagos, Zélie bargains with a rich nobleman for the sailfish, earning more than enough money to pay the tax. But then guards barge into the marketplace, and a girl (Amari) begs Zélie to help her escape. Inspired by Mama Agba's teachings, Zélie agrees, but they're surrounded by guards just outside the city gates. Saved just in time by Tzain, they manage to escape on Nailah. As they do, Zélie locks eyes with the captain of the guard (Inan) and feels a strange, lightning-like sensation travel through her.

Opening Image and Setup/Inan (68–72)

Although we've already seen Inan briefly through Zélie and Amari's perspectives, here is where he's first introduced as a narrator and the novel's third hero. After failing to catch an unnamed fugitive who escaped with a divîner in the marketplace, Inan returns to the palace to face his father, whom he desperately **wants** to prove himself to. As the future king, Inan is extremely hard on himself and now can't stop thinking about the divîner (Zélie) who bested him earlier.

Theme Stated/Inan (73)

"Duty before self" is the motto that the king has drilled into Inan. All of his life, Inan has been taught to believe in his father's oppressive rules. But this belief has inexorably turned him into his father's prisoner. Inan's personal journey in this novel will be about breaking free from his brainwashing, waking up to the truth about the maji and the divîners, and accepting the fact that he is one of them. All of this will require him to betray his loyalty to the king. In other words, put *himself* before duty.

Catalyst/Inan (72–73)

When the king asks Inan if he knows the identity of the fugitive he was hunting today, Inan shamefacedly says no. The king shocks him by revealing that the fugitive is his own sister, Amari.

Catalyst/Zélie (74–77)

Amari reveals herself to Zélie as the princess of Orïsha and shows her the scroll, claiming it can bring magic back. After Amari explains what happened to Binta, Zélie touches the scroll and thinks she feels magic awaken within her. But she crushes "the spark before it can blossom into hope" (77).

Debate/Inan (81–84)

As the king explains that Amari stole a scroll that can bring back magic, Inan doesn't believe it's possible. But the more the king reveals about the history of the war between the kingdom and the maji, the more Inan starts to believe it's true. His Debate question is: What will he do about it? It's here we learn that maji killed the king's first family and that's why he initiated the Raid—to sever the connection between the maji and the gods and keep the maji from becoming too powerful. The scroll must be apprehended before it can be used to awaken any more magic.

Break Into 2/Inan (85)

After Inan discovers the name (Zélie) and village (Ilorin) of the divîner who helped Amari escape, he vows to track her down, find the scroll, and bring Amari back (**Act 2 goal**). The king tells him to burn Zélie's village once he's completed his task.

Debate/Zélie (77–97)

Is it real? Is magic really back? And if so, what will they do about it? These are the questions that populate Zélie's Debate.

When Zélie, Tzain, and Amari return to Ilorin and show the scroll to Mama Agba, it awakens her magic as well, confirming that it's real. Mama Agba, now revealed to be a Seer, summons a vision of Zélie, Tzain, and Amari traveling to the sacred temple of Chândomblé to bring magic back for good (**double bump**). Moments later, the king's guards, led by Inan, arrive and burn the village (**triple bump**). Zélie barely manages to escape alive with Tzain, Baba, Mama Agba, and Amari.

Break Into 2/Zélie (98–101)

Zélie mourns the loss of her village and the people who perished in the fires, feeling responsible for bringing the guards there. Baba convinces her to follow Mama Agba's vision and go on the quest to bring magic back (**Act 2 goal**). Zélie, Amari, and Tzain climb on Nailah's back and set off.

B Story/Zélie and Amari (58–67)

There's a triangle of B Story characters going on in this novel: all three heroes in some way learn their theme from one another. We see the first of this B Story musical chairs happen when Amari and Zélie first meet in the marketplace in Lagos, but their shared fate is sealed once Zélie

Breaks Into 2 and sets off on her quest to bring magic back. Amari is one of Zélie's **twin B Story characters**, the other being Inan, whom she'll meet later.

Zélie immediately dislikes Amari because she's a noble. But over the course of the story, Zélie and Amari will become unlikely friends. It's Amari who most strongly believes in Zélie's power and destiny, providing support when her faith wavers. In turn, Zélie is Amari's B Story character, teaching Amari how to be brave and stand up for herself. Through her own bravery and courage, she will inspire Amari's transformation into a strong and confident warrior.

Fun and Games/Inan (102–223)

Inan's **downward path** begins by the failure to capture Zélie and apprehend his sister in Ilorin and continues when he gets a vision of Zélie and thinks she has infected him with her magic. But he discovers he can use the vision to locate Zélie, and the hunt continues.

B Story/Zélie and Inan (109–115)

Zélie wakes to find herself transported to a strange field of reeds where she meets Inan. But oddly, he now has a white streak in his hair. She quickly realizes that *his* magic has created this vision and transported them both here; she rationalizes that he must have accidentally touched the scroll in the marketplace, which awakened him as a Connector (maji of mind, spirit, and dreams). Inan refuses to believe this.

As Inan's B Story character (and soon-to-be love interest), Zélie will challenge all of Inan's beliefs about divîners and maji, effectively inspiring Inan's journey to defy his father, reject a lifetime of brainwashing, and accept the magic blossoming inside of him.

As Zélie's second B Story character, Inan will challenge *her* belief that all royals are evil and untrustworthy, effectively inspiring Zélie's journey to learn to curb her anger and rage, and to fight for change in a "smarter way."

Fun and Games/Zélie and Amari (116–235)

With their Act 2 goals aligned—to bring magic back—Zélie and Amari's beat sheets merge here as they depart on an **upward path** toward the Midpoint. The journey takes them to new and unfamiliar places, serving as an upside-down world for both of them—especially Amari, who has barely left the palace before. Despite conflict at every turn, both heroes use their wiles and skills to overcome obstacles and get out of binds, all while their flaws are challenged and tested and Zélie and Amari's vastly different upbringings clash.

Their journey takes them first to Sokoto to buy supplies, and then up a mountain to the sacred temple of Chândomblé, which is now in ruins. A Reaper (maji of life and death), Zélie's magic shows her visions of people being slaughtered here. Guided by a sêntaro (a spiritual guardian of the maji) named Lekan, the group is shown into a chamber where a beautiful mural of the gods comes to life and illustrates the origin of the maji. Here we learn about a sacred binding ritual performed by the powerful mamaláwo (leader of the sêntaros) during which three sacred artifacts—the scroll, the sunstone, and the bone dagger—are used to seal the connection of the gods to the sêntaros. This is the ritual that must be performed to bring magic back to Orïsha. But the ritual can be performed only on the centennial solstice (less than one moon away), when a sacred island emerges from the sea. If they miss the centennial solstice, "Orïsha will never see magic again" (164). And King Saran will continue his tyrannical rule.

We now have a ticking clock, increased stakes, *and* a modified goal: gather the three artifacts for the ritual. Lekan has the bone dagger, and Zélie has the scroll, but the sunstone is missing.

When Lekan reveals that the Sky Mother chose Zélie to perform the ritual (by bringing the scroll to her), our superhero is confirmed. As the future mamaláwo, Zélie is the chosen one, destined to restore magic to the kingdom. But Zélie does not feel up to the task, convinced that the Sky Mother's "will is wrong" (165). She resists. But this is part of her life lesson and theme. This is the "smarter way" to fight. If she wants to bring about real change to her world, she will have to accept her destiny and learn to use her power wisely.

After Lekan performs an awakening ceremony on Zélie, connecting her to the Sky Mother and fully awakening her maji abilities, Inan and his guards arrive, forcing them to flee. Lekan is killed, but Zélie, Tzain, and Amari manage to escape across a rickety bridge, which then collapses, trapping Inan and the guards on the other side.

Zélie and Amari's **upward path** journey continues to the desert city of Ibeji, where they track down the sunstone. It's being offered as a prize in a deadly competition—so to get the sunstone, they'll have to win it. Amari thinks it's a lost cause. They'll certainly be killed. But Zélie has a plan to use her Reaper magic to reanimate the dead and command them as an army in the competition. She practices the incantation, failing again and again, until finally she's able to conjure a spirit, giving her hope for the battle to come.

Fun and Games (cont'd)/Inan (102–223)

Zélie and Amari's upward path creates conflict for Inan, whose goal of stopping magic from returning is in direct opposition to theirs. Although he's able to track Zélie to Sokoto and Chândomblé, she keeps evading him. And now the collapsed bridge will take three days to rebuild, keeping them trapped. Essentially, Zélie and Amari's upward path *creates* his downward path (a mark of stellar plotting).

To make matters worse, his own magic is getting harder and more exhausting to hide (**fixing things the wrong way**), and the risk of his secret being discovered mounts daily as Commander Kaea grows suspicious of him. But after seeing Lekan's magic in action and learning more about his own abilities (through the mural in Chândomblé), Inan becomes angry and curses his patron god for poisoning him with magic, vowing once again to destroy it. He realizes how powerful magic is and how vulnerable it would make his father and the kingdom if it were ever to come back permanently. Ironically, though, his best tool to stop it is the magic growing within him.

Midpoint/Inan (222–233)

After failing to apprehend Zélie and Amari (**false defeat**), in a **shift from wants to needs**, Inan chooses to *use* his Connector magic, rather than fight it, to track down Zélie and the scroll, interpreting his decision as putting "duty before self" (theme). He transports himself into a dreamscape and summons Zélie there by thinking of her. The two immediately start arguing, each blaming the other for deaths in their family: Zélie blames Inan's father for her mother's death, and Inan blames Zélie for maji killing his father's first family. Obviously, neither are directly responsible for the other's grief, but in this crossroads beat where **A and B Stories cross**, we see their flaws and prejudices clashing.

Even though Inan has given in to his magic, he still hasn't learned his theme, which is evident from the fact that he's using magic to try to destroy magic. He's still doing his father's bidding, putting duty before self, instead of accepting who he really is and embracing it.

As Zélie and Inan verbally spar, Zélie accidentally (and unwittingly) gives away her location in Ibeiji, which thrills Inan. But the thrill is short-lived when he comes out of the dream and sees Commander Kaea standing there, sword outstretched. Knowing he was using magic, she calls him a traitor and threatens to tell the king. In a **stakes are raised** moment, Inan accidentally kills her with his magic. Inan's motivation to hide his abilities and achieve his goal is renewed as he realizes "I am the very monster I hunt" (231).

Midpoint/Zélie and Amari (234–259)

Twenty-five pages, seven short chapters, two points of view, one epic and thrilling scene. The combined Midpoints of Zélie and Amari feature a deadly battle as Zélie, Amari, and Tzain attempt to win the sunstone. This **Midpoint competition** takes place in an arena filled with water where thirty boats fight to the death. As Midpoints are meant to do, it will challenge our heroes, forcing them to move forward, face fears, battle flaws, and show what they're really made of. Or as Zélie narrates: "There's no backing out now. We either get the stone or we die trying" (242).

In the first of several **false victories**, Zélie raises her army by successfully summoning the spirits of the dead who have perished in this arena. The spirits sink the other ships, but a cannonball lands on Zélie's boat and it, too, starts to go down. As Zélie's magic wanes, she breaks a promise she made years ago to her mother and uses dangerous blood magic. The **stakes are raised** but so is the magic. The rush of power is intense but draining. As her newly created army of spirits saves the sinking boat, Zélie begins to drown.

Tzain jumps in to save her, and Amari (in her own **false victory**) finds the courage to defend Zélie against an enemy captain by plunging a sword into his chest. The team is declared the winners and the sunstone is handed over. But Zélie feels how false this victory is when she thinks about how many people died. "We may have triumphed but this is no victory" (255).

In a **shift from wants to needs**, Zélie looks at Amari and for the first time doesn't see King Saran or Inan; she sees a warrior. And when she takes hold of the sunstone and feels her power electrified, she knows she could now easily take revenge on all the spectators who cheered on the slaughter, but also knows, "That's not what Sky Mother wants. It's not what these spirts need" (256). Slowly, Zélie is letting go of her anger and thirst for revenge and realizing where her true power and strength lie.

In a final nod to their victory, Zélie sees Sky Mother smiling down at her. With the sunstone, scroll, and dagger in her possession, Zélie knows she now has everything she needs to fulfill her destiny and bring magic back.

Midpoint (cont'd)/Amari (260–264)

In the aftermath of the competition, Amari has a personal Midpoint of her own. She feels conflicted about the people still cheering for them in the streets, calling her the Lionaire. She still feels like a coward and an impostor, and she can't shake the loss of all of those deaths.

She considers turning herself in to the guards and going home to the palace, knowing it would free her from danger. But in her own **shift from wants to needs,** she decides against it. She escaped a prison when she left the palace, and she will not return to it. She might have left the palace for Binta, but she's staying for herself. Tzain is glad that she's staying and admits he wants her here, and they share a tender moment as their **love story ramps up.**

Bad Guys Close In/Zélie and Inan (265–397)

Inan and Zélie's beat sheets merge shortly after the Midpoint, when Inan catches up to the group in the Gombe River Valley. He and Zélie face off—Zélie with her staff and Inan with his sword. The fight is interrupted by Amari's scream, and they realize that both of their siblings—Tzain and Amari—have been kidnapped.

Bad Guys Close In/Amari (278–397)

Amari is thrust into a **downward path** as masked men capture her and Tzain and carry them to a nearby divîner camp in the forest. They're interrogated about the scroll and accused of stealing it. Kwame (soon revealed to be a Burner) and Zu (a Healer) don't believe Amari (a noble) when she swears they're on a mission to bring back magic. The clock is ticking down to the centennial solstice. Zélie has five days to perform the ritual or they'll never be able to bring magic back. Tzain is tortured for information, but he and Amari are able to escape when someone attacks the camp.

Bad Guys Close In (cont'd)/Zélie and Inan (281–397)

Despite now having the same goal (to rescue their siblings), Zélie experiences a **downward path** as she struggles with her confidence and her destiny, while Inan experiences an **upward path** as he opens up more to his own magic, learning how to wield it, realizing the truth about his father's brutality, and discovering the kind of leader he wants to be (with Zélie's help).

Regardless, both of them wrestle with their **internal bad guys**, which are closing in. After Inan experiences Zélie's memory of the king's men killing her mother, he realizes he no longer shares his father's vision for Orïsha and vows to be a different kind of king. But despite this rejection, he's still afraid of his own magic (after what he did to Kaea) and refuses to use it. Meanwhile, Zélie is still fighting to overcome her rage, evident by the fact that she brutally attacks a boy associated with the men who took her brother.

Once Zélie and Inan find the camp where Amari and Tzain are being held, they plan an ambush using Zélie's army of the dead. As the time to attack looms, Zélie and Inan grow closer. They confide in each other but still clash in their prejudices: Inan might disagree with his father's oppression, but he still sees magic as a dangerous curse that must be stopped, while Zélie tries to make him understand that magic is the only thing that gives her people power.

When Inan confesses that he hates his magic and thinks of it as a poison, Zélie figures out that the pawn he keeps in his pocket—a gift from his father—is made of majicite (a metal that burns divîners and maji), which is why it always hurt to touch it. His magic has literally been causing him pain because of his ties to his father. He drops the pawn (a symbol of his loyalty) in the dirt, rejecting his father and his upbringing. And that's when his father's creed (and Inan's Theme Stated)—"duty before self"—starts to dissolve. He promises Zélie that when they break into the camp and get the scroll back, she can have it, releasing his primary goal to stop magic from returning.

Inan and Zélie attack the camp. Zélie uses the power of the sunstone to summon animations. For the first time, Inan sees magic not as a curse but as something thrilling. But everything goes awry when Zélie is shot by an arrow and Kwame, the Burner, fights back with fire. Inan saves Zélie's life, proving to truly be on her side. The battle is stopped by Zu, who now realizes that Amari has been telling the truth and that Zélie and Inan are one of them.

Bad Guys Close In (cont'd)/All (338–397)

For the first time, the beat sheets of all three heroes merge as they reunite at the camp, which they soon learn has become a sanctuary for divîners. These chapters leading to the All Is Lost are full of **bouncing balls**. In a moment of personal growth, Zélie forgives Zu for torturing her brother, knowing she would have done the same. But her confidence wavers when Zu offers to hand over the leadership of the camp to Zélie, who has been chosen by the gods. Zélie thinks, "*I can't lead these people. I can barely lead myself*" (343).

Zu, Kwame, and the others agree to help Zélie with her quest to bring back magic, but first they will have a celebration to honor the Sky Mother and awaken the magic in the rest of the divîners at the camp.

In the lead-up to the celebration, Zélie teaches Inan how to embrace and control his magic, bringing them closer together. But a near kiss ignites a fight between Zélie and Tzain, who accuses her of being brainwashed by Inan. The fight escalates, and Zélie, unable to control her magic, almost kills her brother. In the aftermath, Zélie begins to doubt her quest. What if she brings back magic and it falls into the wrong hands? She and Inan have switched viewpoints; now it's Inan who tries to convince her that magic can be good. He imagines a world where magic unites the kingdom instead of tearing it apart. Swept up in this idealized vision, the two share a passionate kiss, only to be interrupted by the sound of a horn.

All Is Lost/All (397–403)

The king's soldiers arrive, demanding the scroll and Zélie. Zu insists that they have neither. In our first of many **whiffs of death** in this beat, Zu is shot by an arrow and the guards unleash a massacre. As Zélie desperately tries to find her brother, Kwame uses blood magic to enhance his Burner powers and fight back. The village erupts in flames, but sadly, so does Kwame. Zélie watches the self-sacrifice in horror, realizing, "We will never have peace. *As long as we don't have magic, they will never treat us with respect*" (403). Just as Amari and Tzain appear astride Nailah, ready to save Zélie, she's grabbed by one of the guards.

Dark Night of the Soul and Break Into 3/Amari (404–406)

Zélie's capture splits up the group and their beat sheets. Amari walks through the sea of corpses in the scorched camp, lamenting everything that has happened, while Tzain sobs over his lost sister. Amari is certain the king will keep Zélie alive to get information about the artifacts. In a **Dark Night Epiphany**, Amari pictures a map in her father's war room with the military bases marked, and suddenly she knows the guards took Zélie to a fortress outside of Gombe.

She Breaks Into 3 with an **Act 3 goal** of rescuing Zélie and a surge of confidence and courage: "I nod, for once not fearing the fight. I was the Lionaire once. For Tzain and Zélie, I shall be her again" (406).

Dark Night of the Soul/Zélie (407–459)

Meanwhile, Zélie is in a prison cell, wallowing in despair over their defeat. Inan enters and begs Zélie to tell him how to destroy the scroll so she can live, but she refuses, saying she'd rather die than give up on magic. After seeing what Kwame did in the forest, however, Inan is still afraid of it and is convinced he can save Orïsha without magic.

King Saran himself enters, and the superhero and nemesis face off for the first time. Saran threatens Zélie, but she does not back down. With majicite chains binding her, though, she has only her words for weapons now: "Your mistake wasn't keeping us alive. It was thinking we'd never fight back" (416).

Dark Night of the Soul/Inan (409–437)

Inan is back in his uniform, back to being his father's son (**return to the familiar**), but he's inspired by Zélie's passion and bravery, standing up to his father when he never could. He still hasn't told his father about his magic. When Zélie is tortured, Inan tries to stop it, only to be called a coward by his father and thrown out of the cell, forced to listen helplessly to her screams.

Zélie breaks and tells Saran that her brother has the scroll. The king now plans to use Zélie as leverage to get the scroll back from Tzain and destroy it. Then he will kill her and parade her body around Orïsha as a warning against rebellion. When Inan proposes using Zélie as an ambassador to unite Orïsha instead, his father gives him an unexpected hug, saying he'll make a good king one day. In a **Dark Night Epiphany**, Inan realizes that his father's approval—the thing he's always wanted—now feels empty.

Break Into 3 /Inan (437)

Inan makes the decision to defy his father and free Zélie (**Act 3 goal**), proving he's learned his theme by putting himself (and Zélie) before his duty.

Finale/Amari (423–514)

Meanwhile, Amari's Finale is already in motion.

In an impressive plotting puzzle spanning the final one hundred pages of the novel, the beat sheets of our three heroes diverge and collide as we track not one, but *three* Five-Point Finales. Are you ready for this? Here we go!

POINT 1: GATHERING THE TEAM. Before Amari can rescue Zélie, she needs help. She and Tzain travel to a bar in Gombe to recruit divîners to touch the scroll and join the quest to free Zélie and bring magic back to all of Orïsha. But it's not an easy feat. Because she's a noble, the divîners are distrustful of her and kick her out of the bar. In a moment of Act 3 **synthesis**, she channels her mother's confidence (Act 1 world) and the strength she's learned from her quest with Zélie (Act 2 world) and reveals herself to be Princess Amari, vowing to one day be the queen of Orïsha and fix the mistakes of her father. Her words work. Amari has her team. But not just any team. A *maji* team.

Finale/Inan (437–509)

POINT 1: GATHERING THE TEAM. Inan waits until after his father is asleep and sneaks into Zélie's cell. The sight of her limp, nearly lifeless body guts him. He now sees that it's his father who is the animal, not the maji.

POINT 2: EXECUTING THE PLAN. As a Connector, he can feel her pain as he carries her out of the cell. She's bleeding badly from the torture and tells him to leave her behind. But he won't. His Act 3 goal is to get her out, and he's determined to succeed. Even as an explosion blasts through the wall of the fortress.

Finale (cont'd)/Amari (423–514)

POINT 2: EXECUTING THE PLAN. It's a storming of the fortress! Amari attacks with her team of newly awakened maji. While others create a diversion with makeshift explosives, Amari, Tzain, and the maji move through the fortress, a Burner knocking guards back with fire, a Welder melting walls, and a Cancer spreading disease. When Saran appears and scolds his daughter, Amari thinks about fighting him but ultimately decides to let him go. She vows to fight him one day, but today, she's here for Zélie.

Finale (cont'd)/Inan (437–509)

POINT 3: HIGH TOWER SURPRISE. The beat sheets continue to weave as Amari's Executing the Plan becomes Inan's High Tower Surprise, stopping his own plan in its tracks. As he watches Amari's maji army take down guards with their magic, he realizes his father was right. Magic is too dangerous to let it come back. He is torn between duty and his love for Zélie. For now, he chooses Zélie, vowing to find a way to stop magic after she's safe. He hands Zélie over to Amari and Tzain. Amari asks Inan to come with them, but he refuses, knowing this isn't his fight and he's not really on their side. Another destiny awaits him: the fight to save Orïsha.

Dark Night of the Soul (cont'd)/Zélie (407–459)

Despite everything happening around her, Zélie is still in her Dark Night of the Soul, still locked in the pain and agony of her defeat, a passive participant in the action. And it's here that we learn why: Zélie's magic is gone.

After finding a safe place to rest, Zélie grieves her lost magic, feeling useless. She tries to **return to the familiar** by escaping into Inan's dreamscape and kissing him, but it doesn't work. Meanwhile, she tells no one that her magic is gone. With the centennial solstice only a day away, she is resigned to giving up. Without her magic, she can't perform the ritual to bring magic back. All hope is lost. When Tzain suggests they run away with Baba and find safety outside of Orïsha's borders, Zélie agrees.

Break Into 3/Zélie (459)

But as Zélie opens her mouth to announce her decision, she can't speak. She realizes this can't be it, after everything they've done. Sky Mother chose her for a reason, and she has to believe that she wouldn't abandon Zélie now. She has to have *faith*. "We're going . . . I don't care what it takes. I won't let them win" (459).

Finale/Zélie (460–523)

POINT 1: GATHERING THE TEAM. To get to the sacred island to perform the ritual (**Act 3 goal**), they need a boat. Zélie, Tzain, and Amari (who, remember, is still in the Executing the Plan point of her Finale!) travel to Jimeta, a lawless city without guards, and commission a group of mercenaries led by Roën (a pickpocket Zélie met at the divîner camp earlier) and secure themselves a fast boat . . . and a team.

POINT 2: EXECUTING THE PLAN. Zélie and Amari's Finales merge as their "plans" become one: Storm the island! And perform the ritual.

But it's not easy. On the journey, they encounter King Saran's warships, en route to the same island to stop Zélie. They peacefully overtake one of the ships—without any blood spilled—which allows them to sneak onto the island undetected.

Through it all, Zélie wonders if Inan is on one of those other warships.

Finale (cont'd)/Inan (444–509)

POINT 4: DIG DEEP DOWN. Inan stares over the railing of one of the warships, feeling trapped between his love for Zélie (who is on a mission to bring magic back) and his duty to save his country (which he believes can be done only if magic is destroyed). It's in this sub-beat that he will finally have to decide once and for all and prove whether he's truly learned his theme. Will he choose duty or self?

He chooses duty, vowing to put Orïsha over Zélie and revealing his journey to be a negative arc. (See page 132 for more on negative arcs.) Instead of overcoming his flaw, he's succumbing to it, reverting to the antagonist he was at the start. Except now, he's even more dangerous to Zélie, because she's let him in. He knows her secrets. Which is why he's able to say to his father with such confidence, "I know how we can get the scroll back" (476). The word "we" is the nail in the coffin of his unlearned theme and launches us into Inan's new plan.

Finale (cont'd)/Zélie and Amari (460–523)

POINT 2: EXECUTING THE PLAN. While Inan works on his *new* plan, Zélie and Amari are still tackling their original plan. As they continue their journey toward the sacred island, Zélie finally confesses to Amari that her magic is gone. Amari falters for a moment, wondering if they should turn back. But her new bravery and her faith in the "superhero" inspires her (and Zélie) to surge on.

They sneak onto the island in uniforms stolen from their captive soldiers. After Roën's mercenaries create a diversion to draw the king's guards away, Zélie, Amari, and the rest of the team enter the magnificent temple. Zélie says one last prayer to the gods to help her before removing the three artifacts and preparing to attempt the ritual. But . . .

POINT 3: HIGH TOWER SURPRISE. Saran and his guards step out of the shadows, along with Inan, who carries a majicite blade. Zélie knows immediately that he has betrayed her, but worse than that: they have Baba. They offer to trade his life for the artifacts.

Zélie blames herself for trusting Inan but knows she can't let her father die. She hands over the scroll and the sunstone before realizing that Inan has never seen the bone dagger. Thinking fast, she gives him a decoy instead. As the trade is made, Zélie accepts the fact that they have lost. She was never meant to bring back magic. The gods chose wrong.

Then, Baba is shot in the chest by an arrow (**team member sacrifice**). As he bleeds out, Zélie sees visions of his life and feels his spirit running through her, deeper than any magic she's felt before. Her powers are restored, stronger than ever.

The guards charge at her, and she easily kills them with her renewed magic, launching a battle between her team and the king's guards. At first, all she feels is rage and revenge, but then she hears Baba's voice in her head, reminding her of why she's here. To bring magic back.

Finale (cont'd) and Final Image/Inan (444–509)

POINT 5: THE EXECUTION OF THE NEW PLAN. In Inan's final chapter, we see how the rest of his new plan plays out. As he watches Zélie attack the guards, he feels her heartbreak over her father and reveals that Baba was never supposed to die. All Inan has been trying to do is make Orïsha a better place. But he knows that to do that he still has to destroy the scroll and keep magic from returning.

Getting an idea, Inan taunts Zélie until her rage gets the better of her and she sends her shadowy magic hurtling toward him. Just in time, he holds up the scroll, and her magic turns it to ash. Here the heroes' Five-Point Finales intersect yet again: Inan's victory is Zélie's failure (and a continuation of her High Tower Surprise). Without the scroll, she's unable to complete the ritual. Inan celebrates with his father, but when a mercenary targets the king, Inan reacts instinctively, killing the attacker with his magic. King Saran realizes the truth: not only is his son a maji, he's the one who killed Commander Kaea. His father plunges his sword into Inan.

Inan's Final Image of the book is seeing the fear and hatred on his father's face as he dies. His father's last words to him are "You are no son of mine" (509).

Finale (cont'd) and Final Image/Amari (423–514)

Amari's Finale splits off from Zélie's as she narrates her final two chapters.

POINT 4: DIG DEEP DOWN. After witnessing her father killing his own son, Amari feels like the sword is piercing her too. She thinks about how her father used to make her and Inan fight each other, believing it would make them stronger. In her mind, she sees her mother, Tzain, Binta, and everyone who tried to fight back against Saran but lost. It gives her the strength to do what she must do . . .

POINT 5: THE EXECUTION OF THE NEW PLAN. Amari accuses her father of being the real monster and raises her sword to him. They spar, but he is no match for the Lionaire! When her father trips, Amari has the perfect chance to end it, but hesitates, realizing she would be no better than him if she killed him. But her father does not show her the same mercy, striking her across the back. She realizes she has no choice. Her father is her **shard of glass**, and he must be removed for good.

In her Final Image, she plunges the sword into his heart, and as he dies, she tells him she will make a far better ruler than him. Amari's first book transformation is complete.

Finale (cont'd)/Zélie (460–523)

POINT 4: DIG DEEP DOWN. Zélie tries desperately to repair the scroll, but it doesn't work, and she can't remember the incantation inscribed on it that she needs to perform the ritual. The centennial solstice begins, filling the temple with light. She's about to lose her chance to fulfill her destiny forever.

Thinking of the connection she felt to Baba when he died (which restored her magic), she wonders if there's another way to reconnect herself with Sky Mother. Perhaps through her mother's ancestors, reaching all the way back to the beginning of magic. Using the bone dagger, she slices through her palms and clutches the sunstone with her bleeding hands, offering the ultimate sacrifice and begging for her ancestors help.

POINT 5: THE EXECUTION OF THE NEW PLAN. It works. She feels her ancestors flowing through her. She feels like she's being torn apart, but she keeps going. The ancestors chant an incantation and she fights through her screams to recite the words, racing against the solstice light that is almost gone.

The sunstone shatters and explodes with light. Zélie witnesses the origin of the gods and realizes that magic connects them all. "We are all children of blood and bone" (519). As the ritual finishes, Zélie feels death coming for her. She hears her mother's voice tell her that she's always been by her side and always will be. Zélie wants to stay there with her mother, where she feels safe, but her mother insists that it's not yet her time. Orïsha still needs her. "It's not over, little Zél. It's only just begun" (523).

Final Image/Zélie (524)

In the epilogue, Zélie wakes aboard a rowboat with Amari, Tzain, and Roën. When she asks if magic is back, no one answers, and Zélie assumes she has failed. But then Amari holds up a hand, which is now swirling with vibrant blue light, and Zélie notices there is a streak of white in Amari's hair. It would seem that magic was not only returned to the maji, but given to others as well, which makes Zélie's blood run cold.

The meaning is clear: Zélie succeeded, but Orïsha is far from safe. Just as Zélie's mother said, "It's not over . . . It's only just begun."

Book 2, anyone?

WHY IS THIS A SUPERHERO?

Children of Blood and Bone contains all three elements of a successful Superhero story:

- **A POWER:** One of many divîners destined to become maji, Zélie is special because she's the one chosen to bring back magic to the kingdom of Orïsha. As the mamaláwo, she alone can perform the ritual and restore the maji's connection to the Sky Mother.
- **A NEMESIS:** King Saran is not a maji. He's threatened by magic and does everything he can to quash it. He's worked hard and tirelessly to banish magic from the world (destroying the artifacts and conducting the Raid eleven years before). Now he hunts down Zélie with tenacity, threatened by her mission and her ability to bring magic back.
- **A CURSE:** Divîners are treated terribly, cast down, beaten, enslaved, and heavily taxed. It's the price of being special, and Zélie feels it harshly, having lost her mother to the Raid.

Cat's Eye View

For quick reference, here's a brief overview of this novel's beat sheet.

OPENING IMAGE/ZÉLIE: Zélie, a divîner, learns to spar with the staff from Mama Agba. When the king's guards arrive to collect a tax on divîners, she loses her temper (flaw), and violence nearly breaks out.

THEME STATED/ZÉLIE: "When your opponent has no honor, you must fight in different ways, smarter ways," Mama Agba tells Zélie on page 18, hinting at the lesson of nonviolence and faith that Zélie will learn.

SETUP/ZÉLIE: Zélie's Baba nearly drowns trying to catch enough fish to pay Zélie's divîner tax so Zélie doesn't end up in the stocks. Zélie and her brother Tzain head to the market to try to sell a recently caught sailfish.

OPENING IMAGE AND SETUP/AMARI: Amari has tea with her critical mother in the palace, where she feels like a prisoner. Her only friend is a servant named Binta who has been summoned to the throne room.

CATALYST, DEBATE, AND BREAK INTO 2/AMARI: After seeing Binta touch a mysterious scroll that awakens her magic and then be murdered by the king, a grief-stricken Amari steals the scroll and escapes the palace.

THEME STATED/AMARI: *"The maji will come for you. When they do, you must be prepared"* (40). King Saran has been grooming Amari to be a warrior, but she's never felt courageous. Her personal journey is about finding that courage but using it against the *real* enemy.

SETUP (CONT'D)/ZÉLIE: After she sells the sailfish, guards barge into the marketplace, and Amari begs Zélie to help her. They escape.

OPENING IMAGE AND SETUP/INAN: After failing to catch an unnamed fugitive who escaped with a divîner in the marketplace, Inan returns to the palace to face his father and thinks about the divîner (Zélie) who bested him earlier.

THEME STATED/INAN: "Duty before self." Inan must break free from his father's brainwashing about the maji and accept the fact that he is one, putting himself before duty.

CATALYST/INAN: The king reveals the identity of the fugitive to be Amari, Inan's sister.

CATALYST/ZÉLIE: Amari shows Zélie the scroll and claims it can bring back magic. Zélie touches it and feels magic awaken within her, but pushes it down.

DEBATE/INAN: When the king explains that Amari stole a scroll that can bring back magic, Inan debates what he will do about it.

BREAK INTO 2/INAN: Inan discovers the name (Zélie) and village (Ilorin) of the divîner who helped Amari escape and vows to track her down, find the scroll, and bring Amari back (Act 2 goal).

DEBATE/ZÉLIE: Is it real? Is magic really back? They bring the scroll to Mama Agba, who is awakened as a Seer. She has a vision of Zélie, Tzain, and Amari bringing magic back. Inan and his guards arrive and burn the village.

BREAK INTO 2/ZÉLIE: Zélie accepts the quest to bring magic back and takes off with Amari and Tzain.

B STORY/ZÉLIE AND AMARI: Amari believes in Zélie's power and destiny the strongest, providing support when faith wavers. Zélie inspires Amari to be more courageous.

FUN AND GAMES/INAN: After failing to capture Zélie and Amari, Inan gets a vision and uses it to find Zélie, but she continues to evade him. As his own magic awakens, he fights to suppress it.

B STORY/ZÉLIE AND INAN: As love interests, the two help each other learn their themes, each challenging the prejudices they have against the other.

FUN AND GAMES/ZÉLIE AND AMARI: After journeying to Sokoto for supplies, they reach the ruined temple of Chândomblé, where Zélie learns from a sêntaro that she has been chosen by the Sky Mother to perform the sacred ritual to bring magic back using three sacred artifacts, two of which she has. They track down the third, the sunstone, in Ibeji but will have to win it in a deadly competition.

MIDPOINT/INAN: After failing to apprehend Zélie and Amari (false defeat), Inan actively uses his magic (no longer resisting it) to track them down, but then accidentally kills a commander who had threatened to report him to the king (stakes are raised).

MIDPOINT/ZÉLIE AND AMARI: In a deadly Midpoint competition, Zélie, Amari, and Tzain battle other boats in a water-filled arena to win the sunstone (false victory), but Zélie had to use dangerous blood magic to do it (stakes are raised).

MIDPOINT/AMARI: Amari thinks of all the death in the arena and considers going home, but decides to stay to prove to herself that she's courageous (shift from wants to needs).

BAD GUYS CLOSE IN/ZÉLIE AND INAN: Inan catches up to the group, and he and Zélie face off before Tzain and Amari are kidnapped. Using Zélie's magic, they storm the camp where they're being held.

BAD GUYS CLOSE IN/AMARI: Amari and Tzain are brought to a secret divîner camp. They swear they are on a quest to bring magic back, but the leader, Zu, doesn't believe them. Tzain is tortured. When Zélie and Inan attack, Zu realizes they were telling the truth.

BAD GUYS CLOSE IN/ALL: As Zélie, Amari, and Inan join forces with the divîner camp, a celebration is planned to honor the Sky Mother and awaken more divîners. Inan and Zélie become closer and share a kiss.

ALL IS LOST/ALL: The king's guards arrive and unleash a massacre on the camp, killing many. Amari and Tzain escape, but Zélie is captured.

DARK NIGHT OF THE SOUL AND BREAK INTO 3/AMARI: Mourning all the deaths, Amari realizes she knows where her father is holding Zélie (Dark Night Epiphany) and vows to rescue her.

DARK NIGHT OF THE SOUL/ZÉLIE: Zélie is tortured in a prison cell. Inan begs her to tell him how to destroy the scroll, but she refuses.

DARK NIGHT OF THE SOUL/INAN: Inan tries to stop the torture, only to be called a coward by his father. He is forced to listen to Zélie scream.

BREAK INTO 3/INAN: Inan decides to defy his father and help Zélie escape, putting himself before duty.

FINALE/INAN: Inan sneaks into Zélie's cell and carries her out.

FINALE/AMARI: Amari gathers more divîners to help. They storm the fortress where Zélie is being kept and, with Inan's help, rescue her.

DARK NIGHT OF THE SOUL (CONT'D)/ZÉLIE: After the torture, Zélie's magic is gone. She is ready to give up on her quest.

BREAK INTO 3/ZÉLIE: But before she can announce her decision, she realizes that Sky Mother chose her for a reason, which renews her faith. She vows to travel to the sacred island and perform the ritual to bring magic back for good (Act 3 goal).

FINALE (CONT'D)/INAN: Torn between his love for Zélie and his duty to his country, Inan decides that Orïsha can be safe only if magic is gone. He chooses to put duty before self (reverse arc) and stop Zélie from completing her quest.

FINALE/ZÉLIE: Zélie, Amari, Tzain, and their team acquire a boat and travel to the island. They evade the king's boats and sneak into the temple, only to be stopped by the king and Inan, who have kidnapped Baba. Baba is killed, but his spirit restores Zélie's magic.

FINALE (CONT'D) AND FINAL IMAGE/INAN: Inan tricks Zélie into destroying the scroll, preventing her from performing the ritual. But when his magic is accidentally revealed, the king kills him, declaring, "You are no son of mine" (509).

FINALE (CONT'D) AND FINAL IMAGE/AMARI: After witnessing her father killing Inan, Amari realizes who the true monster is and kills her father, removing her shard of glass for good.

FINALE (CONT'D)/ZÉLIE: After failing to repair the scroll, Zélie calls on her ancestors to help her complete the ritual. She feels like she's being torn apart, and when she sees her mother, believes herself to be dead. Her mother tells her it's not her time, as there is still much for her to do.

FINAL IMAGE/ZÉLIE: Book 1 in the series ends with Zélie awakening on a boat with Amari and Tzain and asking whether magic is back. Amari reveals a swirling blue light around her hand and a white streak in her hair. Magic has been not only returned to the maji, but given to others as well.

Golden Fleece
Let's Hit the Road!

Grab your maps and your GPS; it's time to go on the road! This genre is all about the destinations that lure us out of our comfort zone and the journeys that change us along the way.

Once upon a time there was a hero named Jason (basically a prince) who led a team called the Argonauts (basically a bunch of sailors) on an epic quest to find and steal the Golden Fleece (basically some really fancy wool). Along the way, Jason and his team encountered all sorts of obstacles and challenges (think wind fairies, dangerous rocks, and boxing matches with kings) before finally securing the fleece and heading home. If you recognized this tale as the ancient Greek myth of Jason and the Argonauts, I'm impressed. (I had to look it up.) But this is not just a well-known ancient myth; it's basically the touchstone for one of the most beloved story types of all time: the road trip!

Road trip stories are extremely popular in young adult fiction. Possibly because teen readers are just starting to explore their own independence. They have driver's licenses! (Or friends with driver's licenses.) They have access to cars! (Or have to steal the keys while they're parents are asleep.) They finally have freedom! (Or the semblance of it.) It's no wonder teens love reading about other teens on the road.

But don't be fooled by the term "road trip." Yes, there's the conventional definition of a road trip: (music, snacks, pitstops at weird restaurants shaped like dinosaurs), but there's also the less conventional definition: basically *any* journey (physical or metaphorical) with a set destination or prize at the end, which means we can lump in quests, heists, treasure hunts, tournaments, and competitions as well.

Now things start to get fun.

Because when you think of a road trip (conventional or not), you don't think of the destination itself. You think of the *road*. The adventure. The people. The unexpected detours. And mostly, you think about what you gain along the way—wisdom, experience, knowledge, and of course, our favorite: personal growth!

In other words, all stories of this genre embody that tired old cliché: it's not the destination, it's the journey!

This is true, but it's not exactly new.

Which is why it's our job, like with all the story genres, to take this tired old cliché and make it fresh. Make it unique. Make it sing.

Think about great young adult novels like *Salt to the Sea* by Ruth Sepetys, *Throne of Glass* by Sarah J. Maas, *The Inheritance Games* by Jennifer Lynn Barnes, *Nyxia* by Scott Reintgen, *Warcross* by Marie Lu, and *The Gilded Wolves* by Roshani Chokshi. These stories span time, genre, and space (some quite literally) and yet, amazingly, at their core they are the same. They all feature a hero (or group of heroes) who goes on an adventure to a destination and winds up transformed.

The distinguishing mark of a Golden Fleece is a defined destination. You'll often see it established as early as the Setup or Catalyst—that faraway landmark, prize, treasure, birthright, trophy, or victory that shines like a beacon in the dark, luring the hero out of their status quo world (usually away from the safety of home) and on to a great adventure!

If this sounds like a journey you want to embark on, make sure you include the three essential genre ingredients to make your Golden Fleece truly golden: (1) a **road,** (2) a **team,** and (3) a **prize.**

Let's get this trip on the road and see what's what.

A ROAD

The road is where our journey takes place. It's the primary setting, and also quite often the **premise** of the novel. A teen boy genius hits the open road for the summer with his best friend after his nineteenth girlfriend named Katherine dumps him (*An Abundance of Katherines* by John Green), or a heartbroken teen girl joins her superstar country-singer best friend on a twenty-four-city tour (*Open Road Summer* by Emery Lord). But the "road" doesn't have to be a literal road. It can be a journey across a city (*Nick & Norah's Infinite Playlist* by Rachel Cohn and David Levithan), a journey across land and sea (*Salt to the Sea*), or a journey across deep space (*Nyxia*). It can be a treasure hunt through a mysterious mansion estate, like in the fantasy novel *The Gilded Wolves* and the contemporary mystery novel *The Inheritance Games*. It can be an adventure through a legendary game or competition, like in the sci-fi novel *Warcross* and the fantasy novel *Caraval* by Stephanie Garber. The road can even be metaphorical.

But because the road is the premise of the novel, the hero (and their team) should probably be *on* the road by the time the Fun and Games hit so you can deliver on the promise of that premise. Which is why in most Golden Fleece novels the Catalyst is either an event that calls the hero onto the road and into the adventure (like the invitation to compete to be the King's Champion in *Throne of Glass*), or an event that somehow *leads* to the road/adventure. Like Avery inheriting Tobias Hawthorne's fortune, which comes with a catch: she must move into the dead man's sprawling mansion, which puts her smack dab in the middle of one of his infamous puzzles.

Either way, by the Break Into 2, we're off! The journey has begun, the games are afoot, the challenge is on! We are on "the road."

The key to defining your own road is the ability to demarcate progress. How will this road be tracked? That's a defining characteristic of the Golden Fleece. Will there be literal road markers and stops along the way (like in *An Abundance of Katherines* and *Open Road Summer*)? Will there be clues and puzzles for the hero to solve (like in *The Inheritance Games*)? Will there be challenges, rounds, or games for the hero to win (like in *Throne of Glass* and *Warcross*)? Or will it be something else? The ability to track the journey is important, because as we demarcate progress along the road, we're also subtly but surely demarcating *growth* in the hero. The closer they get to that final destination (the *external* goal), the more they're changing and evolving (the *internal* goal).

Another thing to consider when crafting your road are the obstacles that the hero and their team will encounter. *Obviously*, this road can't be an easy one. The journey must be full of challenges and setbacks and obstacles. One very common obstacle in Golden Fleece stories is the **road apple**; it usually comes right when victory is in sight (perhaps as part of the All Is Lost beat or the High Tower Surprise in the Five-Point Finale). The road apple is an unexpected roadblock (literal or figurative!) that stops the journey in its tracks. Like the explosion in the Phoenix Riders' dorm in *Warcross* that injures Emika and pulls her out of the game right before the championships. Or Caelena's encounter with the bloodthirsty ridderak and the competitor who's been summoning it right before the final duel in *Throne of Glass*.

But it's a very *purposeful* roadblock, because it forces the hero and their team to look more closely at their strategy, repair any bridges they've burned among themselves, and dig deep down to find their true skills and strengths.

Speaking of the hero's team . . .

A TEAM

The team that joins your hero on their road can be any size you want. It can be large, like the seven refugees en route to board the *Wilhelm Gustloff* ship in *Salt to the Sea*, the four outcasts who join Séverin to seek the Horus Eye in *The Gilded Wolves*, or the Hawthorne brothers who team up with Avery to uncover the secrets hidden within their grandfather's mansion in *The Inheritance Games*. You can also have a team of just two (called a "Buddy Fleece"), like in *An Abundance of Katherines* and *Nick and Norah's Infinite Playlist*. Or your hero can fly solo ("Solo Fleece") and encounter helpers along the way, like Celaena in *Throne of Glass* or Emika in *Warcross* (who has literal teammates in the game, but none of them know about her true mission to track down the hacker until Act 3).

Who you choose to promote to team member status in your own Golden Fleece is not a decision to take lightly. Each of these characters should have a specific purpose on the journey, whether that be a special skill, strength, expertise, wisdom, or experience they possess, or even a more thematic purpose. Chances are one of these teammates is going to play the role of the B Story character and represent the theme of the novel.

Regardless of each team member's role, make sure that they each do have one, that it's unique (otherwise why do you need both characters?), and that it's something the hero doesn't already have. Why does Séverin need to bring four other people with him on the quest to find the Horus Eye in *The Gilded Wolves*? Well, because he needs Laila's gift for reading objects, Enrique's historical knowledge, and Zofia's and Tristan's different "forging" abilities (the power to create and manipulate things in the physical world). Why does Avery need the Hawthorne brothers in *The Inheritance Games*? Because they know the mansion (and their grandfather) far better than she does. At the same time, Avery's growing romantic interest in both Jameson and Grayson plays a thematic role in helping Avery learn an important lesson about her self-worth.

In other words, each team member must possess their own quirks, strengths, flaws, dreams, and possibly even side goals of their own. Which means, with larger teams, it can be difficult to introduce them all and not drag the pace of the story. Creativity and efficient writing are key. Ask yourself how you can introduce each character in a unique and memorable way, possibly making use of the same scene to set up more than one character, as opposed to having to write an entire scene for each member. And how can the scene reveal necessary details about the character(s) in a visual way?

Once your team is assembled, it's time to go after the Golden Fleece itself. Let's take a look at our third genre ingredient.

A PRIZE

The prize is the big goal of the story. It's what the hero and team are after from the moment they hit the road—the far-off destination that put them on the road to begin with. Like the road itself, it can come in many varieties:

To catch a hacker and earn a ten-million-dollar bounty (*Warcross*).

To win a place on the team that will descend to the planet Eden (*Nyxia*).

To secure a treasure (*The Gilded Wolves*).

To find an elusive punk rock concert (*Nick & Norah's Infinite Playlist*).

Or the prize can be more conceptual, like safety (*Salt to the Sea*).

In *Throne of Glass*, Sarah J. Maas merges two prizes together in a creative way. The title of King's Champion is the physical prize that, if won, will earn Celaena her freedom—a conceptual prize.

Whatever the prize, it must be compelling. It must call to the hero, team, and reader like a siren. It has to be enticing enough to pull the hero out of their status quo and onto the road and push them past all of those challenges and obstacles you've thrown in their path. And it has to be alluring enough to compel the reader to keep turning pages. Which means it must feel *primal*. Something we can all relate to, whether the novel is grounded in reality or not.

Even though very few of us will ever fight to become a King's Champion, we can relate to Celaena's desire for more freedom (*Throne of Glass*). Even though we might never get the chance to travel across the galaxy to be a hero on a far-off planet, we understand what it's like to want to prove our worth, *be* valuable, be chosen (*Nyxia*). And even though we might never be on the hunt for a powerful artifact in a nineteenth-century fantasy version of Paris, we can relate to the lure of treasure, power, and wealth (*The Gilded Wolves*).

The prize, however, is the ultimate example of fixing things the wrong way—setting off on a grand adventure for that one thing that the hero *thinks* will solve their problems, only to find that the problems were solved by something much more personal and profound.

In the end, ironically, the prize doesn't really matter. Because, as the tired old cliché reminds us over and over again, it's not the destination. It's the journey.

The prize sets the story in motion, gets us on the road, but it often has less value and/or meaning once it's actually achieved (or not achieved!). By the time Emika earns her bounty and uncovers the true identity of the hacker, Zero, the truth about her employer and his secret plans has changed Emika, teaching her an important lesson about seeing and recognizing *reality* in a largely *virtual* world. By the time Celaena wins the tournament and becomes the King's Champion, it's the friendships and personal connections she's made along the way that have left the most impact.

Even if the hero and team *don't* secure the prize, it's okay, because the prize is not what the story was really *about* anyway. One of the most resonating moments of this genre is when your hero realizes (along with readers) that the treasure they're after pales in comparison to the real treasure they've gained along the way: wisdom, heart, courage, friendship, or whatever other theme you've dreamed up for your story.

A final caution as you set off on your own road: this is a tricky genre to plot. When we read Golden Fleece tales done well, the storytelling feels seamless, straightforward, and even *easy* to replicate. Put them on a road, give them a team and a prize to go after and a lesson to learn. What could go wrong? As it turns out, a lot. About as much as *could* go wrong for your poor hero on that road. Because here's the thing no one tells you about writing road trips and heists and quests: every milestone that your hero reaches along the way, every event that happens, every person they encounter might *seem* unconnected and random at first but should actually be very much connected and very far from random. Ultimately, all of these external plot devices not only lead your hero further down the road but also lead them toward their ultimate realization and change.

Every clue Avery finds and solves in *The Inheritance Games* leads to or informs the next, but also subtly leads to and informs her personal growth. Every contest Calaena competes in leads her closer to the ultimate battle, while also teaching her more about her competitors and strengthening the relationships she's forming.

It's *all* connected. Like a carefully arranged string of dominos, one thing leads to the next, which leads to the next, all the way to the end of the road. Meanwhile, beneath the surface, these events are *also* moving your hero closer to their true goal: transformation.

If you can pull it off, you can truly call yourself a structure master. If you can't, keep trying, keep plotting, keep lining up those dominos until they fall just right. You'll get there. And I bet you'll learn a *lot* in the process. After all, it's not about the destination . . .

To recap: if you're thinking of writing a Golden Fleece novel, make sure your story includes these three essential ingredients:

- **A ROAD** spanning miles, oceans, time, space, a fantasy or virtual world, or even across town—so long as it demarcates growth and tracks the progress of your story in some way. It often includes a road apple that stops the journey in its tracks.
- **A TEAM** (or buddy) that helps guide the hero along the way. Usually, it's those who represent or possess things the hero lacks: skill, experience, or attitude. In the case of a Solo Fleece, the team usually consists of various helpers along the way.
- **A PRIZE** something primal that's sought after: getting home, securing a treasure, freedom, reaching an important destination, or gaining a birthright.

POPULAR YOUNG ADULT GOLDEN FLEECE NOVELS

Nick & Nora's Infinite Playlist by Rachel Cohn and
    David Levithan
An Abundance of Katherines by John Green
Heist Society by Ally Carter
Amy & Roger's Epic Detour by Morgan Matson
The Selection by Kiera Cass
In Honor by Jessi Kirby
Throne of Glass by Sarah J. Maas
Reunited by Hilary Weisman Graham

SIX OF CROWS

BY: Leigh Bardugo
STC GENRE: Golden Fleece
BOOK GENRE: Young adult fantasy
TOTAL PAGES: 462 (Square Fish paperback edition, 2018)

What happens when six criminals take on an impossible heist in a fantasy world? Well, when Leigh Bardugo is writing it, we get a delightful extravaganza of epic worldbuilding, flawless structure, memorable characters, and nonstop action. Not to mention a novel that has sold millions of copies and spawned a hit Netflix original series, *Shadow and Bone* (which combines multiple stories within Bardugo's bestselling Grishaverse novels). As all five POV heroes share the same overarching goal (the heist), this novel is a prime example of a single-track (team) beat sheet (for more on multiple POV beat sheets, see page 116). And although all heroes demonstrate growth, Inej's POV is given the most page time, and her transformation feels the most significant, making her a likely candidate for the novel's one true hero.

This story is truly a marvel of structure, so let's crack it open and see if we can glean some wisdom from master storyteller Leigh Bardugo.

Opening Image/World (3–14)

A new drug called jurda parem is being tested at Councilman Hoede's house. A Grisha named Anya is given the drug to amplify her powers as a Corporalnik healer. When Hoede orders a sergeant to cut off a boy's thumb (to see if Anya can heal it), Anya uses her enhanced power to control the sergeant's mind and compels him to shoot through the glass holding her captive. Hoede tries to have her restrained, and she tells his guards to "wait," freezing them in place. Then she commands Hoede to pick up the knife . . .

While this Opening Image isn't narrated by one of the novel's five primary narrators/heroes, it introduces us to the tone of the novel (dark and suspenseful) and the world of the novel (Ketterdam, one of the countries in Leigh Bardugo's expansive and immersive Grishaverse). The scene also provides context and stakes for the primary storyline that will soon join our five heroes together.

Opening Image/Team

We're introduced to three of our five heroes (Inej, Kaz, and Jesper) on the streets of Ketterdam as their gang (the Dregs) meets with a rival gang (the Black Tips) to discuss control of a lucrative territory called Fifth Harbor. Kaz, the leader of the Dregs, reveals a traitor among his gang and outsmarts the head of the Black Tips to turn the parley in his favor.

In this action-packed scene, we get a taste of life in the "Barrel" (the criminal underbelly of Ketterdam) and the gangs who fight over its turf, and we also learn a little more about Kaz, a cunning "businessman" who always seems to be one step ahead of everyone; Jesper, a sharpshooter who likes to gamble; and Inej (aka the "Wraith"), who's an expert with knives and whose acrobatic climbing skills make her an excellent spy. Inej owes a debt to Per Haskell (Kaz's superior), which she desperately **wants** to pay off so she can be a free woman and control her own destiny.

Setup (15–41)

As Kaz walks home from the parley, we learn the following about him:

- He walks with a limp and a cane due to an injury that's only hinted at.
- He's responsible for turning the Dregs into a powerful gang that others fear.
- He has a mysterious backstory involving someone named Jordie.

When Kaz senses Inej shadowing him, he confronts her, and we get a glimpse at their unique relationship. Kaz relies heavily on Inej as his "thief of secrets" (40), but we get a sense that his feelings for her might go deeper than that.

Catalyst (41–58)

Kaz is attacked in the street and passes out. He comes to, shackled to a chair, in the house of a wealthy merchant named Van Eck who has a proposition for Kaz. Van Eck and the merchant council want Kaz to rescue a Shu man named Bo Yul-Bayur, inventor of the drug jurda parem. A young Grisha—a Tidemaker—demonstrates the drug's capabilities by walking *through* a wall, and Van Eck explains that the drug enables the Tidemaker to change his own state from solid to gas. "No vault or fortress will ever be safe again . . . financial markets would be thrown into chaos. The world economy would collapse," Van Eck explains, establishing the stakes should word of the drug get out (49).

When Van Eck tells Kaz that Yul-Bayur is being held prisoner in the Ice Court in Fjerda, Kaz laughs at the impossibility of the rescue. The Ice Court is impenetrable. But Van Eck offers him twenty million kruge (an exorbitant amount of money), and Kaz thinks about how much he could do with that money. He negotiates the price up to thirty million kruge, and Van Eck agrees. The Golden Fleece **prize** is established.

Theme Stated (57)

As Kaz negotiates, Van Eck, disgusted by Kaz's greed, says, "I do wonder what a boy of your intelligence might have amounted to under different circumstances."

This novel explores how our past traumas turn us into who we are. And even though the statement is directed at Kaz, each team member's shadowy past has shaped them into the criminal they are today and will fuel their motivations for taking on this impossible heist.

For Kaz specifically, as we'll soon learn, that motivation is not greed, but revenge against a man named Pekka Rollins (**wants**) who conned Kaz and his brother Jordie years ago, leading to Jordie's death.

The question, however, is whether our five heroes will choose to break free from the chains of their pasts or continue to let those chains hold them captive.

Debate (59–118)

As Kaz remarked in the Catalyst, "He'd need a very specialized team, a desperate team that wouldn't balk at the real possibility that they'd never come back from this job" (51). So who will make up our Golden Fleece **team**? That's the subject of the novel's Debate.

First up is Inej, who is surprised when Kaz lets her choose whether to join the crew. As an indenture to Per Haskell, her assignments are usually mandatory. During her own personal Debate, we learn that Inej is the only person allowed to see Kaz without the gloves he always wears and that *her* feelings for *him* might also go deeper than she wants to admit.

Next, Kaz recruits Nina, a Heartrender Grisha who specializes in emotions. She agrees to join the crew only after Kaz tells her that he'll also be recruiting a man named Matthias, a Fjerdan Druskëlle (witch hunter) who is currently locked up in Hellgate prison. Nina **wants** redemption for something she did to Matthias in the past (another thematic backstory puzzle that will be slowly pieced together throughout the novel).

Nina, Kaz, and Inej travel to Hellgate, where Nina uses her Grisha powers to knock out a guard, allowing the team to enter Matthias's cell. But when Matthias sees Nina, he tries to kill her, forcing Kaz to intervene. With Jesper's help, they successfully break Matthias out of Hellgate, and Kaz invites Matthias to join the crew. As a Fjerdan, he has special knowledge of the Ice Court that Kaz will need. Matthias says no, refusing to betray his country (not to mention, it's an impossible task), until Kaz offers him the one thing he can't refuse: the ability to become a Druskëlle again. He agrees, but with a secret agenda of his own. As a Druskëlle he'll be able to hunt Nina down and make her pay for what she did to him (**wants**).

Kaz introduces the sixth member, Wylan, a demolitions expert, and along with Jesper, the team is complete. After some debate about whether Wylan is the best demolitions expert available, Kaz—always a step ahead—reveals the real reason he's brought on Wylan. "Meet Wylan Van Eck, Jan Van Eck's son and our guarantee on thirty million *kruge*" (118).

Break Into 2 (119–128)

The heist is afoot! The team begins their plans. As Matthias describes the layout of the Ice Court, and Wylan (who's been there with his father) draws a map of it, we get a sense of just how *impossible* this heist is. But isn't that what make heist stories so much *fun*? The road to this prize will not be easy, but Kaz is ready, explaining that they don't have to break *in*. They only have to break out. Kaz plans for them to enter the prison sector of the Ice Court as prisoners and leave through the embassy sector. They will use the upcoming Hringkälla (a day of celebration when new Druskëlle are welcomed) as their distraction for getting out.

Fun and Games (119–244)

Although the team has a sketch of the Kaz's plan in their mind (as does the reader), the details are left undisclosed, making the rest of the Fun and Games a wild ride of discovery, danger, surprises, and twists as the team heads on an **upward path** toward the Midpoint.

As Inej tries and fails to talk Kaz out of the plan, we get a personal Theme Stated for Inej: "*The heart is an arrow. It demands aim to land true*," she remembers her father telling her (135). Inej must learn to follow her heart and not let herself be controlled by others (namely Kaz). Unfortunately, she doesn't yet know what her heart wants, so she's along for the journey.

First, the ship that they're preparing to board for Fjerda explodes, and the team is attacked by the Black Tips gang. But after Kaz reveals that the ship was a decoy, he leads everyone to the real ship. In the scramble to get there, Inej is gravely injured, but rescued by Kaz. Onboard, as Nina works to heal Inej, Kaz tortures one of the Black Tips gang and learns that it was Pekka Rollins who hired the gang to stop the Dregs from achieving their goal (external conflict). As Rollins is Kaz's antagonist and the source of his deep-seated desire for vengeance, knowing Rollins is also after Yul-Bayur spurs Kaz on even more (and raises the stakes of the story).

As the team is en route to Fjerda, author Bardugo takes some time to develop relationships and reveal crucial pieces of the thematic backstory puzzle. We learn more about Inej's past, as she flashes back to the day she was taken by slave traders and sold to the Menagerie pleasure house. We enjoy some (potentially flirtatious) bickering between Wylan and Jesper, who reveals his motivation for taking this job (to pay off crippling debt from gambling). We also learn how Nina and Matthias met (she was a Grisha in a foreign land, and he was a Fjerdan Druskëlle, trained to hunt Grisha). And we get some secret scheming from Matthias, who plans to betray them all.

Just before arriving in northern Fjerda, Kaz opens up to Inej about his past (growth!) and tells her that Pekka Rollins killed his brother, Jordie. The admission triggers a flashback, which reveals that Jordie and Kaz were conned by a man later discovered to be Rollins, who left them penniless.

B Story (163–171)

Each of our heroes has their own personal B Story character: Inej inspires Kaz to open up and trust others, Kaz pushes Inej to take control of her own destiny, Nina and Matthias challenge each other's ability to move beyond the past, and Wylan pushes Jesper to accept who he really is. But the thematic B Story for the whole team is best represented by the relationship between Nina and Matthias. It's deftly evolved throughout the novel but really kicks into high gear on the journey to Fjerda, where the two are thrust back together, triggering emotions, conflict, and flashbacks. As we'll soon learn, Nina (a Grisha) and Matthias (a Druskëlle trained to hunt Grisha) fell in love despite their ingrained prejudices against one another, but then Nina seemingly betrayed Matthias, leaving behind bitter wounds. Now, in the present, they have the choice and opportunity to either hold on to those past wounds and continue to be tormented by them or move beyond them (a theme for all five heroes). And as Nina and Matthias gradually find their way back to each other, healing the wounds of the past, the theme of the novel is skillfully, and visually, played out.

Midpoint (212–254)

In a **false victory**, the team successfully arrives on the coast of Fjerda, but their quest is far from over. Now they must travel by foot to the Ice Court. During the trek through the treacherous wilderness, more plans are revealed for the upcoming heist and more stakes are raised.

Internal stakes are raised when the team stumbles upon a pyre where Fjerdans burned Grisha, putting further strain on Nina and Matthias's already strained relationship and triggering more flashbacks from their past (**A and B Stories cross**). Here we learn how they went from enemies to friends (and possibly something more) while stranded in this same wilderness after a shipwreck, and how Nina later betrayed Matthias by turning him over to the Kerch and claiming he was a slaver, resulting in his arrest and imprisonment.

External stakes are raised as well when the team is attacked by Grisha under the influence of jurda parem and led by the Shu government, which apparently is *also* after Yul-Bayur. This heist just got a whole lot more complicated.

After seeing the effects of jurda parem firsthand, Nina and Matthias secretly agree to work together to make sure Yul-Bayur doesn't get out of the Ice Court alive. In this single decision, we get not only a **shift from wants to needs** (as the two put aside their differences and wounds of the past to find common ground) but also another **stakes-are-raised** moment (as they make a pact to betray Kaz and the rest of the crew) *and* a new goal for the second half of Act 2.

If that's not structurally romantic, I don't know what is!

Bad Guys Close In (255–294)

The crew reaches Djerholm, and the next part of the heist begins. Using a felled tree and a diversion, they swap places with six prisoners on a prison wagon heading to the Ice Court. That's when things start to go wrong, tipping us into a **downward path**. But do they *really* go wrong? Or is it just Kaz with more tricks up his sleeve? Author Bardugo keeps us guessing, filling the beat with more twists and **bouncing balls**.

First, Kaz passes out from being crammed into the wagon with so many bodies, and we learn (through flashback) that when Jordie died of firepox, Kaz got trapped on a barge surrounded by corpses and was forced to use his brother's body as a flotation device to get to shore. The event left him traumatized and terrified of touching other people (**internal bad guys**).

Then Kaz is punished when the guards find lock picks stuffed into the back of his mouth, but it turns out it was just a diversion to keep the guards from looking too closely at Matthias (who used to be one of their own). Once in their cell, Jesper reveals that he is a secret Grisha Fabrikator and uses the metal of the bars to create new lock picks for Kaz. They break out of their cell and split up. Wylan, Jesper, Matthias, and Inej meet up at the incinerator, where they discover, to their surprise, that it was run recently, which means it's too hot to plant bombs as they'd planned, but Inej still thinks she can climb it.

When Inej reveals that Kaz went to help Nina search the cells for Yul-Bayur (which wasn't part of the plan), Jesper suspects that Kaz is up to something. (Isn't he always?)

All Is Lost (295–300)

Nina and Kaz search the prison cells for Yul-Bayur, but they're running out of time. Their planned rendezvous and escape with the team is drawing near. Nina wonders how she's going to find and kill Yul-Bayur before Kaz gets to him. The two split up, but it becomes more and more evident to Nina that they're not going to find him. It appears the group's plan (to rescue Yul-Bayur) and Nina and Matthias's secret plan (to kill him) have both failed.

In a **whiff of death**, Nina passes by creepy white rooms stained with blood, designed to hold and torture Grisha prisoners. The sight makes her want to run home to Ravka and forget the whole mission.

On her way out, she's unable to find Kaz and instead runs into three Fjerdan guards. She's able to kill them instantly with her Grisha abilities, but not before an alarm bell rings out across the prison, indicating a security breach (**road apple**).

Dark Night of the Soul (301–329)

Inej climbs the incinerator shaft to the roof, planning to throw down a rope for the others. But the scorching-hot shaft is melting her shoes and burning her feet. In a personal All Is Lost (and whiff of death), Inej feels hopeless, convinced they will all die here.

In her despair (and personal Dark Night of the Soul), she thinks about her motivation for being on this mission (to pay off her debt to Per Haskell and go find her family), but even that feels lost. When she hears her father's voice telling her to "*Climb, Inej*," she can't move (309). Her flaw of not knowing where to point the "arrow" of her heart is at an all-time low, and she considers giving up and letting go.

Then Inej feels rain falling from above, cooling the heat of the incinerator and symbolically cleansing her of her past, washing away "the sweat and soot, the coal smoke of Ketterdam, the face paint of the Menagerie . . ." (310). As a girl of faith, Inej thinks of the rain as a blessing (personal Dark Night Epiphany). It gives her strength and a new purpose. In a personal Break Into 3, she decides to use her share of the heist prize to buy her own ship and hunt down slavers. She now has a direction. She knows where to point her arrow. She says goodbye to her past (theme!) and climbs toward her future.

Meanwhile, Kaz is in the prison cells, searching not for Yul-Bayur but for Pekka Rollins. In his personal All Is Lost and Dark Night of the Soul, he feels desperate and unhinged, triggering another flashback, in which we learn about the aftermath of Pekka Rollins's con and Jordie's death. Now we understand how Kaz became the "bastard of the barrel" and when he started planning his revenge on Rollins. He locates Rollins's cell, and in his personal Break Into 3, he finally has the opportunity he's been waiting and planning for. He enters the cell and closes the door behind him. But what he does in that cell we won't discover until the final chapter.

Jesper also experiences a personal All Is Lost as the alarm bells continue to ring and he waits alone for Kaz, ready to give up on him. Finally, Kaz arrives, covered in blood, and they climb the rope up the incinerator to meet the others. Jesper has a Break Into 3 of his own when he reveals his Fabrikator abilities to the entire crew (an identity he's kept secret his whole life), in order to help heal Inej's burned feet.

From the roof, the crew watches the Fjerdan guards react to the alarm bells, feeling hopeless. With the increased security, it'll now be impossible for them to get out. And they still don't know where Yul-Bayur is. "It was like seeing the last bit of their luck drain from a glass," Jesper notes on page 327.

But as they watch guards set up a checkpoint at the White Island where the celebrations are underway for Hringkälla, Inej gets an idea (**Dark Night Epiphany**). She points to the girls from the Menagerie (where she used to work) waiting to enter the checkpoint and announces that she and Nina can enter with them. But it will require her to, once again, become the past version of herself she just vowed to leave behind (**synthesis!**).

Break Into 3 (328–330)

A new plan is hatched! Although we don't get *all* the information about what it entails (because where's the fun in that?), we get enough to piece together the bare bones: Nina and Inej will disguise themselves as Menagerie girls to get onto the White Island and try to find Yul-Bayur, Matthias and Kaz will use "another way" onto the island, and Jesper and Wylan will break one of the gates to trigger Black Protocol (the highest state of emergency) and trap the guards on the island.

How will the crew get out, hopefully with Yul-Bayur in tow? We don't quite know yet. But we know it involves what thieves do best: stealing.

The **Act 3 Goal** is set. Let the epic Five-Point Finale begin!

Finale (331–456)

POINT 1: GATHERING THE TEAM. Kaz lays out the details of the plan to his crew. We are not yet privy to these details, but Inej tells us the plan is "audacious, maybe even mad," and we're excited! Realizing that they might never see each other again, the team share a tender moment of goodbye, reciting the Dregs' motto: "No mourners . . . no funerals" (332).

Inej tells Kaz of her plans to leave the Dregs when this is over. Kaz tries to confess something to her but is unable to. All he can do is let her touch his face without wincing. Inej knows that it's the best he can do, but she also knows that it is not enough for her. In a symbolic gesture, she returns Kaz's gloves to him (which she wore to climb the incinerator). The gloves are Kaz's armor, a way to shield the wounds of his past and keep people at a distance. Now that Inej has overcome her past and discovered her true purpose, she has the strength to leave Kaz.

POINT 2: EXECUTING THE PLAN. As the Elderclock chimes nine bells, the plan is officially in motion. Buckle up, because it's exciting and complicated, full of twists, turns, conflict, fake-outs, false victories, false defeats, and all that you'd expect from a good heist Finale. And along the way, each of our heroes will be tested and challenged to see if they really have learned the theme.

The crew splits into three groups, and author Bardugo uses the chimes of the Elderclock to synchronize their movements for the reader.

Nina and Inej dress in the costumes of the Menagerie girls in preparation for entering the checkpoint. For Inej, this is a symbolic moment of growth as she dons the clothes that represent her **shard of glass,** but this time on her own terms, and in control of her own destiny. Inej is stopped at the checkpoint for further review, and Nina has to go forward with the plan to find Yul-Bayur on her own. When Nina gets to the party, she runs into a face from her past: Jarl Brum, the Druskëlle commander who imprisoned her, whom she believed to be dead.

Kaz and Matthias cross a secret bridge to the White Island where they knock out two guards. Matthias gets the opportunity to shoot Kaz and be free of the Dregs and this mission but chooses not to, and Kaz reveals it was a test to make sure Matthias was truly on their side.

Jesper and Wylan make it to the gatehouse, where banners of cloth made from the uniforms of dead Grisha trigger a flashback to Jesper's **shard of glass** (his father encouraging him to keep his Grisha powers and identity a secret). When Jesper gets in trouble with guards, in a **side character to the rescue** moment, Wylan saves the day using his "schoolroom Fjerdan," a nod to his wealthy upbringing that Jesper has mocked throughout the novel (354). More conflict awaits in the gatehouse, where they find metal chains (not ropes) controlling the gates. Jesper will have to use his recently revealed Grisha powers to weaken the links so they can cut through the chain. Once they succeed, the two boys share a moment and subtly reveal their feelings for each other.

POINT 3: HIGH TOWER SURPRISE(S). This Finale includes not one but *several* High Tower Surprises. Some will prove to be surprises only for the reader, while others will genuinely stop the heroes in their tracks, forcing them to Dig Deep Down and find new solutions.

First, Inej is recognized by Tante Heleen, the owner of the Menagerie, who reveals to the guards that Inej works for Kaz Brekker, an infamous criminal. At first, Inej quails in the presence of Heleen as the horrors of her past comes back to her. But then, in her personal Dig Deep Down, she realizes her own strength, and for the first time fights back against Heleen, attacking her and nearly choking her to death. The guards pull her off and threaten to torture her for information about the mission.

Jesper and Wylan encounter a Grisha Tidemaker on jurda parem, and Jesper (in his own Dig Deep Down) realizes this is a fight he can't win with a gun (his weapon of choice). He has to fight the Grisha . . . *as* a Grisha.

Then, just as Nina thinks she's fooled Jarl Brum into giving up the location of Yul-Bayur, surprise! He throws her into a cell. Matthias appears, confessing that he turned Nina into Brum. "Now our debt is paid," he tells her (378).

And just when we think that Nina and Matthias's reconciliation was a ruse so he could get his revenge, surprise again! Matthias reveals he was only pretending to be on Brum's side so he could rescue Nina and find out where Yul-Bayur is being held. Which he does. But when

Matthias learns from Brum that the Grisha sentenced to death are actually used as slaves in the Ice Court, Matthias has a personal Dig Deep Down, realizing the Druskëlle are the real monsters—not the Grisha. Matthias knocks Brum unconscious and locks him in a cell, proving that he's learned the theme and escaped his past and his former loyalties. "The life you live, the hate you feel—it's poison. I can drink it no longer," Matthias tells Brum (385). He frees Nina from her cell and makes the sacred Druskëlle oath to *her*. His loyalty and heart are forever changed.

They head off to find Yul-Bayur, only to discover (another surprise!) it's not Yul-Bayur in the cell, but his son, Kuwei Yul-Bo, who knows how to re-create his father's formula for jurda parem. Nina prepares to kill him, but in her own Dig Deep Down, she realizes that would make her just as bad as the Druskëlle. Kuwei reveals that he is an Inferni (a Grisha who can manipulate fire), and Nina tells him to destroy the lab with an explosion. The three of them run from the building, only to be captured moments later by more Druskëlle. But (surprise!) one of them turns out to be Kaz in disguise, and together, they escape from the White Island.

It turns out the explosion in the lab was a High Tower Surprise to Kaz, forcing him to improvise their escape. They end up in a gorge, and as Kaz struggles not to drown, he flashes back to how he injured his leg and references his own flaw: "there was no part of him that was not broken, that had not healed wrong, and there was no part of him that was not stronger for having been broken" (401). In his personal Dig Deep Down, he realizes he doesn't have the corpse of his brother to keep him afloat this time (meaning he can no longer rely on his trauma and thirst for revenge to keep him going). Instead, he thinks of Inej and how he was "not so broken that he couldn't pull himself together into some semblance of a man for her" (403).

Meanwhile Inej—with the help of Jesper and Wylan—escapes the guards, and we learn that (surprise!) getting caught was part of the plan. She needed a diamond, and she'd decided to steal the one from Tante Heleen's necklace, which she did when she was choking her. They use the diamond as a drill bit to cut through the Fabrikator-made glass housing the Ice Court arsenal and steal one of the tanks inside. Crashing through the "legendary, impenetrable wall" (414), they leave the Ice Court behind, with the Fjerdan Might banner trailing behind them.

They pick up the others, and the team is reunited once more. But even after shooting out the bridge from the Ice Court, the crew hits their ultimate *team* High Tower Surprise when they reach the harbor and find it blocked by rows of guards pointing guns at them, and a Heartrender Grisha on jurda parem, ready to destroy them.

"I didn't this coming." Kaz admits on page 421. He has officially run out of tricks.

POINT 4: DIG DEEP DOWN. The team all agree they won't be taken alive. They have each been prisoners in the past and they've all had their "fill of captivity." (421). They're ready to fight this army to the death. Nina makes a surprise **team member sacrifice**, taking a dose of jurda parem herself (despite how deadly it can be to Grisha).

POINT 5: THE EXECUTION OF THE NEW PLAN. Nina uses her enhanced abilities to kill the Heartrender and knock all the guards unconscious. A Druskëlle army appears, wearing special armor that protects them against Grisha powers. They open fire on Nina, but she heals herself nearly as quickly as the bullets come. Then she commands the fallen guards to rise and rip the protective armor from the Druskëlle soldiers. Nina starts to kill them as punishment for all the Grisha they've killed but Matthias convinces her to show mercy instead.

The team boards their ship and sets sail for Ketterdam with Kuwei Yul-Bo. They have done the impossible. They have broken into Fjerda's impenetrable prison and, more important, broken out with its most valuable prisoner. But their struggles are not over. Will Nina be able to survive the deadly withdrawal from jurda parem?

When Inej tells Kaz of her plans to get her own ship, he proves that he's changed when he opens up and asks her to stay in Ketterdam with him. It's a big moment in his character growth, but for Inej, it's still not enough. "I will have you without armor, Kaz Brekker. Or I will not have you at all" (434). And when he doesn't respond, she walks away from him. Apparently, he still has some more growing to do. Good thing there's a second book.

The boat docks in Ketterdam, and Jesper, Kaz, Matthias, Inej, and Kuwei go to meet Van Eck to trade Kuwei for their thirty-million-kruge prize. Van Eck appears with a trunk full of cash, and Kaz is ready to claim the team's hard-fought victory. But we get the sense it won't be that easy. There's another twist coming.

Van Eck calls on an army of jurda parem–dosed Grisha and reveals his nefarious plan to use the jurda parem formula for his own personal gains. Kaz is furious that he let himself be conned again. But fortunately, he has one last trick up his sleeve. Just as the Grisha attack, Kaz reveals that Kuwei is actually Wylan (Van Eck's son disguised by Nina). He'll give up Kuwei's location as soon as Van Eck gives up the money.

When Van Eck orders the Grisha to kill everyone but Kaz, Kaz looks at Inej (revealing his weakness to Van Eck). Van Eck kidnaps Inej and gives Kaz one week to bring him the real Kuwei, or Inej will be tortured. It appears Kaz's emotional growth has cost him the very thing that helped him achieve that growth, cleverly setting us up for book 2!

And book 2 is exactly where we're heading. As Kaz stares off in the direction of Ketterdam's harbor, a new plan starts to form in his mind. A plan to rescue Inej and get revenge on Van Eck. But he's going to need the right crew . . .

Final Image (457–462)

In a **mirror beat** to the Opening Image, a single chapter is told from the POV of a new narrator. But it's not a new character.

In his office above the Emerald Palace gambling hall, Pekka Rollins surveys the crew that has requested an audience with him: Kaz, Matthias, Jesper, Wylan, and Nina. It's only now we learn what really happened in Pekka Rollins's cell at the Ice Court. Kaz let him go, vowing that someday Rollins would repay the favor. And now Kaz has come to collect.

Kaz asks Rollins to send a message to the Ravkan capital, then sells Rollins his share of the Crow Club (a gambling hall operated by the Dregs) and Fifth Harbor. They shake on the deal, and Kaz sets off with his crew for another impossible heist. It isn't until Kaz is gone that Rollins realizes Kaz has stolen his watch, wallet, tie pin, pendant, and gold buckles. No one has ever dared to steal from him, but Rollins gets the sense that this is just the beginning.

And he's right.

WHY IS THIS A GOLDEN FLEECE?

Six of Crows contains all three elements of a successful Golden Fleece story.

- **A ROAD:** A journey across the sea from Ketterdam to Fjerda, then through the treacherous Fjerdan wilderness, and finally in, through, and out of the impenetrable Ice Court. The heist to kidnap Yul-Bayur represents the road Kaz's crew must traverse to win their prize.
- **A TEAM:** The Six of Crows is Kaz's team of thieves, criminals, and outcasts. They each possess a special skill that mastermind Kaz needs (Jesper's sharpshooting and secret Grisha powers, Inej's agile acrobatics and climbing, Wylan's knowledge of explosives, Matthias's familiarity with the Ice Court, and Nina's abilities as a Grisha Heartrender), and along the way they each learn a personal life lesson about letting go of the past.
- **A PRIZE:** In exchange for rescuing Yul-Bayur from the Ice Court, Van Eck promises to pay Kaz and his team thirty million kruge. It's enough for all of them to escape their problems, repay their debts, and seek a better life.

Cat's Eye View

For quick reference, here's a brief overview of this novel's beat sheet.

OPENING IMAGE/WORLD: A new and powerful drug, jurda parem, is tested on a Grisha who uses her enhanced powers to overtake her captors.

OPENING IMAGE/TEAM: We meet Kaz, Jesper, and Inej as the Dregs parley with a rival gang, the Black Tips, over the lucrative territory, Fifth Harbor. Thanks to Kaz's wiles, he outsmarts the Black Tips.

SETUP: As Kaz walks home, we learn more about him and Inej (who is shadowing him). We get hints at Kaz's mysterious backstory involving someone named Jordie.

CATALYST: Kaz is kidnapped by Van Eck and offered a job: rescue the Shu inventor Bo Yul-Bayur from the Fjerdan Ice Court (an impenetrable prison) in exchange for thirty million kruge (the prize).

THEME STATED: "I do wonder what a boy of your intelligence might have amounted to under different circumstances," Van Eck says to Kaz (57). This novel explores how our past traumas shape who we are. Each of the five heroes will have to choose to break free from the past or continue to let the past hold them captive.

DEBATE: Who will Kaz choose for his team in this impossible heist? As Inej, Nina, and Matthias are asked to join the crew, we see their personal Debates before they all agree. With Jesper and the demo expert, Wylan, the crew of six is complete.

BREAK INTO 2: The heist is afoot. The team starts planning and prepping. They will enter the prison as prisoners and use an upcoming celebration as their distraction for getting out.

FUN AND GAMES: After their decoy boat is destroyed by the Black Tips and Inej is injured, the team sails for Fjerda. On the journey, we spend some time learning about key pieces of their backstories and furthering relationships between the team.

B STORY: Although each hero has their own personal B Story character, the thematic B Story for the whole team is best represented by Nina and Matthias, who throughout the novel learn to move beyond past wounds (a theme for all five heroes).

MIDPOINT: In a false victory, the crew reach Fjerda and have to travel by foot to the Ice Court. After being attacked by Shu Grisha under the influence of jurda parem, Matthias and Nina make a pact to betray the team and kill Yul-Bayur once they find him (stakes are raised).

BAD GUYS CLOSE IN: The team swaps places with six prisoners and successfully gets into the Ice Court, but not before Kaz passes out from being crammed in with too many bodies (internal bad guys). Jesper reveals he's a secret Fabrikator and uses the cell bars to make lock picks for Kaz. Some of the team meet up at the incinerator to discover it was recently run, ruining their plans, but Inej vows she can still climb it.

ALL IS LOST: Kaz and Nina are unable to find Yul-Bayur, a seeming failure of the team's goal. Nina stumbles upon a blood-stained room where Grisha were tortured (whiff of death) and wants to quit. She kills three Fjerdan guards just before alarm bells ring out across the prison, indicating a security breach.

DARK NIGHT OF THE SOUL: As Inej climbs the incinerator, she feels hopeless and is convinced they will all die. Kaz is revealed to be looking for not Yul-Bayur but Pekka Rollins. He finds his cell and enters. The team reacts to the alarm bells, feeling "the last bit of their luck drain from a glass" (327). Inej gets a new idea of how to get out of the Ice Court (Dark Night Epiphany).

BREAK INTO 3: A new plan is hatched. We don't know all the details, but we do know it involves stealing (because that's what thieves do best).

FINALE: The crew enacts a complicated plan full of twists, turns, and surprises, just managing to escape the Ice Court with not Yul-Bayur but his son, Kuwei Yul-Bo, in tow. But when they're stopped by Fjerdan guards at the harbor, Nina makes a team member sacrifice and takes jurda parem to fight the army, despite the often-deadly side effects. Kaz brings Kuwei to Van Eck to claim his prize, only to be double-crossed by Van Eck. In the fight that ensues, Inej is kidnapped. Kaz starts making a plan to rescue her and get his revenge.

FINAL IMAGE: In a final scene narrated by Pekka Rollins, we learn that Kaz let Rollins go at the Ice Court and now has come to collect the favor he's owed. Kaz asks Rollins to send a message to the Ravkan capital and sells Rollins his share of the Crow Club. Before leaving, he pickpockets Rollins—and Rollins senses this is just the beginning.

Fool Triumphant
Underdogs and Outcasts for the Win!

Ah, high school. A place where your individuality is celebrated, standing out from the crowd is always a good idea, and being different is your best strategy for making friends. Right?

Um . . .

That's not *exactly* how I remember it.

But in the end, that's what the tales of this genre are all about! Not necessarily the "high school" part (although you'll find that a lot of young adult novels of this genre do take place in a more traditional high school setting), but the being different part. This is a genre that celebrates the individual who dares to stand out from the crowd. It doesn't always go well (at first), but eventually, this so-called "fool" is victorious.

In other words, welcome to the age-old story of the underdog. And who doesn't love an underdog?

Fool Triumphant novels tell the tale of a "fool" (an overlooked underdog or outcast) who enters or comes up against some type of establishment or group and whose greatest disadvantage (and secret strength) is the fact that they are disregarded by this establishment.

Look at novels like *Dumplin'* by Julie Murphy, in which the hero—a self-proclaimed "fat girl," comfortable in her own skin—takes on the establishment of her Texas small town's beauty pageant. Or *You Should*

See Me in a Crown by Leah Johnson, in which the hero—an awkward, shy outcast who doesn't fit in in her prom-obsessed Indiana town—takes on the establishment of her high school's cutthroat prom court election. Or even *The Princess Diaries* by Meg Cabot, in which the hero—a gangly "freak" freshman who can't get a date—takes on the establishment of a royal court (literally, she discovers she's the crown princess of small country).

Novels in this genre often have a "fish out of water" vibe. The fool doesn't *appear* to belong in the establishment they're entering (or possibly already in). Their stark difference makes them stand out, perhaps quite awkwardly at first. But it's that contrast that makes these tales so fun to read.

And don't be *fooled* by the word "fool." The genre is called Fool Triumphant for a reason, because in the end, the fool always comes out on top, leaving us with a very important question: Who is the *real* fool here? Is it this refreshingly different individual who dared to disrupt a strict, narrow-minded establishment? Or is it the establishment itself—the group that's been trying so hard to hold on to their outdated conventions, they've managed to completely overlook what was right in front of them? If that sounds uplifting, it is! (Or it should be.) Many of the authors who have ventured into this genre have crafted some memorable, heartfelt, and *highly* successful novels that leave us feeling buoyed, inspired, and thirsty for more.

So if you've got a "victory of the underdog" tale burning a hole in your brain, let's hear it! We need more triumphant fools in the world! Just be sure you're including the essential genre ingredients to ensure that *you* are just as triumphant as your hero: (1) a **fool**, (2) an **establishment**, and (3) a **transmutation**.

Let's dive deeper.

A FOOL

The fool requires one very important criterion: they must be seen as an underdog or outcast at first. This can be represented in a variety of ways: someone who doesn't fit in, someone who is often overlooked, someone naïve to their own potential, someone not expected to succeed or thought to have little chance of winning, or someone who has little status in their society (usually high school, in the young adult variety).

Think about Liz Lighty in *You Should See Me in a Crown*. She starts out insecure, anxious, and desperate to get out of her small Indiana town where everyone is obsessed with prom (and she is decidedly *not*). She spends most of the first act trying to blend in instead of stand out. She's the least likely person who would be in the running for prom queen (even according to her!).

Or think about Willowdean in *Dumplin'*, a plus-size sixteen-year-old whose weight is a constant topic of debate between her and her mother, a former beauty queen who now runs the local pageant. Willowdean abhors the pageant and would never expect herself to enter, let alone win.

The fool is often the hero of the story, although not always. In *Stargirl*, author Jerry Spinelli made the creative choice to tell the tale of his particular fool (Stargirl) from the POV of someone *within* the establishment (the average American high school), giving us a unique perspective on the fool and the way she turns the establishment upside down and, as a result, changes the hero's perspective on his school and himself.

But being the underdog or outcast has its advantages. Because they are often overlooked, they're able to fly under the radar. No one expects *that* person to break the status quo.

In *The Field Guide to the North American Teenager* by Ben Philippe, the fool (Norris Kaplan) is a Black Canadian teenager who moves to a classic American high school in Texas. His sarcastic wit, cynical worldview (which he catalogs in a journal/field guide), and propensity to sweat (a lot) do not make him very popular at his new school. But he doesn't mind. He *prefers* to fly under the radar. He has no intention of rocking the boat. Yet rock it he will.

The fool often feels like the *opposite* of the hero in the Superhero genre. In the Superhero genre, many people *know* that the hero is special, or "the one" and maybe even "destined to change the world." Whereas in Fool Triumphant stories, no one really takes them seriously. Or sees them as a threat. Well, *almost* no one.

There's a common character type found in Fool Triumphant stories: the **jealous insider**. This is an antagonistic character who sees the fool's true potential, feels threatened by it, and works hard to keep it hidden, or even to sabotage the fool. Like the character Callie, another pageant hopeful in *Dumplin'*; Rachel in *You Should See Me in a Crown*, who attempts to use Liz's poverty, race, and sexual orientation against her in the battle for prom queen; or Patrick Lamarra (aka "Hairy Armpits") in *The Field Guide to the North American Teenager*, who bullies and torments Norris right from the start.

The jealous insider, as the title suggests, is typically someone *inside* the establishment that the fool is entering or going up against.

AN ESTABLISHMENT

This is the group of people or subsection of society that the fool either is sent to confront (like the Miss Teen Blue Bonnet Pageant in *Dumplin'*, the prom queen competition in *You Should See Me in a Crown*, or simply an average high school in *The Field Guide to the North American Teenager*), or already exists within and naturally stands out from.

But unlike tales of the Institutionalized genre, the purpose in these stories is not necessarily for the hero to join, escape, or burn down the establishment (although sometimes that happens in the process), but rather to show how one individual can stand out *within* the establishment, simply by being themselves. Their greatest strength (whether they realize it at first or not) *is* their difference. In *Dumplin'*, when Willowdean decides to enter her town's local beauty pageant, she not only shakes up the whole establishment of the pageant but also attracts a group of followers (other misfits, outcasts, and underdogs) who are inspired by her courage and decide to enter too. In *You Should See Me in a Crown*, when Liz finally embraces her identity and challenges the school administration's rules to be able to attend prom with her girlfriend, she's already a winner. And that confidence and sense of self is ultimately what gets her crowned prom queen. And in the novel *Geek Girl* by Holly Smale (whose "fool" is referenced in the title), Harriet Manners, a self-proclaimed "geek," is scouted by a modeling agency at the mall and thrust into the world of haute couture and supermodels.

She knows nothing about fashion, can't walk in high heels, and doesn't have the classic supermodel look. And that's exactly what gets her the coveted job as the new face of a famous fashion house.

When a fool is pitted against an establishment and refuses to change who they are or to be someone they're not, the establishment automatically starts to crumble. You, the author, are essentially poking holes in this group, exposing its flaws and its outdated systems, and ultimately revealing *it* as the true fool of the story.

A TRANSMUTATION

Finally, the transmutation is an essential moment in all Fool Triumphant stories—when the fool *becomes* someone else, either by accident, as a disguise, or to make a point. Like when Willowdean and her fellow underdogs put on dresses and heels and learn how to strut their stuff on stage in *Dumplin'*, and when Liz and Harriet get makeovers in *You Should See Me in a Crown* and *Geek Girl*.

The transmutation doesn't have to last long. It might be a few pages. But it's a key element in the story because it's the moment when the establishment starts to see the fool as someone a little less foolish and a little more like them. Like when Norris dons a fancy tux for prom and becomes a classic American teenager in *The Field Guide to the North American Teenager*.

The transmutation is the opposite of the hero shedding their mask and revealing their true identity. In this moment, the hero *hides* their true identity in order to fit in and "fool" the people who have called them a fool! In a way, it's revealing the establishment as the fool, not the other way around. In *Stargirl*, when Stargirl turns into "Susan" and starts dressing in "normal" clothes, the joke isn't on her. It's on the high school that has squashed the individuality of this unique soul.

But fear not! The transmutation is not permanent. It's just another storytelling device to reveal a deeper meaning. A hidden lesson. Because in the end, all Fool Triumphant stories celebrate the value of being different, the dangers of judging others too quickly, and the lasting difference one person can make just by being courageous enough to go against the grain.

In *Dumplin'*, Willowdean doesn't win the pageant, but that doesn't mean she's not triumphant. She's taught the establishment (and herself) a new definition of beauty, and, through the other outcasts she inspired to join the pageant, she also learns a valuable lesson about friendship. In *You Should See Me in a Crown*, Liz *does* win prom queen, but that's not really the part that resonates with us. It's the fact that the prom queen competition is what allowed Liz to come out of her shell, stop hiding, and embrace who she really is and who she loves. Even in the face of an establishment that might mock her for it.

The Fool Triumphant genre resonates with teen readers the world over because there's something unique and different about every one of us. We've all had to struggle to fit in at some point in our lives. And we've all been told by some establishment (big or small) that we don't belong and that our individuality is a weakness, not a strength.

Thank goodness, we have these tales to inspire us. And remind us that in the end, our greatest triumph is being ourselves.

To recap: if you're thinking of writing a Fool Triumphant novel, make sure your story includes these three essential ingredients:

- A FOOL whose "difference" and innocence is their strength and whose status as an underdog or outcast causes them to be overlooked or ignored by all but a jealous insider who is threatened by the fool's very existence.
- AN ESTABLISHMENT: the people or group the fool comes up against, either within their own environment, or somewhere new, in which they do not fit in—at first. Either way, there's a sense of the fool being a fish out of water.
- A TRANSMUTATION, in which the fool becomes someone or something new, often including a name change that's taken on either by accident or as a disguise, and often leading to the exposure of the establishment as the true fool.

POPULAR YOUNG ADULT FOOL TRIUMPHANT NOVELS

Stargirl by Jerry Spinelli*
The Princess Diaries by Meg Cabot
Into the Wild Nerd Yonder by Julie Halpern
Dumplin' by Julie Murphy
The Season by Jonah Lisa Dyer and Stephen Dyer
Noteworthy by Riley Redgate
The Field Guide to the North American Teenager by Ben Philippe
You Should See Me In a Crown by Leah Johnson
This Will Be Funny Someday by Katie Henry

* Beat sheet follows.

STARGIRL

BY: Jerry Spinelli
STC GENRE: Fool Triumphant
BOOK GENRE: Contemporary
TOTAL PAGES: 186 (Laurel Leaf Books paperback edition, 2004)

At a time when life is all about fitting in, one high school girl dares to go against the grain and do the unthinkable: stand out. A novel beloved among readers, parents, and educators alike, *Stargirl* is the total embodiment of the Fool Triumphant genre. It's told in a retrospective POV, as narrator Leo Borlock looks back on the events of the novel as an adult reliving his high school experience, which gives him a unique perspective on the novel's theme of nonconformity. And the theme resonates. Not only was the book a *New York Times* bestseller, a Parents Choice Gold Award winner, an American Library Association Top Ten Book for Young Adults, and a *Publishers Weekly* Best Book of the Year, but it was adapted as an original movie for Disney+ and even spawned a "Stargirl Society" movement around the world, inspiring young adults to spread Stargirl's positive messages and perform random acts of kindness. I dare you to read this novel and not be inspired yourself. But it's also a great one to study from a structure POV because of its unique customizations to the beat sheet. So let's take a look.

Opening Image (1–2)

In this short prologue, Leo Borlock tells us that he used to collect porcupine neckties. After a small feature was run about his collection in the local paper on his fourteenth birthday, he received a wrapped gift from a mysterious, unknown sender that contained none other than a porcupine necktie. Straight away, the tone here is whimsical, quirky, maybe even a little magical, just like Stargirl herself (whom we will meet shortly).

Although Leo is the narrator, and he does transform in the course of the story, it's the establishment of this Fool Triumphant tale—an average American high school—that will be most changed by our fool, making the establishment itself the central hero of the story.

Catalyst (3–5)

The Catalyst comes right at the start of chapter 1, with the line "Did you see her?" referencing the new girl who has just arrived at Mica Area High School, in Mica, Arizona. (3) (For more on untraditional Catalysts, see page 122). But this is no ordinary new kid. This is Stargirl Caraway, our **fool**. She wears old-fashioned long dresses with ruffles, carries a ukulele strapped to her back, and sings in the cafeteria! This mysterious, formerly homeschooled newcomer causes a stir from the moment she arrives. Little do the students know, Mica Area High School will never be same again.

Setup/Debate (7–25)

Because of the early Catalyst, the Setup and Debate are combined and this joined beat now serves two purposes: to set up the world of Mica Area High and to show how Stargirl's interruption of that world is initially received. So the Debate question becomes: How will the school react to this unique individual invading their very conventional world?

"Mica Area High School—MAHS—was not exactly a hotbed of nonconformity . . . If we happened to somehow distinguish ourselves, we quickly snapped back into place, like rubber bands" (10). Leo paints a picture in our mind of a very average high school where everyone dresses the same, talks the same, and listens to the same music. So the initial arrival of Stargirl elicits suspicion. She doesn't fit into any of the establishment's boxes, so she can't possibly be real.

Leo is pressured by students to put Stargirl on *Hot Seat*, a popular student TV show that he runs with his friend Kevin, but he's reluctant, not wanting to exploit her. Leo's primary **flaw** is that he cares too much about what others think, which has caused his own uniqueness to be smothered. But he's fascinated by Stargirl, perhaps in a different way from everyone else. She speaks to that necktie-collecting goofball he used to be.

Stargirl has an innocence, kindness, and quirkiness that defies conformity, making her a perfect example of this genre's titular **fool**: one who doesn't recognize that they're different or special, but rather innocently goes about their life. And *that* makes them special.

As is often the case with an early Catalyst, there is a second Catalyst (**double bump**) that pushes us closer to Act 2. On page 22, Kevin calls Leo and tells him to come to the football game, quick! There, Leo finds Stargirl on the field, dancing barefoot with the marching band, and joining the football players' warm-up exercises, before grabbing the football and running off the field with it. But perhaps the most extraordinary sight of all is that the students are *cheering*. They love it.

Break Into 2 (25)

At lunch, everyone is shocked to find Stargirl no longer sitting by herself; she's at the cheerleaders' table. It's soon revealed that the head cheerleader has invited Stargirl to join the squad, and she's said yes. The Debate is over. The establishment has officially accepted Stargirl.

B Story/Theme Stated (30–35)

The theme of this novel is conformity and the struggle to let go of what others think and embrace individuality. Although Leo won't fully realize and learn this lesson until he's much older and has acquired the hindsight necessary to narrate the story, it's something the establishment will start to learn before the school year ends. However, as with any hero's transformation, there will be many ups and downs that must happen first.

Archie Brubaker, a local paleontologist and former professor who serves as a mentor and unofficial teacher to many of the kids in Mica (including Stargirl), represents the theme in that he, too, is quirky and different. He challenges Leo's (and the establishment's) beliefs about conformity.

Archie states the theme to Leo when he observes this about Stargirl: "You'll know her more by your questions than by her answers. Keep looking at her long enough. One day you might see someone you know." (35)

Fun and Games (25–70)

Despite being accepted by the establishment, Stargirl is still her beautiful, quirky self. Even as she undergoes her first **transmutation** (putting on the cheerleader outfit), she stands out in the crowd. She doesn't conform, still dressing in long, flowing skirts on nongame days, leaving gifts on students' desks, and serenading people on their birthdays. Definitely an **upside-down world** for Mica Area High.

But there's one person who's definitely *not* having any of it. Hillari Kimble (the **jealous insider**) has been distrustful of Stargirl from the start and resistant to her difference.

By December, Stargirl is the most popular girl in school. Despite her unusual behavior, everyone is drawn to her. She seems to be having a positive effect on the establishment. But is it *real* change? Or is it simply an instance of **fixing things the wrong way**?

It seems like the quintessential upward path. But there's a precariousness about Mica Area High's acceptance of Stargirl. Like one wrong step could cause it to crumble.

And crumble it does.

Basketball season arrives, and Stargirl starts to cheer for *every* basket (including the opponents'). This angers the students of Mica, and the upward path sharply turns into a **downward path** when the cheerleaders ditch Stargirl at the game and the bus leaves without her.

Leo finally agrees to invite Stargirl to appear on *Hot Seat*, and things continue to get worse. The TV show features twelve students as the "jury" members who are allowed to ask nosy and embarrassing questions of the guest. One of those jurors is Hillari Kimble.

Stargirl is bombarded with questions about why she abandoned her birthname (Susan) and why she cheers for the other team. Stargirl's answers make *sense* (she didn't *feel* like a Susan anymore, and she wants all the players to feel happy), but in the context of the establishment, they are nonsense. And as the questions turn to attacks—"Why can't you just be normal?"—we start to catch a glimpse of who the *real* fool is in this equation (67).

Midpoint (70–84)

A collection of closely clustered scenes paints a picture of **false defeat**.

First, Stargirl takes a tomato to the face at a playoff basketball game when she cheers for the other team as Mica is losing.

The next day, Leo receives a card from Stargirl that says, "I LOVE YOU" (**stakes are raised** and **love story ramps up**).

Then Stargirl is kicked off the cheerleading squad, marking the end of the establishment's acceptance of her. It would seem the students of Mica Area High School are no longer willing to put up with the "fun and games" of Stargirl.

Finally, we see a **shift from wants to needs** when Leo overhears people calling him "Starboy" and is secretly thrilled. His attraction to Stargirl is overpowering his concern for what others think of him (theme!). But when he goes to her house, he hides behind a car to avoid seeing her, proving his flaw is still holding him back. However, the scene serves to shift the focus of the story from Stargirl's relationship with the establishment to her relationship with Leo.

Bad Guys Close In (85–132)

This **upward path** beat is filled with cute, flirty scenes between Stargirl and Leo, who declares he is "loopy with love" for her (85). Stargirl takes Leo to her "enchanted place" and teaches him how to meditate. He finds it difficult at first but eventually feels himself "stepping over a line . . . taking one step into territory new to [him]" (94). Leo is officially stepping over the line from the first half of Act 2 to the second half, where his beliefs and flaws will be challenged, events will have more meaning, and he'll be forced to confront emotions he's never had to confront before. His internal bad guys.

At school, Leo exists in a state of ignorance, love, and bliss, at first failing to notice that no one speaks to him and Stargirl. But soon it becomes apparent that the rest of the school is "shunning" Stargirl (a word used by B Story character Archie to describe the behavior). Leo becomes paranoid about this, while Stargirl, true to form, doesn't even seem to notice. The establishment has officially turned against the fool. This shunning serves as the **bouncing ball** and primary source of conflict for the beat. Leo feels pulled between the bliss of their blooming relationship and the pressure to conform to the establishment (his flaw). Or as Archie puts it, "Whose affection do you value more, hers or the others'?" (104).

Stargirl continues to show Leo how she sees the world and teaches him a different way to live, like how to notice and appreciate the simple things in life. In her room, Stargirl has a "happy wagon" filled with pebbles that each represent a happy day in her life. It's never been fuller. When Stargirl tells Leo that she reads the "filler" sections in the newspaper to find out what's happening in people's lives, Leo realizes it was she who sent him the porcupine necktie on his fourteenth birthday.

But the "bad guys" (both external and internal) are never far away. The students' reactions to Stargirl are getting worse, and when Leo thinks of the question Archie asked him, about whose affection he values more, he becomes angry. He doesn't want to choose. After Stargirl hangs a huge sign—"Stargirl loves Leo"—on the school bulletin board, the shunning escalates, and Leo succumbs to his **internal bad guys** and starts to ignore Stargirl.

When she corners him to ask if they're breaking up, Leo insists something has to change. He can't handle the shunning. He cares too much about what everyone else thinks, a concept Stargirl has trouble grasping. In her delightfully innocent way, she restates the theme: "But how do you keep track of the rest of the world? Sometimes I can hardly keep track of myself" (136).

After Leo sadly breaks the news to Stargirl that no one at school likes her, she vanishes for two days and returns transformed. Now she wears normal clothes, jewelry, and makeup. No more ukulele, no more pet rat, no more Stargirl. She's changed her name back to her birth name, Susan (her second **transmutation**). Leo notes, "She looked magnificently, wonderfully, gloriously ordinary" (139–140). So ordinary, in fact, that he didn't even see her in the lunchroom. She blended right in. She *conformed*.

The reader immediately recognizes how sad this is. But Leo, still as flawed as the establishment he represents, is thrilled. He struts around school with her, proud to be her boyfriend. Their relationship continues its upward path as Leo and "Susan" start going on "normal" dates to the movies and the mall.

But despite Leo's happiness, the next time he goes to Stargirl's house, he notices that her "happy wagon" only has two stones in it. And strangely, the transmutation seems to be fooling only Leo. The rest of Mica Area High are still shunning her. Even Dori, Stargirl's biggest supporter, is angry at her for betraying herself.

After Stargirl has a vision in her enchanted place, she becomes convinced that if she wins the upcoming state oratorical competition, she'll become popular, and the students will finally like her. She practices her speech in preparation for the big day, and Leo attends the competition with her. During the semifinal round, however, Leo is surprised when Stargirl improvises a brand-new speech unlike the one she practiced. One that is much more reminiscent of the old Stargirl, who is slowly reemerging, unable to be trapped for long in the conformity of her Susan disguise.

For the final round, Stargirl changes her speech yet again. This time, she just talks to the audience. But it's so unique and sincere (like Stargirl herself), it moves Leo to tears and earns her raucous applause and the championship trophy. Afterward, Stargirl is mobbed by strangers wanting autographs and TV crews wanting to interview her. She even appears on the front page of the *Arizona Republic* the next morning. It seems Stargirl has finally been accepted for who she really is.

That is, until she returns to Mica Area High.

All Is Lost (158–161)

As they drive back to school, Stargirl is already planning her big entrance to the fanfare that she is sure awaits her. But when they pull into the parking lot, they find only two teachers and Dori, who is crying and holding a congratulations sign for Susan. Stargirl's trophy slides off her lap and falls to the ground. The wonderful, unique, kindhearted girl who was so quick to cheer for *everyone* has no one to cheer for her.

In a **whiff of death**, we sense that this will be the end of "Susan."

Dark Night of the Soul (160–166)

By Monday, Stargirl is back in full force, wearing her usual clothes and serenading people with her ukulele. It's a **return to the familiar** that we applaud but that makes Leo angry. When he suggests to her that she back off the Stargirl persona and not come on so strong, she kindly restates the theme yet again: "Because we live in a world of *them*, right? You told me that once" (162).

Stargirl kisses his cheek and tells him she knows he's not going to ask her to the upcoming Ocotillo Ball, and that's okay. She accepts him for who he is, even if he can't do the same. This only makes him angrier. The relationship is clearly over. Just as Leo foreshadowed back in the Setup/Debate, he is that rubber band. He "somehow happened to distinguish [himself]," only to be "snapped back into place" (10).

That night, Leo wallows and stews in his bedroom, pulling down the shade to block the moonlight for the first time ever (creating a *literal* dark night). As he slinks further back into hiding, returning to his place among the establishment, he starts to recognize what a coward he is (**Dark Night Epiphany**).

Break Into 3 (166–169)

The Ocotillo Ball arrives, and Leo doesn't attend at all. Instead, he rides his bike past the event and remarks on the conformity of the scene: "I could not identify individuals, only stirrings of color. Much of it was powder blue" (166).

True to her unique and glorious self, Stargirl arrives in the most nonconformist way: riding in a bicycle sidecar decorated with flowers like a parade float and driven by her number-one fan, Dori. She wears a buttercup-yellow gown (a distinct clash with the school's powder blue) and is accompanied by her pet rat. Everything about her appearance is a **synthesis** of the Stargirl we have come to know and love over the past 160 pages. To say this is the climax of Stargirl (the book and the person) is an understatement.

Finale (169–183)

Even though it's doubtful Stargirl has a master plan of how the events of the Finale will unfold (given her spontaneous nature), as she enters the ball and smiles at everyone, her **Act 3 goal** is clear: be magnificently, wonderfully, gloriously *un*-ordinary. Stargirl, the fool, is just being herself. The question is: Will the establishment do the same?

POINT 1: GATHERING THE TEAM. Stargirl dances with abandon, completely on her own. No one speaks to her, but they can't help looking at her, finally taking notice, instead of ignoring her outright. And as the night goes on, the students start to get the feeling that they are "more alone than she [is]" (170).

A boy named Raymond asks her to dance, and suddenly, Stargirl is no longer alone. More boys rush to dance with her.

POINT 2: EXECUTING THE PLAN. Stargirl requests the bunny hop from the band, and before long, she is leading a long line of dancers across the floor. Stargirl improvises funny moves that echo down the line behind her, creating a dancing line of "fools." In another moment of Act 3 **synthesis**, Stargirl becomes the cheerleader (Act 2 self) of nonconformity (Act 1 self). But instead of gawking at her in confusion and disbelief, they follow her lead. The line eventually wanders off the tennis court and disappears into the desert.

Back at the dance, Hillari (who certainly did *not* join the bunny hop) tries to get the band to play "regular music," but they refuse. She drags her boyfriend onto the dance floor and tries to dance "normally" to the song, but it becomes a lost cause. Normalcy doesn't fit here anymore.

The bunny hoppers finally return from the dark desert (like a moment of rebirth), looking "more energized than before," with eyes that "sparkled in the lantern lights" (174).

POINT 3: HIGH TOWER SURPRISE. Hillari Kimble tells Stargirl, "You ruin everything," before slapping her across the face (175).

This stops the fun in its tracks. Everyone goes quiet. Stargirl and Hillari face off.

POINT 4: DIG DEEP DOWN. When Stargirl finally moves, Hillari flinches, expecting to be slapped back. But Stargirl kisses her on the cheek, showing the establishment what true compassion looks like, and proving to them once and for all that Stargirl is real. It's not an act.

Moments later, she disappears on her flower-covered bicycle and is never seen again.

What comes next is up to *them*.

POINT 5: THE EXECUTION OF THE NEW PLAN. Leo tries to find Stargirl after the dance, but her family has moved away. When Leo asks Archie if she was real, Archie responds, "As real as we get" (177). Archie then tells Leo how lucky he was to have known her and that she temporarily gave up herself for him. He says Leo won't fully understand what that means until much later in his life.

Years pass. Leo gets a job on the East Coast as a set designer, inspired by his time in Stargirl's enchanted place. Whenever he comes home to visit, he talks to Archie about Stargirl. On one visit, Archie takes Leo deep into the desert and buries his favorite rodent skull with a scrap of paper that he says contains a word. Although he won't tell Leo what that word is, we're fairly certain it has something to do with Stargirl and the legacy she left behind.

Final Image (184–186)

In the epilogue, we learn more about that legacy. The students still talk about Stargirl at high school reunions. And the establishment of Mica Area High has changed. There's now a club dedicated to performing kind acts for others; there's a ukulele player on the marching band. The fans at the basketball games have a strange tradition of cheering for the opposing team's first basket.

Leo, too, has been transformed. He drops change on the sidewalk and reads the "filler" sections of the newspaper. He notices the little acts of kindness that most people miss. He may never have another chance at love with Stargirl, but he's okay with that. She left her mark, and he's been changed for the better because of her. They all have.

Despite not having a family of his own, Leo doesn't feel alone. Because he knows he's being watched by more than just the stars.

And he's right. In a perfect **mirror image** to the prologue, he receives a porcupine necktie in the mail for his birthday.

WHY IS THIS A FOOL TRIUMPHANT?

Stargirl contains all three elements of a successful Fool Triumphant story.

- **A FOOL:** Stargirl's innocence, kind heart, and eccentricity at first elicit curiosity and even appreciation from her classmates, but when her behavior steps too far outside the confines of their "normal" high school box, they turn on her. In the end, though, it's that very innocence and kind heart that prove her unique ways weren't as foolish as they once seemed.
- **AN ESTABLISHMENT:** Mica Area High is an average American high school where conformity is the name of the game. Students rarely distinguish themselves in any lasting way, as fitting in is the only way to avoid being shunned. Stargirl's appearance shakes things up and eventually reveals the establishment to be the true fool in this story.
- **A TRANSMUTATION:** Stargirl experiences two transmutations. First, when she becomes a cheerleader and dons the uniform. Although she now *dresses* like the others, it does little to hide her eccentricities. It's not until her second transmutation—when she turns into "Susan," the average American teenager—that she truly blends in. But it doesn't last long, because it soon becomes clear that Stargirl can't be anyone else but Stargirl.

Cat's Eye View

For quick reference, here's a brief overview of this novel's beat sheet.

OPENING IMAGE: In a whimsical, quirky prologue, we meet Leo, who represents the establishment of an average American high school (the novel's true hero). After a newspaper article ran a story about his porcupine necktie collection, he received one as a gift from an unknown sender.

CATALYST: A new girl arrives at Mica Area High School, and Stargirl (our fool) is definitely *not* like the rest of the kids in this establishment. Mica will never be the same again.

SETUP/DEBATE: How will the students react to this newcomer? In a combined beat, the author sets up the average world of Mica Area High while also showing how Stargirl's arrival disrupts it. In a double bump, Stargirl dances barefoot on the football field during a game and elicits cheers. The students appear to *like* her.

BREAK INTO 2: When the head cheerleader invites Stargirl to join the squad, it's official. The establishment has accepted Stargirl.

B STORY/THEME STATED: "You'll know her more by your questions than by her answers. Keep looking at her long enough. One day you might see someone you know" (35). Archie, a local paleontologist and mentor to Mica Area High kids, states the theme of nonconformity and letting go of what others think of you. He also represents this by being a little bit of a quirky outsider himself.

FUN AND GAMES: At first, the students accept Stargirl and she becomes popular, but when she starts cheering for the other team at basketball games, they begin to turn on her. Leo puts her on *Hot Seat*, a local TV show at school, and she's attacked.

MIDPOINT: Someone throws a tomato at Stargirl's face during a basketball game, and she's kicked off the cheerleading squad (false defeat). She tells Leo she loves him in a card (love story ramps up). The focus of the novel shifts to Stargirl and Leo's relationship.

BAD GUYS CLOSE IN: Stargirl and Leo are "loopy with love" (85), but their relationship is strained by the shunning at school. When Leo confronts Stargirl about it, she transforms herself into the very average "Susan," which pleases Leo but doesn't fool the other students. Stargirl competes in the state speech competition, but it's only when she gives a speech from her heart that she wins the whole thing.

ALL IS LOST: Susan/Stargirl returns to school victorious, only to find that no one has shown up to cheer for her. We get the sense that this is the end of Susan (whiff of death).

DARK NIGHT OF THE SOUL: Susan becomes Stargirl once more, which makes Leo angry. They break up, and Leo wallows in his room, pulling the shades to create a literal "dark night."

BREAK INTO 3: The Ocotillo Ball arrives, and Leo rides his bike past it to watch Stargirl arrive in a gloriously nonconformist way (riding in a bicycle sidecar and wearing a color that clashes with the other students').

FINALE: At the dance, Stargirl leads the entire school in the bunny hop. When jealous insider Hillari slaps her in the face, Stargirl kisses her in return, showing everyone what real compassion looks like. Then she disappears forever.

FINAL IMAGE: Stargirl left a legacy at Mica Area High, and the establishment is forever changed. There's a club dedicated to performing random acts of kindness, and a tradition of cheering for the other team at basketball games. In a mirror image, Leo receives a porcupine necktie in the mail for his birthday.

Dude with a Problem
When the Odds Are NOT in Your Favor

There's nothing more primal and inspiring than a story about one of the most basic human instincts: survival.

Apocalypses, secret spy organizations, droughts, famines, deadly attacks, alien invasions—these are just some of the problems that test the human spirit and our willingness to do what it takes to overcome insurmountable odds.

This genre—named for the ordinary dude or dudette who finds themselves facing extraordinary circumstances and must rise to the challenge—might be better known for its movies than its novels. Think big-budget action thrillers where the average Joe Schmoe or Jane Schmane is thrust into a plot they definitely didn't expect or deserve and now must battle for their life and their sanity. Like *North by Northwest, Speed, Air Force One, Armageddon, Gravity, Castaway,* and the like. And although the genre is definitely rife with novels as well, there are decidedly fewer to be found in the young adult space. But that doesn't mean these tales can't or shouldn't be written for teens. After all, you'll find some of the most successful and acclaimed novels proudly sporting this genre label (like *The Hunger Games* by Suzanne

Collins and *The Hate U Give* by Angie Thomas). So clearly there's a demand for teenage dudes and dudettes with problems!

All stories that fit into the Dude with a Problem genre are stories of a lone hero or lone group facing incredible odds, whose survival often includes a life-or-death battle. These are the types of novels where the Catalysts are *big* and the stakes are even *bigger*, but the hero is not so different from you and me.

While novels of the Superhero, Fool Triumphant, or even Institutionalized variety might fill some aspirational teen fantasies about being chosen, special, different, or destined to do great things (like take down an evil government), the Dude with a Problem stories can be just as inspiring, but for a very different reason. Because these are stories that feature *ordinary* heroes who start out as nothing more than average, but who take on unexpected, dangerous, and often death-defying challenges!

In other words, the heroes of these stories are us! We're all ordinary dudes, and we're all aware that life as we know it can change in the blink of an eye, thrusting us into situations that test our strength, courage, determination, and will to survive.

Inspiring, indeed!

In fact, one hallmark of a Dude with a Problem *is* the hero's innocence and seeming averageness. These are not superheroes gifted with special abilities. These are just average teens, going about their daily lives, minding their own business, not asking for any trouble, when suddenly . . . BAM! Trouble falls upon them—usually through no fault of their own.

So what do they do? (Besides panic.) They rise to the challenge, of course. Even though the odds seem impossible and death is a very probable outcome. But what else are they going to do? Lie down and let death come for them? I think not!

That's what makes these stories so dang exciting. We are watching heroes *seemingly* ill-equipped to handle the situation . . . handle the situation! Note the emphasis on the word "seemingly." All Dudes of this genre *do* have what it takes to overcome this world of hurt that's been suddenly thrust upon them. They just don't know it yet. The adventure, the fun, the thrill comes in watching them figure it out as the battle for survival rages on.

But "survival" is an interesting word that can be interpreted several different ways. This genre doesn't just include battles for *physical* survival. The life-or-death battle that's often at the heart of these stories can, yes, be about the continued existence of an individual life (like in *The Hunger Games* or *The 5th Wave* by Rick Yancey) or the continued existence of an entire city, state, or population (like in *Alex Rider: Stormbreaker* by Anthony Horowitz, *Dry* by Neal Shusterman and Jarrod Shusterman, or *Illuminae* by Amie Kaufman and Jay Kristoff). These represent the typical action thriller facet of this genre. But the life-or-death battle can also be about the continued existence of a family, group, or society, like in *The Hate U Give* or *All American Boys* by Jason Reynolds and Brendan Kiely, both of which deal with issues of racism and police brutality and the impact they have on an entire community, school, and society at large. It's through inspiring novels like these that we're seeing this genre expand and adapt to the young adult space, going beyond the typical action thriller to tell a slightly different kind of survival tale that teens want and need to read about.

So if you think you have what it takes to *survive* this genre, be sure to include these necessary ingredients to make it impactful and inspiring: (1) an **innocent hero**, (2) a **sudden event**, and (3) a **life-or-death battle**.

AN INNOCENT HERO

The innocent hero of these tales *is* our titular "dude." But dudes don't have to be . . . well, *dudes*. The word "dude" is meant to convey their averageness. They're not destined to save the world (at least not at first!). They're like you and me. Starr Carter in *The Hate U Give* and Rashad Butler in *All American Boys* are just average Black teens attending high school. Brian Robeson in *Hatchet* by Gary Paulsen is just an average teen boy whose parents are going through a divorce. And Alyssa Morrow in *Dry* is just an average teen girl living in a quiet suburban California neighborhood.

But of course, your hero's "averageness" is relative to the world you've put them in. Katniss Everdeen in *The Hunger Games* is just an average teen living in the dystopian world of Panem. Kady Grant and Ezra Mason in *Illuminae* are just your average ex-boyfriend and girlfriend living in a mining space colony on the planet Kerenza.

What may be average to your dude might not seem average to the reader.

The key factor, therefore, is the hero's innocence. The problem that's about to befall them is not their fault and was not asked for; in some cases, the hero doesn't even know how they got involved.

Katniss was minding her own business, doing what it takes to make ends meet in District 12, when BAM! Prim's name is *randomly* drawn for the reaping. Rashad was popping into a convenience store to buy some snacks when a woman *accidentally* crashed into him, causing a police officer to wrongfully arrest him for theft and then beat him unconscious. And it was just another average day for Alyssa in Southern California when *suddenly* the taps stopped working.

The suddenness or unexpectedness of the event is important. It helps define the hero's innocence. But it's also the key quality of our second genre ingredient.

A SUDDEN EVENT

These moments come nearly without warning (often at the Catalyst beat) and thrust the hero into a whole new heap of trouble, leaving them very little time to think or even process what's happening.

However, *because* the hero is innocent, this sudden event might even speak to a greater injustice or societal issue in your hero's world. Rashad wasn't *just* innocent when he was wrongfully arrested and beaten by a police officer. He was the victim of racial profiling and police brutality. Katniss's sister wasn't just *randomly* selected to fight to the death; she and Katniss are both victims of a dystopian government that pits children against each other for the entertainment of the rich.

The sudden event that you choose to thrust your hero into the action has the potential to take us on a much more thought-provoking journey than just an old-fashioned high-stakes thrill ride. Of course, that's always an option, but in the world of young adult fiction, especially in today's climate, publishers, librarians, teachers, parents, and even teen readers themselves are looking for thrill rides that don't just thrill, but also inspire us to take a closer look at our own world.

Regardless of your chosen route, the sudden event is the moment that catapults us into the main conflict of the story and consequently introduces the "problem" part of the Dude with a Problem.

When the pilot of Brian's plane has a heart attack in *Hatchet*, it sends Brian plummeting to earth and leaves him stranded and alone in the middle of the Canadian wilderness. (Huge problem.) When the space colony where Kady and Ezra live is attacked by a rival mining company, it sends the two exes on the run for their life through the galaxy while a deadly virus runs rampant on the spacecrafts. (Another huge problem).

In other words, we're dealing with *big* problems here. If you're not sure if your problem passes the test, try pitching it to someone else. If their first reaction is "Dude, that's a *huge* problem," and their second reaction is, "What would I do if I were in the hero's shoes?" then you got yourself a winner, my friend.

Because that's *exactly* what we want our readers to be thinking too!

The problem *must* be big, because it's inevitably going to lead to our third and final genre ingredient.

A LIFE-OR-DEATH BATTLE

This is a genre of high risk and high stakes. The very existence of something or someone has to be on the line here, or you're probably looking at a different genre. These are the ultimate stories of *survival*. But again, survival can be interpreted in different ways. Some battles are life-threatening (*Hatchet, The 5th Wave, The Hunger Games*), some are world-threatening (*Dry, Stormbreaker, Illuminae*), and some threaten the existence of a neighborhood, community, school, group, or society (*The Hate U Give, All American Boys*).

But regardless, these battles often include a struggle for the hero's own sanity, as they're forced to do things they never thought they could do (or have to).

A little hint: it's easier to pull off *big* problems with *big* stakes when you've got bad guys at play in your story. That's why this genre tends to include more classic antagonists, villains, or opposing forces. Whether that be the Gamemakers pulling the strings behind the scenes of *The Hunger Games*, the natural elements at play in *Hatchet*, a deadly virus and the A.I. who will do anything to contain it in *Illuminae*, or the aliens invading earth in *The 5th Wave*, these are the bad guys that will serve as your source of conflict throughout the story, keeping that life-or-death battle front and center of your story.

In stories where the bad guy is more of a widespread concept than a person, like racial inequality in *The Hate U Give*, it's helpful to give that concept a face in the form of an antagonist (like the character of Hailey, Starr's former best friend, whose racism becomes increasingly apparent throughout the novel).

Regardless of who you nominate to play the role, the golden rule of bad guys still applies: the badder the bad guy, the greater the heroics, the better the story. In other words, bad guys should get progressively worse and put *more* pressure on your hero as the story goes on, which makes the plot more exciting and the ending feel all the more earned.

But of course, it's not *all* bad all the time. In fact, this genre comes with a common beat called the **eye of the storm**, when the hero gets a little moment of reprieve amid all the chaos and life-or-death battling. This is when the action slows down for a chapter or two and the hero gets a chance to take a much-needed breath. And this moment is *usually* (although not always) shared with a common Dude with a Problem character, the **love interest**. Yes, most thrillers do have a little romance to keep things interesting, especially those of the young adult variety.

Think about the moment in *The Hunger Games* when Katniss and Peeta kiss in the cave when Peeta is recuperating before the final show-down with the remaining tributes. Or the moment in *The 5th Wave* when Cassie and Evan kiss right before setting off to rescue her brother from the aliens who captured him.

These moments are important to include—*sparingly*—to keep the plot from feeling too repetitive and give us a break from the A Story. All action, all the time, can get tiresome, and slower moments like this can help refresh your pacing and provide ample time to develop a romance or friendship. But a word of warning: these moments need to feel *organically* plotted. A hero who stops running from killer robots *just* to snog the love interest might not feel realistic. Make sure you're building in believable reasons for your hero to take these reprieves, or you risk sabotaging the urgency of your own plot.

And remember, these reprieves can't last forever. By definition, the eye of the storm is a temporary calm. The storm is still raging all around your hero. The bad guys are still out there. The life-or-death battle must be fought—and hopefully won!

Yes, dudes often *do* overcome their problems in this genre, although it's not a hard-and-fast rule. The concept of victory is always up for interpretation, especially if you're setting up a series. But if you opt for an ending where the dude doesn't win, make sure there's a good reason.

And don't forget that Dude with a Problem stories celebrate the triumph of the human spirit and the idea that even ordinary people, when faced with the right circumstances, can push themselves to do extraordinary things. So it's important to brainstorm your dude and your problem strategically, taking into account your hero's background, traits, and skills to match the right dude with the right problem. Because although your hero may *seem* ill-equipped to handle the problem, it turns out they are the *perfect* person to take on this challenge.

Katniss may seem like a long shot (even to herself!) to win a televised fight to the death, but what do we see her doing in the Setup beat? Hunting! She may not be a soldier trained from birth like some of the "career tributes" from the wealthier districts, but she's smart, she's scrappy, and she's proven to be very good with a bow and arrow, something author Suzanne Collins cleverly sets up from the beginning.

And Alex Rider may not seem like he's cut out to be a spy and save the world; even the people who recruit him don't have much faith in his success. But his grandfather was a spy too, and little did Alex (and the reader) know, he's been secretly grooming Alex the whole time.

It's all about giving your hero a problem that's *just* hard enough for *them*, to make victory seem improbable but not impossible. Impossible problems make for very short novels. Dude, problem, death. But *improbable* problems make for riveting reads full of conflict, struggle, stakes, and a triumph that feels earned.

So give your dude the abilities they'll eventually need to conquer their problem, but hide those abilities from your hero and your reader, ensuring that your hero doesn't realize their true potential until just the right moment. When the Finale is upon us, the bad guys are armed and ready, and the ultimate test of strength, courage, individuality, brawns, and brain is all that stands in the way of victory.

Because in the end, every Dude with a Problem has a similar message that teens can resonate with: deep inside, we all have untapped skills, untested courage, and the ability to persevere and overcome. And even the most "average" of us can become heroes.

To recap: if you're thinking of writing a Dude with a Problem novel, make sure your story includes these three essential ingredients.

- **AN INNOCENT HERO** (or heroes) who is dragged into the mess without asking for it—or possibly even being aware of how they got involved—but in some way has the skills to overcome the problem, even if those skills are buried at first.
- **A SUDDEN EVENT** that thrusts the innocent(s) into the problem. It should be *big* and come without warning.
- **A LIFE-OR-DEATH BATTLE** that threatens the continued existence of an individual, group or society, during which the hero is pitted against bad guys or opposing forces who get stronger and more dangerous as the story goes on.

POPULAR YOUNG ADULT DUDE WITH A PROBLEM NOVELS

Hatchet by Gary Paulsen
Stormbreaker by Anthony Horowitz
The Hunger Games by Suzanne Collins*
Across the Universe by Beth Revis
Monument 14 by Emmy Laybourne
The 5th Wave by Rick Yancey
Illuminae by Amie Kaufman and Jay Kristoff

All American Boys by Jason Reynolds and Brendan Kiely
The Hate U Give by Angie Thomas
Dry by Neal Shusterman and Jarrod Shusterman

* Beat sheet follows.

THE HUNGER GAMES

BY: Suzanne Collins
STC GENRE: Dude with a Problem
BOOK GENRE: Young adult sci-fi/dystopian
TOTAL PAGES: 374 (Scholastic Press hardcover edition, 2008)

No guide about teen fiction would be complete without an analysis of what is unquestionably one of the most successful, memorable, and market-defining YA novels of all time. *The Hunger Games* has sold more than one hundred million copies worldwide, has been translated into more than fifty languages, and has spawned a movie franchise which garnered box office receipts totaling more than three *billion* dollars. You could even argue it's one of the primary reasons the young adult market is as massive as it is today. *The Hunger Games* created a voracious audience of teen (and adult) readers hungry for more content spotlighting teen protagonists.

And it all started with a single seed of an idea in one writer's brain. Talk about inspiring!

But I didn't choose to break down *The Hunger Games* in this book solely based on its staggering success. As a former television writer, Suzanne Collins knows how to structure and pace a story, and the novel remains to this day one of my favorite examples of structure and one of the very *best* examples of the beat sheet in action.

Opening Image (1–4)

Katniss wakes up in her house in District 12 on the day of the "reaping." We're quickly introduced to Katniss, her sister Prim, her mother, and her underprivileged life. They are poor and often hungry.

In this first glimpse into Katniss's world, we see her one and only priority: survival.

We also see glimpses of Katniss's very close relationship with her sister, Prim, of whom Katniss is very protective. When Prim brought home a scrawny kitten, Katniss tried to drown him because it was just another mouth to feed. But Prim begged and cried, and Katniss spared his life (Save the Cat!).

Katniss dresses for a day of hunting and slips out of the house.

Setup (4–20)

Katniss sneaks off and meets Gale, her friend and hunting partner. We learn that Katniss knows how to hunt with a bow and arrow and it's allowed her to keep her family fed (**wants**). Gale is attractive even though Katniss claims there is nothing romantic between them.

Life is tough in "The Seam" (the poorer area of District 12), and Gale and Katniss are both the providers for their families. They both feel disdain toward the Capitol but dare to voice it only while they're alone in the woods together. When Gale suggests that they should run away, Katniss immediately dismisses the idea as "preposterous," establishing her as someone who is not prepared to take risks to defy the Capitol, as much as she might dislike them.

In this Setup, we get a sense of one of Katniss's primary flaws. She's distrustful of most people and doesn't like to accept help from others. Her distance is understandable. When her father died, her mother turned "blank and unreachable, while her children turned to skin and bones" (8), leaving Katniss to fend for and rely on herself to feed her family.

Katniss returns home to prepare for the reaping, which we learn is the process of choosing (by a type of lottery) one teen boy and one teen girl from each of the twelve districts of Panem to compete in a televised fight to the death (the Hunger Games). It is explained to be a punishment for an uprising among the districts seventy-four years ago and a reminder that the Capitol holds all the power.

The unfairness and brutality of the Games angers Katniss, but as she remarks on page 19, "there's nothing you can do." Here we get another hint of Katniss's sense of powerlessness in the face of the Capitol. She believes in order to survive, you simply have to keep quiet and play by the Capitol's rules. But that belief will certainly change by the end of the novel.

Catalyst (20–25)

Katniss's little sister, Prim, is chosen as the girl tribute for the Hunger Games and Katniss jumps in to volunteer as tribute to protect her sister. Things will never be the same again.

Debate (25–58)

The question is not whether Katniss will go to the Hunger Games (she already volunteered). The question is: Can she win?

With a single Catalyst, Katniss's goal changes. Or rather amplifies. While moments ago, her goal of survival was all about keeping her family fed, now it's about fighting twenty-three other tributes to the death (much more difficult). And we're about to meet one of those tributes.

Right after Katniss volunteers to take Prim's place, the boy tribute is chosen. It's Peeta Mellark. Katniss remarks that she knows the name but has never spoken to him, and then flashes back to a day after her father was killed in a mining accident and her family was starving and Peeta (whose parents own a bakery) tossed her a burnt loaf of bread.

Eventually, in Act 2, Peeta will become Katniss's love interest and B Story character, but at this point in the story, all Katniss can hope is that "*someone else will kill him before I do*" (33). Because at this point of the story, she is already debating how she might be able to win—and thinking solely about survival.

The Debate covers all the preparations for arriving at the Capitol, including saying goodbye to her friends and family, getting some last-minute advice from Gale, and the train ride with Haymitch (Katniss and Peeta's alcoholic mentor).

But before Katniss leaves to board the train, her friend Madge (the mayor's daughter) gives Katniss a Mockingjay pin, and Katniss promises to wear it in the arena. Katniss doesn't know it at the time, but this pin represents resistance to the Capitol. It's a symbol of revolution and rebellion. And by wearing it, Katniss is marking herself as the revolutionary that she needs to become.

During the train ride, Haymitch tells them he can help them in the arena, but only if they do exactly as he says. But as we've already established, Katniss is not great at trusting others . . .

Break Into 2 (58–60)

The train passes through a dark tunnel, and when it emerges on the other side, we are in a completely different world. An **upside-down world**. It is completely unlike District 12. Everything here is glamorous, luxurious, indulgent, colorful, and the people are gluttonous and clueless. Welcome to the Capitol.

This is where Katniss's **Act 2 goal**—win the Hunger Games—will play out.

Peeta waves at the crowd, already playing the game and trying to get sponsors. This only serves to remind Katniss that, just like all the other tributes she'll face in the arena, Peeta is not to be trusted.

Speaking of Peeta . . .

B Story (130)

During a televised interview with Caesar Flickerman before the Games begin, Peeta confesses that he's in love with Katniss, effectively elevating his status to love interest and B Story character. Even though he was introduced in Act 1, this is where their relationship gets really interesting and Peeta becomes much more important to Katniss and her internal journey.

His confession leads the audience to believe that Katniss and Peeta are star-crossed lovers, doomed to die. At first Katniss is furious that he did this and thinks it will make her appear weak. But Cinna (her stylist) and Haymitch assure her that it's only helping her hardened, unlikable image (flaw). So already he's acting as a "helper character."

But Katniss is confused. She's unsure of her true feelings for Peeta. She'd rather just hate him, because she knows once they step into the arena, they will become enemies. But it's admittedly hard for her to do that. Up until this point, he's been nothing but nice to her, but she's been able to convince herself that it's all for show and he'd just as soon kill her when they enter the arena.

As the B Story character, Peeta represents Katniss's struggle with trusting others. This is one brilliant element of the love story Suzanne Collins has crafted: readers must figure out whether Peeta *is* trustworthy. Does he really love Katniss? Or is he just playing the game in order to survive—just as Katniss is doing?

Eventually, as all good B Story characters should do, Peeta will teach Katniss her theme: there's more to life than just survival.

In fact, he's the one who will state it.

Theme Stated (142)

Although the theme is hinted at several times throughout Act 1, here it's stated most overtly.

In a poignant moment on the roof of the training center, Peeta tells Katniss that he knows he's not a real contender in the Games—and then, "I keep wishing I could think of a way to show the Capitol that they don't own me. That I'm more than just a piece in their Games." Peeta wants to die with his dignity intact. He wants to defy the Capitol. But Katniss dismisses the idea. "But you're not. None of us are. That's how the Games work" (142).

Katniss's whole life has been about survival—playing by the Capitol's rules to protect her family and come home alive. But by the end of the novel, she'll learn that to truly "win," she'll have to defy the Capitol, not just survive it. This story is so much bigger than just surviving. It's about being more just a piece in the Capitol's Games.

Despite what Katniss said on page 19 about the injustice in Panem, there *is* something she can do about it.

She can rebel.

And by the end of the book, she will.

Fun and Games (61–183)

The first half of the Fun and Games is spent in preparation for the seventy-fourth annual Hunger Games. Here we really see Katniss floundering in her upside-down world.

First, she grits her teeth through a makeover session where stylists work on transforming her from the simple, disheveled provincial girl from a poor district to a beautiful, polished, sparkling tribute (an upside-down version of herself!).

Then Katniss and Peeta undergo training and mentoring. They make a noteworthy entrance at the opening ceremonies in "fiery" costumes, foreshadowing Katniss's nickname throughout the series: "The Girl on Fire." Katniss wows the Gamemakers during her private assessment, earning an almost unprecedented score of 11. Which might seem like an upward path for Katniss, but it instantly puts a target on her back (**bouncing ball**).

The *literal* fun and games—the Hunger Games—begins when Katniss and the other tributes are raised into the arena on platforms. This is the **promise of the premise** (and of the title). Twenty-four teens fighting to the death.

Despite securing herself a backpack with supplies, and other small wins, Katniss is on a clear **downward path** toward the Midpoint. She suffers from dehydration and, after the Gamemakers create a wall of fire to push her closer to the other tributes, smoke inhalation and burn wounds.

She's also shocked to see that Peeta has joined an alliance of "Career" tributes. She thinks his talk about dignity the other night was just another game to mess with her head. He is clearly in it to win it.

While Katniss is tending to her burn wounds in a pond, the Careers find her and chase her up a tree. They try to climb after her, but fail. They decide to wait it out and kill her in the morning.

Midpoint (183–194)

In a **false defeat**, Katniss is trapped. "All my bravado is gone. I'm weak from pain and hunger but can't bring myself to eat. Even if I can last the night, what will the morning bring?" (183) It seems like the end. Surely she won't be able to escape the Career tributes who have been hunting her ever since the Gamemakers put that target on her back.

But then she notices a pair of eyes in the darkness. They belong to Rue, the twelve-year-old tribute from District 11 who reminds Katniss of her sister. Rue points out a nest of tracker jackers (a genetically modified wasp). Katniss saws the nest free, and it falls on the Careers, unleashing chaos and killing two tributes. Katniss gets stung three times and has horrific hallucinations, but still manages to pry the bow and arrow from the hands of one of the fallen tributes. Given her archery skills, this marks a clear turning point in her path and her chances of survival.

Tormented by the tracker jacker stings and the hallucinations, Katniss staggers and falls. She spots someone coming for her through the trees. It's Peeta. But instead of stabbing her with his spear—which she expects—he pushes her up and tells her to run.

In a brilliant crossroads where the **stakes are raised**, the **A and B Stories cross**, *and* Katniss **shifts from wants to needs**, Katniss realizes that Peeta just saved her life.

Why would he do that if he were just playing the game, as she once believed? Maybe he *can* be trusted. Maybe he really *does* have feelings for her.

But Katniss still knows (as does the reader) they can't both win. So what's the point in loving someone who will have to die if you are to survive?

Well, the answer, as Katniss will learn, is our theme.

Bad Guys Close In (195–232)

Things get decidedly better for Katniss in the arena as we round the turn into an **upward path**.

Once she's worked the tracker jacker venom out of her system, Katniss finds food and forms an unexpected alliance with Rue. This is a big moment of growth for Katniss, as one of her primary flaws is her distrust of others.

They share information about the other tributes and the arena. Rue tells her that she doesn't think Peeta's lover boy act is an act. They make a plan to destroy the Careers' food supply to starve them out of the Games (**modified goal**).

Katniss and Rue set their plan in motion. During her mission, Katniss learns that one of the Careers injured Peeta and left him for dead. Katniss is worried about him, but still unsure what to make of his actions at the Midpoint.

Katniss blows up the Careers' supplies. The explosion causes her temporary hearing loss, but the plan is a success!

Until . . .

All Is Lost (232–236)

Katniss hears a young girl screaming and runs to find Rue stuck in a trap. The boy tribute from District 1 stabs Rue with a spear, and Katniss kills him with one of her arrows (her first kill in the Games). Rue makes Katniss promise she'll win for both of them. Katniss sings a song for Rue as she dies (**whiff of death**).

Dark Night of the Soul (236–244)

Katniss's anger toward the Capitol erupts. She feels that same impotence she felt at the start of the novel, but now, mourning Rue, it's even stronger. She wants her revenge for this injustice, but what can she do?

That's when, in a **Dark Night Epiphany**, she remembers Peeta's words: "I keep wishing I could think of a way . . . to show the Capitol that they don't own me. That I'm more than just a piece in their Games."

She remembers her theme.

And takes her first step toward proving that she's learned it.

To shame the Capitol and honor Rue, Katniss decorates her dead body with flowers, knowing the Gamemakers will have to show it to all the viewers. She receives a gift of bread from District 11 (Rue's district) and says thank you to them. She remembers her promise to Rue and vows to win for her.

Break Into 3 (244)

When it is announced that there's been a change of rules and now two tributes can win the Hunger Games if they are from the same district, Katniss involuntarily calls out Peeta's name.

At the Break Into 2, she vowed not to trust him. And now he's her only ally and her best chance at winning. What a difference an act makes!

With this rule change, we also get a goal change. Katniss's **Act 3 goal** is to find Peeta so they can win together. She rationalizes her decision by telling herself she's teaming up with Peeta only to maintain the "star-crossed lover" façade so the audience will keep rooting for them and sending gifts, but we get the sense there might be more to it than that. Only time (and the Finale) will tell.

Finale (262–373)

POINT 1: GATHERING THE TEAM. Katniss sets off to find Peeta and tracks him to a stream bed where he's camouflaged himself in mud. His wounds are bad and he's nearly dead, but she manages to get him moving, and they settle in at the mouth of a cave. Katniss and Peeta are now a team. They must work together if they want to win.

POINT 2: EXECUTING THE PLAN. At first it seems Katniss's plan is working. She kisses Peeta, and Haymitch sends down a pot of broth, signaling to Katniss that if she wants more gifts, she's going to have to keep up the love act. Despite everything, Katniss still hasn't completely learned her lesson; she is still faking it to try to survive. Or so she thinks.

Peeta is getting worse. The Gamemakers announce that all the remaining tributes need something that will be available in a backpack in the center of the arena. Katniss knows they're trying to lure the remaining tributes together to keep the action going, but she doesn't have a choice. She knows Peeta's medicine will be there, but Peeta won't let her risk her life to get it. She drugs Peeta to get him to sleep so she can go get the medicine. This is a momentously unselfish act for Katniss, who's typically distrustful of others and thinks only of survival. But now, she's doing this not in the name of survival, but for Peeta.

Just as Finales should be, this one is packed with conflict. As Katniss goes for the medicine, she's attacked by another tribute who nearly kills her. But Thresh, the other tribute from Rue's district, kills the tribute instead. He spares Katniss's life as a thank-you for what she did for Rue, but Katniss is bleeding badly from the attack.

Katniss gets the medicine to Peeta and passes out from the blood loss. When she wakes, Peeta is much better, and the two share stories from their past. Katniss realizes that Peeta might *really* be in love with her, which only confuses her.

The two manage to survive until there are only three tributes left: Katniss, Peeta, and Cato. Their Act 3 plan is still working!

The Gamemakers drive the three remaining tributes together and unleash genetically mutated wolves on them. Cato is killed.

POINT 3: HIGH TOWER SURPRISE. Just when Katniss and Peeta believe they've won the Hunger Games and their plan has worked, the Gamemakers announce that they are revoking the revision of the rules. Only one tribute can win.

Katniss is furious that she was tricked by the Gamemakers, yet again.

Peeta grabs his knife, and Katniss aims her bow and arrow. Peeta throws his knife in the lake and tells Katniss to kill him. But she can't. She knows she won't be able to live with herself if she does.

POINT 4: DIG DEEP DOWN. "We both know they have to have a victor," Peeta says (343–344), and suddenly Katniss realizes what she has to do. She can't just survive. She has to rebel.

The lesson is learned.

She gathers poisonous berries and tells Peeta that they will eat them together, so that there will be *no* victor. Katniss demonstrates that she's willing to forfeit her life—her goal of survival—in order to defy the Capitol, die with dignity, and prove that they don't own her.

POINT 5: THE EXECUTION OF THE NEW PLAN. Katniss and Peeta prepare to swallow the berries, but the Gamemakers stop them just in time and announce that they have both won. They are lifted out of the arena and separated to recover before returning home. The Capitol organizes a celebratory reunion of the two lovers on television, and Katniss plays it up for the cameras. She is still unsure of her feelings for Peeta, but she has to continue the charade because the Capitol is furious at her for making them look like fools with the berry stunt. When Peeta discovers that Katniss has been "faking it" for the cameras, he is crushed. He really does have feelings for her. But he agrees to continue the charade for the press. Was Katniss really faking it, though? She's still not sure. She vows to figure it out after this is all over and she's safe at home.

Final Image (373–374)

Katniss and Peeta join hands for the cameras as they prepare to disembark the train that has brought them back to District 12. She is returning home a victor. She doesn't know what will happen—will the Capitol seek their revenge on her or let her be?—or even how she feels about Peeta. But one thing is certain: She is not the rule-playing, survival-obsessed girl she was before. She is a rebel.

WHY IS THIS A DUDE WITH A PROBLEM?

- **AN INNOCENT HERO:** Katniss is an ordinary girl, living in District 12 and playing by the Capitol's rules. She doesn't start out as a rebel and often feels powerless against the Capitol's unjust laws. The lottery that pulls her into the events of the novel is completely random, making her a truly "innocent" hero.
- **A SUDDEN EVENT:** When Prim's name is randomly selected at the reaping, everything changes for Katniss. This sudden event has enormous consequences for Katniss and her family.
- **A LIFE-OR-DEATH BATTLE:** Katniss volunteers to take her sister's place and enters the Hunger Games, where she must fight against twenty-three other teens in a life-or-death battle for survival.

Cat's Eye View

For quick reference, here's a brief overview of this novel's beat sheet.

OPENING IMAGE: Katniss wakes up in District 12 on the morning of the reaping. She is poor and often hungry, and she thinks solely of keeping her family alive (wants).

SETUP: We get a glimpse of Katniss's world in District 12. It's a tough life. She has to hunt illegally in the woods to make ends meet. She is very protective of her sister, Prim, and distrustful of most others (flaw), and although she's angry about injustices of the Capitol, she feels powerless to do anything about it.

CATALYST: Prim's name is called at the reaping for the Hunger Games. Katniss volunteers to take her place.

DEBATE: Can she win? The boy tribute, Peeta, is chosen. Katniss says goodbye to her family and her friend Gale, who gives her some advice on how to win, and boards the train to the Capitol at which time she meets her alcoholic mentor, Haymitch.

BREAK INTO 2: The train arrives in the Capitol. It's an upside-down world compared to District 12. Peeta waves at the crowd, reminding Katniss that he's already playing the game.

B STORY: Peeta declares his love for Katniss on TV, identifying him as the novel's love story and B Story character. He helps Katniss not only earn support and win the games but also face up to her flaw of distrust and learn the theme: to truly win the games, you have to do more than just survive.

THEME STATED: The night before the Hunger Games begin, Peeta tells Katniss, "I keep wishing I could think of a way to show the Capitol that they don't own me. That I'm more than just a piece in their Games" (142). She dismisses this as irrational, but in the end, that's exactly what she'll do: show the Capitol that they don't own her.

FUN AND GAMES: Katniss receives a makeover and trains for the games. The Hunger Games begin, and she struggles with dehydration and burn wounds. She discovers Peeta has allied with the "Career" tributes, confirming her suspicion that he can't be trusted.

MIDPOINT: In a false defeat, the Careers chase Katniss up a tree, where she will surely meet her end. But shockingly, Peeta saves her life, proving that his love for her might not be an act (stakes are raised and love story ramps up).

BAD GUYS CLOSE IN: Katniss forms an alliance with Rue, and the two manage to blow up the supplies of the Careers, a big win for both of them.

ALL IS LOST: Rue is caught in a trap and killed (whiff of death).

DARK NIGHT OF THE SOUL: Rue's death fuels Katniss's anger and sense of impotence against the Capitol's injustices. In a Dark Night Epiphany, she realizes she *can* do something to defy them. She buries Rue in flowers to honor her fallen ally and shame the Capitol.

BREAK INTO 3: When the Gamemakers announce a rule change—now two tributes from the same district can win—Katniss calls out Peeta's name. The same boy she vowed to distrust at the Break Into 2 is now her only ally and best chance at winning.

FINALE: Katniss finds Peeta badly injured and nurses him back to health. They manage to survive until they are the only two left. But when the Capitol announces another rule change—now only *one* tribute can win—Katniss proves she's learned the theme by threatening to eat poisonous berries, which would leave the Capitol with *no* victor. The Gamemakers stop them and declare both the winners.

FINAL IMAGE: Katniss rides the train home to District 12 with Peeta. She is returning home not just a victor, but a proven rebel.

Out of the Bottle
A Magical Twist on Reality

Everyone makes wishes, right? We blow out birthday candles, hoping for something to change. We see a shooting star and think, *What if . . . ?* We find a penny on the street and wonder if it really is lucky. We believe in magic.

And that's what this genre is all about.

Magic.

Typically, though, when we think about "magic" in young adult fiction, we think witches, wizards, fairies, elves, summoners, vampires, and demons. We think *fantasy*.

But what about magic that happens right here in the real world? To ordinary heroes? What about the average down-on-their-luck teenager who makes a wish for something that will make all of their problems go away—and *poof!* It comes true.

Named for the magic wish-granting lamp in *Aladdin*, Out of the Bottle stories explore what it's like for an ordinary hero to be *temporarily* touched by magic and leave the encounter transformed.

The magic can come in all shapes and sizes—wishes granted, curses bestowed, bodies swapped, guardian angels dispatched, parallel universes and time loops explored—but they all tend to serve a common purpose: to fix a problem or highlight something wrong with the hero's life. Magic can be a fun way to escape reality for a while (for the reader *and* the hero!). But in the end, all Out of the Bottle stories have a similar lesson: you can escape "reality" for only so long. Eventually you must face it. Because even though the hero is only *temporarily* touched by magic, they are *permanently* changed by it.

The magic in Out of the Bottle stories is typically used as a story-telling device to play out life's biggest "what if" questions. What if I was reliving the same day over and over? (*Opposite of Always* by Justin A. Reynolds and *Before I Fall* by Lauren Oliver.) What if I had made another choice? (*The Love That Split the World* by Emily Henry.) What if I could still talk to someone after they're dead? (*You've Reached Sam* by Dustin Thao.)

Which is why stories of this genre are often tagged as "magical realism" rather than fantasy or sci-fi. Once the magic is bestowed on our hero, they eventually have to learn that they didn't need it after all! In the end, reality is where it's at. So this genre typically isn't about exploring a new, fantastical world. Most Out of the Bottle heroes come from *our* world and are temporarily gifted (or cursed) with magic before returning to reality as a changed person.

So these tales tend to resonate in a very specific way. Who among us hasn't wished for a touch of magic to fix life's problems? Who hasn't wondered *what if*? In these novels, we get to play out a magical twist on a reality we know all too well: our own reality. And in the end, we are left riveted and inspired by the message that even magic can't fix the problems of the real world. Only we can do that.

Having penned five Out of the Bottle novels myself (two for teens and three for tweens), I know from experience that they can be a blast to write and a fun way to put a creative spin on some age-old lessons about growing up and facing that brutal foe we call *reality*. We just have to make sure we're gearing our Out of the Bottle stories toward the right audience. The key is choosing a type of magic that will appeal to teen readers and the experiences they're having at this time of their lives. And, as the magic in these stories is just a creative vehicle to explore deeper issues, be sure that those issues resonate with the twelve-to-eighteen crowd.

To do that effectively, you'll need the following three ingredients: (1) a **hero deserving of the magic**, (2) a **spell** (or touch of magic), and (3) a **lesson**.

Let's *spell* them out.

A HERO DESERVING OF THE MAGIC

As in all stories, the hero must fit the plot. And in Out of the Bottle tales, this specifically relates to the magic. Why does your hero deserve this magic?

In *You've Reached Sam*, teenage Julie had her life all planned out with her boyfriend, Sam, until Sam died in a car accident. Now she's having a hard time dealing with the loss of Sam and all their big plans. Her instinct is to throw away everything that reminds her of him and try to forget. This makes her the perfect candidate for discovering that she can still talk to Sam through their phones, which are magically connected. She needs to learn that her grief can't be dealt with by forgetting or hanging on but only by *moving* on. Something that Sam helps her do through the magic that's bestowed on her.

In *Instant Karma* by Marissa Meyer, the hero, Prudence, likes to cast judgment on those around her, thinking she's taking the moral high ground. When she's magically gifted with the ability to bestow karmic justice on vandals, bullies, and other no-good-doers, we get it. It fits. But when the magic backfires, Prudence learns a valuable lesson about virtue and vanity and the gray area in between.

In *Instructions for Dancing* by Nicola Yoon, the hero, Evie, was once a romance novel junkie, but stopped believing in love after she walked in on her dad cheating on her mom. How appropriate that she would receive the magic ability to *see* the entire span of people's relationships—how they began, the highs, the lows, and the end. And how even *more* appropriate that for most of the novel, Evie thinks of these visions as a curse and proof that all love stories eventually end. But she'll discover that perhaps that's not what the visions are really there to teach her.

The key to nailing this ingredient is answering the question "Why *this* magic for *this* hero?"

Perhaps your hero is down on their luck and desperately in need of a change in fortune (also called an **empowerment** story), or they're sitting on a high horse and desperately in need of a wake-up call (also called a **comeuppance** story). Either way, when the magic strikes (usually at the Catalyst or the Break Into 2), the reader should be saying "Oh yeah, that's *exactly* what they deserve!"

Which brings us our second genre ingredient.

A SPELL

How are you going to bend the laws of nature to give your hero (and readers) the adventure of a lifetime? What magic are you going to pull out of your bottle? Will your hero be caught in a time loop (*Opposite of Always* and *Before I Fall*)? Cast into a parallel universe or dimension (*The Love That Split the World*)? Experience alternate outcomes of the same choice (*Ask Again Later* by Liz Czukas)? Be gifted (or cursed!) with a special power, ability, or magical visitor (*Instant Karma*, *Instructions for Dancing*, and *Pet* by Akwaeke Emezi)? Discover a magical device that connects them to a lost love (*You've Reached Sam*)? Kicked out of their body or thrust into a new one (*If I Stay* by Gayle Forman and *Airhead* by Meg Cabot)? Or will you invent something completely new?

Regardless of what you choose, choose wisely, because this magic will most likely be the whole **premise** of your novel—the reason the reader was drawn to the book in the first place. In fact, it's probably going to define the upside-down nature of your Act 2 world.

Out of the Bottle stories typically follow a similar structure (although not always). The hero receives the magic at the Catalyst, debates whether the magic is real or tries to figure out how it works in the Debate, and finally accepts it and starts interacting with it more willingly at the Break Into 2, making your Fun and Games the beat where the magic is most prominent. Because it's new, it's exciting (or it's a drag), but it's what you promised the reader, so you must deliver!

That shouldn't be too hard to do. Just make sure you're building your A Story (external story) *around* the magic. After all, the Act 2 world is supposed to be about fixing things the wrong way, right? Well, Out of the Bottle stories just put a magical twist on that concept. Your hero is literally using *magic* to fix things. Of course, it's the wrong way. But it can really put the *fun* in Fun and Games!

The Fun and Games in *Instant Karma* is when Prudence dishes out karmic justice left and right and in *You've Reached Sam* when Julie talks on the phone with Sam for hours at a time, even visiting their favorite places with him. But even she senses the wrongness in this solution to her grief, saying "It's the not the same, Sam. Not at all . . ." (88).

When inventing your own magical premise, don't be afraid to get creative! The Out of the Bottle story might be familiar, but the magic is where you get to strut your stuff and put your own unique twist on things. *Before I Fall* and *Opposite of Always*, both make use of time loop magic, but with a different spin. In *Before I Fall*, Samantha is trapped in the day she dies and tries to stop it. While in *Opposite of Always*, Jack is stuck in a stretch of time, between the day he met Kate and the day she dies, trying to prevent not his own death but another's. Same magic, fresh twist.

The novel *Pet* puts a unique spin on the genre by placing the story in a utopian society that has supposedly rid itself of all the "monsters" (people who harm others). But the magic begins when an angel named Pet visits the hero, Jam, and tells her that he's there to hunt a monster hiding in the midst of this seeming paradise.

Whatever fresh twist you choose to throw at it, one thing you must do is clearly establish the **rules of the magic**. Yes, yes, Out of the Bottles by definition *break* the rules by having magic in the first place, but you still have to give yourself some guidelines and stick to them!

Every time an author writes a novel, they enter into a contract with the reader. The reader promises to suspend disbelief and go along with whatever make-believe stuff the writer conjures up, only if the writer agrees to do it well and play fair. This contract is especially important in Out of the Bottle stories, where the make-believe stuff you're conjuring up really is *make-believe*. It bends the laws of nature! So your reader has to suspend disbelief even more than usual. If you choose to break your own rules to better serve your plot, your reader will likely feel betrayed.

In *You've Reached Sam*, author Thao sets up his rules well, establishing that only Julie and Sam's phones are connected by this magic, and they can only talk, not text message. Additionally, it's established that if Sam ever calls and Julie *doesn't* pick up, it will sever their connection completely. And in *Instructions for Dancing*, after some trial and error, Evie figures out that her visions are triggered only when she first sees a couple kissing, and they must be in love for it to work.

To establish the magic (and the rules), sometimes it's helpful to include one of two types of common Out of the Bottle characters: a *confidante* (someone the hero confides in about their strange nature-defying situation) or a *guide* (someone who either already knows about the magic or perhaps is somewhat responsible for bestowing the magic).

Both can be useful in guiding the story and/or getting the hero out of their head. Because heroes are often alone in this magical predicament, it can be easy for authors to rely solely on internal reflection when narrating the story, but this can get tedious. Having a guide or confidante gets the narration out of the hero's head and into dialogue.

In *You've Reached Sam*, Sam serves as the guide, helping establish not only the rules, but also the stakes of the magic: Sam thinks that if Julie tells anyone else about their connection, it might weaken it and threaten their ability to talk to each other.

In *Instructions for Dancing*, we see both. A strange woman is present when Evie first picks up the book *Instructions for Dancing*, which she determines is somehow linked to her visions. She believes the woman knows something about it, so when she sees the guide again, she gets some much-needed answers and advice from her. But almost immediately after the magic is bestowed, Evie confides in her best friend, Martin, who helps her Debate how the magic works and whether it's real, making him a fun confidante to share the experience with.

One additional piece of advice: be careful not to *overexplain* the magic, which can be tempting when writing an Out of the Bottle story. Because we're dealing with magic here, we often feel the need to *prove* to the reader that it works, with a deep dive into the mechanics. The reader doesn't need proof. They *know* it's magic. They're game! Sticking to the rules is enough to convince them to go along for the ride. The *how* of the magic is not as important as what the magic does for the story and the hero. The *purpose* of the magic. Which is to deliver the third genre ingredient.

A LESSON

How will this magic *transform* your hero? What does it mean to be a human in the *real* world? That's the stuff that great magical tales are made of. And that's ultimately what all Out of the Bottle stories are about.

It's not the magic that will fix the hero's life for good. The magic just shows them *what* needs to be fixed. Now they have to do it themselves.

In *You've Reached Sam*, Julie can't stay connected to Sam forever. Eventually she must learn how to let go and move on. But the magic gives her a chance to say goodbye—something she didn't get in real life. Only then can she *choose* not to pick up when Sam calls—the very thing that will sever their connection forever and cast her back into the real world.

In *Instructions for Dancing*, the guide helps Evie realize that she's been looking at the visions all wrong (fixing things the wrong way). She was looking at it as a curse, only focusing on how love ends, when really it was a gift, allowing her to *see* love. This relates directly back to the lesson Evie must learn: "It doesn't matter that love ends, it just matters that there's love." (278)

And in *Pet*, Jam must come to terms with the fact that "monsters" are still out there and that refusing to see them or believing that they don't exist is the surest way to *allow* them to exist. A lesson she learns only with an angel's help. Still, when Pet wants to kill the "monster," Jam stops him, choosing instead to expose the "monster" to the town and forcing *everyone* else to see him too. She now knows this is the only way to prevent more of them.

Magic can be a fun distraction. It's easy to sweep our problems under the rug when magic is involved. But in the end, we all know it's cheating. After all, if magic were the ultimate solution to problems, what does that mean for us readers who live in the real world, who will never experience that magic? How will we relate to the story?

We won't.

That's why this third ingredient—the lesson—is so important. And why many Out of the Bottle tales include a moment in the Finale when the hero has to **do it without the magic**. It's a test to prove if they've really learned the lesson and truly understand that the magic, while maybe cool, wasn't necessary after all. They already had the power to transform themselves. It was inside them all along. And *that* is pretty magical.

To recap: if you're thinking of writing an Out of the Bottle, make sure your story includes these three essential ingredients:

- **A HERO DESERVING OF THE MAGIC:** whether you're empowering an underdog or delivering a comeuppance to a worthy recipient, make sure it's clear to the reader that this hero needs *this* specific supernatural boost.
- **A SPELL OR TOUCH OF MAGIC:** regardless of how the magic comes to be (via a person, place, object, or other), make sure you're setting up this illogical thing with logical rules that you stick to, lest you risk betraying your reader's trust.
- **A LESSON:** what does your hero learn from this magic? And how do they ultimately fix things the right way (without the magic)?

POPULAR YOUNG ADULT OUT OF THE BOTTLE NOVELS

Split by a Kiss by Luisa Plaja
Airhead by Meg Cabot
If I Stay by Gayle Forman*
Before I Fall by Lauren Oliver
Through to You by Emily Hainsworth
Parallel by Lauren Miller
Ask Again Later by Liz Czukas
The Love That Split the World by Emily Henry
The Square Root of Summer by Harriet Reuter Hapgood
Two Summers by Aimee Friedman
Me and Me by Alice Kuipers
Pretty in Punxsutawney by Laurie Boyle Crompton

Opposite of Always by Justin A. Reynolds
Pet by Akwaeke Emezi
Instant Karma by Marissa Meyer
Instructions for Dancing by Nicola Yoon
You've Reached Sam by Dustin Thao

* Beat sheet follows.

IF I STAY

BY: Gayle Forman
STC GENRE: Out of the Bottle
BOOK GENRE: Young adult contemporary/magical realism
TOTAL PAGES: 234 (Penguin Publishing, paperback edition, 2010)

What if you could choose to live or die? That's the what if? question at the center of this poignant, heartbreaking Out of the Bottle (and out of the body!) tale. After Mia suffers a terrible car accident, she wakes up outside of her body and finds herself facing the most difficult choice of her life: to live or die. Not coincidentally, she was also facing a gut-wrenching choice before the accident, creating a past/present mirror of Mia's theme about life's impossible choices and the courage it takes to make them. *If I Stay*, which has sold more than two million copies and has been adapted into a major motion picture starring Chloë Grace Moretz, is a beautiful and poetic example of a flashback-driven narrative as Mia jumps back and forth in time, weighing her decision whether to go or stay.

Opening Image (1–11)

Mia wakes to a blanket of snow. School is canceled, and Mia's family decides to visit friends. The Catalyst comes quickly in this novel, so the Opening Image does a lot of great Setup work. For instance, we learn that at **home,** Mia is very close with her parents and younger brother Teddy. At **play,** Mia is in a serious relationship with Adam, the lead singer of a rising punk rock band called Shooting Star, but complications have recently been cropping up between them. And at **work,** Mia is a high school senior and a skilled cellist who **wants** to go to Juilliard. Her recent audition went well, but she knows that if she gets in it'll further complicate her relationship with Adam (**stasis = death**).

Setup (11–15)

As everyone piles into the car and launches into their usual debate about what music to listen to, it becomes clear that, even though they have very different tastes, this is a family bonded by their love of music. They compromise and agree to take turns listening to their preferred stations. Mia chooses a classical station, and when Beethoven's Cello Sonata no. 3 comes on, she considers it a cosmic coincidence, since it's the piece she's supposed to be practicing today.

Cosmic coincidence or just bad luck, this piece will be the soundtrack to the most devastating moment of Mia's life.

Catalyst (15–18)

"Eviscerated" is the word Mia uses to describe the car after a pickup truck plows into the passenger side. Mia describes the horrific sounds of the accident and then the silence, broken only by the sonata still playing from the speakers. After finding both her parents dead, she searches for Teddy but instead finds her own body.

Debate (18–86)

"Am I dead?" Mia asks as the paramedics arrive on the scene, posing the first Debate question (19). As with most Out of the Bottle stories, this Debate is centered on figuring out whether the magic is real and if so, how it works.

First, convinced it's a dream, Mia tries to wake herself, but can't. As the paramedics work on her, we experience the first of many flashbacks that author Gayle Forman uses throughout the novel to give us context about Mia's life and pose the thought-provoking question at the heart of this novel's theme, premise, and title: Do I stay or go? Each flashback serves to either inform Mia's ultimate choice or show us how the theme of choice has affected other parts of her life.

Theme Stated (27)

During the first flashback, Mia shares the story of her first cello recital. She was so nervous, she almost didn't go on stage. When she asked her dad (a former rock musician) how he got over the performance jitters, he said, "You don't. You just work through it. You just hang in there" (27).

Sometimes there are no shortcuts, no easy ways around. Sometimes the only way out is through. In this story, Mia will have to find the courage to face the hardest, most devastating struggle of her life: deciding whether to stay and fight for her life or let go and die. Both choices will require heartbreaking sacrifices. Several times, she'll want to give up the choice, wishing someone else would make it for her, because it's just too hard. But, as we'll soon see, that's not how this magic works. This magic puts Mia in the driver's seat of her own destiny. And just as her dad said, there is no easy way out. She'll have to work through it.

Debate (cont'd) (18–86)

On route to the hospital via helicopter, the doctors confirm that Mia's parents are dead, but that Teddy is still alive. Mia concludes that she is *not* dead (answering the first Debate question) and while doctors operate on her body, she tests out the **rules of the magic**, trying to figure out how it works. She tries to walk through walls and transport herself places, but she can't do either. Why, then, is she here? What is the point of this magic?

The answer will soon become clear.

In another flashback, we're introduced to the big choice Mia was facing before the accident: go to Juilliard or stay with Adam. When she got offered an audition for Juilliard, she was so torn about how to feel, she didn't even tell Adam she was applying, which felt like a betrayal. A subsequent flashback reveals that Mia has always loved going to Adam's shows but felt out of place in his world, and that their first intimate encounter recently upped the stakes of their relationship, making her choice even harder.

Back in the present, Mia is in ICU in "grave condition," and a social worker warns her family (and her best friend, Kim) that Mia is comatose and might never wake up. When Gran and Gramps visit Mia, Nurse Ramirez tells them that Mia can hear them and is aware of everything going on. "'You might think that the doctors or nurses or all this is running the show,' she says, gesturing to the wall of medical equipment. 'Nuh-uh. *She's* running the show'" (82). Acting as the **guide** of this Out of the Bottle tale, Nurse Ramirez starts to illuminate why Mia has been touched by this particular piece of magic and why she's really here.

Break Into 2 (86–89)

"*I* decide. I know this now . . . If I stay. If I live. It's up to me" (88).

And with this terrifying realization, we're thrust into the premise of the novel (and the **Act 2 goal**): choosing to live or die.

B Story (101)

Adam arrives at the hospital. Although he has been part of Mia's world long before she breaks into Act 2, both the accident and the realization of the choice she must make suddenly cast him in a new light and thrust him into a new role. He is an integral part of the choice she must make, but also a symbolic representation of that choice. If she stays, she gets to be with him (and with Teddy), and find out whether she got into Juilliard, but she'll also have to live without her parents. If she goes, she'll have to say goodbye to her future, which might include Adam.

Fun and Games (89–138)

Mia's condition improves: she's able to breathe without the ventilator, kicking off the **upward path** of this beat.

Another flashback mirrors this upward path, as we see the early days of her relationship with Adam, and how he helped her come out of her shell. Back in the present, when Adam and Kim are told they can't visit Mia in the ICU (because they're not immediate family), they hatch a plan to sneak in. Meanwhile, through more flashbacks, we learn how instrumental Kim was in reviving Mia's passion for the cello when it once waned, serving to inform both Mia's choice before the accident

(Juilliard or Adam) and her choice now (stay or go). Choosing to go would also mean sacrificing her music.

Midpoint (138–152)

With a little help from Nurse Ramirez (the guide), Adam and Kim create a diversion and successfully slip past the nurses to get to Mia (**A and B Stories cross**). In a **false victory** (and a lot of commotion), Adam dramatically makes it to Mia's room and reaches for her hand. Mia didn't realize how much she wanted to feel his touch until now that it's so close. But before he can make contact, he's dragged away by guards. A family friend, Willow, arrives and uses her clout as a nurse to convince the guards to release Adam and promises to find a way to help Adam see Mia.

That's when Mia has a heartbreaking realization: Willow was taking care of Teddy at another hospital. She would never just leave him. If Willow is here, that means Teddy is dead. Mia's choice just got a whole lot harder (**stakes are raised**).

Bad Guys Close In (152–194)

In a flashback to the day Teddy was born, we get another look at how close Mia is with her brother and how devastating this loss is for her. Her internal distress creates an external reaction in her unconscious body, which goes into cardiac arrest. She's immediately rushed into surgery (**downward path**). It's the first time we've seen disembodied Mia have some kind of influence over the state of corporeal Mia, and she realizes there is a connection between the two, which makes her looming choice feel more immediate and real.

But she doesn't want to choose. "Why can't someone else decide this for me? Why can't I get a death proxy?" (180). She'd rather opt out of the choice—a sign that she has yet to confront her **internal bad guys** (wanting to run away from a challenge).

The rest of the beat is spent exploring the theme of choice and sacrifice.

Later, as Gramps cries over her body, he tells her he will understand if she chooses to go, even though he wants her to stay. Then, through flashbacks, Mia thinks about when her dad quit his band after Teddy was born. He even changed his look and went back to school to become an English teacher. When young Mia asked her father if he was sad about his choice, he said no. "Sometimes you make choices in life and sometimes choices make you" (192). Her dad was able to make his choice with no regrets. Will Mia be able to do the same?

All Is Lost (194–198)

Willow lobbies for Adam to be allowed to visit Mia in the ICU. But Mia doesn't want to see him, because she knows it will make her decision harder. "I'm trying to summon the courage to do what I have to do. And Adam will complicate things" (194). She has already started to let go (**whiff of death**), but she's not yet ready to face the sacrifice of that choice. In other words, she hasn't yet learned the theme.

She tries to run away from the ICU before Adam arrives, but she finds she no longer has the strength to move. When he takes her hand, she's overcome with the desire to touch him, but knows that even if she could, it would be too hard. He pleads with her to stay.

Dark Night of the Soul (198–220)

Through flashbacks, Mia recalls the downturn of her relationship with Adam that started after her Juilliard audition. The choice that hung over them—if she were to be accepted—created tension between them.

When Mia talked to her mom about the decision, her mom restated the theme: "I'd understand if you chose love, Adam love, over music love. Either way you win. And either way you lose" (211). The advice is relevant to Mia in the present too, as she faces another seemingly impossible choice with heartbreaking sacrifices: if she stays, she lives in a world without her family (love); if she goes, she says goodbye to Adam and music (also love). At the same time, her mother is offering her unconditional support, which serves to remind Mia that even if she chose to stop fighting and go, her mom would understand.

In another flashback, Mia remembers a conversation with Adam when he pressed her about Juilliard. "If you get in, the choice is already made, isn't it?" (211). She admitted that it was. She would go.

As Mia processes her decision to "go" in the present, these flash-backs comfort her and support her. But it becomes clear, as she thinks about her family, Kim, and Adam, that Mia is making peace with her imminent death and saying goodbye.

Break Into 3 (221–228)

In the final full flashback, Mia recounts the impromptu Labor Day party her family had the past summer. Mia remembers thinking to herself, *"This is what happiness feels like."* (225). As present Mia makes her choice to go, we get one last glimpse of the reason: her family. She doesn't want to live without them.

The scene ends with Adam and Dad convincing Mia to play her cello with them. At first she refuses. She doesn't fit into their punk-rock world (a fear she's always struggled with). But when she finally gives in, she's surprised to hear how good the music sounds. She really did fit in after all. And it makes her decision to go with her family all the more powerful.

Finale (228–234)

In only one scene and six pages, author Forman powerfully hits *all* five sub-beats of the Five-Point Finale.

POINT 1: GATHERING THE TEAM. It's morning. A new dawn. And Mia notes how different the hospital feels. She's made her choice, and soon this will all be over, which relieves her. She's tired. She prepares to go, but waits for Adam so she can say goodbye (**Act 3 goal**).

POINT 2: EXECUTING THE PLAN. Adam returns, and Mia can tell he's been crying. He tells Mia that if she stays, he'll do whatever she wants. He'll quit the band and go to New York with her. But he'll also leave, if that's what she wants. He understands that returning to her old life (including him) might be too painful, and he's willing to go away if that's easier for her. "I can lose you like that if I don't lose you today. I'll let you go. If you stay" (231).

In this thematic declaration (and **B Story Sacrifice**), Adam proves that he's willing to make the hard sacrifice, the painful choice, because of his love for Mia. It's a lesson Mia is about to learn as well: some things are worth living for, even when they come with pain. Adam bursts into sobs, and Mia can't watch. She covers her ears and closes her eyes. But then . . .

POINT 3: HIGH TOWER SURPRISE. Mia hears music. Adam has placed headphones over unconscious Mia's ears and is playing a Yo-Yo Ma cello piece. And Mia can *hear* it. Once again, the mystical connection Mia has with her body is used at a pivotal point in the story.

POINT 4: DIG DEEP DOWN. Mia's reaction is like an explosion. She flashes forward and back to countless moments of her life as it was and how it would be if she stayed. She sees her family, Kim, Adam, her music. The flashes come so fast, she can't keep up. And she can't take them any longer.

POINT 5: THE EXECUTION OF THE NEW PLAN. There's a blinding flash and a moment of pain and Mia realizes she can *feel* Adam's hand. For real. She's been thrust back into her body. Now she fully feels the pain of what she's lost, and it's nothing compared to the grief she felt when she was detached from her body.

She feels the powerful need to hold Adam's hand. She aims all of her energy into her right hand. She's weak, and it's difficult. But she uses all the love she's ever felt from her family and friends. She pictures that same hand stroking Teddy's hair and grasping her cello bow and holding Adam's hand.

And she squeezes.

Final Image (234)

Exhausted from the effort, Mia slumps back, unsure if she's done what she intended to do. But then Adam gasps and speaks her name, and Mia can truly *hear* him for the first time since the accident.

Even though the novel ends here, without a resolution of what might happen in the aftermath, Mia has made the difficult choice. The one she didn't think she was strong enough to make. She's staying.

WHY IS THIS AN OUT OF THE BOTTLE?

If I Stay contains all three elements of a successful Out of the Bottle story:

- **A HERO DESERVING OF THE MAGIC:** Before the accident, Mia was struggling to make the toughest decision of her life: to go to Juilliard and or stay with her boyfriend. Suddenly, that choice feels trivial compared to the out-of-body decision she's now given: live or die. It's a piece of magic that will test her strength and courage like no other choice she's ever faced.
- **A SPELL OR TOUCH OF MAGIC:** When Mia wakes up outside of her body, she's magically able to see and hear everything around her while no one is able to see or hear her. Over time, she discovers that she can manipulate what's happening to her unconscious body, putting her in the driver's seat of this daunting decision.
- **A LESSON:** To live without her family—or die with them and leave behind a life she loved. Mia doesn't want to make this terrible choice. She'd rather someone else make it for her. But that's not how life (or this magic) works. In the end (with the help of her B Story character), she'll learn a lesson about courage and sacrifice, and that some things are worth living for, even when they come with pain.

Cat's Eye View

For quick reference, here's a brief overview of this novel's beat sheet.

OPENING IMAGE: Mia wakes to a blanket of snow and a canceled day of school. Her close-knit family all decide to go visit friends. We learn that Mia is a skilled cellist who wants to go to Juilliard, but if she gets in, it'll complicate her relationship with her boyfriend, Adam.

SETUP: The family piles into the car. On the road, they take turns choosing what music to listen to. Mia picks a classical station.

CATALYST: A pickup truck plows into the passenger side of the car. Mia's parents are both killed. She goes to look for her brother, Teddy, but instead finds her own body.

DEBATE: "Am I dead?" The Debate is centered on Mia's figuring out what's happening to her, how it works, and most important, *why.*

THEME STATED: "You just work through it. You just hang in there" (27). There is no shortcut to being brave and making hard choices. Something Mia will learn throughout the novel as she faces the hardest choice of her life: To stay or go.

BREAK INTO 2: "*I* decide. I know this now . . . If I stay. If I live. It's up to me" (88). Mia realizes why she's in this predicament. She has to decide whether to stay or leave (Act 2 goal).

B STORY: Adam arrives at the hospital. The accident and looming choice cast him in a new light. He represents the choice and sacrifice Mia will eventually have to make.

FUN AND GAMES: Mia's condition improves, and Adam and Kim (Mia's best friend) hatch a plan to break into the ICU to see her. Through flashbacks, we learn more about Adam, Kim, and Mia's music (all variables and stakes in her choice).

MIDPOINT: Adam and Kim create a diversion and slip into the ICU (false victory) but are apprehended by guards before they can get to Mia. The appearance of Willow (a family friend who was with Teddy at another hospital) confirms that Teddy is dead, making Mia's choice even harder (stakes are raised).

BAD GUYS CLOSE IN: Mia's grief over her brother's death causes her body to go into cardiac arrest, a sign that she has some control over the situation she's in. But she doesn't want to choose. She would rather back away from the challenge (internal bad guys).

ALL IS LOST: Mia gives up and starts to let go (whiff of death). Adam finally gets into the ICU to see her and pleads with her to stay.

DARK NIGHT OF THE SOUL: In processing her decision to go, Mia flashes back to her *other* choice, the one she was facing before the accident—to go to Juilliard or stay with Adam.

BREAK INTO 3: As Mia makes her choice to go, we get one last glimpse, through flashback, of the reason: her family. She doesn't want to live without them.

FINALE: Mia prepares to go but waits for Adam so she can say goodbye. Adam cries and says he's willing to leave her if that makes it easier for her to stay. Mia hears music and realizes Adam has put headphones over her ears and is playing one of her favorite cello pieces. The music pulls her back into her body. She tries to squeeze Adam's hand.

FINAL IMAGE: Adam calls Mia's name, and she hears him for real. She has made her choice. She's staying.

Whydunit

The Dark Truths We Hide

A crime has been committed! Who did it? And more important . . . *why*?

Welcome to the Whydunit—Save the Cat's version of the classic mystery novel.

When we think of the classic mystery novel, we think of greats like Agatha Christie, Sir Arthur Conan Doyle, Gillian Flynn, Ruth Ware, Stieg Larsson. In other words, we think *adult* novels. Not *young adult* novels. But that doesn't mean teens don't love a good whodunit as well, as evidenced from the recent rise of bestselling young adult mystery novels like *One of Us Is Lying* by Karen M. McManus, *A Good Girl's Guide to Murder* by Holly Jackson, and *Firekeeper's Daughter* by Angeline Boulley, among others.

But as we look more closely at all of the best whodunits (regardless of intended age group), we find that it's not the *who* that draws us in and keep us desperately turning pages until the end. It's the *why*. It's the reason *behind* the crime. The motivation.

Yes, we were all shocked to learn *who* killed Andie Bell in *A Good Girl's Guide to Murder* or to learn *who* was behind the deadly meth operation in *Firekeeper's Daughter*. But the who on its own is sort of irrelevant. It makes very little sense. It was the *why* that kept us reading. The trail of secrets and truths that lead us further and further into the dark side of humanity. That's what makes this genre work, and so, aptly, that's where it gets its name.

Why was the crime committed? And what does that tell us about human nature?

These are the two questions that lie at the heart of the Whydunit genre.

Because although, as readers, we turn to mysteries to be thrilled and surprised and shocked, we also turn to them to learn something about ourselves. About our flaws, our shortcomings, our dark urges, and what might become of them if left unchecked. These things may look *slightly* different in an adult novel versus a young adult novel, but in the end, your goal in writing this genre is the same: to lure your reader through a series of increasingly dark rooms, skillfully **turning the cards** (or revealing the clues) to twist the story and send it in new, unexpected directions, until finally we reach the truth at the center. A truth that will change us forever.

Sound easy? Yeah, not so much. Plotting a successful mystery is no simple feat. But with a little study, a lot of writer elbow grease, and this handy genre checklist, it can be done. I believe in you!

All successful YA Whydunits share these three genre ingredients: (1) a **detective**, (2) a **secret**, and (3) a **dark turn**. Ensuring that your novel has them too will instantly start you down the right path. So let's take a look at *why* each of these belong in your whydunit, and how they apply to a young adult audience.

A DETECTIVE

If a crime has been committed, someone's gotta solve it. This first ingredient is where we're going to find our biggest divergence from the whydunits of the adult variety. Sure, you could conceive of a world in which a teenage protagonist is an actual detective, in the professional sense of the word—Encyclopedia Brown, although younger than a teen, was technically *paid* for his detective work—but detectives don't have to be professionals. Amateur, aspiring, or even unwilling detectives count here too. You just need someone who's up for the task of solving a crime (whether they realize it at first or not). In *A Good Girl's*

Guide to Murder, hero Pippa decides to investigate the disappearance of Andie Bell (and alleged suicide of her boyfriend/killer) for her senior capstone project, a decision that leads her (and the reader) through a maze of twisty clues and shocking reveals about what the police thought was a closed case. In *A Study in Charlotte*, author Brittany Cavallaro has imagined a world where the infamous Sherlock Holmes and James Watson are real, and Charlotte Holmes and Jamie Watson, the teen detectives of the novel, are their real-life descendants.

Depending on how you've crafted your narrative, the *reader* might be the primary detective in your story. In *One of Us Is Lying*, because there are four points of view, the reader is privy to information the other characters don't have, making them the number-one gumshoe of the investigation, even as the teen heroes also scramble to put together the clues.

Whatever creative wizardry you use to devise your teenage detective(s), two things must be true of them: they must be wholly unprepared for what they're getting into (regardless of how prepared they *think* they are), and they must be somehow connected to the mystery (even if the connection isn't evident or even existent at first). Remember my earlier advice: Why *this* hero for *this* plot? The same applies to whydunit mysteries! Nothing slows the pace of a good mystery more than a detective who is not connected to the plot somehow. An unconnected detective has nothing to lose. Nothing at stake. No reason for being in the story other than to be a clue delivery service.

Think about Daunis in *Firekeeper's Daughter*. After her best friend Lily is shot, the FBI recruits her to be a confidential informant for their investigation into a suspected meth operation on Sugar Island, home to many members of the Ojibwe people. Daunis has no prior experience solving crimes or going undercover, making her completely unprepared for what she's getting herself into. Despite this, she's also the perfect "detective" for the job. As the daughter of an Ojibwe father and a white mother, Daunis straddles two worlds, giving her both an insider's and an outsider's perspective, something the FBI considers an asset. But as author Boulley cleverly turns the cards, giving Daunis (and us) more shocking clues about this mystery, we realize just how connected Daunis really is.

In *A Study in Charlotte*, both detectives are being framed for murder! They are connected to the mystery as key suspects, something Jamie (a novice detective) is not prepared to deal with. Even Charlotte, who has already solved several cases, is stumped by this one.

Showing us how unprepared *this* detective is for *this* mystery and how intricately the two are linked will prove to your reader that this story has novelty and most of all, *purpose*. Yet their personal connection to the case ensures that without this detective, the mystery would never be solved. Without this hero, the ultimate dark secret could never be believably revealed.

A SECRET

The secret is what lies at the end of this series of dark rooms. When we open the last door, what will we find? The real reason Andie Bell disappeared that night (*A Good Girl's Guide to Murder*)? The true story behind the illegal drug operation on Sugar Island (*Firekeeper's Daughter*)? Who really killed Lee Dobson, and why they're framing Charlotte and Jamie for it (*A Study in Charlotte*)?

And it's rarely what we thought we'd find. The secret is the heart of the whydunit. It's the reason we keep reading. Because we have to know. But it's not just the *why* that's revealed here. It's the who, what, where, and how, too. All of this adds up to a delightful, *surprising* reveal. And yes, "surprising" is the operative word here. You, the writer, have the task of making the secret good—and unexpected.

The key is complexity.

Secrets should start out small, contained, and seemingly—dare we think it—*simple*. But as the detective digs deeper and gets more and more entrenched in the case, the secret expands, perhaps even with layers of secrets built into it.

In *A Study in Charlotte*, as Charlotte and Jamie chase down drug dealers, sneak into morgues, discover hidden cameras, and interview students on campus, the mystery grows, leading us to dead ends, red herrings, and layers of intrigue.

In *A Good Girl's Guide to Murder*, as Pippa follows the clues and interviews more people associated with Andie Bell, her "persons of interest" list grows. Not just in number, but in complexity. How do all of these people fit together? Who is lying? Who is telling the truth? Who is covering for someone else? The American cover of the novel shows us a dizzying crisscross pattern of threads, linking each clue to the other in a web of complexity.

That's the essence of a good secret.

In fact, a popular (although not required) element of a whydunit is a **case within a case** or a secret within a secret. Often, there's not one mystery happening, but two. Whether that second mystery is set up from the very beginning (like the suspicious death of Daunis's uncle in *Firekeeper's Daughter*) or it's another case or secret that's uncovered along the way (like the hit-and-run accident revealed in *A Good Girl's Guide to Murder*), the second mystery adds a layer of complexity to the story—maybe even serving as a red herring—and helps remind us of the theme universal to all whydunits: things are rarely what they seem. There's always a darker secret lurking beneath the surface.

And as the secret grows, so does our detective's desire (and possibly even obsession) to get to the bottom of it, leading to . . .

A DARK TURN

This is the moment (usually in the second half of the novel) where the detective makes a decision that goes against their own rules, morals, ethics, loyalties, or common sense. This can also be a breaking of society's rules or the rules of the case, or knowingly putting oneself in danger.

In *A Good Girl's Guide to Murder*, even after Pippa's dog is kidnapped and turns up dead, Pippa goes against her better judgment (telling her to drop the case) and keeps hunting down the truth, despite the threatening notes she's received. Her dark turn is even hinted at in the title! How far will this "good girl" go in pursuit of this harrowing truth?

In *A Study in Charlotte*, as Jamie and Charlotte work together and develop a friendship, a trust develops between them. So when Jamie breaks that trust and investigates a secret in Charlotte's past (even though she repeatedly warned him not to), it creates a rift between them. But this dark turn also ultimately leads to the discovery of the murderer's identity, making it arguably a worthwhile choice. That's what makes the dark turn so useful in plotting. It not only helps reveal complexity but also helps build stakes. If the detective isn't forced into a dark turn situation, it might mean you haven't built enough conflict and danger into your story.

As the case grows darker and the secrets grow more twisty, the detective doesn't shy away, even if perhaps they should for their own safety. Instead, they plunge on, a decision that usually leads to dangerous consequences. This genre ingredient is sometimes milder in young adult whydunits than in those of the adult variety, but it still marks an important moment in the story. Because no matter how dark you go with your dark turn, the purpose is the same: to show just how deep your hero's obsession with the case has become and just how desperate they are to solve it. The dark turn is why readers care about this particular case. Because the pull of *this* secret has become so strong, even the "good girls" and straight arrows are helpless against it.

Yet ironically (or not?), it's usually this dark turn that ultimately leads the detective not just to discovering the secret and solving the case but to an important thematic lesson as well. Because ironically (or not?), all heroes must travel through the darkness to find the light, in pursuit of both the truth—and themselves. Isn't that what good storytelling is all about? Isn't *that* what makes any novel (mysteries included) worth reading?

When we put our three ingredients together, we get a riveting, twisty tale that ultimately shows us something about the dark side of human nature. Whether it's greed and the lives it ruins (*Firekeeper's Daughter*), revenge and how far someone will go to seek it (*A Study in Charlotte*), the lengths we'll go to keep our secrets hidden (*A Good Girl's Guide to Murder*), or whatever else your clever writer brain can devise, it's these little glimpses into our own dark sides that transform us as readers and keep us hungry for more whydunit action, even if the craving makes us feel just the slightest bit uneasy.

To recap: if you're thinking of writing a whydunit novel, make sure your story includes these three essential ingredients.

- **A DETECTIVE:** whether that's a professional, an amateur, or even the reader. It just needs to be someone with a case on their hands. A case that they are not fully prepared for, but somehow connected to (whether they realize it or not).
- **A SECRET:** the key to unraveling the whole thing. What is inside the last, darkest room of our hunt for the truth? It should be complex and illuminate something about the dark side of humanity.
- **A DARK TURN:** the moment when the hero or detective finds themselves so deep into the mystery that their own rules, morals, loyalties, and/or ethics are compromised. The hero must do something (usually in the second half of the novel) that somehow breaks the rules or threatens their integrity, their innocence, or even their own life.

POPULAR YOUNG ADULT WHYDUNIT NOVELS

Remember Me by Christopher Pike

The Curious Incident of the Dog in the Night-Time by Mark Haddon

Pretty Little Liars by Sara Shepard

Ten by Gretchen McNeil

Liars, Inc. by Paula Stokes

A Study in Charlotte by Brittany Cavallaro

One of Us Is Lying by Karen M. McManus*

The Cheerleaders by Kara Thomas

Sadie by Courtney Summers

Truly Devious by Maureen Johnson

A Good Girl's Guide to Murder by Holly Jackson

Grown by Tiffany D. Jackson

Firekeeper's Daughter by Angeline Boulley

The Ivies by Alexa Donne

The Agathas by Kathleen Glasgow and Liz Lawson

* Beat sheet follows on page 334.

ONE OF US IS LYING

BY: Karen M. McManus
STC GENRE: Whydunit
BOOK GENRE: Young adult mystery
TOTAL PAGES: 360 (Delacorte Press hardcover edition, 2017)

Four heroes, one crime. Who is telling the truth? And who is lying? Welcome to the world of Karen M. McManus's runaway bestseller, which explores the dark side of stereotypes, high school gossip, and social media. Released in 2017, the book quickly became a *USA Today* bestseller, an *Entertainment Weekly* and *Buzzfeed* Best Book of the Year, and a *New York Times* bestseller, spending more than three years on the list. In 2021, the TV adaptation was released on Peacock.

Not only does this novel have the perfect whydunit title, which sows the seeds of constant doubt and suspicion in the reader's mind, but it also has a tautly paced structure that all mystery authors can aspire to. Using a single-track beat sheet to chart all four points of view, it's a stellar example of multiple POV plotting (for more on multiple POV beat sheets, see page 116). So let's delve into the dark hallways of Bayview High and find out exactly who is lying, and more important, why.

Opening Image (3–8)

It's Monday afternoon, and Bronwyn (the first of our four heroes) is doing what every other student at Bayview High is doing: reading About That, the gossip app created by Simon Kelleher. From sex tapes to cheating scandals—in this world, no secret is safe.

Bronwyn, introduced as an overachiever who cares too much about what people think (flaw) and never breaks the rules (supposedly), is on her way to detention for being in possession of a phone she swears isn't hers. Bronwyn is the first narrator we meet, is given the most page time in the story, and is the character responsible for bringing all four heroes together in the second half of the novel, making her a likely candidate for the "one true hero" of this tale.

In detention, we meet our other three heroes, Addy and Cooper (who also claim they were wrongfully accused with planted phones), and Nate, the resident troublemaker. The fifth student in detention is Simon Kelleher.

Themes Stated (7 and 11)

The first chapter introduces two themes: a general theme for the novel and a personal theme that applies to all four heroes.

On page 7, Mr. Avery tells the detention students to "write a five-hundred-word essay on how technology is ruining American high schools." This novel explores the dark side of technology and social media and how far it will go to ruin *this* American high school, particularly the lives of the five people in this room.

Then, on page 11, Simon states the personal theme of the novel, saying to Addy, Cooper, Bronwyn, and Nate respectively: "She's a princess and you're a jock. And you're a brain. And you're a criminal. You're all walking teen-movie stereotypes." These four heroes have been locked in a prison of how others perceive them. So much so, they often play *into* those stereotypes. But, as we'll soon learn, they all harbor secrets that either go against their stereotypes or arose because they were too afraid to break free from them. These secrets reveal deeper wounds and personal flaws that they must deal with. The character transformations for Addy, Cooper, Bronwyn, and Nate will come from overcoming these flaws, breaking free of their stereotypes, and proving to the rest of the school (and themselves) that they are more than meets the eye.

Setup (8–25)

Before the Catalyst hits, we read narrations from the other three heroes in which we get quick glimpses into their lives, flaws, and **shards of glass**. Cooper is a star baseball pitcher under constant pressure to do well, especially from his dad. Addy is emotionally dependent on her boyfriend, Jake, which is not surprising, given her mom's belief that Addy needs to be pretty enough to attract a man to take care of her for life. Nate has a rough home life, with a single dad who drinks and an absent mom whom he refuses to talk about but whom everyone believes died in a car accident.

As the teens work on their detention assignment, Simon complains that his water bottle is missing, and Mr. Avery tells him to grab a cup from the sink. Before he can drink, a fender bender in the school parking lot pulls everyone's attention to the window. Simon drinks from the cup and collapses to the floor, wheezing with an allergic reaction. His EpiPen is missing from his bag, and when Cooper is sent to the nurse's office to fetch one, he finds the box mysteriously empty. Simon is taken to the hospital in an ambulance.

Catalyst (25)

In a classic phone call Catalyst, Bronwyn's phone rings later that afternoon with the news that Simon is dead.

Debate (25–78)

All four heroes react to the shocking event, and when they're all called into to the principal's office to be interviewed by the police, the Debate question is established. The officer reveals that Simon died from a peanut allergy and the cup he drank from contained traces of peanut oil. Was this death really an accident?

Throughout this Debate we get hints about what secrets our four heroes are hiding, along with more information about each character and the **things that need fixing** in their lives. Bronwyn feels pressured to hold up a family tradition and get into Yale (**wants**), but her strategies for acing chemistry might be suspect. Cooper **wants** to play major league baseball after high school (or maybe that's just what his father wants), and he might be cheating on his girlfriend, Keely, with someone named Kris. Nate's mother was bipolar and a cocaine addict who walked out on the family years ago, leaving Nate and his father to fend for themselves. Nate started selling painkillers to make ends meet. And Addy cheated on her boyfriend, Jake, with TJ, a mistake she regrets terribly. But we also learn that Jake is very controlling, dictating what Addy wears and even how long she keeps her hair.

When a new Tumblr page is published by someone claiming to be Simon's killer (**double bump**), the stakes of the story are raised, and the Debate question changes from "*How* did peanut oil get into Simon's cup?" to "*Who* put the peanut oil in his cup?" The post spreads through the hallways of Bayview High, and suspects start to pop up. Addy is questioned by the police about the EpiPens missing from the nurse's office, because she went there earlier that day. But when another Tumblr post is published implying that Simon's "killer" was in the room with him when he died, the police haul all four heroes in for questioning.

Break Into 2 (78–98)

Two chapters, four heroes, four police interviews.

They're all shown an unpublished post from Simon's app that was supposed to be posted the day he died. It contains secrets about *all* of them:

- Bronwyn stole tests to improve her chemistry grade.
- Nate has been violating his probation by selling drugs at school.
- Cooper did steroids to improve his baseball game.
- Addy cheated on Jake with TJ.

While Bronwyn, Nate, and Addy all admit (to the reader) that the accusation is true, Cooper is the only one who is surprised and somewhat relieved about what was written about him, hinting that this is not his *real* secret.

The police have determined that someone put that peanut oil in Simon's cup. There are only four people who could have done that, and they all had reason to keep Simon quiet. This isn't just an investigation into an accidental death. This is an investigation into a murder. All four deny having anything to do with it, but the title of the book is *One of Us Is Lying*, so . . .

Let the murder mystery begin!

B Story (54–58)

Technically all four characters qualify as B Story characters to each other. They all come into one another's lives as a result of the murder investigation (Act 2) and they all push each other beyond their stereotypical boundaries, helping one another learn the theme.

But the relationship that seems to embody this the most (and gets the most page time in the story) is the romance between Bronwyn and Nate, which really kicks off on page 54 when Nate unexpectedly shows up at Bronwyn's house and Bronwyn plays the piano for him. She's surprised by how easily she's able to play a song that usually gives her trouble.

Nate, the "criminal," and Bronwyn, the rule-following "brain" would never have formed an attachment in the status quo world. But because they've been thrown into this investigation together, their shared experience results in an unlikely friendship—and more. The A Story forces them to see past their own limited worldviews and break free from the stereotypes holding them hostage. Just as all four heroes must do throughout the story.

Fun and Games (89–157)

Who killed Simon? And which one of them is lying? As usual with a whydunit mystery, the **Act 2 goal** (figuring out the truth) is not just for the heroes; it's also a goal for the reader.

All four heroes experience a **downward path** as they're plunged into the upside-down world of a murder investigation. Things get progressively worse for all of them.

Addy comes clean to Jake about her affair with TJ, and Jake breaks up with her, leaving her to deal with a murder investigation without the boyfriend she's so heavily relied on for emotional support. (What a perfect opportunity for growth!) Jake then turns their group of friends against her, and Addy goes from popular to outcast.

Bronwyn meets with a lawyer who warns her not to talk to the other suspects, a rule the rule-follower disobeys the moment she gets to school and sees Nate. He gives her a burner phone so they can communicate.

Cooper's *real* secret nearly comes out when a text from Kris pops onto his phone and his girlfriend, Keely, sees it. Cooper lies that it's a guy he knows from baseball.

Nate has to stop selling drugs due to the investigation. His phone calls with Bronwyn become more personal, and they both confess that the secrets Simon wrote about them are true. But they swear they had nothing to do with his death.

As Nate and Bronwyn grow closer, they start to cross the invisible lines of their stereotypes (B Story), but they're still doing it in secret—that is, **fixing things the wrong way**—because Bronwyn is still worried about what people will think (her flaw), and Nate is still hesitant to let Bronwyn get too close to him (his flaw).

Then Simon's unpublished post (with all four heroes' secrets) gets published on the Tumblr page, and the stakes are raised again when the police announce they'll be interviewing *all* the students at Bayview High. The four heroes are brought together in the principal's office and start speculating on other possible suspects. Author McManus throws some red herrings at us, highlighting characters like Aidan Wu, who had to transfer out of school after his secret was posted on Simon's app, and Leah Jackson, who attempted suicide after her secret was posted.

As we near the Midpoint, Addy hits a personal **false defeat** when she admits to her sister that she *did* go to the nurse's office the day Simon died, but it was to get Tylenol for Jake. (So one of them *was* lying.) She breaks into sobs, realizing how much of a doormat she was in her relationship. Afterward she feels lighter and admits that though she still misses Jake, she doesn't miss being controlled by him (**shift from wants to needs**).

Bronwyn's sister, Maeve, hacks into the access panel of Simon's gossip app and discovers that there are two files with Cooper's name—the secret that was posted (about using steroids) and another file that's encrypted.

Midpoint (157–161)

At a **Midpoint party**, Cooper learns that Simon's parents have invited students from Bayview to their house to take some of Simon's things to remember him by. Guess which four students *haven't* been invited (**false defeat**)?

Then the **stakes are raised** when it's revealed that all four of them have been named "persons of interest" in a local newspaper article, which also included the secrets exposed on the Tumblr page. This mystery (and its repercussions for our four heroes) is no longer contained to Bayview High.

Bad Guys Close In (162–273)

The local newspaper article sparks a media backlash, marking the start of the Bad Guys Close In. Author McManus continues her theme of the dangers of technology by ramping up the stakes, using not traditional "bad guys" but modern society in general. Although none of the four heroes have been proven guilty, they instantly come under attack by the media, even attracting the attention of a popular national news show called *Mikhail Powers Investigates.*

But the backlash brings the four heroes closer together, and their developing bond tracks the **upward path** of this beat. They all step outside the borders of their cliques and stereotypes (theme!) and find friendship and support in each other. The media even gives them a nickname—"The Bayview Four"—unifying them symbolically. The more society pushes them away, the closer they become. And by the end of the beat, all four are sitting together at lunch. "The whole murder club at one table," says Addy on page 260. Without this murder investigation, they probably never would have talked to each other. *That* is the romantic waltz of structure. External events triggering internal growth.

In fact, we see a lot of internal growth in this beat, as more secrets and lies are revealed and each hero battles their own **internal bad guys**.

Addy chops off all her hair, a clear departure from her old "beauty queen" self who was emotionally dependent on Jake. Later, during a tense meeting with Jake, she disagrees with him for the first time and remarks on how freeing it feels. When Addy befriends Janae, Simon's best friend and someone Addy never would have spoken to before, Janae asks her if she misses her old life. Addy replies, "Nobody I hung out with ever really cared about me . . ." (245).

Bronwyn gradually combats her flaw as her relationship (and physical intimacy) with Nate deepens and she takes more emotional risks, sneaking him into her house, asking him to be her boyfriend, and even, by the end of the beat, kissing him in the cafeteria in front of everyone, clearly no longer caring what others think.

Nate shocks Bronwyn (and the reader) when his mother shows up, revealing that despite his claims, she's not dead. (Hmmm. Another one who's been lying.) Nate found it easier for people to believe she was dead than for them to know the truth. Her appearance forces Nate to deal with the traumatic past he's avoided (and lied about) for years. He shows growth when he opens up to Bronwyn about it and even begrudgingly gives his mother the opportunity to explain her actions over dinner. But when Bronwyn asks Nate to be her boyfriend, he balks, proving that he's still pushing people away and has some more growing to do.

Cooper breaks up with Keely, knowing he doesn't really love her and never will. Only at page 212, when it's revealed that Cooper is in love with a boy named Kris, do we truly understand how much of his identity he's been hiding. Cooper hasn't come out because he knows his dad would never accept him, and he's well aware how few openly gay players there are in major league baseball. But external events will push him to confront his fears when the police decrypt the other file on Simon's app, revealing his real secret. This serves as a personal All Is Lost for Cooper and drives him to come out to his father—who, as Cooper predicted, doesn't react well. News quickly spreads at school. Other students heckle and ridicule the once untouchable Cooper. Surprisingly, it's Nate who stands up for him, showing just how far all four of these characters have come.

Oh, and let's not forget about the A Story! There's still a murder mystery going on here. And a twisty one at that! Between the *Mikhail Powers Investigates* show, the Tumblr page (supposedly written by Simon's killer), and the actual police investigation, suspicions bounce around wildly. Among other suspects, Bronwyn is thrust into the police's spotlight when they find an old comment she left on one of Simon's posts about her sister, Maeve. It tells Simon to "F**k off and die" (205). And Cooper's secret was the only one swapped out for a fake one. What else could he have done to keep Simon quiet?

When Bronwyn gets the idea for the "Bayview Four" to get together and compare notes, the Act 2 goal kicks into high gear. They brainstorm other possible suspects and theories and by the end of the meeting, Nate remarks, "One: I like all of them more than I thought I would . . . And two: I don't think any of them did it" (269). Not only are they pushing beyond the boundaries of their stereotypes, but they're also starting to trust each other. They've become a team.

Maeve finds some disturbing comments that Simon wrote in an online forum, in which he criticized a school shooter for being "unoriginal" in his revenge scheme. This, combined with Mikhail Powers's scathing criticism of the Bayview police in outing a gay student during their investigation, turns media attention away from the Bayview Four. In a stunning reversal, the police are now the bad guys and the focus of the case is on Simon, himself. It seems our four heroes are finally in the clear and life can go back to normal. Nate and Bronwyn even start fantasizing about going on a real date and being a real couple when this is all over.

But then . . .

All Is Lost (273–275)

Nate is arrested, bringing the story crashing down from its upward path peak. This is a personal All Is Lost for Nate and even Bronwyn (who's started falling in love with him), but it's also a low point for all four heroes, who have bonded and become a team. As Nate is a member of the Bayview Four, his arrest is a loss for all of them. None of them believe he actually did it. And despite the title, the reader probably doesn't believe it either.

Dark Night of the Soul (275–300)

Although all three remaining heroes react to the news, the focus of this beat is mostly on Bronwyn. After the shock wears off, she reacts by doing what Bronwyn does best: taking action. She convinces Eli Kleinfelter, a lawyer from a nonprofit called Until Proven, to take Nate's case.

Eli reveals that an anonymous tip called in to the police prompted them to search Nate's locker, where they found Simon's water bottle and the missing EpiPens. They also found a laptop in Nate's closet with all of the Tumblr posts on it. Bronwyn finds this suspicious because (1) Nate would never be stupid enough to hide evidence in his locker, (2) his locker and house were already searched after Simon died and nothing was found, and (3) Nate's house is never locked, so anyone could have planted that computer in his closet. She also experiences her own personal Break Into 3 when she confides in her mom about everything, realizing that keeping secrets doesn't end well.

Meanwhile, Addy has her own personal Break Into 3 when her mom pushes her to date TJ (whom she's been growing closer to), and Addy finally stands up to her mother (**shard of glass**), asserting that she doesn't need a guy to be happy and she just wants to be alone so she can learn not to be afraid of it.

Despite Eli Kleinfelter's warning to not get involved in Nate's case, Bronwyn invites Cooper and Addy over to her house to finish what they started and to try to make sense of everything. Bronwyn wants to prove that Nate didn't write those Tumblr posts, so the three pore over them, looking for clues. In a **Dark Night Epiphany**, they find a post describing something that none of them remembers ever happening: Detective Wheeler eating a pile of donuts in the interrogation room. Addy recognizes this as a lie she'd told Jake.

Break Into 3 (300)

This epiphany kicks off a full-scale investigation. Not by the police, but by Bronwyn, Addy, and Cooper. Jake is definitely involved, but how? It's time to get to the bottom of this murder once and for all. If they can figure out what really happened, they can get Nate out of jail (**Act 3 goal**).

Finale (300–347)

POINT 1: GATHERING THE TEAM. Bronwyn, Addy, and Cooper meet up again at Bronwyn's house. This time, Bronwyn's sister, Maeve, comes too.

POINT 2: EXECUTING THE PLAN. They write down all the details they know on sticky notes and put them on the wall, trying to connect the dots. Why would whoever killed Simon drag the four of them into this? But no matter how they rearrange the notes, nothing seems to make sense.

Cooper is able to track down the red Camaro that had the fender bender in the school parking lot the day of Simon's death. He gives the license number to Bronwyn, but instead of turning it over to the authorities, she tracks the car herself, to Eastland High's parking lot, where the owner, Sam, reveals that someone paid him to have that accident.

POINT 3: HIGH TOWER SURPRISE. Bronwyn is certain Sam must be talking about Jake, but Sam reveals that it was Simon who paid him. (Is there anyone in this story who *wasn't* lying?)

POINT 4: DIG DEEP DOWN. The team meets at a coffee shop to discuss this new twist. But this time, Cooper brings Kris (showing how far he's come, to be out in public with his boyfriend), and Addy brings her sister. The stereotypical lines are long gone as the three heroes' worlds collide to solve this thing once and for all (**synthesis!**).

They go over the notes again, adding the new detail. It's Kris—the outsider—who's able to make a connection that the rest of them missed. Simon was pulling the strings all along, orchestrating this whole thing. This was "Simon's version of a school shooting. Kill himself and take a bunch of students down with him" (314). And Jake was his accomplice.

Upset at the thought of Jake framing her for murder, Addy bolts from the coffee shop. But later, when she digs deep down, past the manipulation, past Jake's hold over her, she remembers how Jake offered to carry her bag the morning of Simon's death. That's when he slipped in the fake phone that landed her in detention. She finally sees the *whole* truth about Jake and what he's capable of. Her emotional dependence on him was even more dangerous than she realized.

POINT 5: THE EXECUTION OF THE NEW PLAN. Cooper drives Addy to Janae's house in hopes of getting more information about what Simon and Jake did. Janae cracks and admits that she helped Simon with his plan. She produces his "manifesto," which she was supposed to send to the police a year from now. In its pages, Simon brags about how creative he was, orchestrating this whole thing without anyone knowing what happened.

"Why?" Addy asks on page 327, getting to the heart of the genre.

Janae explains that Simon felt depressed, overlooked, and underappreciated at school. And he had reason to be angry at three of the heroes: Bronwyn for cheating on the test and making it impossible for him to compete with her for valedictorian; Nate for hooking up with a girl Simon liked; and Cooper for getting Simon uninvited to a party and humiliating him. But Addy was different. When Jake found out Simon was rigging votes to get himself on the junior prom court, Simon used his knowledge of Addy's sleeping with TJ to keep Jake quiet and get him to participate in the plan. He lured Jake in by promising he could get revenge on Addy by pinning the murder on her. Then Jake blackmailed Janae into helping, insisting that she plant all the evidence on Addy. But after Addy started being nice to her, Janae couldn't do it and planted it on Nate instead.

The mystery of the title has been solved. We know now who is lying. It's everyone!

When Jake shows up at Janae's house a few minutes later, Addy gets the idea to hide in the other room and record their conversation to use as proof against Jake. It seems to be working until Addy receives a text and her recognizable ringtone gives her away. Here we see the general theme of the (literal) dangers of technology reach its climax.

Addy runs. Jake gives chase. She twists her ankle and falls. Jake catches her. She fights back valiantly, but Jake slams her head against a rock and then tries to strangle her. Cooper appears and takes Jake down. Jake is arrested, and Nate is released from prison.

Cooper finally makes a decision about his future: he wants to play college baseball, not pro like his father wanted. His dad hasn't completely accepted him, but Cooper notes that he's "looking me in the eye again" (339). And that's a start.

Addy recuperates from a fractured skull. Needing to get away from her mother and get a fresh start, she moves in with her sister, who's getting over a failed relationship of her own.

Bronwyn agrees to do an interview on *Mikhail Powers Investigates*; she admits publicly to cheating and gives a heartfelt apology. But when she goes over to Nate's house and puts her heart on the line, saying she still wants to be with him, he rejects her. "It's time to go back to normal right? And we're not each other's normal" (346). Apparently he's the only one who hasn't yet learned the theme. But don't worry. There's still thirteen pages to go.

Final Image (348–360)

Bronwyn narrates the epilogue, in which she tries to go back to normal (even dating the boy she was crushing on at the beginning), but too much has changed. She performs in a piano recital and impresses everyone (including herself) with her emotional performance. Cooper and Addy come to support their new friend, but there's one person conspicuously missing.

It isn't until Bronwyn is leaving with her family that Nate arrives and apologizes, explaining that he never really had anyone else and always thought that Bronwyn would be better off without him in her life. His dad is back from rehab and his mom has moved back from Oregon. Things are going better for him. Then, to prove that he, too, has completed his transformation, he says, "You were the best thing that ever happened to me, and it freaked me out. I thought I'd ruin you. Or you'd ruin me. That's how things tend to go in the Macauley house. But you're not like that" (355).

Bronwyn, however, is not quite ready to forgive him. So he asks her to watch a movie with him as friends, and she agrees. But from the smile on both of their faces as they say goodbye, it's pretty clear the lines between them have vanished for good.

WHY IS THIS A WHYDUNIT?

One of Us Is Lying contains all three elements of a successful Whydunit story.

- **A DETECTIVE:** Although the reader is the primary detective of the story, with more information than any of the heroes (due to the multiple POV narration), once the Bayview Four start working together in the second half of Act 2, they all become detectives too. As primary suspects in the case, they are all directly connected and wholly unprepared for what befalls them.
- **A SECRET:** Secrets play a huge role in this story, and all four heroes are hiding something, which eventually comes out. But the biggest secret of all, which unlocks the mystery, is Simon's plan

to commit suicide and bring the four heroes down with him as payback for the secrets they kept.

- **A DARK TURN:** Bronwyn, the "rule breaker," breaks the rules when she continues to investigate the murder, even after Nate's lawyer warns her not to several times. When she goes to confront the owner of the red Camaro herself (instead of turning the information over to the authorities), she sets off a chain of events that endangers not just herself but everyone. Addy also takes a dark turn when she confronts Janae and tries to trap Jake into a confession, leading to her being attacked and hospitalized.

Cat's Eye View

For quick reference, here's a brief overview of this novel's beat sheet.

OPENING IMAGE: Bronwyn reads About That, the school's infamous gossip app created by Simon Kelleher. Bronwyn, Addy, Cooper, and Nate (the four heroes) all meet up in detention for crimes they swear they didn't commit. Simon is also there.

THEME STATED: "She's a princess and you're a jock. And you're a brain. And you're a criminal. You're all walking teen-movie stereotypes," Simon says to the four heroes on page 11. They are all harboring secrets that either go against their stereotypes or arose because they were too afraid to break free from them. These secrets reveal deeper wounds and personal flaws that they must deal with.

SETUP: Narrations from the other three heroes give us quick glimpses into their lives, flaws, and shards of glass. In detention, after a fender bender in the parking lot, Simon drinks from a cup of water he got at the classroom sink and collapses. He's sent to the hospital in an ambulance.

CATALYST: Bronwyn's phone rings later that afternoon with the news that Simon is dead.

DEBATE: Was Simon's death really an accident? The police interview the four heroes, and we learn that the cup Simon was drinking from contained traces of peanut oil, triggering a deadly allergic reaction. As each hero reacts to the news, we learn more about them, the secrets they're hiding, and what needs fixing in their lives. A Tumblr post is published, written by Simon's supposed killer, and the police bring all four heroes in for questioning.

BREAK INTO 2: The four heroes are shown an unpublished post from Simon's app that was supposed to be posted the day he died. It contains secrets about *all* of them. Each one of them has a motive to kill Simon and becomes a suspect in what is now being treated as a murder case.

B STORY: Although all four heroes serve as B Story characters to each other, the theme is best represented by the romance between Bronwyn and Nate, who help each other see past their own limited worldviews and break free from the stereotypes holding them hostage.

FUN AND GAMES: The upside-down world of the murder investigation is tough for all four heroes, as more secrets are revealed and more students are questioned. Addy and Jake break up, and she becomes an outcast at school. Cooper's real secret is almost discovered. Bronwyn and Nate grow closer.

MIDPOINT: At a Midpoint party, it's discovered that all four heroes have been named "persons of interest" by the press and their secrets were revealed in a newspaper article. This mystery has expanded beyond the hallways of Bayview High (false defeat and stakes are raised).

BAD GUYS CLOSE IN: Pressure and allegations from modern society and the media (the bad guys) close in on the heroes and tensions mount. Despite this, the four heroes bond, stepping outside the borders of their stereotypes and cliques as they each continue to battle (and overcome) their internal bad guys. Bronwyn brings all four heroes together to try to solve the mystery and clear their names.

ALL IS LOST: Nate is arrested for Simon's murder. As he's a member of the Bayview Four (who all believe he's innocent), it's a loss for all of them.

DARK NIGHT OF THE SOUL: The three remaining heroes react to the news. Bronwyn takes action, convincing a lawyer from Until Proven to take on Nate's case. When Bronwyn, Cooper, and Addy meet up, they find something in the Tumblr posts that indicates Jake might be involved in Simon's murder (Dark Night Epiphany).

BREAK INTO 3: Bronwyn, Cooper, and Addy decide to investigate this turn of events and get to the bottom of this murder once and for all (Act 3 goal).

FINALE: After tracking down one of the cars from the fender bender in Act 1, Bronwyn discovers that Simon orchestrated the whole thing, killing himself and pinning it on the heroes for revenge. Addy confronts Janae, Simon's friend, who comes clean about her and Jake's involvement. But Jake shows up and attacks Addy, putting her in the hospital with a fractured skull. Bronwyn asks Nate to be with her, but he rejects her.

FINAL IMAGE: Bronwyn performs in a piano recital, with Cooper and Addy in the audience. Nate shows up and apologizes, confessing that he was scared of messing things up. Bronwyn agrees to hang out with him as friends, but the reader senses that the lines between them have vanished for good.

Monster in the House
Now THAT's a Scary Story!

For as long as teenagers have been able to drive themselves to the movie theater, there's been an endless supply of the teen horror flicks to keep them chilled and thrilled. From *Scream* to *The Cabin in the Woods* to *Halloween*, Hollywood just loves to trap teens in enclosed spaces and throw a monster into the mix. (And teenage audiences eat them up!) Which is why it might surprise you to learn that the YA novel equivalent of the teen horror flick—the Monster in the House—is not as popular as some of the other Save the Cat! genres we've been studying. (Although a handful of these movies *have* been based on young adult novels, like *I Know What You Did Last Summer*, the cult classic based on the novel by Lois Duncan, and *There's Someone Inside Your House*, the hit Netflix movie based on the novel by Stephanie Perkins.)

Historically, though, this genre has been dominated by books for adults: from iconic horror novels like Stephen King's *It* and William Peter Blatty's *The Exorcist* to classic novels like Mary Shelley's *Frankenstein* and Shirley Jackson's *The Haunting of Hill House* to sci-fi thrillers like Michael Crichton's *Jurassic Park*.

These novels tap into that primal fear that lives within all of us (regardless of age). The fear that we might be trapped somewhere with a monster . . . and it might somehow be our fault.

This describes the basic premise of all novels that fit into the Monster in the House genre. And despite the skew in age demographic, some stellar young adult authors have ventured into this genre, with bone-chilling success.

But be forewarned: the YA variety of the Monster in the House isn't just a collection of cheap thrills and escapist chills (although you'll find those too). Many of the books in this genre carry important messages and themes, dealing with big issues like climate change, feminism, rape culture, racism, substance abuse, and more—proving once again that even in a horror novel, young adult authors are pushing boundaries and creating complex characters with real-world problems that mirror our own, even in worlds that are not our own. Maybe *especially* in worlds that are not our own.

If you're looking to venture into this scary genre, you best be prepared with courage, determination, and, of course, your three genre ingredients: (1) a **monster**, (2) a **house**, and (3) a **sin**. Let's see why these three things add up to a chilling read that teens simply can't put down.

A MONSTER

First up, don't let the term "monster" fool you. Monsters can come in many forms beyond the classic "boogeyman in the closet" variety. They can be evil incarnations like the "Collector," who feeds on young girls, in *Sawkill Girls* by Claire Legrand. They can be ghosts or spirits, like Anna, the murdered girl in the bloodstained white dress who takes her revenge on anyone who enters her house in *Anna Dressed in Blood* by Kendare Blake, or "the Hag," an urban legend who haunts the town of Cedarville in *White Smoke* by Tiffany D. Jackson. They can be diseases or viruses—manmade, natural, or supernatural—like the Tox in *Wilder Girls* by Rory Power or the deadly bacteria in the water in *Contagion* by Erin Bowman. Or the monsters can be human. After all, the world is full of real-life monsters. Like the serial killer terrorizing a small Nebraska town in *There's Someone Inside Your House*, or a wronged victim with an ax to grind and a thirst for revenge like Lillian, the girl who terrorizes Kayla and Esme in *The Lake*. Or it could be a terrifying combination of more than one type of monster, like Naughty John in *The Diviners* by Libba Bray, who is the *ghost* of a serial killer summoned back into the world of the living.

In other words, there are no limits on the type of monster you can create. But the key to creating your monster is to go scary or go home. Monsters should exhibit behavior that goes beyond the realm of natural human behavior, making them literally *supernatural*. Which means that, although paranormal or magical monsters fit the bill, so does the serial killer in *There's Someone Inside Your House* or Lillian in *The Lake*. Their thirst for violence or revenge, while potentially justified, is exaggerated to the point of scariness.

The supernatural quality of these villains is what makes them monsters. They're driven by motivations that go against the laws of nature. And *that's* terrifying. Because whether they're human, subhuman, or far from human, they make us fear for our *own* humanity. And often they make us fear not just for our lives, but for our very *souls*.

Anna in *Anna Dressed in Blood* doesn't just kill the people who try to enter her house. She dooms them to an eternity trapped in the house with her. (Not fun.) The Collector in *Sawkill Girls* isn't just a scary demon who likes to snack on young girls. He's been feeding off their souls, using them for his own strength, and making each one his "queen." (Yikes!) And the bacteria on the planet Achlys in *Contagion* doesn't just infect people and kill them; it turns them into wild, monstrous versions of themselves. It steals their humanity.

Which is *so* much worse.

One way to up the fright factor is to introduce an optional character called the **half-man** or **half-person**. This character has gone to battle with the monster before and lived to tell about it. However, they've usually come away from the encounter damaged, traumatized, or maimed. The half-person helps demonstrate the monster's abilities, raise the stakes of the story, and deliver important information about the mythology of the monster in a non-info-dumpy way. In *Contagion*, for example, author Erin Bowman gives a sporadic POV to Coen, a boy who's been living on Achlys alone for two months since the outbreak that killed his entire mining crew. These short chapters not only provide context about what the monster is capable of but also create stakes and conflict, as we question whether Coen is a danger to the heroes.

The half-person can be a mentor who gives the hero important information that will eventually help them destroy the monster, or even a nemesis like Val's mother in *Sawkill Girls*, who had her chance to stand up to the Collector but, just like the women who came before her, didn't have the strength or courage. And now she's a dark, miserable, and corrupted soul.

Whether you introduce this character or not, what's even scarier than the monster itself is the fact that the hero is in some way stuck with it. And that's our second genre ingredient.

A HOUSE

The *house* is a metaphor. It can be any type of confined space or restrictive circumstances, keeping the hero (or heroes) trapped with the monster. It can be an island like in *Wilder Girls*, a distant planet like Achlys in *Contagion,* a summer camp like in *The Lake*, or even a whole town, like in (despite its title) *There's Someone Inside Your House*. Or it can be an *actual* house, like the "house on the hill" that Naughty John is spiritually bound to in *The Diviners*, or even multiple houses, like the boarded-up homes on Maple Street that "the Hag" is rumored to haunt in *White Smoke*.

The key, however, is giving the "house" a compelling reason to exist and to make sure it really is keeping your hero from leaving, or is in some way linking the monster *to* your hero. Otherwise, what's the point? Where's the connection? Why this hero for this plot? And why this monster for this house?

In *The Lake*, Lillian is targeting Kayla and Esme, who left her to burn in an accidental fire years ago. But she didn't hunt them down and attack them in their own towns. She waited for them to return to the scene of the crime—the summer camp where it all went down years before.

In *Sawkill Girls*, we actually find two types of houses, both intricately linked to not only the plot but also the monster's mythology. First, the Collector must be anchored to a host (to feed and build strength), which is currently Val, one of the novel's three heroes. On top of that, the Collector is also confined to the island of Sawkill Rock and is trying to build up enough strength to leave it. But Sawkill Rock isn't just a random island where a random evil incarnate happens to live. The Rock is the location of an *obscurae* (a tear in the dimensions) through which the monster has been able to pass. The Rock is also a sentient being, with a feminine, maternal energy, that needs the help of all three heroes—Marion, Zoey, and Val—to vanquish the monster from its shores. And for that very reason, the Rock won't let the three girls leave.

In *Anna Dressed in Blood*, we also get two types of houses. Anna is confined to the house she was killed in, yes, but in a fun twist, we eventually discover that Anna isn't the only ghost in town and her house isn't *the* house. At the Midpoint, Cas, the ghost-hunting hero, frees Anna from her imprisonment and thinks he's done the job he's come to do (false victory, anyone?), only to discover, at the All Is Lost, that there's a bigger, badder monster after him. One that's been trapped in the "athame" he uses to kill ghosts. And worst yet, it's linked directly to *him*. So even if he tries to leave town, the monster will follow him.

As you brainstorm your own "house," make sure there's a good, valid reason that it exists and that your heroes are stuck there. Otherwise, you risk your reader asking, "If it's so scary, why don't they just leave?" And what would be the fun in *that*?

The key here is the feeling of being trapped. We can't run. We can't hide. I guess the only way out of this situation is to confront the monster head-on and destroy it. And that's exactly what nearly all Monster in the House heroes eventually do. (Or at least they *try*.)

But as anyone who's done battle with a monster will tell you, that's easier said than done. Most monsters are not so easily defeated. The key to destroying your monster lies in our third ingredient.

A SIN

The sin is the reason the monster exists in the first place. Or the reason the monster is attacking *this* hero. Or *this* "house." Someone is responsible for creating this monster, letting it loose, or luring it into *this* story. It can be the hero or heroes themselves, like Kayla and Esme in *The Lake*; their irresponsibility, fear, and cowardice led them to start a fire in the forest and leave a girl there for dead. It can be a certain group or institution, like the Sterling Foundation in *White Smoke*, who were trying to run Black residents out of their homes so they could "reinvent" the town. It can be generations past that are to blame, like the Mortimer girls in *Sawkill Girls*, who sold their souls to the Collector in exchange for beauty and power, or Anna's own mother in *Anna Dressed in Blood*, who killed her daughter and cast a spell to keep her spirit locked inside the house forever. Or it can be the fault of humanity in general. Like the corporate greed in *Contagion* that pushed mining crews deeper into space in search of the valuable element corrarium, only to discover a monstrous bacteria that infects humans.

In the end, that's what this third ingredient comes down to: humanity's weaknesses, fears, ignorance, and/or darkness made manifest in fiction. Some great human sin has led to the creation of a monster who is haunting us for our mistakes. The "sin" serves as a warning to readers. But it's also what makes the monster the scariest of all.

Supernatural evil that threatens our very soul? Scary, yes. Being trapped with said supernatural evil? Also scary. But knowing you (or your human counterparts) are responsible or partly responsible for its creation? Downright terrifying!

The point is, this monster wasn't created randomly. We are not merely innocent victims here. And that's what often distinguishes this genre from its close relative, the Dude with a Problem, in which the hero is usually innocent and brought into the storm of trouble through no fault of their own. For the Monster in the House, however, that shouldn't be the case! Someone (or multiple someones) is to blame here.

Yet all hope is not lost. We can all learn from our mistakes or evolve from the errors of generations past. Because as frightening as the beast's raison d'être might be, it's also often the key to the beast's undoing.

If we can figure out *how* the monster was made, we can free ourselves from it. In fact, it's often not *until* we figure out the sin that created the monster that we have any clue on how to take it down. This important moment of discovery is often (but not always) linked with the **Dark Night Epiphany** and then the Break Into 3. Because what is the sin, if not a theme or a life lesson that your hero must learn? That we *all* must learn.

The sin is what gives your story purpose and depth and what often leads to the ultimate resolution.

It's not until Val breaks free of the Collector (with the help of Zoey and Marion)—something she admits she and her ancestors have been too weak to do—that she can share his secrets with the other girls and come up with a plan to defeat him (*Sawkill Girls*). It's not until Kayla and Esme face the very fears that led them to flee that night of the fire that they have the strength to enter the forest and confront Lillian and their past (*The Lake*). It's not until Marigold realizes that the Sterling Foundation's racism and greed is the *true* monster of the tale that she becomes resolved to expose them and bring them down (*White Smoke*).

This is what makes the sin such a compelling genre ingredient. If it was humanity that somehow created the monster, does that make us any less innocent than the monster itself? If we are to blame, then who is the real monster here? It's a question that dates back to one of the earliest examples of the genre, *Frankenstein* by Mary Shelley—a question still explored in examples today.

This may be why some authors choose *not* to defeat the monster in the end. Or to leave their endings ambiguous. To impart the message that good does not always conquer evil. And that good and evil are not always as black and white as we want them to be.

Should Kayla and Esme be fully redeemed for the part they played in the fire years ago? Or is Lillian justified in her revenge? Read *The Lake* to see how the author chose to answer this, and form your own opinions as well. That is the ultimate goal of any Monster in the House worth its salt: to get our readers thinking.

Yes, we want to scare them. We want to thrill them. We want to send them running to the kitchen to stash the book in the freezer. But we also want them to ask themselves the big questions, think the big thoughts, ponder the big stuff.

Wow, that's one scary monster. But what does it say about us?

To recap: if you're thinking of writing a Monster in the House novel, make sure your story includes these three essential ingredients:

- **A MONSTER**: made scary by their "supernatural" powers—even if its strength derives from inhuman obsession or irrationality.
- **A HOUSE**: that is, an enclosed space, which could be a literal house, a family unit, an entire town, or the world. Somehow your hero is stuck with this monster and can't escape.
- **A SIN**: Someone is guilty of bringing the monster into the house (or invading the monster's territory)—a transgression that can include ignorance and often relates to the theme the hero must learn, while at the same time hinting at who the real monster might be.

POPULAR YOUNG ADULT MONSTER IN THE HOUSE NOVELS

Anna Dressed in Blood by Kendare Blake
The Diviners by Libba Bray
Asylum by Madeleine Roux
Kalahari by Jessica Khoury
Sweet by Emmy Laybourne
There's Someone Inside Your House by Stephanie Perkins
Contagion by Erin Bowman
Sawkill Girls by Claire Legrand
Wilder Girls by Rory Power*
The Lake by Natasha Preston
White Smoke by Tiffany D. Jackson

* Beat sheet follows on page 358.

WILDER GIRLS

BY: Rory Power
STC GENRE: Monster in the House
BOOK GENRE: Young adult horror
TOTAL PAGES: 353 (Ember paperback edition, 2020)

What's worse than being trapped on an island with a monster? Becoming "monstrous" yourself as a result. In Rory Power's debut novel, which became an instant *New York Times* bestseller, we see all the elements of a chilling Monster in the House tale played out through a truly modern, young adult lens. This isn't a story where our young heroes learn to follow the rules and run to the adults for help. In fact, it's the opposite. It's a tale about learning to fend for yourself and protect your own when the adults who promised to take care of you fail. Receiving numerous starred reviews, the novel has been described as a feminist *Lord of the Flies* and praised by NPR for being "as sharp as a blade used to cut out corruption." In a market where teen readers are becoming more savvy and sophisticated and wanting their horror novels to go deeper than just blood and gore, *Wilder Girls* delivers.

Opening Image (3–5)

The Raxter School has become a nightmare. Hetty, our hero and primary narrator, stands guard on the roof with her best friend, Byatt, rifles raised and aimed at a giant animal stalking between the trees. They are on "Gun Shift," while the "Boat Shift" returns from their trip across Raxter Island to the dock where the Navy delivers rations. The Boat Shift girls are the only ones allowed to go outside the quarantine fence around the school.

Hetty prides herself on being the best shot at Raxter, despite having only one working eye. Her right eye went dead in a recent "flare-up." It's sealed shut, and she can feel something growing under the lid. In fact, all of the girls at Raxter are sick with strange symptoms like this.

Setup (6–42)

Through a sequence of gripping, disquieting scenes, we learn that a mysterious disease called the Tox has taken all but two teachers (Headmistress and Ms. Welch) and about fifty students. The students who survived have been left *changed*. Extra spines growing on top of flesh, scaly hands, weeping sores, and tremoring limbs. By using the Monster in the House feature of the **half-person** (all of the surviving students have gone to "battle" with the monster and lived to tell about it), author Rory Power builds suspense and stakes, showing exactly what the monster is capable of.

So far, no cure for the Tox has been found, but every day the girls hope and pray (**wants**) and follow the Navy's orders to stay inside the fence to keep safe from the deadly animals who have also been changed by the disease. A letter from the Navy, promising to keep the girls safe and find a cure, is pinned to a bulletin board; the girls, including Hetty, touch it for good luck as they pass. They believe help is coming. They have no reason to doubt the adults and authority figures who have *seemingly* protected them for this long. And Hetty suffers from this flaw most of all. Despite the Navy's sending food, there is never enough, leading to fights.

Flare-ups of the Tox come in cycles, each worse than the last, and often the girls don't survive it. Hetty's best friend Byatt is due for her next flare-up any day (**stasis = death**). The girls each keep a single bullet casing full of gunpowder in a pocket. They've been taught how to crack it open to ingest the powder in the event that they ever "need to die" (29). Ingesting gunpowder is lethal when you have the Tox, and it's better to die on your own terms.

Talk about **things that need fixing!**

The surviving girls have formed small groups, like clans. "Reese and Byatt, they're mine and I'm theirs," Hetty explains on page 10. Bonded by the dangers and uncertainty of the Tox, these makeshift families look out for each other and protect their own.

Hetty, Reese, and Byatt are roommates and friends, but Hetty secretly wishes she could be more with Reese. She's never expressed it, however, because Reese is distant and hardened. Reese grew up on Raxter Island with her father, Mr. Harker, who used to be the groundskeeper, but after the Tox turned him violent, he fled the school and hasn't been seen since.

At shooting practice, a girl named Mona experiences another flare-up. Gills appear on her neck and start pulsing. As she's dragged away, the other girls resume shooting, as though nothing has happened.

If you're starting to feel uneasy, I imagine that's intentional. The author successfully sets up the terrifying fragility of the Act 1 world. Believe it or not, this has become the **status quo** for these girls. But it feels like any moment now one wrong step could bring it tumbling down.

Theme Stated (39)

While walking by the tide pools, Hetty and Byatt find a local species of crab called a Raxter Blue, which triggers a memory for Hetty of the days before the Tox, when they dissected these crabs in biology. "See how a body will change to give you the best chance it can," their teacher said, pointing out that the crab had both lungs and gills.

This is a clue to understanding the monster that has been ravishing the island, but also a clever nod to the theme and life lesson that Hetty will eventually learn in this story about survival and knowing whom to trust. When you're face-to-face with a monster (which we'll soon learn can come in many forms), the only people you can rely on are yourself and your own family (including one you choose). Essentially, to give *herself* the best chance to survive, Hetty must adapt, just like the Raxter Blue crab. She must trust in herself and her girls. Because the adults and the authorities she's been taught to rely on are not always looking out for her.

Catalyst (42–45)

There is an open spot on Boat Shift, and Reese desperately wants it. She hopes that being able to leave the quarantine zone will give her an opportunity to look for her dad. But when Hetty gets chosen for Boat Shift instead, Reese violently attacks her. Hetty admits that they've fought before over rations, but nothing like this.

The incident shifts the dynamic of Reese and Hetty's relationship and sends the plot in a new direction. With Hetty chosen for Boat Shift, for the first time in eighteen months she'll be able to leave the fenced area and see the rest of the island.

Debate (45–54)

The Debate question is not "Will she go?" but rather "What should she expect?" Hetty spends the beat preparing for her first journey, asking questions, wondering what she'll encounter, and flashing back to the earliest days of the Tox. We're getting ready to leave an old world behind and enter a new one.

Quite literally, in this case.

Break Into 2 (55–59)

The moment Hetty steps outside the fence, she is overwhelmed by how much it's changed. This island that used to feel familiar is now foreign and strange. "It all feels forgotten, like we're the first people here in a hundred years" (59). With the Tox left to spread and blossom on its own, the island has turned *wilder*, and Hetty feels as though none of them belong there anymore.

Welcome to the **upside-down world** of Act 2.

Fun and Games (60–185)

The **Act 2 goal** is clear: get the supplies. Accompanied by Ms. Welch, Hetty and the Boat Shift girls travel across a dangerous and overgrown island that has been ravaged by the Tox. Where there used to be tame animals, there are now claw marks on the trees and giant, hungry bears with faces half gone. If you're looking for horror, look no further than this **promise of the premise**, as Hetty comes face-to-face with what the "monster" has done to her home.

Despite the danger, the girls arrive safely at the dock to collect the supplies (**upward path**), but Hetty is shocked to see Ms. Welch throw most of the food into the sea, claiming it's "off." Welch warns Hetty not to tell anyone about what she's seen, and even though Hetty feels wrong about it, she agrees, believing Ms. Welch must know what's best (**flaw**).

As they head back to the school, an encounter with a Tox-ravaged bobcat separates the group. While hiding in the trees, Hetty finds a mysterious cooler containing a vial of blood labeled "Potential RAX009."

Back at the school, Hetty fights the urge to tell her "family" (Byatt and Reese) about the discarded food but chooses to follow Ms. Welch's orders and keep it a secret (**fixing things the wrong way**). But things take a turn for the worse when Byatt is sent to the infirmary with a flare-up.

B Story (93–95)

Reese attempts to comfort Hetty about Byatt, marking an important pivot point in their relationship. Although Reese has been part of Hetty's world since she arrived at Raxter, their new dynamic is very much a product of the Act 2 world. After the Catalyst drives them apart, Byatt's flare-up and absence bring them together in a different way. As their relationship deepens into more than just a friendship, it becomes clear that Byatt has been an unintentional blockade between them. Now that they're alone—even though Byatt's absence guts Hetty— they can explore feelings for each other in a way they never could in a group of three.

As the B Story character, Reese helps Hetty learn an important lesson about relying on yourself and your chosen family, instead of on the adults and authorities who promised to protect you. And later, by having to say goodbye to her father (the adult authority in her own life), Reese is a perfect representation of the theme.

Fun and Games/cont'd (60–185)

When Hetty sneaks into the infirmary to visit Byatt, she makes a shocking discovery: Byatt is gone. Hetty refuses to believe she's dead, and an overheard conversation between Welch and a mysterious male voice on the radio supports her suspicions that something else is going on. The man confirms "receipt" of a "replacement," to which Welch responds that they need to make a "return." The man tells Welch to "drop her at the Harker house" (107) at this time tomorrow.

And just like that, we have a new Act 2 goal! Convinced that they're talking about Byatt, Hetty makes plans to sneak outside the fence to find her. After some coaxing, she convinces Reese to join her. But we get the feeling that Reese's motivation isn't *just* to find Byatt, but also to look for her dad. From the start, Reese has wanted to leave the quarantined area and find her father but has never had the courage to break the rules and leave on her own.

The narration then switches to Byatt. Her sporadic POV throughout the novel serves to widen our view of the story, the theme, and the world, giving us a unique perspective on the "monster" that lurks on Raxter Island.

Byatt wakes up in a strange, hospital-like room, her confusion presented through choppy, disjointed phrasing, lack of punctuation, and creative sentence structure. When Byatt tries to answer questions posed to her by a boy in a hazmat suit (Teddy), her voice causes him physical pain, so she writes her answers instead. Byatt believes she's in Camp Nash, the Navy base on the mainland. She remembers fighting against Welch when she brought her here, trying to run away, and being shot by a dart. Byatt is given a pill labeled RAX009; from the way the doctors watch her, they clearly believe it's supposed to be a cure. Instead, Byatt experiences another flare-up, this one giving her a sense of power and strength. While trying to tamp it down, she narrates, "Only part of me doesn't want to. I can hear it, snarling and low, telling me to let go. Telling me this has always been inside me and that these doctors are trying to take it away" (129). She screams, causing everyone to fall to their knees in pain, until Byatt is finally tranquilized.

Byatt's POV explores the novel's theme from a different angle. As we'll soon learn, the Navy has been experimenting on the girls to find a cure for the "monster" discovered on Raxter Island. Byatt's voice—her power—is being stolen by the very people she's been taught to trust.

Back in Hetty's POV, Hetty and Reese prepare to venture outside the fence. They steal a rifle, and Hetty teaches Reese to shoot, leading to a romantic moment, an admission of mutual feelings, and a kiss (upward path). Later, in a moment of growth, Hetty breaks her promise to Welch and tells Reese about the food that's being thrown away.

When we return to Byatt's POV, we learn that Byatt's parents sent her to Raxter because she lies and manipulates people. Interesting, then, that the Tox has made her voice *literally* painful to hear. Dr. Paretta restates the theme when she shows Byatt a Raxter Blue crab they've been studying and points to its gills and lungs. "It's pretty amazing, right? So it can survive anywhere. And I think it's pretty amazing, too, that you girls are part of it now . . . Imagine how we could use this. Imagine the people we could help" (163).

It's clear that Dr. Paretta and the other scientists see these girls as test subjects that they can use to protect the greater good from an imminent threat. But the theme of the novel is about protecting one's own, not the greater good. About adapting to take *back* one's power, not to give it away. Something that's reflected later when Byatt thinks about the other modifications the girls at Raxter have undergone and realizes that the Tox is "trying to make us better, if only we could adapt" (169).

Is it possible the "monster" is trying to change these girls for the better? Which raises the question posed in so many Monster in the House tales: Who is the real monster here?

Byatt lies to Teddy that the Tox can't infect him, convincing him to take off his mask. She kisses him, and the next day Teddy has his first flare-up.

Midpoint (189–210)

Armed with rifles and knives, Hetty and Reese sneak out of the school to find Byatt. In a **shift from wants to needs**, Hetty thinks of the pinned-up note from the Navy, promising that help is coming, and realizes "we have to help ourselves" (191). The two make it to Harker house (**false victory**); soon after, Welch arrives with a student named Taylor, dragging a body bag. Hetty is devastated, thinking it's Byatt, but after Welch and Taylor leave, they open the bag to find Mona. This is the "return" Welch was talking about on the radio (**Midpoint twist**).

Knowing someone is coming to pick up the body, the girls wait so they can follow them to where Byatt is being kept (presumably at Camp Nash). **A and B Stories cross** and **love story ramps up** when Hetty and Reese talk and Hetty realizes Reese isn't out here risking her life for Byatt; she's out here risking her life for Hetty. Moments later, the **stakes are raised** when the shape of a man emerges from the trees.

Bad Guys Close In (211–286)

It's Reese's father, but the Tox has turned him into another of the island's monsters. He attacks, plunging the story into a **downward path**, Hetty is forced to kill Mr. Harker, driving an emotional wedge between her and Reese and their blossoming relationship.

Back in Byatt's POV, she wakes up drugged, restrained, and unable to talk, and learns that her body has rejected another potential cure. The study is shut down and the facility evacuated. Byatt is given an oxygen mask filled with a deadly gas that she knows will kill her, but she has no fight left. This feels like a personal All Is Lost for Byatt. After breathing in the gas, she studies her reflection in the mirror and sees a pulsing bulge under the flesh of her arm, like a "darkness . . . trying to flee" (243). She cuts herself and removes a long, wormlike parasite. It's the Tox, but perhaps something else as well. When she looks back in the mirror, she notices something is missing. In her personal Break Into 3, Byatt rids herself of the monster that lives inside of her, but she's forced to take a piece of herself too.

Her slow death is personified in the collapse of her sentence structure. Punctuation falls away and the spacing between words expands as the phrases grow more and more fragmented and make less sense. Until she's gone.

Back at Raxter School, the downward path continues. Hetty heads out with Boat Shift for another supply run, only to find not food, but a canister of deadly gas. Welch knows this means the Navy is never coming back. In her defeated state, Welch rambles on about how she tried to protect the girls and warns them not to trust the CDC or the Navy. Then she kills herself.

The Boat Shift girls decide to take the canister back to the school to let Headmistress decide what to do with it, once again trusting the authority figures to have their best interest at heart (which will prove to be another mistake). After returning to the school and telling Headmistress what happened, a Tox-ravaged bear gets inside the quarantine fence. Hetty realizes she was so distracted by Welch's confession and death that she forgot to close the gate. The bear gives chase, and

Hetty tries to sacrifice herself, but Reese grabs her and pulls her to safety. The bear gets another student instead.

All Is Lost (287–296)

After waking everyone up, Hetty and Reese look for someone to take charge. Hetty goes to Taylor (the student that Welch and Headmistress trust the most), once again putting her faith in the wrong person, instead of in herself and her family.

The girls build barricades to keep the bear from getting inside the school. Hetty looks on, frozen and helpless, realizing this is all her fault. Because this is the All Is Lost, she does the *opposite* of the theme and listens to Headmistress, the last remaining adult. Headmistress lines up the girls and leads them into the music room before ordering Taylor to "take" Reese. After attacking Reese and dragging her from the room, Headmistress locks the door behind her and, in a *literal* **whiff of death**, gas fills the room.

Girls start to drop dead. Not from the Tox, but from Headmistress's betrayal and Camp Nash's gas. The face of the true "monster" is revealed. And the size of the "house" has just shrunk down to a room that's filling with deadly gas. Hetty's internal bad guys (trusting the wrong people) have led to the external bad guys (seemingly) winning.

Hetty smashes out a window in the door, and the surviving girls stagger into the hallway.

Dark Night of the Soul (297–310)

Hetty mourns the dead. Sixteen girls lost to the monster. She leaves to find Reese, who's locked in the infirmary. Speaking through the door, Reese tells her that Headmistress and Taylor took her because they wanted to know how to get off the island (and she knows Raxter best). Hetty struggles to open the door but is stopped by Taylor, who attacks her with a knife. They fight, and Hetty surprises herself by stabbing Taylor. In her shock and paralysis, she thinks of Welch and Mr. Harker, wallowing in all of the death she's responsible for. "This stain will never wash out" (305).

After finally getting the infirmary door open, Hetty and Reese stumble back to the others. The bear breaks through the barricade and attacks. Hetty saves one of the younger girls, feeling like it's the least she can do to offset all the death she's caused.

Hetty is surprised when Reese tells her she *does* know a way off the island (**Dark Night Epiphany**).

Break Into 3 (310)

Reese explains that she's never tried to escape because she didn't think she could get past the fence and never had the strength to leave her home before. But now, with Hetty, she does. They have both learned where to find true strength: in themselves and in each other. Now, with an **Act 3 goal** (escape Raxter) set in motion, they'll have to prove it.

Finale (311–349)

POINT 1: GATHERING THE TEAM. Hetty gets the idea to steal supplies from Headmistress's office. When Headmistress scolds her for barging in, telling her she's not allowed, Hetty laughs. "Like that matters anymore" (311). Hetty is no longer beholden to Headmistress's authority.

This "gathering the supplies" beat soon becomes a "gathering the information" beat, as Hetty confronts Headmistress about trying to kill them and Headmistress explains more about what's been happening on Raxter. After noticing the effects of climate change on the island years ago, the Navy and CDC decided to run some experiments. Headmistress swears she never thought it would be dangerous for the girls, but Hetty, having now learned her theme, can tell she's lying. Headmistress sacrificed the girls to experimentation while secretly planning her own escape. Then Hetty notices that the stash of water bottles in the office are laced with gunpowder (which kills those infected with the Tox), and Headmistress reveals that Camp Nash has sent jets to bomb the island. Raxter has become too big of a risk, and the Navy is shutting it all down. Headmistress also reveals that they failed to find a cure. They tried to experiment on the girls with the food they delivered, but Welch wouldn't let them. It turns out there was one adult looking out for the girls all along. And she's dead now.

The weight of all of this sends Hetty over the edge. She forces Headmistress to drink from a contaminated bottle and watches her die. There may not be a cure for the Tox, but Hetty has slayed at least one monster in this house.

POINT 2: EXECUTING THE PLAN. Hetty and Reese leave the school, hand in hand, vowing to stay together. They head to Harker house, where Reese's dad kept a boat hidden along the shore. At the house, Tox-ravaged foxes are eating Mr. Harker's body. Reese shoos them away before saying a quick goodbye to her father (and her life on the island). They stumble down to the shoreline until they find Mr. Harker's dinghy. Hetty can just make out the mainland on the horizon. They're nearly safe.

POINT 3: HIGH TOWER SURPRISE. But a sight on the north side of the island stops them short. The Raxter visitor center has been covered by some type of tent. Hetty finds this strange. The visitors' center is supposed to be empty.

POINT 4: DIG DEEP DOWN. Everything clicks for Hetty. She always thought the CDC and the Navy were on the mainland, but they've been here the whole time. An outpost on Raxter ensured that the Tox wouldn't spread to the mainland and made it easier to get access to test subjects from Raxter School.

Suddenly Hetty knows Byatt is not on the mainland. She's in the visitors' center. And Hetty knows what she must do.

POINT 5: THE EXECUTION OF THE NEW PLAN. Hetty and Reese reach the abandoned outpost and find Byatt's room and the parasite she pulled out of her arm. Hetty realizes it's the Tox and that they each have one inside of them too. In Byatt's chart, they find a graph tracking climate change on Raxter. Hetty remembers reading about prehistoric creatures trapped in ice, releasing terrifying things as the ice melts. She concludes that's how the Tox got here: a prehistoric parasite was released, infecting small things first, "until it was finally strong enough to reach into the wilderness. Into us" (342).

After exploring the lab, they learn that Byatt was the ninth test subject—RAX009. There were eight others, including Mona, but the cure worked on none of them. Following a trail of blood, they find Byatt's body on the ground. But she's not dead! The gas didn't kill her, because Byatt had removed the parasite the gas was targeting.

The sound of the jets jolts them into action. They help Byatt to her feet, but fatigue and injuries make moving difficult. When Hetty loses her will to go on, Reese calls out her name, giving her strength to continue (like a good B Story character!). They reach the boat and push off, floating farther away and closer to safety, until the jet sound fades away. They've escaped the monsters that live on the outside, but what about the ones that still live *inside* them?

Final Image (349–353)

They cut the engines and float. Hetty experiences another flare-up and feels something lodged in her throat. Reese reaches into her mouth and pulls out a beating human heart. Hetty thinks about the Raxter Blue crabs with both lungs and gills, and realizes that perhaps the monster isn't trying to destroy them. "It's trying to make me better, but I can't take it" (352).

Reese assures Hetty it will be okay, promising to save her life just as Hetty has saved hers. As they float, Hetty thinks of a simpler time, before the Tox, when they were just friends, not victims of a monster. She vows to make it that way again.

Much is left uncertain in the final pages of this standalone novel, but one thing is not: together, these three girls have defeated a monster. And maybe, just maybe, they can do it again.

WHY IS THIS A MONSTER IN THE HOUSE?

Wilder Girls contains all three elements of a successful Monster in the House story.

- **A MONSTER:** The monsters take many shapes in this story, from the contagious virus known as the Tox, which leaves its survivors changed and often violent, to the Tox-infected animals who lurk just outside the fence, to perhaps the scariest monster of them all: the authorities (including Headmistress) who knowingly subjected the girls of Raxter School to the horrors of the Tox and the Navy's experimentation for the cure.

- **A HOUSE:** Raxter Island is isolated from the mainland by its location and the government's quarantine. Furthermore, within the island's confines, the Raxter School serves as an even smaller "house" that the girls are not allowed to leave.
- **A SIN:** The author hints that climate change (made worse by humanity's damage to the environment) is responsible for creating the Tox, melting ancient ice and awakening prehistoric creatures and parasites into the wilderness of Raxter. But we also see the "sin" of selfishness and self-preservation, even in the theme Hetty must learn. Headmistress sacrificed the Raxter girls to save herself, yet Hetty and Reese must do what it takes to survive, themselves, even if that means leaving the others behind. The result is a morally complex story that leaves teen readers with much to think about in a time when the world seems so uncertain and the adults don't appear to have all the answers anymore.

Cat's Eye View

For quick reference, here's a brief overview of this novel's beat sheet.

OPENING IMAGE: Hetty stands guard on "Gun Shift" with Byatt as the "Boat Shift" girls return from their supply run. She has one working eye; the other went dead in a flare-up.

SETUP: The Tox has ravaged the school and the island, infecting students and animals and leaving them changed. There is no known cure, but Hetty and the other girls wait patiently in their quarantine for the Navy to find one (wants), trusting that the authorities will take care of them (flaw). At shooting practice, a girl named Mona has a flare-up and is dragged away.

THEME STATED: "See how a body will change, to give you the best chance it can" (39) says a teacher in a flashback referring to the Raxter Blue crabs found on the island. By the end, Hetty will need to adapt to give herself the best chance to survive. She must trust in herself and her girls. Because the adults and the authorities she's been taught to rely on are not always looking out for her.

CATALYST: Hetty is chosen to join Boat Shift (a role Reese desperately wants), which changes the dynamic in their relationship and also means that, for the first time in eighteen months, Hetty will be able to leave the quarantine area around the school.

DEBATE: What should she expect outside the fence? Hetty spends the Debate preparing for her first journey, asking questions, wondering what she'll encounter, and flashing back to the earliest days of the Tox.

BREAK INTO 2: The moment Hetty steps outside the fence, she is overwhelmed by how much the once-familiar island has changed. With the Tox left to spread and blossom on its own, the island has turned *wilder*, and Hetty feels none of them belong there anymore (upside-down world).

FUN AND GAMES: Hetty goes to the dock to pick up supplies and sees how the Tox has ravaged the island and its animal inhabitants. She watches Ms. Welch throw away most of the food but is warned not to tell anyone about what she saw. Later, after Byatt has a flare-up and disappears from the infirmary, Hetty makes a plan with Reese to sneak out and find her. Byatt wakes up in a medical facility where scientists test a potential cure on her, but it only causes another flare-up. We learn that the Navy has been using Raxter girls as test subjects for the Tox.

B STORY: Through their blossoming relationship, Reese helps Hetty learn whom to trust and rely on (not the adults and authority figures they've been taught to trust). By having to say goodbye to her father (the adult authority in her own life), Reese is a perfect representation of the theme.

MIDPOINT: Hetty and Reese arrive at Harker house (false victory) where they believe Byatt is being taken, only to find a body bag containing Mona. Stakes are raised when a man (Reese's father) emerges from the trees.

BAD GUYS CLOSE IN: Hetty is forced to kill Reese's father, who's turned monstrous from the Tox. On the next Boat Shift, there's no food, only a canister of gas. Knowing this marks the end, Ms. Welch kills herself. Hetty accidentally leaves the fence open, and a Tox-ravaged bear gets into the school. Meanwhile, the medical facility where Byatt is being held is shut down, and Byatt is given deadly gas to breathe.

ALL IS LOST: Headmistress locks all the girls in a room and takes Reese hostage. The room fills with toxic gas, and girls start to drop dead (literal whiff of death). Hetty breaks a window to rescue the remaining students.

DARK NIGHT OF THE SOUL: Hetty mourns the dead and goes to find Reese, who's been tortured by Headmistress because only she knows a way off the island. After saving one of the younger girls from the bear, Hetty discovers that Reese *does* know how to get off the island (Dark Night Epiphany).

BREAK INTO 3: Reese has never tried to escape before because she didn't have the courage to leave home. Now, with Hetty, she does. They have both found strength in each other and make a plan to escape Raxter (Act 3 goal).

FINALE: After learning from Headmistress more about the Tox and the Navy's experimentation on the girls, Hetty kills Headmistress (one of the true monsters) and escapes the school with Reese. Sailing away from the island on Reese's dad's boat, they notice something strange at the Raxter visitor center and go to investigate. There they find Byatt. She's been on the island all along, not on the mainland. And despite what we've been led to believe, she's not dead. The three girls escape on the boat just as the Navy's jets appear to bomb the island.

FINAL IMAGE: The three girls float away from the island. Hetty realizes the Tox is still inside her and has been trying to make her stronger, but her body can't take it. Reese assures Hetty everything will be okay, but since the ending is left ambiguous, we can't be sure. Either way, a monster has been slayed.

Selling Your Novel
How to Pitch Your Book to Agents, Editors, and Readers

So you've made it through the beat sheet and the genres! You've written a stellar novel that ticks all the boxes and gives readers the same thing, only different. Or at least you're well on your way.

Now what?

Well, I've got some good news and some bad news for you. Which do you want first?

Bad news it is! (Hey, I had a 50/50 shot.)

The bad news is that it's not enough to *write* a stellar novel. You also have to *sell* your stellar novel. Whether your goal is to traditionally publish (sign a deal with a major publisher), self-publish (in eBook or in print), or perhaps just post your manuscript online somewhere for free and see where it goes, somewhere along the line you're going to have to convince someone to read this book.

Meaning you're going to have to answer that terrifying question:

What's your book about?

And sorry, this time you can't just say, "It's about transformation!" (Even though that's technically true, and I would be so proud!) Answering this question is all about shrinking your novel into a bite-size piece of information that quickly and effectively conveys everything awesome about your book, to make someone not just *want* to read it but *need* to read it.

This is about the *pitch*.

What Is a Pitch?

Think about the last novel you purchased. What made you buy it? Was it the cover? That probably had a lot to do with it ("don't judge a book by its cover" is the *least* followed advice in the book industry). But what did you do after you were drawn in by that intriguing cover? Did you turn the book around and read the summary on the back? Or scroll down to the description on the sales page? Or click "read more" on your eReader?

Whether you realized it or not, you were pitched.

That summary you read is the book's formal, *written* pitch. As opposed to a more informal *verbal* pitch, which is usually what you'll hear when an author speaks at an event about their book or talks about their book during a live chat online. All good pitches have one thing in common:

They leave the reader wanting to know more.

They *hook* people!

Which is why you never want to reveal the *whole* story in a pitch. You want to include just enough to make them want to read it. Or better yet, buy the book that instant with a click of a button!

You gotta paint a picture of your story that's so intriguing, so riveting, so *hooky* that readers will scream, "Just take my money already!"

Does that sound hard? It is. And here's why:

Most authors cringe at the thought of pitching their book. Not because they're not natural-born salespeople (which, let's face it, most authors aren't), but because the idea of distilling all of those words into a single compelling page of text is so daunting, they give up. We authors get way too caught up in the magnificence of the trees (our character quirks and subplots and five-hundred-year-history of the warring villages) to even *see* the forest. Let's be honest, most authors would rather write another 300-page novel than write a one-page sales pitch.

I can't tell you how many times I've asked an author, "What's your book about?" and twenty minutes later, they're still talking, and I still don't know the answer.

If you're starting to feel a little panicky and are thinking, *I thought she said there was* good *news . . .*

There is!

Pitching your book *is* hard for most authors. Fortunately, *you're* not most authors. Because *you're* holding this book.

If you've already worked out the fifteen beats of your Save the Cat! Beat Sheet, you already have your pitch.

The method I've been guiding you through in this book is designed to help you see your story from a macro level—to distinguish the forest from the trees. This automatically makes it easier for you to craft an engaging pitch for your novel once you've reached this point in the process.

In this chapter, you'll learn how you can take the beats you already have and use them to craft two kinds of pitches: the logline and the short synopsis. Both will be instrumental to your novel-writing journey, regardless of where you're headed on that journey.

Why Pitches Are Important for ALL Novelists

As the author, you are essentially the first link in a very long chain of people who will have to sell your novel to someone else. There are lots of people who have to convince other people that your book is awesome. Which is why I call it the "chain of awesome."

For instance, if you're pursuing a traditional publishing path, to get a book deal with a major publisher you first have to get a literary agent. And to get a literary agent, you have to convince an agent that your book is awesome, so they'll represent you. The agent will then have to convince an editor at a publishing house that your book is awesome, so they'll buy it. But to buy the book, the editor has to convince a whole team of people at the publishing house—sales, marketing, publicity—that the book is awesome.

Once the book is sold to a publisher, the chain splits off and expands into multiple chains of awesome. The sales team has to convince the booksellers to stock the book, and the booksellers have to convince the readers to buy the book. Meanwhile, the publicity and marketing teams are selling the book to reviewers, bloggers, vloggers, and the media, and—for young adult novels—the school and library teams are selling your book to schools, libraries, and book fairs. And let's not forget about your agent, who's still out there selling your book to foreign publishers and movie producers!

And if you're planning to self-publish, you're going to need to convince a lot of people—primarily readers—that your book is awesome!

And guess what? *All* of that is done with the pitch.

But your pitch isn't just important for *selling* your book. Even if you never plan to put this book up for sale or public consumption, there's another very crucial reason why you must master your pitch.

It's a test.

Albert Einstein said, "If you can't explain it simply, you don't understand it well enough." If you can't pitch your story succinctly, then you haven't quite figured out what you're trying to say yet.

Your pitch is a way to check that your novel and your beats are in line, impactful, and working. If you use your beats to craft your pitch, and that pitch falls flat, that might mean your beats don't have enough punch. They aren't doing the job they're meant to do and might need a revision.

So let's put your story to the test.

The Logline

The "logline" originated as an old Hollywood term. Movie studios would log screenplays into a book with a single line (or sentence) that served as a quick summary of the story. Now loglines are commonly used by screenwriters and novelists alike. Because not only can a logline help us pitch our story quickly (to agents, editors, readers, or even big movie studios!), but it can also help us distill our story to its very essence, its very core, which allows us to see if our story is working. If you can pitch your book in one sentence, you can be sure you're on the right track.

Wait a minute. Did you just say one *sentence?*

That I did.

A logline is a single-sentence description of your book. And to prove it can be done, let's play a little a game. Can you tell me what young adult novel this is?

> *On the verge of her sister's departure for college, a teen girl, secretly in love with her sister's boyfriend, starts a fake relationship with the most popular boy in school in order to hide her crush; but when the relationship starts to feel a little too real, she must confront all of her emotions head-on before she breaks more hearts than her own.*

If you said, *To All the Boys I've Loved Before* by Jenny Han, you're right!

Let's do another one. Name this novel (no peeking at the answer!):

> *On the verge of eviction from her apartment, a teen bounty hunter, grieving her father's death, accepts an invitation to go undercover in the world championships of the most popular virtual reality game in order to track a dangerous hacker; but when an assassination attempt is made on the game's elusive young creator, she must learn to see beyond the perception of reality and discover the unsettling truth behind the game, before it turns deadly.*

Recognize that one? It's *Warcross* by Marie Lu!

Now, those two novels are *quite* different stories in quite different genres, yet they could each be described in a single sentence. And you might have noticed that they were very *similar* sentences. You might have even noticed that they followed the same pattern. (Are you sensing a pattern in all of this pattern-making?) That's because I was using the Save the Cat! *beats* to build the logline.

Which means, if you already have your beats, you are one step closer to building your own logline.

And you can do that using the handy-dandy Save the Cat! logline template!

THE SAVE THE CAT! LOGLINE TEMPLATE

> On the verge of a **stasis = death** moment, a flawed hero
> **Breaks Into 2**; but when the **Midpoint** happens, they must
> learn the **Theme Stated** before the **All Is Lost**.

Simply plug in the beats of any story of any genre, and presto! You have a logline.

The template works because it does four essential things:

- Creates urgency (with the phrase "on the verge of" and a mention of how stasis = death)
- Delivers on a hook or premise (by referencing Act 2)
- Hints at stakes (with a nod to the Midpoint and All Is Lost)
- Proves your story has purpose by showing that *this* hero is essential to *this* plot and vice versa (with a hint of the Theme Stated)

All of that delivered in *one* sentence.

Of course you can (and should) feel free to change up the language and make it your own. If the wording feels awkward, the logline won't be able to do its job. So play around with the actual wording and syntax to ensure it's clear and reads well.

However, if you're finding yourself rewriting and tinkering too much, make sure it's not the wording that's the problem. Often, it's the beats themselves that aren't working. If your logline is just not coming together, it's worth looking at those beats again and asking yourself: *Are they serving the purpose they're meant to serve? Am I able to check off all the boxes of the checklists for each beat at the end of chapter 2?*

Perhaps your Break Into 2 isn't a clear enough departure from Act 1. Or your Midpoint isn't big enough to raise the stakes and send the story in a new direction. Or your All Is Lost doesn't feel low enough. Or you don't have enough urgency built into your Setup, and change doesn't feel *essential*.

Again, the logline is not just a sales tool; it's a fantastic test to make sure your beats are as compelling, impactful, and functional as they need to be to tell an engaging story. And you don't have to wait until the book is finished. Forcing myself to write a logline for every book I write (even *while* I'm still writing it) is incredibly illuminating. It never fails. If the logline is giving me problems, the book is giving me problems. And it usually means *both* need work.

Just for fun, let's plug some more stories into the template and see what we get.

The Sun Is Also a Star by Nicola Yoon

On the verge of her family's deportation, a teen girl who would rather trust in facts than fate is thrown into the path of a cute stranger, which sets off a life-changing adventure through the streets of New York City as she attempts to stop the deportation; but when she starts to actually fall in love with this boy, she must come to terms with the reality that destiny might have a plan for all of us, even if it's not what we planned.

The Hunger Games by Suzanne Collins

After her sister is chosen to compete in a televised fight to the death, a hardened teen girl struggling to make ends meet volunteers to take her sister's place as a tribute in the arena; but when she starts to fall in love with a fellow competitor whom she must kill if she wants to win, she must realize who the true enemy is and outsmart them before more lives are lost and she becomes just another pawn in their deadly games.

Children of Blood and Bone by Tomi Adeyemi

Under the rule of a ruthless king set on suppressing her kind, a young maji girl with a power to raise the dead and a thirst for revenge sets off on a quest to restore the magic that was stolen from her world; but when she realizes how much blood has been spilled in the fulfillment of her destiny, she must embrace a more peaceful way to bring about change before more innocent lives are taken and magic is lost forever.

If you're worried the logline gives away too much, consider this: Did any of these loglines make you want to read the book *less*? Loglines speak to that innate story DNA that all of us share. Just like when we read a good story, when we read a good logline with all the right beats in all the right places, that DNA hums within us like a beautiful melody.

That said, if your Midpoint reveals a big twist with a *huge* spoiler, consider providing a hint at that twist instead of spelling it out. Just try to avoid a logline that reads like this:

> *Under the rule of a ruthless king set on suppressing her kind, a young girl with a powerful ability sets off on an important quest; but when things turn deadly, she must find another way to bring about change before more innocent lives are taken and her hopes of succeeding are lost forever.*

In case you didn't pick up on it, this is *also* a logline for *Children of Blood and Bone,* except I hid all the good parts, including the hook! Did you notice how much less compelling this is because of its ambiguity? It lacks focus and clarity. There's nothing for me to grasp on to as a reader.

So be careful about hiding *too* much, or it can lead to a muddled and confusing logline, not to mention a missed opportunity to hook your reader. I'm not suggesting you spoil your entire book; just don't leave out the very thing that's going to convince your reader to click "Buy Now" because you're afraid of a *small* spoiler.

One writer's small spoiler is often another writer's big selling point.

However, you may or may not end up using the logline to actually sell your book directly to readers. Perhaps you'll only use it for yourself, to test your story, or internally within your publishing house, to rocket your book along the chain of awesome.

But this next pitch we're going to work on is one you will most *definitely* use to sell your book to readers. In fact, along with your book's cover and title, it will probably be the most important sales tool in your arsenal.

The Short Synopsis

The short synopsis goes by many names: book description, book summary, jacket-flap copy, back blurb, and so on. But in the end, we're all talking about the same thing: a two- to three-paragraph summary of your novel designed to pull readers in and make them want to read more.

Want some examples? Fortunately, you have access to *tons* of them right now. Just walk over to your bookshelf, pick up a paperback, and flip it over, or pick up a hardcover and read the inside jacket flap. There it is! The short synopsis is there for you to read, devour, and most of all *study*.

Understandably, a lot of pressure goes into writing a short synopsis. After all, it might be what stands between you and an agent, you and a publishing deal, or you and a reader clicking "Buy Now." If agents and editors are the gatekeepers of the publishing world, then the short synopsis is the key that gets you through the door—or keeps you locked out in the cold. Because the short synopsis is *also* what makes up the majority of your query letter (the letter you must send to agents before they'll agree to read your book and consider you for representation).

That's a lot of pressure for three little paragraphs.

So much pressure, in fact, that I've heard writers say this is the part of the novel-writing process that they dread the most. I've heard of magnificent, life-changing novels that were never sold to publishers or never offered to readers because the writer couldn't get past this very crucial step.

And that is just *wrong*.

But it all changes now.

Because, as you might have predicted, I have another template for you! (Oh, how you know me so well now!) And just like the logline template, it uses beats you already have.

Before I give you the template, though, let's take a look at some short synopses of popular young adult novels, taken straight from the back covers or jacket flaps of the books, and see if we can identify the beats that are being used to pitch these books. This will help you understand where the template comes from and how easy it is to use it to craft your own short synopsis.

Red Queen by Victoria Aveyard

Mare Barrow's world is divided by blood—those with common, Red blood serve the Silver-blooded elite, who are gifted with superhuman abilities. [Setup] Mare is a Red, scraping by as a thief in a poor rural village [flawed hero and stasis = death], until a twist of fate throws her in front of the Silver court. Before the king, princes, and all the nobles, she discovers she has an ability of her own. [Catalyst]

To cover up this impossibility, the king forces her to play the role of a lost Silver princess and betrothes her to one of his own sons. [Break Into 2] As Mare is drawn further into the Silver world, she risks everything and uses her new position to help the Scarlet Guard—a growing Red rebellion [Fun and Games]—even as her heart tugs her in an impossible direction. [B Story]

One wrong move can lead to her death [whiff of death], but in the dangerous game she plays, the only certainty is betrayal. [All is Lost hint/Theme Stated hint]

The Inheritance Games by Jennifer Lynn Barnes

Avery Grambs has a plan for a better future: survive high school, win a scholarship, and get out. [Setup and flawed hero] But her fortunes change in an instant when billionaire Tobias Hawthorne dies and leaves Avery virtually his entire fortune. [Catalyst] The catch? Avery has no idea why—or even who Tobias Hawthorne is.

To receive her inheritance, Avery must move into sprawling, secret passage–filled Hawthorne House, where every room bears the old man's touch—and his love of puzzles, riddles, and codes. [Break Into 2] Unfortunately for Avery, Hawthorne House is also occupied by the family that Tobias Hawthorne just dispossessed. This includes the four Hawthorne grandsons [B Story]: dangerous, magnetic, brilliant boys who grew up with every expectation that one day they would inherit billions. Heir apparent Grayson Hawthorne is convinced that Avery must be a con woman, and he's determined to take her down. His brother Jameson views her as their grandfather's last hurrah: a twisted riddle, a puzzle to be solved. [Fun and Games] Caught in a world of wealth and privilege, with danger around every turn [Midpoint and All Is Lost hint], Avery will have to play the game herself just to survive. [Theme Stated hint]

***The Hate U Give* by Angie Thomas**

Sixteen-year-old Starr Carter moves between two worlds: the poor neighborhood where she lives and the fancy suburban prep school she attends. [Setup and flawed hero] The uneasy balance between these worlds is shattered when Starr witnesses the fatal shooting of her childhood best friend Khalil at the hands of a police officer. Khalil was unarmed. [Catalyst]

Soon afterward, his death is a national headline. Some are calling him a thug, maybe even a drug dealer and a gangbanger. Protesters are taking to the streets in Khalil's name. Some cops and the local drug lord try to intimidate Starr and her family. What everyone wants to know is: What really went down that night? And the only person alive who can answer that is Starr. [Fun and Games]

But what Starr does—or does not—say could upend her community. [Midpoint] It could also endanger her life. [All Is Lost hint]

Inspired by the Black Lives Matter movement, this is a powerful and gripping YA novel about one girl's struggle for justice. [Theme Stated hint]

Pretty uncanny, right? The way the same beats appear again and again? It's almost as if the publisher who wrote these synopses was pulling from a Save the Cat! Beat Sheet. (Spoiler alert! They probably weren't.) But hopefully, this is another example of how the beats are just there, whether we realize it or not, baked into all good stories. And when we pull out the right ones and present them succinctly in the right order, we can once again speak to that innate story DNA inside all of us and entice anyone to read our novels.

Which brings us to . . .

THE SAVE THE CAT! SHORT SYNOPSIS TEMPLATE

- **PARAGRAPH 1:** Setup, flawed hero, world, and Catalyst (2–4 sentences)
- **PARAGRAPH 2:** Break Into 2 and/or Fun and Games with optional B Story (2–4 sentences)
- **PARAGRAPH 3:** Theme Stated hint, Midpoint hint and/or All Is Lost hint, ending in a cliffhanger (1–3 sentences)

Voilà!

Isn't it a beaut? It's also a lifesaver!

Notice this is not a beat-by-beat *summary* of your entire story. This is a sales pitch. The short synopsis is designed to give the reader just enough information to understand the essence of the plot, the hero, the stakes, and the transformation, while still leaving the reader wanting more.

In paragraph 1, we introduce a flawed hero and their world [Setup] to give the reader a sense of who the hero is and why they need to change. We also reference the wrecking ball that will swoop in to change that world [Catalyst].

In paragraph 2, we plunge into the upside-down world of Act 2 to show the general direction of the plot; prove that it does, in fact, go somewhere; and lure the reader in with the hook [promise of the premise/ Break Into 2/Fun and Games].

And in paragraph 3, we hint at the stakes, the urgency [Midpoint/ All Is Lost], and the internal journey [Theme Stated], which combine to make up the *why* of the whole novel. And then we conclude with a well-placed cliffhanger to entice the reader to keep reading.

Unlike the logline template, this template includes a Midpoint *hint* and/or an All Is Lost *hint*. Because the short synopsis is typically used to pitch directly to readers, we do want to be more careful about spoilers here. A hint of the Midpoint or All Is Lost, combined with the other information we've provided about the hero, world, and plot, is usually effective enough to give a sense of the stakes and the looming danger (either physical or emotional), and allows us to *tease* the reader instead of spoil things for them.

As you can see, the short synopsis template gives us a bit more room to move around and stretch our creative muscles than the logline template. Again, feel free to customize this to fit *your* story and *your* beats. Synopses work best when they follow the template and include a sense of tone and style. Notice how these examples each had a little different voice and emphasis. Depending on the genre, some synopses might focus more on the characters, others on the world, and others on the events of the plot. Some might only hint at the beats, while others might reference them more directly.

So play around with it. Make it your own. But make sure those beats are included and that you don't exceed a single double-spaced page. If you can't effectively pitch your novel in one page or less, then you haven't quite figured out what you're trying to say.

Don't be surprised if your short synopsis takes a few drafts to perfect. The template definitely makes it easier, but synopsis writing is still an art form that might take practice. Here's the best part, though: Once you master your short synopsis, you can use it over and over again. On your book's sale page (if you're self-publishing), in your agent query letter (if you're traditionally publishing), on your website (when you're marketing), even in an email to friends and family (when you're soliciting feedback and early readers). The short synopsis can be used anywhere and anytime you need to pitch your book succinctly and engagingly. It will become a key tool in your novel-selling tool-box. And you'll be grateful you took the time to get it just right.

Like the logline, the short synopsis is also a test to make sure you've nailed your beats and your story resonates. If you've followed the template and your short synopsis doesn't have that oomph that you're looking for, go back and check your beats again.

Using your short synopsis and logline as a test is one of the easiest (and cheapest!) ways to self-check your own manuscript. Sure, you could hire a freelance editor (and you might have to at some point, which is fine). But try this first. Distill your story down to its core. Figure out what you're really trying to say. Write a short synopsis and watch how the problems bubble up to the surface.

If you want to get better at writing synopses, I recommend studying others. A *lot* of them. Preferably those in your genre. So grab some novels from your bookshelf, visit your local library or favorite bookstore, or hop onto Goodreads and start analyzing.

The more practice you have analyzing other stories, the more natural it will be for you to break down your own. And the easier it will be for you to find problem areas in your manuscript and your pitch.

Going Beyond the First Book
Using Save the Cat! to Develop and Plot
Your YA Book Series

You can't write a craft book about young adult fiction without including a chapter about series. Well, you *can,* but it probably won't be well received. Young adult is a glorious hotbed of series. In fact, you could argue that one of the primary reasons young adult is so popular today is because of successful series like Twilight, the Hunger Games, and Divergent, among so many others.

Of course, there are plenty of successful standalone novels in the young adult space that deserve their rightful attention, but for many readers and writers, the term "young adult" comes with the word "series" attached like a necessary appendage. That's probably because teen readers love to immerse themselves in a world and stay there. They fall in love with characters and don't want to say goodbye. And a series is the perfect way to indulge that. So let's talk about them.

Types of Series

First up, there are three main types of book series. We'll talk about two briefly and one in *much* more detail.

STATIC SERIES

Static series are books featuring the same character or group of characters but the stories aren't connected and there's typically not an overarching storyline, thread, or character arc. Think the Babysitters Club, Nancy Drew, or Hardy Boys series. These are not YA, I realize, probably because static series are not as popular in young adult fiction. You find them more prominently in the middle grade space and in the adult mystery space.

ANTHOLOGY SERIES

These are books connected by setting, world, theme, or even a character relationship but aren't necessarily tied together by an overarching storyline. Some authors, for example, choose to set multiple novels in the same town, high school, or fantasy world but not necessarily tie those stories together, except for maybe a few nods to or mentions of the other novels. This type of series is very popular among adult romance novelists and *does* appear in young adult (like the Giver quartet and the DC Icons series), but because each novel typically stands alone, you would plot these books the way you would plot any other book, not necessarily concerned with connecting them through a larger story thread.

For both static and anthology series, the books can usually be read in any order. A reader can start with book 1 or with book 10 and still have a relatively pleasant (and sensical) reading experience. The same cannot be said about the third type of series.

DYNAMIC SERIES

You could also call these "sequential" series because the books *must* be read in sequential order for them to make sense. (I still get nightmares about readers reading book 2 in my Unremembered trilogy before book 1.)

Books in a dynamic series are connected by an overarching storyline, usually featuring some or all of the same primary characters in each installment. In this category you'll find most of the young adult series on the shelf today. Think the Twilight saga by Stephenie Meyer, the Hunger Games trilogy by Suzanne Collins, Legacy of Orïsha by Tomi Adeyemi, Arc of a Scythe by Neil Shusterman, To All the Boys I've Loved Before by Jenny Han, An Ember in the Ashes by Sabaa Tahir, and so on. In these series, the plot and character(s) continue over the span of multiple novels, and the overarching conflict and/ or goal usually doesn't get resolved until the very last book. Because of this, the series as a whole tends to feel like one *long* story or saga. There might be smaller goals reached or smaller conflicts dealt with in each book, but typically the story doesn't feel "over" until the end of the last book.

This is the type of series we'll focus on in this chapter.

But first, one more note about series types: you *can* have a series within a series. The Shadow and Bone trilogy by Leigh Bardugo, for example, is a dynamic series that's also part of a larger anthology series called the Grishaverse, which houses other dynamic series like Six of Crows, King of Scars, and even some standalone novels, all set in the world of the Grisha. Similarly, the Mortal Instruments series by Cassandra Clare is a dynamic series set within the larger Shadowhunters anthology series along with other dynamic series like the Infernal Devices, the Dark Artifices, the Bane Chronicles, and others.

The Series Beat Sheet

You might have figured out already that if you're writing multiple books in a series, you're going to need multiple beat sheets—or maybe you were just *hoping* I wouldn't say that. (But there, I've said it.) Whether the series is static, dynamic, or an anthology, every time you want to structure a well-told story with a beginning, middle, and end, you need a road map.

But because dynamic series, in particular, act as one long story with a beginning, middle, and end, you also need a road map to track *that* story and make sure you're structuring your series soundly and delivering on your *series* premise in an engaging way.

That's when a series beat sheet will come in handy.

A what?!

That's right. A dynamic series can (and probably *should*) have more than one beat sheet. A trilogy should have a total of four (three novel-length beat sheets to help you track the events of each book, and one series-length beat sheet to help you track the events in the entire series). A tetralogy (four books) should have a total of five beat sheets, and so on. Of course, if you've got multiple points of view within those novels, each with their own beat sheets, the numbers start to multiply like rabbits left alone in a hutch for too long.

But don't stress out. I included this chapter for a reason: charting a successful dynamic series is complicated, but it can be done. And a road map never hurts.

Your series beat sheet doesn't necessarily need to include *all* of the fifteen beats (however, my cowriter and I *did* include all fifteen in our System Divine series beat sheet, which I've included at the end of this chapter), but it should track a larger arc for your hero, heroes, or world. One that stretches over the entire series. I find it most helpful to use the **foundation beats** to plot a series. We talked about these in more detail back on page 105, but here they are again:

- Catalyst
- Break Into 2
- Midpoint
- All Is Lost
- Break Into 3

These are the major turning points of the story, so you can think of them as the major turning points of the series as well.

THE TRILOGY BEAT SHEET

Let's look at the Hunger Games trilogy.

In book 1 (whose beat sheet can be found on page 295), there's a Catalyst (Prim's name is called at the reaping). But what happens at the *end* of book 1? Katniss defies the Capitol in the arena and wins the games. Doesn't that moment kind of feel like a Catalyst for the world as a whole? The events of the Panem revolution can be tracked all the way back to *that* single event. If Katniss had simply died in the arena, or killed Peeta and won on her own, I'm not sure the revolution would have happened. It was the way she won the games—that act of defiance—that lit the spark.

It was a *series* Catalyst.

And when Katniss departs on her victory tour in Book 2 and starts to witness the unrest that's brewing in the other districts, doesn't that *feel* like a Break Into 2 for the whole series? The event that takes her on a journey to a new world and takes her one step closer to becoming the Mockingjay and leading the revolution? These are beats within the individual books, yes, but they are also turning points of the series. Look!

The Five Foundation Beats of the Hunger Games Trilogy

- **CATALYST:** Katniss wins the Hunger Games by defying the Capitol in the arena, which triggers a domino effect of unrest among the districts. (End of book 1—*The Hunger Games*)
- **BREAK INTO 2:** Katniss sets off on a victory tour of Panem (a journey!) in an attempt to quell the unrest, per President Snow's warning (series Act 2 goal), but her presence seems to only rile people up more. (Beginning of book 2—*Catching Fire*)
- **MIDPOINT:** After failing to ease the unrest, in a false defeat that raises the stakes of the series, Katniss finds out she's being sent back into the arena for the Quarter Quell and will likely die there. (Middle of book 2—*Catching Fire*)
- **ALL IS LOST:** Peeta is captured by the Capitol and, in a whiff of death, Katniss wakes up in a District 13 hospital to discover her entire district has been bombed by President Snow. (End of book 2—*Catching Fire*)

- **BREAK INTO 3**: Katniss finally agrees to be the Mockingjay, the face of the revolution, to try to save Peeta and take down President Snow and the Capitol for good (series Act 3 goal). (Beginning of book 3—*Mockingjay*)

Woah! It's almost like Suzanne Collins did that on purpose!

You'll notice that she chose to end books 1 and 2 on the Catalyst and the All Is Lost, respectively, which creates a cliffhanger of sorts. Something *big* has happened, but we don't quite know what Katniss is going to do about it or what the reaction in Panem will be. Because remember, the Catalyst and the All Is Lost are both external, action beats, which trigger a reaction (Debate or Dark Night of the Soul) and then a decision (Break Into 2 or Break Into 3). Some trilogy authors might choose to end books on those decision beats instead, creating a slightly different type of cliffhanger.

Like in *To All the Boys I've Loved Before* (whose first book beat sheet can be found on page 151). This is what the foundation beats of the full trilogy looks like:

The Five Foundation Beats of the To All the Boys I've Loved Before Series

- **CATALYST**: Lara Jean and Peter share their first real kiss in a hot tub, and an untrue rumor spreads that they had sex, mortifying Lara Jean but kicking off a series-long transformation for Lara Jean and her relationship with Peter. (Toward the end of book 1—*To All the Boys I've Loved Before*)
- **BREAK INTO 2**: Lara Jean decides to write a love letter to Peter to reconcile their relationship and be a *real* couple. (End of book 1—*To All the Boys I've Loved Before*)
- **MIDPOINT**: Lara Jean receives a letter from an old crush that turns the series in a new direction, introducing a new love interest who will raise the stakes of her relationship with Peter and put pressure on both of them to figure out what they need from each other (Middle of book 2—*P.S. I Still Love You*)
- **ALL IS LOST**: In the lowest moment of their relationship, Lara Jean and Peter break up (a relationship whiff of death), and Lara

Jean tells Peter she wishes they had never gotten together at all. (Toward the end of book 2—*P.S. I Still Love You*)

- **BREAK INTO 3:** Lara Jean and Peter reconcile, Peter says "I love you" for the first time, and they agree to go "all in" and be vulnerable to each other. (End of book 2—*P.S. I Still Love You*)

Notice how Jenny Han has created a very different kind of cliffhanger in her series, by ending the first two books on the decision beats. It's no longer a question of "What will the hero do?" It's about *how* they will do it and how it will play out. When book 1 ends with Lara Jean starting her letter to Peter, we're scrambling to read book 2 to see if the letter works and how their new "real" relationship fares when put to the test. And isn't that promise of the series premise? When book 2 ends with Lara Jean and Peter going "all in" and deciding to be vulnerable to each other no matter how much it might hurt or how dangerous it might feel, we're then scrambling to read book 3 (*Always and Forever, Lara Jean*) to see how *that* decision plays out. And book 3 serves as one grand Finale of their relationship, with all the ups and downs of a powerful Finale and even, dare I say it, a five-point Series Finale!

Regardless of how you slice and dice your trilogy beats, the trilogy beat sheet tends to fall naturally along the same lines, looking something like this:

Possible Series Beat Sheet for a Trilogy:

- Book 1 = Series Act 1
- Book 2 = Series Act 2
- Book 3 = Series Act 3

Trilogies are easy to conceptualize in a series beat sheet because they naturally and mathematically follow a three-act structure. Three books, three acts. The first book in a trilogy often serves as an Act 1 book, setting up the series world, introducing the main players, and establishing the overarching goal and/or conflict. The second book in a trilogy often feels like the roller coaster ride of Act 2, with a Fun and Games, a stakes-raising Midpoint, Bad Guys who Close In, and an All Is Lost for the entire series, which eventually leads to book 3 or Act 3 of the series. Don't third books in trilogies often feel like one giant Finale?

With the highest stakes, the bloodiest battles, the ultimate showdowns, the highest body counts, and the most rewarding victories!

But what about other series lengths? Duologies, tetralogies, pentalogies, and more?

Well, it works the same way; the math is just a little different.

THE DUOLOGY BEAT SHEET

Let's look at the duology Six of Crows by Leigh Bardugo.

In the first book (whose beat sheet can be found on page 249), we see Kaz and his crew setting off on a great heist to apprehend a kidnapped Shu scientist in exchange for a large sum of money. Do they succeed? Yes! They capture Kuwei Yul-Bol, bring him back to Ketterdam, and at the very end of the novel, meet up with Van Eck to make the exchange. Does this feel like a *false* victory? That's probably because it is! In a *series* Midpoint twist, Van Eck double-crosses them, reveals that he has no intention of paying out the money, *and* takes Inej hostage in the process. Oh, and did I mention she's taken hostage by Grisha, who can now *fly*? And that Kaz has finally dropped his guard and let himself feel real feelings for her? Talk about raising the stakes, both emotionally and within the world of the story!

In the second book, *Crooked Kingdom*, we see a new goal introduced (often the case after the Midpoint): get revenge on Van Eck (the new villain of the story) and get the money that was promised them. (After rescuing Inej, of course.) That plan plays out in the series Bad Guys Close In but goes afoul in the series All Is Lost when it's revealed that Pekka Rollins (a villain from Kaz's past) has now teamed up with Van Eck to create a supervillain duo! Together they stop Kaz and his crew from achieving their new plan, forcing them to regroup yet again and come up with an Act 3 goal. At the series Break Into 3, Kaz announces the most audacious, complex, twisty, and surprising heist of the entire series. In the Series Finale, we see the epic plan unfold, involving a rigged auction, fake bullets, swapped bodies, Grishas in disguise, and plenty of gasp-worthy moments (seriously, read this series; it's jaw-droppingly amazing). Until finally, *finally* the team gets their reward: the same thirty million kruge promised them at the start of the series.

If you want to see it in a quick overview, here you go:

The Five Foundation Beats of the Six of Crows Duology

- **CATALYST:** Kaz gets a job offer from Van Eck to track down a Shu scientist who's being held captive in an impenetrable Fjerdan prison, in exchange for thirty million kruge. (Start of book 1—*Six of Crows*)
- **BREAK INTO 2:** Kaz, Inej, Nina, Matthias, Jesper, and Wylan (the Six of Crows) set off for Fjerda to apprehend the scientist and bring him home to claim their reward. (Book 1—*Six of Crows*)
- **MIDPOINT:** Kaz and his crew deliver the Shu scientists to Van Eck (false victory), but he double-crosses them, revealing he was never planning to pay the reward (Midpoint twist), and kidnaps Inej (stakes are raised). This sets the story in a new direction, introducing a new villain (Van Eck) and several new goals (rescue Inej, get revenge on Van Eck, and secure the promised thirty million kruge reward). (End of book 1—*Six of Crows*)
- **ALL IS LOST:** Their plan to destroy Van Eck's sugar supply (by sabotaging his silos) goes sour when Pekka Rollins (a villain from Kaz's past) and his gang interfere, revealing that he's now working with Van Eck. Both bad guys have seemingly won. (Book 2—*Crooked Kingdom*)
- **BREAK INTO 3:** A new plan is concocted, involving a rigged auction, in an attempt to recover their money once and for all and destroy Van Eck's reputation. (Book 2—*Crooked Kingdom*)

The math of a duology series beat sheet might even be simpler than that of a trilogy. Because the beat sheet naturally splits at the Midpoint, sending the story in a new direction, duologies tend to do the same. And because the Midpoint usually raises the stakes of the story with some kind of twist, we often see the first book in a duology end with a big twist and/or cliffhanger that leads us into book 2 with a new goal at the ready.

Possible Series Beat Sheet for a Duology:

- Book 1 = Series Act 1 and Act 2A (up until the Midpoint)
- Book 2 = Series Act 2B and Act 3

Who knew you'd be doing so much math in a writing craft book! But while we've got our calculators out, let's look at a tetralogy.

THE TETRALOGY BEAT SHEET

I'll use the popular YA sci-fi series the Lunar Chronicles by Marissa Meyer, whose foundation beats look like this:

The Five Foundation Beats of the Lunar Chronicles

- **CATALYST:** Cinder learns she's the lost Lunar princess Selene and is supposed to be on the throne of Luna instead of the evil Queen Levana, whom she's just discovered is plotting to marry Prince Kai and kill him. (Toward the end of book 1—*Cinder*)
- **BREAK INTO 2:** Cinder makes a decision to break out of prison, find out the truth about her past, and attempt to stop Queen Levana from enacting her evil plans. (End of book 1—*Cinder*)
- **MIDPOINT:** The stakes of the series are raised when Queen Levana orders her mutant wolf soldiers to attack Earth to pressure Prince Kai to marry her, and Cinder vows to hone her Lunar gift of mind manipulation, find the girl who can reveal Queen Levana's secrets (Cress), and stop hiding. (End of book 2—*Scarlet*)
- **ALL IS LOST:** After Cinder and her crew have infiltrated the palace and stopped the royal wedding, Queen Levana, in a whiff of death, retaliates by declaring war on Earth. (End of book 3—*Cress*)
- **BREAK INTO 3:** Cinder decides she's going to Luna to start a revolution, fulfill her destiny as the heir to the Lunar throne, and defeat Queen Levana for good. (End of book 3—*Cress*)

So cool, right? But it gets even cooler when you start filling in the plot of the series *between* these foundation beats.

After Cinder finds out she's the long-lost princess Selene and the rightful heir to the throne (the event that launches the entire four-book series), she Breaks Into 2 with her decision to escape prison and find out more about her past so she can eventually defeat Queen Levana. That's sounding suspiciously like an Act 2 goal! And it is. It's a *series* Act 2 goal. (I'm telling you, goals are the key to *everything*.)

This proactive decision that Cinder makes at the end of book 1 is exactly what we see play out in book 2, *Scarlet*. We even get an **upward path** as the series Fun and Games happens. By the end of book 2, Cinder *does* learn more about her past, as well as achieve other goals—like finding Scarlet Benoit, a newly introduced hero who *also* has her own goal of finding her grandmother (which she achieves). All of this goal achievement makes for a satisfying false victory *series* Midpoint. But like all Midpoints, it comes with a raising of the stakes: Queen Levana attacks Earth, putting more pressure on Prince Kai to marry her, and Cinder makes yet another decision, which launches us into Book 3 (and the second half of the series Act 2). Now that Cinder has learned about her past and come to terms with being the lost Lunar princess Selene, she vows to practice her Lunar gift of mind manipulation, find Cress (who has secrets about Levana), and stop hiding who she really is from the world. Not surprisingly, this feels a lot like a **shift from wants to needs**, especially for a hero whose series-long arc is all about coming into her own, fulfilling her destiny as the rightful heir to the Lunar throne, and defeating the evil queen.

Since we saw an upward path in Book 2, *Scarlet*, we naturally see a **downward path** in book 3, *Cress*, as the series Bad Guys literally Close In. The new goal of finding and rescuing Cress goes sour, leading to injury and the disbanding of Cinder's team. Scarlet is captured and then imprisoned and tortured on Luna. Cress and her companion, Thorne, barely survive a satellite crash to earth that leaves Thorne blinded, then travel endlessly through the desert before Cress gets kidnapped. Definitely a downward path. Book 3 concludes with a series All Is Lost and whiff of death—Levana declaring war on Earth—and a series Break Into 3: Cinder vowing to go to Luna and start a revolution.

Which leads us to . . . ta-da! The revolution! Book 4, *Winter*, is the series grand Finale, in which we see the revolution play out and Cinder and Queen Levana finally go head to head in an epic battle.

So how does that all shake down in a series beat sheet?

Possible Series Beat Sheet for a Tetralogy

- Book 1 = Series Act 1
- Book 2 = Series Act 2A (up until the Midpoint)
- Book 3 = Series Act 2B
- Book 4 = Series Act 3

Once again, we find the Save the Cat! Beat Sheet splitting up nicely, as there are natural breaks between Act 1, Acts 2A and 2B (divided by the Midpoint), and Act 3. Four breaks, four books!

So it should come as no surprise that the *majority* of young adult series are duologies, trilogies, or tetralogies, because the natural structure of story breaks down so neatly for two, three, and four books.

But what happens if you want to write a series with five books, six books, even seven or more books?

Three acts, fifteen beats, seven books? That math is not so pretty.

The trick, as always, is to look at our foundation beats. These beats help us nail in those major turning points of the series, which we can then use to slot the other books between.

Let's see what that might look like.

PLOTTING LONGER SERIES

Regardless of how long your series is, there are a few things that longer series tend to have in common: The series Catalyst tends to happen by the end of the first book (to pull the reader into the next book), the series premise is usually delivered on by the second book (to keep the reader hooked), and the last book usually consists entirely of the series Finale.

Of course, there are exceptions to every rule, including this one, but keeping these three things in mind, we could chart out longer series beat sheets, like these.

Possible Series Beat Sheet for a Pentalogy

- Book 1 = Series Act 1
- Book 2, 3 = Series Act 2A (to the Midpoint)
- Book 4 = Series Act 2B
- Book 5 = Series Act 3

Possible Series Beat Sheet for a Hexalogy

- Book 1 = Series Act 1
- Book 2, 3 = Series Act 2A (to the Midpoint)
- Books 4, 5 = Series Act 2B
- Book 6 = Series Act 3

Possible Series Beat Sheet for a Heptalogy

- Book 1 = Series Act 1
- Book 2, 3, 4 = Series Act 2A (to the Midpoint)
- Books 5, 6 = Series Act 2B
- Book 7 = Series Act 3

Feel free to play around and make adjustments to fit *your* series. These are just some rough guidelines to get you started. Use those foundation beats as your anchors and see where the rest of the beats (and books) fall.

In the end, what's the lesson here? (Besides an unexpected math lesson.)

There are many ways you can slice and dice the beats of a series, depending on how many books there are, how you want the events to play out, where you want to leave your reader hanging, and the larger thread you're tracking. There's also a lot more flexibility in how the beats fall compared to a single novel. The series beats don't have to (and probably won't) adhere to the percentage guidelines in chapter 2. Bottom line: don't get too bogged down in the nitty-gritty details. Use these series beat sheets as guidelines to help you track major events in the story and ensure there's a natural and exciting pace to your series as a whole.

Threading Your Books Together

You might have noticed that in the examples we just studied we were tracking much more than just a single character's journey through a story.

In the Hunger Games trilogy, we tracked not just Katniss's journey but the journey of the entire nation of Panem.

In Six of Crows, we tracked not one, but six heroes' journeys to heal the wounds of their past and find a family among each other, while at the same time tracking both a series-wide goal to claim a monetary reward and the two villains who stand in the way of that goal (Van Eck and Rollins).

When you're plotting a dynamic series, there has to be a larger thread holding the books together. And that thread usually comes in the form of an overarching goal, conflict, or oftentimes both.

In the Hunger Games trilogy, the uniting thread and overarching goal is the revolution of Panem, defeating the Capitol, which comes with an overarching conflict that stands in the way of that goal (President Snow). Similarly in the Lunar Chronicles, it's a Lunar revolution and the overthrowing of an evil monarch/arch enemy.

In a contemporary or romance series, we might not see such world-changing stakes as we would in an epic fantasy or sci-fi series, but we still have a unifying thread that ties it all together. In the To All the Boys I've Loved Before series, the overarching goal is Lara Jean and Peter's relationship. And although conflicts come and go throughout the novels (like Peter's ex-girlfriend Genevieve, Lara Jean's other crushes, Josh and John, and, in the last book, the choice of where to go to college), the overarching conflict is teenage life itself. How do you make young love last in our contemporary world?

Each book in a series must have its own set of goals and conflicts to be won, lost, or resolved by the ends of each installment, but the series must also track a larger, overarching goal and conflict throughout all the books. This is extremely important for reader satisfaction and engagement. If you chose to track *only* a series-wide goal and conflict and therefore have *no* resolution whatsoever in any of the individual books, your readers will most likely feel frustrated and misled and might eventually give up on the series.

That's why Katniss *does* win the Hunger Games by the end of the first book and why she *does* get out of the arena by the end of the second book. Because without these smaller resolutions—book-long goals and conflicts—we'd feel cheated and eventually lose interest. Yet these smaller resolutions feed into the larger goal and conflict (defeating President Snow and overthrowing the Capitol for good) that is not resolved until the final book.

In Six of Crows, the crew *does* achieve their book 1 goal of apprehending the kidnapped Shu scientist by infiltrating the impenetrable Fjerdan Ice Court. But the achievement of that goal and the twist on its result set us up for another book with new goals and new conflicts of its own.

Figuring out your overarching goal and conflict as you plot and write your series will help you not only thread your books together cohesively but will also help you figure out those smaller book-wide goals and conflicts that can serve as building blocks to the larger series-wide ones.

Tracking Character Arcs and World Arcs

That's already a lot to keep track of in a series. But we're not done yet. The overarching threads help us string our books together, and the foundation beats of the series beat sheet help us track the major events of our series and improve the pacing. But since you've read this far, you know that good story isn't just about goals, conflicts, major events, and pacing. It's also about *change*.

Actually, it's *primarily* about change.

Just as a single novel in your series must transform someone (or multiple someones), so must your series as a whole.

If you're having trouble conceptualizing the scope of such an epic and daunting task, let's look at it in reverse and see if that helps.

Look at Katniss Everdeen toward the end of the Hunger Games trilogy. She leads a team of rebels through the burning streets of the

Capitol, kills President Coin, and helps usher in a new Panem. Would she have done all of that (or *any* of that) at the start of book 1? Of course not. She was feisty, but she wasn't *that* feisty. Katniss may have been destined to become a revolutionary and change the course of Panem's history, but she had a *lot* of growing to do to get there.

With each book in the trilogy, she moves closer to becoming the ultimate version of herself, taking steps forward (and back) along the way. And in each book, the major events trigger those steps. (The romantic dance of structure strikes again!)

In book 1, *The Hunger Games*, it's Rue's death and the Capitol changing the rules on her at the last moment that trigger Katniss to stop playing by those rules. She defies the Capitol by threatening suicide with Peeta. This is her first big step toward becoming the Mockingjay (a revolutionary symbol and leader), but it's still only a *step*.

In *Catching Fire*, however, when President Snow threatens her family if she doesn't pretend that her act of rebellion was an act of love (in order to quell unrest in the districts), Katniss agrees to once again play by their rules. She doesn't want war. She just wants to protect the ones she loves. This doesn't feel like a step *toward* her ultimate transformation; it actually feels like a step *backward*. Progress is never a straight line, after all. And good thing too, as it would make for very boring fiction. But then, when President Snow throws Katniss and Peeta back into the arena, in a series Midpoint twist, the fire is lit inside her once again, triggering more forward growth. When she shoots an arrow through the force field of the arena, there's no doubt this is not an act of love. It's an act of outright rebellion.

But when the series All Is Lost hits, and Katniss discovers she's been rescued from the arena while Peeta has been taken captive by the Capitol (not to mention her entire district has been wiped out), it sends her into a series Dark Night of the Soul at the start of book 3, *Mockingjay*, in which she mourns her losses and wallows around the hallways of District 13, feeling helpless. It's not until she sees Peeta on a TV interview, seemingly under the Capitol's control and manipulation, that she knows what she has to do. In a series Break Into 3, and another forward step in her growth, she vows to be become the revolutionary symbol Panem needs. But it's not easy. She stumbles and falters, and the events of book 3 test her resolve and force her to prove that she has really changed—just as any good Finale should do!

There you have it. Transformation over three books. Each book pushing the hero forward (and sometimes backward) until they reach their ultimate destiny.

SMALL STEPS LEAD TO BIG CHANGE

Think of it as baby steps toward a destination. Your hero must change by the end of the series, but they also must change in each individual installment of that series, which means that the character arc in each individual installment is actually a *piece* of the larger character arc.

It's a much more complex and nuanced undertaking than simply transforming your character over the course of one book. But it also gives you more room to play with your characters and explore the scope of your theme. And there are so many creative ways you can accomplish a series-wide transformation, especially when you think about human nature and our natural resistance to change.

In the Six of Crows duology, Kaz battles with human connection—a flaw caused by the **shard of glass** of his brother trusting the wrong man and ending up dead because of it. The flaw is externalized by Kaz's fear of actual human touch. He wears gloves to avoid any contact. But this flaw is also internalized by the fact that Kaz refuses to let himself feel his true feelings for Inej, because he sees such emotions as a weakness to be exploited. By the end of book 1, however, he's changed. He starts to allow those feelings to surface and to explore what they might mean for their future together. But this creates a vulnerability for Kaz, which leads to Inej getting kidnapped.

So what does Kaz do in book 2? He backpedals, vowing to tamp down those feelings because the events at the end of book 1 proved his former worldview was correct: Emotions create weakness, and weakness leads to loss and pain. The result is an internal tug of war with his feelings and his fears throughout book 2, until finally he overcomes them and they find a way to be together, as themselves.

After your hero learns a lesson in book 1, how does that lesson get tested, subverted, expanded, or even overcorrected in the subsequent books? There's a reason heroes often dabble in the dark side in later books of a series. They're testing the limits of what they've learned in book 1.

The more Cinder comes into her own and learns to wield her Lunar gift of mind control in the Lunar Chronicles, the more she starts to see *herself* in the villain, Queen Levana, and to become afraid of her own tendencies. And the more Lara Jean makes herself vulnerable to Peter in the series To All the Boys I've Loved Before, the more challenging the relationship becomes, causing her to explore darker sides of herself and fears she never knew existed before she fell in love.

Themes presented in book 1 often expand in future books, as the character explores more of their world and puts their new and improved self to the test. After all, change is never a one-and-done thing. Life lessons learned often lead to more questioning, more exploring, more lessons along a similar track or theme.

EXPANDING YOUR WORLD

The key to tracking arcs in a series is *expansion*. Books 2, 3, or even 6 and 7 always push the boundaries of things. Sometimes that's accomplished by expanding the world of the story. Heroes explore new countries, territories, or lands perhaps previously mentioned but not yet visited. Like Katniss's tour of the districts in *Catching Fire*, Cinder's adventures in the European Federation, the African Union, and finally Luna itself in *Scarlet*, *Cress*, and *Winter*, or even Kaz's crew venturing into new parts of Ketterdam in *Crooked Kingdom*. Taking your hero farther from home organically triggers new realizations about themself and often leads to forward (or backward!) progress along their arc.

Expansion can also happen from exploring other characters within the world. This is why you'll often find new points of view introduced after book 1 in the series, often with goals and smaller arcs of their own.

In the Lunar Chronicles, Scarlet struggles to find her kidnapped grandmother while also learning how to trust after being betrayed one too many times. Cress helps Cinder expose Queen Levana with her clever hacking skills, while also learning how to live in the real world after being held captive in a satellite for most of her life. And Winter aids Cinder in the revolution against her stepmother, Queen Levana, while also learning how to deal with her own Lunar gift that she's been repressing for years.

In *Crooked Kingdom* (Six of Crows book 2), even as Kaz, Inej, Jasper, Matthias, and Nina (the primary heroes of book 1) are continuing their own personal arcs to overcome past tragedies and heal from past wounds, we also get a new POV from Wylan Van Eck, who has to come to terms with his father's betrayal and the discovery that his mother is still alive. Combined, the theme of the series *expands* into an important lesson they all learn about finding a home and a family in each other.

But characters aren't the only elements that can change in the course of a series.

THE WORLD ARC

World arcs are popular arcs to track alongside character arcs. They work similarly to character arcs, but instead of tracking the change in a character, you're tracking the change in a world, group, community, or political system as a whole.

Revolution is a popular world arc in young adult fiction. The world of the story goes from dystopic, tyrannical, oppressive, unjust, and so on to something new and improved. Just as a character digs deep down and solves their life problems, so can a world. And often the same major series events that trigger internal changes in your character also trigger changes in your world.

The Catalyst in the Hunger Games trilogy (Katniss winning the Hunger Games by openly defying the Capitol) doesn't just set Katniss on a series-wide journey of transformation; it's also the incident inciting unrest in the districts. And when Katniss and Peeta go on their victory tour in the series Act 2, the fire of rebellion only spreads. The Midpoint (sending Katniss and Peeta back into the arena) leads to more revolt and the Capitol's attempt to quash it by bombing District 12. The All Is Lost (Peeta's capture) and the Break Into 3 (Katniss's decision to become the Mockingjay) are the final turning points of the revolution, leading Panem to a hard-won victory and, eventually, a new nation.

We see a similar world arc happening again and again in countless young adult series. Revolutions are part of our human history, so they will probably never cease to be part of our fictional stories as well.

But not all world arcs are revolutionary. In Six of Crows, the world arc plays out on the streets of Ketterdam, not to revolutionize the political system but to shift the power dynamics in that influential city. A "coup de ville," if you will, instead of a coup d'état. By the end of the series, Kaz has ushered out the old power players and ushered in a new reign (himself).

Even in a realistic fiction series like To All the Boys I've Loved Before, Lara Jean's *world* changes as the story flows from book to book. Her sister moves away to Scotland, she falls in love (more than once), her father falls in love, she applies for college. In a story about a girl growing up and facing the *real* world, not surprisingly the real world changes and expands to give her more challenges and chances to prove herself.

The point is, when you track a successful series, you're typically tracking so much more than just a single character. After all, you probably already did that in book 1. Series are about going beyond book 1, into new worlds, new characters, new angles and perspectives of a theme. And to do that, the events of your series (the turning points of your series beat sheet) must have larger repercussions, make bigger waves, affect more people, and maybe even change the world.

SERIES BEAT SHEET FOR THE SYSTEM DIVINE TRILOGY BY JESSICA BRODY AND JOANNE RENDELL

The following graphic is a visual breakdown of my cowritten young adult sci-fi trilogy, System Divine, for which we took inspiration from Victor Hugo's *Les Misérables* for the character storylines and the French Revolution for the world storyline. With this graphic, you can see exactly where the beats fall across all three books.

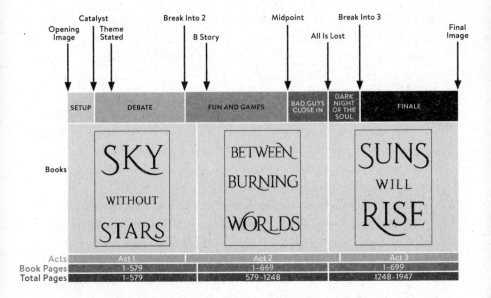

I've also included a high-level beat sheet for the entire series, which highlights the major events of the story and primarily tracks the "world arc" across all three installments, while also referencing the emotional arcs for the three POV heroes.

THE SYSTEM DIVINE TRILOGY

Book 1: *Sky Without Stars* (579 pages)
Book 2: *Between Burning Worlds* (669 pages)
Book 3: *Suns Will Rise* (699 pages)
BY: Jessica Brody and Joanne Rendell
STC GENRE: Institutionalized
BOOK GENRE: Young adult sci-fi/space opera
TOTAL SERIES PAGES: 1,947 (Simon and Schuster hardcover editions)

Opening Image (Book 1: 1–15)

In a dirty, crime-infested marketplace in the capital city of Vallonay, a thief named Chatine Renard steals a medallion off a well-dressed man from the Second Estate. She is almost caught by Inspecteur Limier and his Policier droids but narrowly escapes. In this Opening Image, we get a glimpse of what the planet of Laterre looks like at the start of the series. It's corrupt, unjust, and divided. In short, it's miserable.

Theme Stated (Book 1: 70)

"Every estate has its place and purpose. The First Estate rules us, like the brain governing the body. We, the Second Estate, are the heart, providing the power and pulse. While the Third Estate are the legs on which we all stand. Laterre is the envy of the System Divine because of how well our beautiful body functions."

Stated by General Bonnefaçon, the head of the Ministère (the governing and military body of Laterre). This is the guiding principle by which all Laterrians live and the "truth" that the Regime wants everyone to believe (especially the Third Estate). But, in truth, it's an illusion. The "institution" of the three estates is a construct to keep people divided and, more important, keep people in their place. The reality is that the Third Estate hold the true power. And should they ever come to realize that, the Regime will certainly fall.

Which is why the theme of the series is about realizing and taking hold of your true power. It's played out not only in the revolution storyline but also in the emotional transformations of all three heroes.

For Chatine, the theme is represented in her series-long arc, from a selfish thief who thinks only of herself and hides her emotions behind a carefully constructed wall, to a selfless rebel who finally lets down her guard, confronts the monsters of her past, and opens her heart to love.

For Marcellus, the theme plays out in his transformation from doting protégé of General Bonnefaçon and loyal servant of the Regime to a fully awakened rebel following in the footsteps of his father.

And for Alouette, the theme of embracing your power comes through in her transformation from a naïve, sheltered girl who's been kept hidden away from the outside world to a strong, wise, and resilient rebel leader who discovers the truth of her heritage and learns how to harness both her political power and her personal power.

Setup (Book 1: 1–67)

For those who live in Ledôme, the climate-controlled biodome in Vallonay, Laterre is a beautiful, prospering, majestic, *dry* planet full of opportunity, luxury, and prosperity. For the remaining 95 percent of the planet (the Third Estate), Laterre is a cold, dark, wet, wretched place where clouds block all the light from the system's three suns, hunger and crime run rampant, and the only hope of rising above it all comes from the annual "Ascension" lottery, which chooses one member of the Third Estate to "ascend" to the Second Estate and live out their days in sunshine and decadence.

We learn that seventeen years ago the Rebellion of 488 had nearly toppled the Regime when a rebel group called the Vangarde tried to bring about change. Their leader, Citizen Rousseau, was captured and imprisoned, the rebellion died, and the Vangarde were believed to have died with it.

Throughout this Setup, the planet, its primary players and politics, and the world of the series are established, with several **stasis = death** moments, including:

- A city full of crumbling tenement housing structures called "Frets" that look like they're on the verge of collapse
- Morgues filled to the brim with bodies of workers who have died due to the terrible conditions of the factories and mines
- A prison moon (Bastille) where convicts endure harsh and deadly conditions to mine a precious element called zyttrium
- People starving in the streets

Something needs to change here, and something is about to.

Catalyst (Book 1: 68–70)

The planet of Laterre is shaken when the Premier Enfant (the only child and heir of Patriarche Lyon Paresse) is murdered, causing the Ascension lottery to be canceled. The first riot in seventeen years breaks out in the streets.

Debate (Book 1: 70–527)

The majority of the remainder of book 1 is centered around this Debate question: How will the planet react to this unexpected turn of events?

The answer comes in the form of several major plot points in book 1, including the arrest and public execution of the Premier Enfant's alleged murderer, which incites more rioting, and the bombing of the factory that makes TéléSkins (screens implanted in the arms of every Third Estater).

This beat also serves to further introduce and establish the three heroes. As they each interact with the unfolding events, we learn more about them and get better insight into their goals, flaws, and backstory.

Break Into 2 (Book 1: 527–530)

When two women are caught breaking into the office of the warden of Bastille, it's revealed that the Vangarde rebel group are not dead, as everyone believed. They are very much alive and have been planning their next move carefully, biding their time. But the events of the Catalyst and Debate forced them to move quickly. By breaking into the warden's office, they were attempting to free their imprisoned leader, Citizen Rousseau, but their attempts failed (or so it seems).

The Debate question has now been answered. The Vangarde have taken a significant first big step toward their envisioned future for Laterre. They have seized their opportunity to initiate change. How that decision will fare (and how it will affect the three heroes) we won't know until the next beat and the next book.

Fun and Games (Book 1: 531–571 and Book 2: 1–349)

Sky Without Stars (book 1) wraps up with uncertainty in the aftermath of the Vangarde's attempted break-in. Book 2, *Between Burning Worlds*, picks up a few weeks later, in the midst of the beat's **downward path**. The Patriarche has turned the planet into a police state (in reaction to the murder of his daughter and the events of book 1), which only seems to be riling people up more. Marcellus discovers that his grandfather, General Bonnefaçon, is attempting to overthrow the Regime on his own and is developing a new weapon to facilitate his aims. Marcellus sets off with Alouette on a quest to learn more about it. Meanwhile, a new rebel group, the Red Scar, has surfaced, seeking to bring about change through violence (compared to the Vangarde's peaceful tactics). The Vangarde make another *seemingly* unsuccessful attempt to break Citizen Rousseau out of Bastille.

B Story (Book 2: 162–172)

Chatine spends the majority of book 2 living with an off-grid community called the Défecteurs who serve as the B Story characters of the series. The Défecteur community represents the series theme of harnessing one's own power by rejecting the institution and choosing to live outside of its laws. Living off-grid, they literally harness their own power. The community's very existence proves that Laterre's system is not the only way to live. But they also represent the opposite of the theme by refusing to stand up against injustices, instead choosing a code of nonengagement. By the end of the series, however, they too will harness their unique power to stand up against the Regime.

Midpoint (Book 2: 350–390)

In a **false defeat**, the general's weapon is revealed to be a new update to the TéléSkins, which will give him full control over the entire population of the Third Estate, turning them into his own personal army (**stakes are raised**).

Bad Guys Close In (Book 2: 391–662)

After discovering that the general plans to use his weapon to kill the Patriarche and take control of Laterre, Marcellus, Alouette, and Chatine team up and make a plan to stop him. The plan is thwarted when the general activates the weapon, instigating a bloody battle. Alouette shuts down the TéléSkins (and as a result, the general's weapon) by accessing a DNA-locked kill switch after discovering she is the Patriarche's long-lost daughter and shares his DNA. The Patriarche flees, Alouette is captured by the general, and it's later revealed that the Vangarde's plan to free their imprisoned leader from Bastille was actually a success. Citizen Rousseau is safely back at the Vangarde headquarters, recuperating and waiting to be revealed to the world. The Vangarde is finally ready to launch their peaceful revolution for a new Laterre (**upward path**).

All Is Lost (Book 2: 663–669)

The Red Scar capture the Patriarche and behead him in the public marketplace. Book 2 ends with a literal **whiff of death** as the smell of burning flesh from the laser guillotine fills the air.

Dark Night of the Soul (Book 3: 1–194)

Book 3, *Suns Will Rise,* picks up three months after book 2 ends, in the middle of Laterre's Dark Night of the Soul. But ironically, it doesn't *feel* dark. It feels just the opposite.

The general has taken provisional command of the planet and has cleaned it up significantly. The streets are safer; the people are happy, clothed, and fed; and there hasn't been a riot in months. From the outside, it would seem Laterre is flourishing.

With no Patriarche and no heir, the System Alliance (a coalition of delegates representing the twelve planets of the System Divine) are tasked with naming a new leader for Laterre. The Red Scar kill three cousins of the Patriarche, favored to be chosen by the Alliance.

Alouette, who has been imprisoned by the general for the past three months, manages to escape. Shortly after, the System Alliance appoints General Bonnefaçon to be the next leader of Laterre.

Break Into 3 (Book 3: 214–224)

Despite Alouette's safe return (and her status as the rightful heir to the Regime), the Vangarde decide it's too dangerous for her to be part of their plan. If she steps forward as the Patriarche's daughter, the Red Scar will surely kill her. They make a plan for Citizen Rousseau to lead the revolution on her own.

Finale (Book 3: 224–691)

The Vangarde hijack the general's coronation; Alouette defies the Vangarde's orders and steps forward as the Patriarche's only living heir, but the Red Scar attempt to kill her by inciting a riot. The general escapes the mayhem and crowns himself emperor (with the support of the System Alliance). After the Vangarde release footage revealing the general's crimes, their headquarters is bombed. The Red Scar lead a horde of Third Estaters to attack Ledôme, where the First and Second Estate live. Alouette stops the march and convinces them not to fight, but instead to build barricades to protect the resources they provide for the planet (the source of their true power). The general's last attempt to destroy the barricades fails when his own troops turn on him.

Final Image (Book 3: 692–699)

The République of Laterre is founded. Alouette sits down to record its history in the new Chronicles of Laterre. In an Epilogue dated "Ten Years Later," and written in the style of Alouette's Chronicles, we see the Final Images of all three heroes as well.

WHY IS THIS AN INSTITUTIONALIZED?

The System Divine trilogy contains all three elements of an Institutionalized story:

- **A GROUP:** Inspired by the "ancien régime" of prerevolutionary France, the Laterrian "Regime" (divided into three "estates") is the oppressive institution at the heart of this story. It's what brings the three heroes together and turns the people of Laterre into heroes as well when they fight to take it down.
- **A CHOICE:** The brando of this series is the Third Estate collectively, the "people of Laterre" who have a choice to make: either fight against the Regime that has kept them chained for five hundred years (represented by the "company man," General Bonnefaçon), or keep living under its oppression.
- **A SACRIFICE** leading to one of three possible endings: join, burn it down, or escape. Many lives are sacrificed by the end of the series, but as one primary character says before he dies, "It was worth it" (*Suns Will Rise*, page 652). The Laterrian people have "burned down" the institution with their bravery, unification, and willingness to finally harness the power they've held all along.

Final Image
Where We End . . .

Well, we've reached the end of our journey together. The Final Image of our deep dive into young adult storytelling.

How do you feel?

About your novel? About storytelling? About *yourself*?

It is my sincere hope is that I leave you feeling transformed. Just as our external stories are the vehicles of change for our heroes, the stories we endeavor to tell are vehicles of change for ourselves. Every novel I tackle helps me grow, every character I develop makes me think deeper about the person I want to become, and with every story I feel like a different writer.

So, before I send you off to tell that story I know you're destined to tell, one final word about change:

It is inevitable.

Your story *will* change as you write and rewrite and rewrite it. Your hero will grow in your mind just as much as they grow on the page. Your beats will be revised many times before you reach the final draft. Your Catalyst might bounce around in the story. You might not even *realize* your theme until the fifth draft. Your Fun and Games might start out as an upward path, only to be revised as a downward path. And don't even get me started on the Midpoint! Oy! I can't tell you how many times the Midpoint has changed in my novels. *It's a false victory! No, it's a false defeat! There's a twist! No, there's a ticking clock! No, there's a Midpoint party! Ooh, what if there's all three!?*

These are the joys and struggles of life as a writer. There are an infinite number of combinations, and you can't possibly expect to get it right on the first try.

Because here's the thing. Whether we're plotters, pantsers, or something in between, we are *all* discovery writers in some way. Some of us are just discovering more as we go; some of us are trying to discover as much as we can before we start. But through writing and revising more than twenty novels, I've learned that discovery is part of the process. We can never figure out *everything* before we start, because we can't predict the future. The harder you try to hold on to the story you *think* you want to write, the more you will struggle to write it. So be flexible. Let the beats and characters change when they need to. Don't be afraid of this change. Embrace it as an inevitable, beautiful part of the process.

Novels don't pour out of us fully formed. They come out of us in awkward chunks and disjointed ideas. Despite the grandeur and brilliance we've created in our minds, the truth is, stories emerge as messy piles of words that bear no resemblance to those masterpieces we envisioned. It's then our job to puzzle them all together into the semblance of a story.

And it takes *time*.

So as you read and study the novels on your shelf, remember that these are *finished* works. Works that have gone through the same discovery process that you will go through. Works that have been written and rewritten and revised again and again. Works that have been agonized over and fretted over and torn apart and stitched back together. There's a reason they're called "works."

So never compare your first, second, or even seventh draft to someone else's finished masterpiece. That will only discourage you. Don't be discouraged! Be inspired! This is what your book can eventually *become*. With effort, determination, flexibility, study, trial and error, and most of all discipline.

Inspiration only gets you started. Discipline gets you finished.

Hopefully this book has helped spark some of that inspiration. The rest is up to you.

So let's get to work.

ACKNOWLEDGMENTS

When it comes to "saving the author," I have many people to thank.

First and foremost, thank you to the wonderful team at Save the Cat! (B. J. Markel, Jason Kolinsky, and Rich Kaplan) for trusting me to carry the torch of this wonderful method to novelists everywhere. And of course, to Blake Snyder, without whom there would be no method (and I doubt any of my own novels would exist).

Buckets of love and gratitude to Jim McCarthy, my fabulous literary agent for more than ten years now. (*Gah! Has it really been that long?*) Thank you for talking me through countless Dark Nights of the Soul. Here's to many more years and books together!

I'm eternally grateful for the people at Ten Speed Press who helped this book become a reality, including Ashley Pierce, Nicole Sarry, Betsy Stromberg, and Dan Meyers, as well as Mikayla Butchart and Ken DellaPenta. Thank you to Courtney Mocklow and Brianne Sperber for your publicity and marketing genius. Extra sparkly thanks to Kristi Hein, copyeditor extraordinaire, whose little notes in the margin always made me smile (even when I'm tackling copyedits, which is no easy feat!). And a confetti-and-fireworks-filled thanks to my editors Matthew Inman and Fariza Hawke, who deftly shepherded this project from a seed of an idea to the (*slightly* longer than intended) finished book. Also thank you to Nick Martorelli, Christina Rooney, and the talented team at Penguin Random House audio for your amazing work on the Save the Cat! audiobooks.

I also want to take a moment to thank all the writers in my Writing Mastery Academy. I learn more from you every day than I could ever hope to teach you. I am forever inspired by your dedication to your craft, your courage to try new things, and all the wonderful milestones you've achieved. And gigantic thanks to the team that helps me keep it running: Chelle, Peggy Sue, Sarah, and Charlie. You are all truly amazing!

Every author needs a "crew," and I have one of the best. Shout-outs to my "J Crew": Jessica Khoury, Joanne Rendell, and Jennifer Wolfe. I couldn't have written this book—or any book for that matter—without your support, cheerleading, and mood-boosting gifs. And to all my YA author friends whom I've toured with, retreated with, and plotted with (sometimes nefariously) and who have inspired me greatly throughout my career, including (but certainly not limited to) Marissa Meyer, Leigh Bardugo, Emmy Laybourne, Marie Lu, Anna Banks, Morgan Matson, Len Vlahos, Alyson Noël, J. R. Johansson, Dhonielle Clayton, Tamara Ireland Stone, Suzanne Young, and Lish McBride.

No one knows how stressful it is to write beat sheets better than my husband, Charlie, who has to actually *live* with me while I write beat sheets. You *are* my B Story. You inspire me to be a better version of myself every day. May we never stop chasing Golden Fleeces together. And thank you to my parents for always being ready with a hug or an episode of *The Great British Bake Off* when I need it.

But the biggest thanks of all goes to you, the person holding this book. Your passion for storytelling and determination to be the best writer you can be is the reason this book exists. When the writing got hard and the reading list felt never-ending, I thought about you, and it kept me going. Don't ever forget that the world needs your story, and no one can write it as well as you. So, go forth and tell beautiful tales, my friend.

ABOUT THE AUTHOR

Jessica Brody is the author of *Save the Cat! Writes a Novel* and an internationally bestselling author of more than twenty novels for teens, tweens, and adults, including *The Chaos of Standing Still* (Rites of Passage), *The Geography of Lost Things* (Golden Fleece), *52 Reasons to Hate My Father* (Fool Triumphant), *I Speak Boy* (Out of the Bottle), the Unremembered trilogy (Superhero), and the System Divine trilogy (Institutionalized). Her books have been translated in more than twenty languages, and several have been optioned for film and TV. Previously, she worked for MGM Studios as manager of acquisitions and business development, and she is now the founder of the Writing Mastery Academy, an innovative online learning platform for fiction writers. She lives near Portland, Oregon, with her husband and dogs.

Visit her online at JessicaBrody.com or WritingMastery.com and follow her on Instagram or Twitter @JessicaBrody

INDEX

Published in the United States by Ten Speed Press, an imprint of the Crown Publishing Group, a division of Penguin Random House LLC, New York. TenSpeed.com

Ten Speed Press and the Ten Speed Press colophon are registered trademarks of Penguin Random House LLC.

Typefaces: Linotype's Sabon LT Pro, HDV Fonts' Brandon Text, and Nicole Sarry's YA Novel

Library of Congress Cataloging-in-Publication Data
Names: Brody, Jessica, author.
Title: Save the cat! writes a young adult novel : the ultimate guide to
   writing a YA bestseller / Jessica Brody.
Other titles: Ultimate guide to writing a YA bestseller
Description: First edition. | California : Ten Speed Press, 2023. |
   Includes index.
Identifiers: LCCN 2022048830 (print) | LCCN 2022048831 (ebook) |
   ISBN 9781984859235 (trade paperback) | ISBN 9781984859242 (ebook)
Subjects: LCSH: Young adult fiction--Authorship. | Young adult
   fiction--Technique. | LCGFT: Handbooks and manuals.
Classification: LCC PN3377 .B7 2023 (print) | LCC PN3377 (ebook) |
   DDC 808.3--dc23/eng/20230127
LC record available at https://lccn.loc.gov/2022048830
LC ebook record available at https://lccn.loc.gov/2022048831

Trade Paperback ISBN: 978-1-9848-5923-5
eBook ISBN: 978-1-9848-5924-2

Printed in USA

Editor: Matthew Inman | Assistant editor: Fariza Hawke | Production editor: Ashley Pierce
Designer: Nicole Sarry | Design manager: Betsy Stromberg
Production manager: Dan Myers
Copyeditor: Kristi Hein | Proofreader: Mikayla Butchart | Indexer: Ken DellaPenta
Publicist: Courtney Mocklow | Marketer: Brianne Sperber

1st Printing

First Edition